Perspectives on International Fixed Income Investing

Edited by

Frank J. Fabozzi, CFA
Adjunct Professor of Finance
School of Management
Yale University

Published by Frank J. Fabozzi Associates

Cover design by Scott C. Riether

ISBN: 1-883249-31-7

Printed in the United States of America

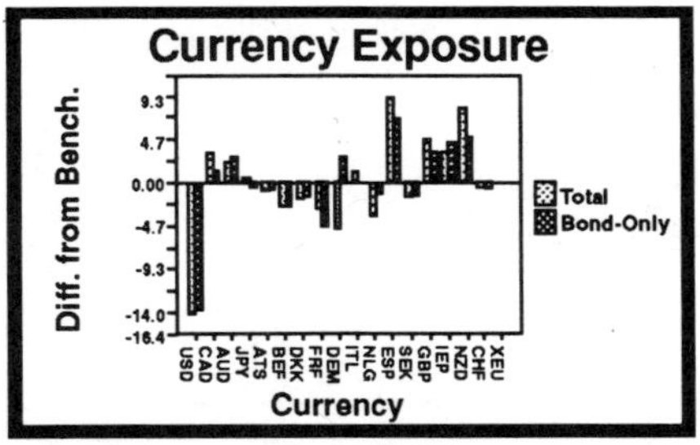

The Wilshire Axiom provides a global approach to multi-currency portfolio management featuring extensive portfolio analytics for risk management.

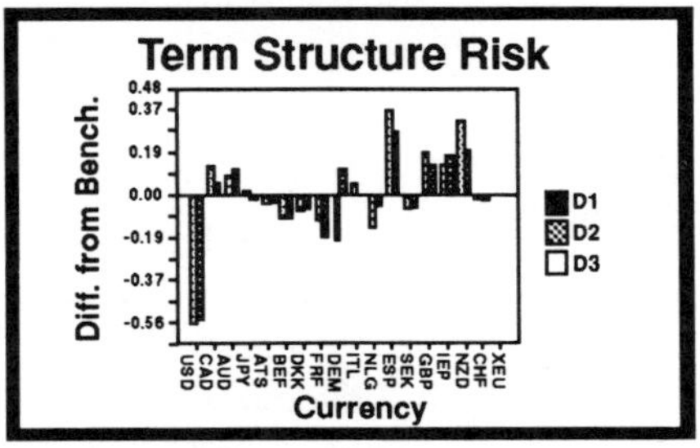

Wilshire's term structure model measures three basic types of yield curve shifts: level (DI), slope (D2) and curvature (D3).

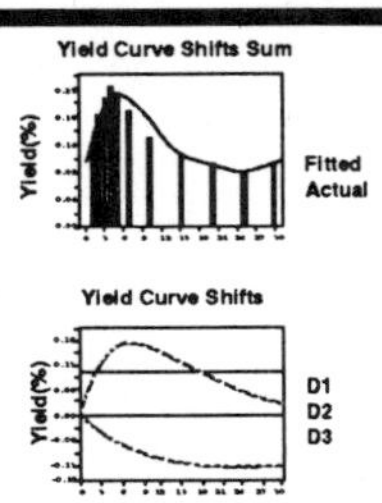

Yield Curve Shifts

Time	Start	Shift	End
D1		0.11	
D2		-0.13	
D3		0.18	
0.5	5.39	0.08	5.47
1.0	5.68	0.14	5.82
2.0	6.06	0.18	6.24
3.0	6.23	0.21	6.45
4.0	6.36	0.23	6.59
5.0	6.43	0.22	6.65
7.0	6.61	0.19	6.80
10.0	6.75	0.15	6.90
15.0	6.95	0.12	7.06
20.0	7.08	0.11	7.19
25.0	7.11	0.09	7.20
30.0	6.94	0.10	7.04

Axiom delivers daily term structure data and provides an analysis of yield curve movements.

W I L S H I R E

Now in Windows™ NT and 95

For more information please contact:

WILSHIRE ASSOCIATES INCORPORATED
1299 Ocean Avenue, Santa Monica, CA 90401
www.wilshire.com
e-mail: quantum @wilshire.com
voice mail: 310.319.2501

Santa Monica	London
TEL 310.451.3051	TEL 44.171.814.7355
FAX 310.458.0520	FAX 44.171.814.6611

SANTA MONICA ▪ NEW YORK ▪ PITTSBURGH ▪ MINNEAPOLIS ▪ LONDON ▪ AMSTERDAM

Table of Contents

Contributing Authors

Roveen Bhansali	BARRA, Inc.
Chris P. Dialynas	Pacific Investment Management Company
Steven I. Dym	Steven I. Dym & Associates
Anthony L. Faillace	Pacific Investment Management Company
Gifford Fong	Gifford Fong Associates
Lisa Goldberg	BARRA, Inc.
Jonathan M. Kelly	Fidelity Investments
Robert C. Kuberek	Wilshire Associates Incorporated
Luis R. Luis	Scudder, Stevens & Clark
J. Hank Lynch	BankBoston
Luis F. Martins	Fidelity Investments
Ellen Rachlin	Aubrey G. Lanston & Co. Inc.
Jonathan Reiss	Sanford C. Bernstein & Co., Inc.
Christopher B. Steward	Putnam Investments
Lee R. Thomas	Pacific Investment Management Company
Ram Willner	Pacific Investment Management Company
Daihyun Yoo	Gifford Fong Associates
Zandra M. Zelaya	Gifford Fong Associates

Chapter 1

Trading International Bond Markets

Christopher B. Steward, CFA
Senior Vice President
Putnam Investments

INTRODUCTION

Trading international bond markets can be an exciting and exhausting enterprise. Markets are traded virtually around the clock and a portfolio manager must keep abreast of economic, political, and market factors across 20 to 30 countries to effectively compete with other global bond managers. Issuers of debt have also become truly global with most large borrowers generally indifferent whether they raise funds in U.S. dollars, German marks, Japanese yen, or Italian lira. Barriers to foreign investment have been reduced as countries have taken steps to make their markets more liquid and transparent in order to attract global institutional investors. The drive for diversification and the search for additional expected returns have fueled interest in cross-border investing with fixed income portfolio managers now willing to invest capital in a variety of countries, including some that did not exist a decade ago. Some innovations, such as the development of the asset-backed debt market, have spread from the United States to other countries, and others, such as the issuance of inflation-indexed bonds, have been adopted by the United States.

The investment opportunities presented to those investors who venture outside their own borders, however, can be overwhelmed by the challenges and risks posed by unfamiliarity with market conventions in other countries. Successful navigation of the international capital markets requires both education and experience. As Francis Bacon wrote: "Travel, in the younger sort, is a part of education; in the elder, a part of experience. He that travelleth into a country before he hath some entrance into the language, goeth to school, and not to travel." And education in the global bond markets can be costly.

This chapter can provide only some of the flavor of international bond investing and highlight a few of the issues that confront global bond investors. First, the various instruments available for investment are described, including Eurobonds, and emerging market instruments. In the next section, issues concerning the trading of international bonds are addressed. Lastly, the impact of currency on international fixed income investing is addressed, particularly the attribution of international bond market returns between bonds and currencies. Investors should be aware of these issues, if not fully understand them, before venturing into markets outside of their normal investment universe.

INSTRUMENTS

The global bond portfolio manager is presented with a wide array of investment opportunities. The Salomon World Government Bond Index (WGBI) is comprised of 17 different markets with return data provided on an additional three market indexes not included in the WGBI. As can be seen in Exhibit 1, the large industrial countries comprise the lion's share of the world's bond market with the G3 bond markets of the United States, Japan, and Germany accounting for 72% of the $21.5 billion publicly issued bonds in the 23 largest bond markets. [1] The G7 market comprised 88% of outstanding bond issues in 1996, where it has maintained a fairly stable market share over the past 25 years.

Deregulation has removed barriers to foreign investment in many countries and increased the transparency of domestic markets to appeal to both foreign and domestic institutional investors alike. Italy, one of the last major bond markets to open its domestic market to foreign investors, did not remove its capital controls until 1990. [2] Initially, much of the deregulation was driven by the growth of the Eurobond market which is outside the jurisdiction of domestic securities regulators. More recently, the drive for European Monetary Union where many countries will share a common currency, has spurred further measures to attract investors.

This competition for trading activity has also led governments to expand the types of instruments that they issue. For example, the U.S. government began issuing index-linked Treasury notes which offer a real rate of return over the inflation rate in 1997, following in the footsteps of the United Kingdom, Canada, and Australia. Germany and Spain introduced a strips market in July 1997. In Germany, where there was no bill market, the Bundesbank began to issue short-term instruments. And in the United Kingdom, the government allowed for the creation of a repo market and the stripping of long bonds.

---

[1] This and other data on the size of the international bond market are from data published by Salomon Brothers, Inc. in *How Big is the World Bond Market? —1997 Update*, published in September 1997.

[2] See Michael Mussa and Morris Goldstein, "The Integration of World Capital Markets," in *Changing Capital Markets: Implications for Monetary Policy*, published by the Federal Reserve Bank of Kansas, 1993, and "Regulatory Reform in the Financial Services Industry: Where Have We Been? Where Are We Going?" in *Financial Market Trends 67*, OECD Paris, June 1997, for a historical perspective.

Exhibit 1: Size of Major Bond Markets at Year-End 1996

(Nominal Value Outstanding; Billions of U.S. Dollars or Equivalent)

Bond Market	Total Publicly Issued	As a Pct. of Public Issues in All Markets	Central Govt.	Central Govt. Agency & Govt. Guaranty	State & Local Govt.	Corp. (Incl. Cvts.)	Other Domestic Publicly Issued	Intl. Bonds[b] Foreign Bonds	Intl. Bonds[b]	Intl. Bonds[b] Euro-Bonds	Private Place. Unclass.
U.S. Dollar	$9,583.4	**44.5%**	$2,682.3	$2,634.5	$1,049.6	$1,910.0	$346.9	$175.9		$784.3	—
Japanese Yen	3,655.9	**17.0**	1,951.5	197.4	96.6	410.0	655.2	105.9		239.3	$717.4
Deutschemark	2,303.1	**10.7**	699.8	55.8	83.0	2.1	1,158.7	—	$303.7[c]	—	552.5
Italian Lira	1,274.4	**5.9**	978.4	20.4	—	4.6	182.5	3.3		85.0	—
French Franc	1,044.0	**4.8**	509.7	219.3	2.8	152.7	—	6.5		153.0	—
U.K. Sterling	661.8	**3.1**	446.5	—	0.1	32.7	—	6.7		175.9	—
Canadian Dollar	446.3	**2.1**	202.8	—	110.3	61.2	0.7	0.4		71.0	—
Dutch Guilder	400.8	**1.9**	196.8	—	2.7	119.9	—	5.0		76.4	82.6
Belgian Franc	386.9	**1.8**	216.9	5.7	—	16.2	110.4	36.6		1.2	—
Danish Krone	288.0	**1.3**	104.2	—	—	—	175.1	—		8.7	—
Swedish Krona	253.4	**1.2**	117.4	—	1.0	7.4	123.9	—		3.7	—
Swiss Franc	241.4	**1.1**	26.3	—	22.5	27.9	64.8	99.8		—	68.3
Spanish Peseta	234.4	**1.1**	171.8	—	13.4	17.6	16.2	15.4		—	—
Australian Dollar	163.6	**0.8**	74.4	37.0	—	13.9	—	0.4		37.8	—
Austrian Schilling	132.5	**0.6**	57.0	1.8	0.5	4.5	66.4	2.4		—	5.3
European Currency Unit	130.0	**0.6**	65.6	—	—	—	—	—		64.4	—
South African Rand	74.4	**0.3**	57.4	13.4	1.9	—	—	—		1.7	—
Portuguese Escudo	58.7	**0.3**	35.2	—	1.3	6.3	7.7	8.2		—	—
Greek Drachma	57.6	**0.3**	55.7	—	—	—	—	1.4		0.5	—
Finnish Markka	56.4	**0.3**	38.6	—	0.9	5.4	9.6	—		1.8	—
Norwegian Krone	49.0	**0.2**	19.1	2.3	6.8	3.3	16.8	0.4		0.3	—
Irish Pound	30.0	**0.1**	27.5	0.9	—	1.0	—	0.2		0.3	—
New Zealand Dollar	21.5	**0.1**	12.9	1.3	—	3.0	—	0.2		4.2	—
Total	**$21,547.4**	**100.0%**	**$8,747.9**	**$3,189.8**	**$1,393.3**	**$2,799.8**	**$2,934.9**	**$468.5**	**$2,481.6**[d]	**$2,013.1**	**$1,426.1**[e]
Sector as a Pct. of Public Issues in All Markets	**100.0%**		**40.6%**	**14.8%**	**6.5%**	**13.0%**	**13.6%**		**11.5%**		

[a] Exchange rates prevailing as of December 31, 1996: ¥116.0/US$; DM1.5548/US$; Lit1,530.6/US$; Ffr5.237/US$; £0.5889/US$; C$1.3696/US$; Dfl1.6859/US$; Bfr32.005/US$; Dkr5.945/US$; Skr6.871/US$; Sfr1.3464/US$; Pta131.28/US$; A$1.2555/US$; ATS10.954/US$; Ecu0.7988/US$; R4.6825/US$; Esc156.38/US$; Dr247.02/US$; Fmk4.6439/US$; Nkr6.4425/US$; Ir£0.5948/US$; and NZ$1.4156/US$. [b] Includes straight, convertible and floating-rate debt. [c] The German bond market does not distinguish between Euro and Foreign international issues. [d] Includes both Foreign and Eurobond totals. [e] In addition, an unspecified amount of privately placed issues of the private sectors exists.

Source: *How Big is the World Bond Market? — 1997 Update*, Salomon Brothers Inc., September 1997.

As of this writing, it appears likely that the European Union (EU) will launch a single European currency called the *Euro* on its planned start date of January 1, 1999. The composition of countries that will be included in the first round of European Monetary Union, or EMU, will be decided by the summer of 1998, but is nearly certain to include many of the largest European countries including Germany and France. The United Kingdom, which, although a member of the EU, is unlikely to join EMU in the first round as it was granted an "opt-out" clause from the single currency during the negotiation of the Maastricht Treaty on monetary union in the late 1980s. The adoption of the Euro would continue to place pressure on national bond markets to coordinate their trading conventions; however, significant differences are likely to persist for some time. Credit analysis will also become increasingly important to international bond portfolio managers investing within a common currency area.

The global bond markets are difficult to divide into distinct sectors, especially as new instruments, such as global bonds, further blur the distinctions. As a first cut, bond markets are divided by currency with the U.S. bond market including all fixed income instruments issued in U.S. dollars. One way to classify bond market sectors within each currency of issue is *internal* and *external*, where internal refers to all bonds issued under the laws of the domestic market regulators. Another classification system, based primarily upon the domicile of the issuer, is *domestic* and *international*, where bonds issued by foreign entities are considered international even though they may be subject to national securities market regulations. This latter system will be followed in the discussion below, beginning with a discussion of the domestic bond markets. The emerging markets are discussed in a separate section.

Domestic Bond Markets

Nearly all developed countries, and many emerging countries, have well-developed domestic bond markets. The market conventions, including issuance and settlement procedures, taxation issues, and yield calculations can vary substantially from market to market. As a rule of thumb, bonds in the dollar-bloc markets including the United States, the United Kingdom, Canada, Australia, and New Zealand, pay interest semiannually, whereas bonds in most other markets have annual coupons. Some markets, however, will issue bonds with both semiannual and annual coupons. This difference in yield calculation can skew comparisons between bond yields, understating yields on semiannual pay bonds by 10 basis points or more unless they are restated on a comparable basis.[3]

Exhibit 2, from J.P. Morgan, shows how much market conventions in the 21 largest bond markets can vary. Even the nomenclature can be confusing to international bond investors. For example, in the United Kingdom, bonds are known as *stocks* and equities are known as *shares*. To avoid trading and settlement errors, and to realize the maximum value from investing overseas, a thorough understanding of the individual instruments available in the major markets is required.

---

[3] 0When comparing yields of bonds which pay interest annually and semiannually, generally the semiannual yields are converted to annual yields using the formula: Annual yield = $(1+ \text{Semiannual yield}/2)^2 - 1$. Annual yields can also be converted to a semiannual basis using the formula: Semiannual yield = $2 \times [(1+ \text{Annual yield})^{1/2} - 1]$

Exhibit 2: Conventions In Major Government Bond Markets

	Australia	Austria	Belgium	Canada	Denmark	Europe	Finland	France		Germany	
Instrument	*CGSs*	*Bund*	*BGBs* *OLOs*[6]	*Canadas*	*DGBs*	*ECUs*	*Markkas*	*OATs, Emprunts*	*BTANs*	*Bund*	*Schätze, Bobls*[6]
Accrued interest											
Coupon (date)	semi (15)	ann	ann	semi	ann	ann/semi	ann	ann	ann (12)	ann	ann (18-22)
Odd first	yes	yes	yes	yes	no	yes	yes	yes	yes	yes	no
Special calculation	yes	yes	no	yes	no	no	no	yes	yes	no	no
Odd last	no	no	no	no	no	no	no	no	no	no	no
Ex-dividend (days)	yes (7)	yes	no	no	yes (30)	no	no	no	no	no	no
Accrual basis	actual	30E	30E	actual	30E	30E/actual[7]	30	actual	actual	30E	30E
Year basis	actual	360	360	365	360	360/actual[7]	360	actual	actual	360	360
Coupon custody [1]	value	value	value	value	value	value/trade[7]	value	value	value	trade	trade
Settlement date [2]											
Domestic [3]	T+3M	T+2M	T+3M	T+2M, T+3M	T+3M	T+3M/domestic	T+3M	T+3M	T+1M	T+2M	T+2M
International	T+3M	T+3M	T+3M	T+3M	T+3M	T+3M	T+3M	T+3M	T+3M	T+3M	T+3M
Value date [2]											
Domestic	settlement	settlement	settlement	settlement	settlement	domestic rule	settlement	trade	settlement	settlement	settlement
International	settlement	settlement	settlement	settlement	settlement	settlement	settlement	settlement	settlement	settlement	settlement
Trading basis											
Quotation	yield	price	price	yield	price	price	yield	price	yield	price	price
Tick	bp	.01	decimal	decimal	decimal	.01	bp	decimal	decimal	.01	.01
Denomination	1,000	varies	20,000 (1mil)	1,000	1,000	1,000	1-5(mil)	2,000	1 mil	varies	5,000 (100)
Bid/offer spread	2-5 bp	.10	.40 (.10)	.05-.10+	0.10+	.10-.25	3bp	.05-.10	2bp	.04-.10	.05-.08
Commission (%)	0	.75	.02-.05 (0)	0	0	0	0	0	0	0+	0-.50
Tax (nonresident, %)[4]	10	0	0	15	0	0	0	0-10	0	0	0
Transaction (millions)	10	50	10-25 (100-250)	10-25	25-50	5-10	10-50	100-500	100-250	25	25
Price/Yield method	U.S. (sa)	ISMA	ISMA	U.S. (sa)	ISMA	ISMA	ISMA	ISMA	ISMA	ISMA/Braeß	ISMA/Braeß
Size (US$ billions)[5]	74	43	145	195	102	99	29	300	149	500	88 (108)

	Ireland	Italy	Japan	Netherlands	New Zealand	Portugal	South Africa	Spain	Sweden	Switzerland	United Kingdom	United States
Instrument	*IGBs*	*BTPs, CTOs CCTs, CTEs*	*JGBs*	*DSLs*	*NZGs*	*OTs*	*Gilts Semi-gilts*	*Bonos,*	*Statsobliga-tionslån*	*SGBs, SGNs*	*Gilts*	*Treasur*

Exhibit 2 (Continued)

	Ireland	Italy	Japan	Netherlands	New Zealand	Portugal	South Africa	Spain	Sweden	Switzerland	United Kingdom	United States
Instrument	*IGBs*	*BTPs, CTOs CCTs, CTEs*	*JGBs*	*DSLs*	*NZGs*	*OTs*	*Gilts Semi-gilts*	*Bonos,*	*Statsobligationslån*	*SGBs, SGNs*	*Gilts*	*Treasuries*
Accrued interest												
Coupon (date)	semi/ann	semi/ann	semi (20)	ann (1, 15)	semi(15)	semi/ann	semi	semi/ann	ann	ann	semi	semi
Odd first	yes	no	yes	no	yes	no	no	no	no	no	yes	yes
Special calculation	yes	yes	yes	no	no	no	yes	yes	no	no	yes	yes
Odd last	no	no	yes	no	no	no	no	no	no	no	no	no
Ex-dividend (days)	yes [8]	no	yes(7)	no	yes	yes(4)	yes	no	yes	no	yes(7)	no
Accrual basis	actual/30E	30E	actual	30E	actual	30	actual	acutal	30E	30E+	actual	actual
Year basis	365/360	360	365	360	actual	360	actual	actual	360	360	365	actual
Coupon custody [1]	value	value	value	value	value	value	value	value	value	trade	value	value
Settlement date [2]												
Domestic [3]	T+1M	T+3M	T+3M	T+3M	T+2M	T+4M	T+2nd Th	T+1M	T+3M	T+3M, T+3M	T+1M	T+1M
International	T+3M	T+3M	no	T+3M	T+3M,T+7M	T+4M	no	T+7C	T+3M	T+3M	T+3M	no
Value date [2]												
Domestic	settlement	T+3M+1C	settlement	settlement	settlement	settlement	settlement	settlement	settlement	settlement	settlement	settlement
International	settlement	T+7C	no	settlement	settlement	flexible	settlement	settlement	settlement	settlement	no	no
Trading basis												
Quotation	price	price	yield (simple)	price	yield	price	yield	price	yield	price	price	price
Tick	decimal	decimal	.5bp	decimal	bp	decimal	bp	decimal	.5-1bp	decimal	1/32	1/256-1/32
Denomination	varies	varies	varies	10,000	10,000	10,000	1,000	10,000	100,000	1/5/50/100 thou	varies	1,000
Bid/offer spread	.05-.20bp	.01-.10	.5-3 bp	.10-.20	5bp	10 bp	1-5bp	.05-.10	3bp	.10-.50	2-4/32+	1/128-4/32
Commission (%)	varies	0	.25-.40	varies	0	0	0	0	0	varies	0	.004
Tax (nonresident, %)[4]	0	0	10	0	0	0	0	0	0	0-35	0	0
Transaction (millions)	1-10	5-25	500-5,000	2.5 - 50	5	500-1000	2-20	500-1,000	20-500	.5-5	5-100	1-500
Yield method	ISMA	ISMA (ann)	simple	ISMA	U.S. (sa)	ISMA	U.S.(sa)	ISMA	ISMA	ISMA	varies (sa)	U.S. (sa)
(US$ billions)[5]	27	1.22(tril)	1.95(tril)	186	15	17.2	42	166	85	27	326	2,380

[1] Date that determines coupon custody in domestic market transactions.
[2] T, M, C denote trade date, market days, and calendar days, respectively; Value date is the date the buyer begins to earn interest; Settlement date is the day on which settlement usually takes place.
[3] In Canada, the first rule is used for bonds with remaining maturities of less than three years. In Switzerland, the second rule is for SGNs.
[4] Effective rate from U.S. investor's perspective.
[5] As of date indicated in individual market outlines.
[6] Figure in [brackets] is for Bobls (OLOs) where it differs from Schätze (BGBs).
[7] Actual/actual day count basis for French, ECU, OAT issues; value date same as trade date for domestic clearing of such issues.
[8] Wednesday nearest 3 weeks before the coupon is paid.
[9] Reimbursement can be claimed.

From the perspective of a U.S. investor, the most important consideration when investing in a bond is whether it is denominated in U.S. dollars or some other currency. The U.S. fixed income market remains one of the most sophisticated including a large array of instruments such as mortgage bonds, strips, floaters, plus a very liquid derivatives market which includes swaps, options, caps and collars. The U.S. dollar-pay market is still dominated by domestic issuers with the U.S. Treasury, federal agencies, and corporate issuers accounting for 90% of the U.S. fixed income market. The issuance of international bonds, including the Yankee and Eurodollar sectors of the U.S. dollar-pay market, has increased as issuers in other countries have been attracted by the liquidity of the U.S. market.

Most domestic bond markets also include issues by state and local governments and government agencies; some are fully guaranteed by the sovereign, others are not. Most states in the United States and many local governments issue bonds, many of which are tax advantaged for high tax bracket investors. In Australia, the seven state governments issue bonds known as *semi-governments*, and in Canada, provincial bonds are issued by the 10 provinces. Many bond markets have issues by government agencies, or other government guaranteed issuers. U.S. agencies, such as Fannie Mae and Freddie Mac, issue mortgage backed securities. Other countries, including Canada, Australia, and Denmark have mortgage bond markets as well. Examples of other government guaranteed issuers include Germany's Bank for Reconstruction and Development, Kredit fur Weideraufbau, known as KfW, established after World War II as a clearing bank for Marshall Plan money.

International Bond Markets

Within one bond market, international bonds are defined as those issued by a foreign borrower. These can be *foreign bonds*, issued under national securities market regulations, *Eurobonds*, issued outside of any national securities market regulations, or *global bonds*, designed to trade in both national bond markets and the Eurobond market simultaneously.

Foreign Bonds

Foreign bonds are bonds issued in a domestic market by non-domiciled issuers under the jurisdiction of the domestic regulatory authorities. The *Yankee* market is the foreign bond market for the United States. Foreign bond markets in other countries also have nicknames, in the United Kingdom they are referred to as *Bulldogs*, in Japan they are called *Samurais*, and in Spain, *Matadors*. Regulations on foreign bond issuance may include restrictions on sizes, or the structure of issues, disclosure and reporting requirements, and minimum credit quality restrictions.

In the United States, the international bond sector includes Yankee bonds and Eurodollar bonds. Yankee bonds are SEC registered bonds that are issued in the United States by a foreign entity. Eurodollar bonds, a sector of the Eurobond market which is traded offshore, are not subject to SEC registration, and are mostly held by non-U.S. investors. This is primarily because the SEC's Regulation S locks out U.S. investors from purchasing Eurodollar bonds at auction, requiring a "seasoning period" of 40 days before they can be sold in the United States. The main differences between Yankee bonds and Eurodollar bonds are summarized in Exhibit 3.

The Yankee market experienced exceptional growth in the 1980s, expanding more than eight-fold from 1980 through 1990, compared with a four-fold increase in the U.S. fixed income market as a whole. The Eurodollar market, which attracts investors in U.S. dollar-denominated debt who prefer to deal outside of the United States where the regulatory environment is less stringent, has experienced far less growth, remaining less than one quarter the size of the Yankee market. However, in other countries, the Eurobond market tends to be much larger than the foreign bond market with Eurobonds accounting for 80% of all international bonds, both foreign bonds and Eurobonds.

Eurobonds

Eurobonds, which are traded offshore, and hence not subject to the oversight of national securities market regulators, are denominated in many different currencies. One defining characteristic of Eurobonds is that they are underwritten by an international syndicate. "Bought deals" brought by one issuer, are not uncommon, and Euro Medium Term Note (EMTN) programs have become increasingly popular in recent years. EMTNs allow for issuance in different currencies and maturities under one umbrella agreement. The ability of borrowers to use EMTNs to tap the markets more quickly and efficiently than with traditional Eurodollar bonds which require separate documentation for each bond issue has fueled strong growth in EMTN issuance which reached $223.9 billion in 1996. In recent years, EMTNs have been used for underwritten deals as well, further blurring the distinction between EMTNs and traditional Eurobonds. As the majority of all Eurobond issues are swapped into floating-rate debt, and market opportunities to obtain favorable swap terms can be fleeting, borrowers appreciate the flexibility of EMTN programs.

Exhibit 3: Differences Between Yankee and Eurodollar Bonds

Yankee Bonds	Eurodollar Bonds
• Non-U.S. issuer	• Any issuer
• SEC registered	• Not subject to national securities laws
• Registered (book entry) securities	• Issued in bearer (unregistered) form
• Semiannual interest payments	• Annual interest payments
• Traded mostly in the U.S.	• Traded offshore, primarily in London

U.S. dollar-denominated bonds comprise the largest segment of the Eurobond market, accounting for 37% of outstanding bond issues. Eurobonds denominated in currencies of the G7 countries comprise 83% of Eurobonds outstanding. The issuers in the Eurobond market constitute a broad mix of sovereign, supranational, corporate, and financial borrowers. Supranational agencies, such as the World Bank and the European Investment Bank, borrow frequently in the Eurobond market, reflecting their constant need for development financing and their lack of a "home" issuance market. Sovereign and sovereign-backed borrowers, such as Finland, Italy, and Sweden, are also regular issuers of Eurobonds. Governments in emerging markets have also been issuers of Eurobonds, as investors are willing to accept more credit risk to offset declining global bond yields. Such diverse borrowers as Russia, Poland, and Lebanon, have tapped the Eurobond market in recent years

Most Eurobonds are known as "straights" or plain vanilla fixed-rate coupon bonds. Many Eurobonds are convertible into common stock or have been combined with warrants on either debt, equities, or currencies. Warrants, like options, allow the holder to purchase the stock, bond or currency in the future at a set price. Most warrants are detachable from the underlying bond and can be traded independently.

Many large regular issuers of Eurobonds, such as sovereigns and supranationals, have become very sophisticated in securing the lowest all-in financing costs for their debt issues. As nearly all issuers swap debt issues into their home currency, most Eurobond issuers are indifferent as to the currency in which they issue, searching out the lowest cost of funds. For example, relatively wide swap spreads in the 5-year area of the German bond market attracted a large volume of issues by non-residents and German-based specialized financing entities. Issuers would then typically enter into a swap where they receive a fixed rate and pay a floating rate, thus transforming their liability from a fixed rate one to a floating rate one, but at a more attractive rate than they could have obtained in their home market because the difference between the fixed rate on the bond that they issued and the fixed rate received on the swap allowed for lower funding costs relative to the London Interbank Offer Rate or LIBOR.[4] Eurobonds are also issued as floating-rate notes, usually linked to LIBOR. The coupon is typically stated as a spread over LIBOR, although it may use another reference rate, such as the London Interbank Bid Rate or LIBID.

Dual Currency Bonds *Dual currency bonds* have the coupon payments denominated in one currency and the principal repayment denominated in another. This reduces the foreign exchange risk borne by the investor from that of holding a foreign bond while allowing for higher income than domestic bonds. A surge in issu-

---

[4] Nearly all Eurobonds are swapped into Eurodollars before being swapped back into the issuer's home currency as liquidity is usually far less for cross-currency swaps not involving the U.S. dollar. Thus, most issuers will assess funding opportunities in terms of all-in spread relative to U.S. dollar LIBOR.

ance of dual currency bonds during 1995 and 1996 was driven primarily by Japanese investors seeking income opportunities not available domestically due to extremely low interest rates. In the Japanese case, most of the dual currency bonds were priced in yen with the principal denominated in Australian or New Zealand dollars and coupon payments paid in yen. *Reverse dual currency bonds*, with the principal denominated in yen and the coupons payable in another currency were also issued, but in fewer numbers.

Global Bonds

The distinction between Yankee and Eurodollar bonds has become increasingly blurred in recent years with the advent of the "global bond." Global bonds were designed to be placed simultaneously in both the Yankee and the Eurodollar markets to broaden the pool of potential investors. The first global bond was a $1.5 billion World Bank issue launched in 1989. The success of global bond issues is further evidence of the melding of the Euro and domestic markets that has accelerated to accommodate the increasing movement of capital across international borders. In 1996, the issuance of global bonds more than tripled to $118.3 billion from the year before.[5]

The early development of the global bond market was dominated by issues from central governments and supranational organizations. However, in recent years U.S. borrowers, especially U.S. agencies, have begun to dominate global bond issuance. In reviewing developments in the global bond market during 1996, the OECD noted that "residents of the United States continued to account for the lion's share of issuing activity (68% of all issues). In spite of the dominance by borrowers from the United States, it has been a noteworthy trend this year that borrowers from a wider selection of countries have tapped the market for global bonds"[6] including Canada, Germany, Ireland, Mexico, Argentina, and Brazil. Much of the strong growth of global bond issuance in 1996, however, was driven by special purpose vehicles for asset-securitization deals.

Emerging Markets

A combination of improving credit quality and privatization programs in the emerging markets and a scramble by investors to offset declining yields in the developed bond markets has increased investor appetite for emerging market bonds. Emerging market investments for the fixed income investor was mostly limited to the Brady bond market; however, in recent years local currency investments, such as Mexican Cetes, have become more popular. In those emerging markets that lacked a developed local bond market, many investors created synthetic bank deposits using the forward foreign exchange market. These instruments can be in the form of non-deliverable forwards, or incorporated into a structured note which can pay a coupon.

---

[5] As reported in *Bank for International Settlements, 67th Annual Report*, p. 128.

[6] *Financial Market Trends 66*, OECD Paris (March 1997), p.62.

Brady Bonds The Brady bond market was born out of the Latin American debt crisis which left the New York money center banks with large amounts of nonperforming loans to sovereign borrowers. Brady bonds were named after Treasury Secretary Nicholas Brady who fostered a market-oriented approach to the Latin American debt crisis by repackaging nonperforming bank loans into marketable securities in the late 1980s.

The first Brady agreement was reached with Mexico, and the bonds were issued in March 1990; however, Aztec bonds, a similar privately arranged restructuring of Mexican debt by J.P. Morgan, were issued two years earlier. The Mexican Brady plan offered the commercial banks two options in return for their Mexican loans: a *Discount* bond issued at 65% of face value paying a floating market coupon of LIBOR+13/16, and a *Par* bond issued at full face value, but paying a below-market fixed coupon of 6.25%. The banks were also given a third alternative, allowing them to carry existing loans on their books at face value if they agreed to provide new lending to Mexico of at least 25% of their existing exposure over the next three years. Both Discount and Par bonds have their principal repayment backed by zero-coupon U.S. Treasuries plus a rolling interest guarantee covering, in many instances, 18 months of interest payments. Today, 12 countries have issued Brady bonds, although Latin American countries still dominate the Brady market with 86% of debt outstanding. The size of the Brady market has grown from $30 billion in 1990 to $136 billion in 1995, with the debt divided evenly between fixed- and floating-rate bonds.

There is no generally accepted delineation between an emerging and a developed market. Mexico and the Czech Republic, considered by many to be emerging markets, are now members of the OECD. Some emerging markets have issued bonds in the Eurobond market. Generally the distinction is left up to the credit rating agencies who determine whether a country is investment grade: Moody's Baa3, Standard and Poor's BBB–, or better. Even the credit rating agencies sometimes cannot agree. For example, South Africa has a split rating of Baa3/BB+ meaning that Moody's regards the credit as investment grade, whereas Standard and Poor's does not.

The market risk of holding emerging market securities is generally much higher than holding developed country credits, regardless of currency denomination. The turmoil in the Pacific Rim currencies including the Thai baht, and the Philippine peso during the summer of 1997, and the Mexican crisis in late 1994 and early 1995 which spread to other Latin American markets, serve as a vivid reminder of the risks associated with holding emerging market debt. The pressure on the Pacific Rim currencies stemmed from concern about the Thai banking system. The 1994-1995 Latin American debt crisis was triggered by concerns about the Mexican peso's ability to stay within its stated devaluation band in the face of extremely large current account deficits and declining reserves. These concerns prompted many Mexican residents to move money out of the country. When the sentiment of international investors turned as well, the reaction was quick and harsh. On December 19, 1994 the Mexican peso was devalued. By March of 1995, the peso had lost half of its value against the dollar, and Mexican Par bonds had also fallen by 50%. By the end of 1995, market prices had recovered substantially, as investor confidence improved and liquidity returned to the emerging markets.

Local Currency Emerging Market Debt Local currency investing has become the fastest growing segment of the emerging fixed income market driven both by investor demand and rapid development of domestic capital markets in developing countries. Examples include Argentina's Bocons, Ecuador's government bonds, Brazil's NTN-Ds, and Russian GKOs with an embedded foreign exchange hedge, to name but a few. At the end of 1996, according to data from the World Bank and IMF, 75 developing nations had local bond and or money market instruments whose value exceeded $850 billion. This number compares with $230 billion in Brady bonds and Eurobonds issued by the same countries. Local markets instruments offer a wide selection of tenors (although most are in the 28-day to 1-year range) and structures (e.g., floating, fixed, or inflation-linked). With the deepening of these local markets, investors who choose to do so have become increasingly able to hedge their foreign exchange risk via forwards, and in some cases, options. The most developed local bond markets can be found in Argentina, South Africa, Chile, and the Czech Republic.

One of the attractions to investors of local currency emerging market debt is its low correlation to the developed bond markets, especially the United States. Because Brady bonds are U.S. dollar denominated and most are partially collateralized by U.S. Treasuries, Brady bonds have a high correlation to changes in U.S. interest rates. Even floating-rate Brady bonds, although not collateralized, exhibit significant sensitivity to U.S. interest rate shifts. Local currency emerging market debt not only shows less correlation with the U.S. bond market, but also generally shows less cross market correlation to other emerging markets. However, during periods of crisis, such as during the speculative attacks on the Thai baht and other Pacific Rim currencies in 1997, there can be a contagion effect from market attacks across countries, or even regions. The 1994 Mexican peso devaluation also resulted in pressure on several currencies including the Philippine peso, the Thai baht, and the Czech koruna. However, the Mexican peso devaluation had little impact on other Latin American currencies, and its impact on the bond and equity markets in some of these countries tended to be short lived.

TRADING INTERNATIONAL BONDS[7]

Over the past several years, the trading of international bonds has increasingly become incorporated into the mainstream of fixed income portfolio management. Once used only to "flavor" domestic bond portfolios, international bonds have

[7] I am greatly indebted to John McCarthy, Senior International Trader at Colonial Management Associates, for the structure of much of this section.

assumed an important role as either a dedicated or tactical asset class, finding their way into many different types of portfolios. The increased acceptance of trading international bonds is clearly observable in the trading volumes, both in cash instruments and futures contracts, as well as the increase in international derivatives available which compliment the trading of these assets.

Trading international bonds poses an array of challenges due to differences between markets in trading hours, taxation issues, interest calculations, as well as issuance and settlement procedures, to state a few. In addition, local economic situations, political developments, and in general any news, both local and international, will have varying degrees of influence on the trading of bonds in different countries.

Withholding Taxes

A number of countries have in the past imposed withholding taxes on coupon income for non-resident bondholders. These taxation policies provide an extra source of revenue for the sovereign government and often were established to discourage international investors from investing in a given country. Regardless of the motivation for establishing withholding taxes, international investors can leave a significant amount of "money on the table" unless they are aware of these policies and the implications that these policies have on their investments. Most global bond portfolio managers are successful in avoiding payment of withholding taxes which can help in keeping a competitive edge in the performance rankings.

Anomalies in withholding tax laws can also provide international investors with opportunities for enhancing performance. The removal of withholding taxes in Italy provides a good example of how different tax treatment can significantly alter total returns on individual bonds. Most Italian bonds were subject to a 12.5% withholding tax which was levied at the source on both coupon payments and the original issue discount. Investors from countries which had a treaty against double taxation with Italy needed to apply for a tax refund, which typically took 45 days after the date of the coupon payment to process. U.S. investors, prior to 1997, did not qualify for withholding tax refunds. When Italy removed its withholding tax on interest paid to non-residents at the beginning of 1997, only bonds that had already made a coupon payment in 1997 were exempt from withholding taxes. Thus, individual bond selection would have made a significant impact on total returns from holding Italian bonds.

In contrast to the many countries, like Italy, which have relaxed or removed withholding taxes on non-resident bondholders, Australia has tightened the legislation governing its withholding tax procedures. The Australian fixed income market is arguably one of the more mature and liquid fixed income markets in the global fixed income universe. However, because of its taxation policy, some investors avoid the Australian bond market. The Australian authorities apply a 10% withholding tax on coupon interest paid on all Australian fixed interest securities held by non-residents; but dual tax treaties exist with many countries and therefore give relief of this withholding tax to those countries. International investors have essentially two methods of avoiding withholding tax altogether in Australia. One method is selling the fixed income instrument 2 to 6 weeks before the coupon clipping period and buying another comparable fixed income instrument that already has relief from the coupon tax until the next clipping date. This method, known as "coupon washing," avoids the tax on the coupon, however the investor is in essence forced to pay the bid/offer spread (i.e., the difference between the price that someone will bid you for the instruments you hold and the offer whereby someone will offer you the new instruments you want to purchase).

The second method of avoiding Australian withholding taxes is through the Euro Australian dollar market. Euro Australian dollar bonds are free of withholding tax and hence provide a viable alternative to domestic instruments that are subject to withholding taxes. As a consequence of the instruments having no withholding tax on the interest paid, the bonds yield somewhat less than those instruments that are not free of withholding taxes. In practice, the withholding tax imposed on non-residents generates little extra revenue, as most investors avoid the withholding tax by selling the issue being taxed and buying one that is ex-withholding or investors buy offshore issues or avoid the market entirely.

Liquidity

With the increasing size of international capital flows, the liquidity of an individual bond market plays an important role in the portfolio manager's decision as to whether or not to invest in a particular market. Many global bond portfolio managers tend to be active traders, shifting positions between markets frequently to take advantage of short-term shifts in market sentiment. Thus, although the yield or macroeconomic outlook for a given bond market may seem attractive, if the liquidity of that market is restrictive, then that particular market is more likely to be ignored as an alternative investment.

The Finnish government bond market provides an interesting example of how liquidity can work for and against bond market valuations. Although small by international standards, the Finnish government bond market offered attractive yield levels, but only surfaced as a viable and liquid market in recent years. Representing less than one half of 1% of the world bond market capitalization, the Finnish bond market was too small to generate much interest from international investors. Liquidity concerns were accentuated by the dominance of local investors in the Finnish bond market. This fact was dramatized when international investors who had invested in Finland's bond market were not able to liquidate their investments quickly enough, due to the lack of liquidity, to avoid the damaging effects of the 1993 devaluation of the Finnish markka.

The liquidity of the Finnish bond market has increased substantially since 1993, due to the introduction of a more orderly auction process, the development of a repo market, and an increase in the number of primary dealers. In July 1996, the liquidity of the Finnish bond market was particularly enhanced by the inclusion of Finnish bonds into the Salomon World Government Bond Index. Because many global funds are managed to outperform a global bond index, many fund managers will match a particular index with an over or under weighting in particular sectors of that index. Hence, when a market is added to one of the major global bond indexes, the demand from managers who track those indexes tends to increase the liquidity of that particular market.

Liquidity can be severely reduced around holidays or other market events; trading on Fridays ahead of long weekends can be extremely thin. In Australia, for example, the market effectively shuts down during the running of the Melbourne Cup horse race. In Germany, trading of bonds OTC virtually stops during the "fixing" of bond prices on the Frankfurt exchange from 11:30 to 12:30 Frankfurt time. In some Muslim countries such as Egypt, Fridays and Saturdays are holidays and Sunday is a work day. Hence these subtle but important constraints must be taken into consideration not only for liquidity reasons, but also for settlement of securities to ensure that the appropriate transfer agents are open for business.

Domestic Investors

In most bond markets domestic investors tend to constitute the bulk of the investment flows and international fixed income portfolio managers typically represent the marginal buyer or seller. Thus, the positioning and outlook of domestic investors can be very important in determining whether a particular market is over or undervalued. Understanding who the major players are in each bond market and what influences the investment decisions of domestic investors is important. In foreign markets, domestic investors may act and react differently to certain information and data than a particular investor is used to seeing in the investor's home market. Thus, in addition to the traditional factors that enter into an investor's decision making process, it is important to note other domestic items of investment interest namely holiday schedules, the importance of particular economic data releases, and the role of certain officials or think tanks, to name a few.

Futures Trading

The presence of a liquid futures market is to a certain extent an indication of how mature a country's bond market is. Because futures may be utilized to influence investment decisions in many ways, the availability of futures in a given market enhances that market's attractiveness to foreign investors. Dealers are able to offset their risks by engaging in futures trading and investment managers are able to adjust their duration exposure through the futures market. Especially in fast moving markets, investment managers can use the futures market to hedge or gain additional exposure much more easily than they could through shifting positions in the cash market.

The development of futures markets is often driven by competition among financial centers. In Germany, for example, it was not too long ago that the government bond market did not have a futures market. During the mid to late 1980s, because of Germany's attractive yield levels and the desire of global bond investors to diversify their holdings, Germany's fixed income markets began to draw great attention. During this time period there were no futures markets in the fixed income markets or the equities markets. The present German futures exchange, the Deutsche Termin Boerse, or DTB, remained on the drawing board. As market deregulation of the 1980s continued to evolve, international investors became more anxious to get various German futures contracts functioning. This pressure increased with the introduction of a 10-year German bund contract on the London International Financial Futures Exchange (LIFFE) in the fall of 1988. London's dominance in the trading of bund futures continued for a number of years, while the Germans developed their own futures exchange. During this time period, German investors mostly remained in the German cash bond market, whereas foreign investors gravitated more and more toward the London market. The German fixed income market as a whole was becoming more efficient but the efficiency was being forced upon the Germans by foreign means. In early 1990, the Germans issued their own 10-year bond contract on the Deutsche Termin Boerse, or DTB, the newly developed German futures market. However, much of the trading of German bunds and bund futures remained in London, as domestic foreign investors had become comfortable dealing outside of Germany in the London cash and futures markets.

Trading Hours

Trading hours can be divided into three distinct periods, broadly defined by the domestic trading hours of the major bond markets: the Far East, Europe, and the United States. During these hours the majority of trading and the largest volume of that region's domestic instruments are exchanged. Obviously the transition from one time zone to the next results in a similar transition in liquidity from the instruments of one region to the next. The dividing lines of trading hours in the various regions/time zones have become increasingly blurred, however, with investors able to transact in U.S. Treasuries and other major bond instruments in the major trading centers of the three time zones, namely New York, London, and Tokyo. Thus, the impact of any one particular dominant "player" in any region has become more diluted as international investors increase their holdings of foreign bonds and trade them more frequently outside of their home markets.

The derivative markets, especially the futures market, have been instrumental in moving international fixed income markets in the direction of around the clock trading. Trading in the domestic Australian futures market, for example, runs from 8:30 a.m. to 4:30 p.m., with a 1½ hour break for lunch. After the close of the domestic futures market, trading of the same futures contract begins in the overnight market, called SYCOM (Sydney Computerized Overnight Market), running from 4:40 p.m. to 7:00 a.m. Sydney time. Thus, international investors have nearly around the clock access to Australian bond futures, which is one reason why the Australian bond market has the reputation of being one of the most liquid and global markets in the investment industry.

Around the clock futures trading is also available through Globex, which supports after-hours trading in futures contracts that trade on the Chicago Mercantile Exchange. These contracts on foreign bond markets, which may be fairly liquid when traded during U.S. hours, lose liquidity during local trading hours when domestic futures markets are open. Granted, these markets are not as liquid and cannot support as much flow as their domestic contracts are able to; however, for the global investor these markets provide a viable alternative for managing their investments risks.

Settlement

Settlement of international bond trades are generally more complicated than domestic bond trades, if only because most bond trades also require a currency trade as well. Most international bond trades are electronically transferred by one of the two major clearing systems: Euroclear, and Cedel. That is, on settlement day, the buyer of a security receives a credit to his security account and a debit to his cash account and likewise the seller of a security receives a debit to his security account and a credit to his cash account. With electronic settlement nothing is physically exchanged and the settlement process becomes much less laborious than in the case of physical delivery. In physical delivery, the actual cash and security are moved in some form from one location to another and exchanged on the settlement date.

The settlement of securities in emerging markets tends to be riskier where in many markets securities are still physically delivered. In South Africa, for example, settlements take place in Johannesburg, where many of the South African banks are headquartered. South Africa is presently moving toward electronic security settlement on the third business day after the trade date. However, in the not too distant past, physical settlement of all securities trades took place on the second Thursday after the trade date. This trade date was chosen so that investors would have enough time to organize the actual physical delivery of the securities and cash. This laborious chore of coordinating delivery of the securities between counterparties turned Johannesburg into somewhat of a scooter rally on settlement days as bank employees would zoom around the city on motor scooters with backpacks full of securities to deliver.

THE IMPACT OF CURRENCY

Perhaps the greatest challenge in international fixed income investing is in managing foreign currency exposures. For a U.S. dollar-based investor, the total return on an unhedged foreign bond position will increase as the dollar depreciates against foreign currencies and will decline if the value of the dollar rises. International bond portfolio managers tend to worry more about currency exposures than their counterparts in the international equity markets because the volatility of currency returns is generally far greater than that of bond market returns, but not dissimilar from that of equities. However the significant returns that can be gained from just one correct currency call lures most international fixed income portfolio managers into active currency management.

Exhibit 4: Average Annual Returns of Salomon Brothers Non-U.S. Bond Index by Components

	Local Market Return	Currency Return	Unhedged US$ Return	Hedged US$ Return
1985-1996	9.14	5.24	14.45	8.75
1985-1988	9.24	13.54	25.15	10.23
1989-1992	8.45	1.23	7.91	6.60
1993-1996	9.75	1.41	11.00	9.45
1988-1996	8.87	0.46	8.63	8.14

One misconception about international fixed income investing is, at least for U.S. dollar-based investors, that the lion's share of the returns from global bond indexes have come from currency gains. Although it is true that the dollar has been in a trend decline against most major currencies since the breakup of the Bretton Woods system in the early 1970s, currency gains have tended to be lower than bond market returns. Exhibit 4 shows the breakdown of returns from the Salomon Brothers Non-U.S. Government Bond Index into local bond market returns and currency returns.[8] The unhedged average annualized U.S. dollar return of 14.45% during the first 12 years of the non-U.S. index was composed of a 9.14% local bond market return and a 5.24% currency return. Thus, bonds accounted for roughly 63% of the total gains from holding unhedged non-U.S. bonds, while gains from currency accounted for approximately 36%. However the average annualized volatility of the gains due to currency was more than two and a half times the volatility of both the local currency and hedged bond returns.

Breaking up the returns into three 4-year periods shows that currency returns for a U.S. dollar-based investor were concentrated in the late 1980s. Currency returns were one and a half times higher than bond market returns during the first period, but in the two later periods bond returns were nearly seven times higher than currency returns. The strong currency gains in the mid to late 1980s were due to the rapid decline of the U.S. dollar from its 1984 peak. If we exclude the first three years of the Salomon Non-U.S. Bond Index, years of extreme dollar weakness, the returns due to currency for the 9-year period from 1988 to 1996 drop to below one half of 1%. The individual annual returns in Exhibit 5 illustrate how much more volatile currency returns have been relative to bond market returns. In seven of the 12 years of the Non U.S. Index, bond market returns were larger than currency returns. In addition, currencies had four years where they

[8] The unhedged U.S. dollar return is not the sum of the local bond market return and the currency return because returns from currency include hedge costs or benefits which are determined by short-term interest rate differentials. The currency return was interpolated from the Salomon Brothers Hedged and Unhedged Non-U.S. Bond Indices using the formula (1 + unhedged return)/(1 + hedged return) − 1. The Salomon hedged index uses a rolling 1-month hedge.

subtracted from unhedged returns — a total of 23.37%. Bond markets, on the other hand, posted only one year of negative returns, losing 3.26% in 1994. The return disparities between bonds and currencies become even more distinct when the first three years of the index are excluded. From 1989 on, currencies posted double digit returns twice, in 1990 and 1994. International bond markets had twice as many double digit gains, rising strongly in 1991, 1992, 1993, and 1995.

The index return data in Exhibits 4 and 5 represent the returns that would have been obtained from a passively managed indexed portfolio. The actual performance of global bond portfolios can vary substantially from the index, as most international bond portfolio managers actively manage both bond and currency exposures and often invest in markets outside the index. Nevertheless, the data in Exhibits 4 and 5 show that not only is currency often a less important contributor to total returns than bond market returns, but that currency returns also tend to be much more volatile. Investing in hedged international bonds can significantly lower overall portfolio volatility, but has historically returned far less than unhedged international bonds.[9] For example, the average annualized volatility of hedged non-U.S. bond index over the 12-year period from 1985 through 1996 at 3.77% was nearly one third the 10.97% volatility of the unhedged index. However, the hedged non-U.S. bond index lagged the unhedged index by an average of 570 basis points per year over the same period, outperforming the unhedged index in only 4 out of the 12 years.

Exhibit 5: Average Annual Returns of Salomon Brothers Non-U.S. Bond Index by Components

	Local Market Return (%)	Currency Return (%)	Unhedged US$ Return (%)	Hedged US$ Return (%)
1985	11.08	21.48	35.01	11.14
1986	11.22	17.93	31.36	11.39
1987	7.66	23.68	35.15	9.27
1988	7.06	-6.21	2.34	9.12
1989	2.47	-7.23	-3.41	4.11
1990	4.61	11.59	15.29	3.32
1991	14.24	4.60	16.22	11.11
1992	12.97	-3.01	4.77	8.03
1993	17.52	1.50	15.12	13.42
1994	-3.26	10.44	5.99	-4.02
1995	16.13	1.38	19.55	17.92
1996	9.89	-6.92	4.08	11.82

[9] See Chapter 2.

CONCLUSION

Investors who have ignored the international fixed income markets have missed out on significant opportunities for return as well as risk reduction through diversification. Investing internationally, however, involves managing the additional risk of currency and country allocation, and requires a thorough knowledge of market conventions in foreign markets. These include government regulations, issuance and settlement procedures, accounting practices, custody fees, yield conventions, commissions, and the behavior of domestic investors. An understanding of these issues will not necessarily reduce the risks of investing internationally, but rather will increase the chances of success in increasing returns while reducing the potential pitfalls which can result in failed trades, lost money, and underperformance.

Chapter 2

International Bond Portfolio Management

Christopher B. Steward, CFA
Senior Vice President
Putnam Investments

J. Hank Lynch, CFA
Vice President
BankBoston

INTRODUCTION

Management of an international bond portfolio poses more varied challenges than management of a domestic bond portfolio. Differing time zones, local market structures, settlement and custodial issues, and currency management all complicate the fundamental decisions facing every fixed income manager in determining how the portfolio should be positioned with respect to duration, sector, and yield curve.

The following fundamental steps in the investment process apply to domestic and international investing alike:

1. setting investment objectives
2. establishing investment guidelines
3. developing portfolio strategy
4. constructing the portfolio
5. monitoring risk and evaluating performance

The added complexities of cross-border investing magnify the importance of a well defined, disciplined, investment process. The chapter is organized to address each of these challenges in turn.

To provide a broad overview of the many aspects of international fixed income investing within the scope of one chapter implies that many topics do not receive the depth of discussion that they deserve. The topic of currency management alone has provided material enough for many books and articles. Wherever possible, footnotes are provided referencing additional sources that offer a more detailed discussion of each topic.

INVESTMENT OBJECTIVES

Most investors are attracted to global bonds as an asset class because of their historically higher returns than U.S. bonds. Others are drawn to global bonds because of their diversification value in reducing overall portfolio risk. The investor's rationale for investing in international bonds is central to developing appropriate return objectives and risk tolerances for a portfolio. Broadly speaking, investor objectives can be divided into four categories: total return, diversification or risk reduction, current income, and asset/liability matching. Each of these investment objectives has implications for the management of an international bond portfolio and should be reflected in the investment guidelines. At a minimum, investment guidelines should include return objectives, risk tolerances, benchmark selection, and an appropriate time horizon for judging performance.

Return objectives are often expressed in terms of the benchmark return, e.g., benchmark return plus 100 basis points after management fees. The investment objectives will indicate not only the most appropriate benchmark, but also the most suitable management style. Investors who are primarily concerned with diversification may wish to place tight limits on the size of positions taken away from the benchmark to ensure that the diversification benefit is not weakened. A total-return oriented investor might be far less concerned with how the portfolio composition differs from the benchmark, but may be more critical of shortfalls in performance.

Investment guidelines should be flexible enough to allow the portfolio manager sufficient latitude for active management while keeping the portfolio close enough to the benchmark to ensure that the portfolio remains diversified. The guidelines should address allowable investments including, the countries in the investment universe, minimum credit ratings, and the use of derivatives such as futures, options and structured notes. The time horizon over which investment performance is to be measured is also important. A short-term time horizon, such as a calendar quarter, may encourage more short-term trading which could diminish the natural diversification benefit from international bonds as an asset class. Investors who emphasize the risk reduction, or diversification aspect of international bond investing should have a longer time horizon of perhaps two to three years. As differences between economic cycles can be prolonged, this would provide enough time for a full economic cycle to play out and the diversification benefit to take effect be realized.

Benchmark Selection

Benchmark selection for an international bond portfolio has many ramifications and should therefore be done carefully. As is the case when choosing an international equity benchmark index, the choice of a pure capitalization (market value) weighted index may create a benchmark that exposes the investor to a disproportionate share in the Japanese market relative to the investor's liabilities or diversification preferences. While international equity indices chosen for benchmarks are most often quoted in the investor's local currency (i.e., unhedged), international bond benchmarks may be hedged, unhedged, or partially hedged depending on the investors objectives.[1] The choice of a hedged, unhedged, or hybrid benchmark will likely alter the risk and return profile of the resulting investment portfolio and should thus be done with careful consideration of the primary rationale for investing in international bonds.

Benchmarks can be selected from one, or a combination, of the many existing bond indices: global, international (ex-U.S.), currency-hedged, G7 only, 1-3 year, 3-5 year, 7-10 year, emerging markets, Brady bonds, etc., or a custom index can be created. The most frequently used benchmarks are the J.P. Morgan Global Government Bond Index, or the Salomon Brothers World Government Bond Index, although many other investment houses such as Merrill Lynch, Lehman Brothers, Goldman Sachs, and UBS offer full index services as well. The benchmark often provides both the return objective and the measure of portfolio risk.

Benchmark Currency Position

Currency management is a matter of much debate in the academic literature.[2] The natural currency exposures incurred through international investing require portfolio managers to adopt either an active or passive approach to currency management. Many managers are attracted to active currency management because of the large gains that can be attained through correctly anticipating currency movements. Some international fixed income portfolio managers, however, prefer not to actively manage currency exposures. This may reflect doubts about their own ability to add value through active currency management, or a belief that no one can forecast currency movements with any degree of reliability. The former often hire outside currency overlay managers to manage the residual currency risk determined by the bond allocation, the latter often run fully hedged or unhedged portfolios as a matter of policy. Both approaches, in our opinion, are sub-optimal[3] as compared to an integrated approach that determines bond and currency allocations simultaneously. Although many international fixed income portfolio managers place greater emphasis on bond market allocations while managing currency exposure as a residual, the same fundamental economic factors which influence bond prices also impact currency levels. The integrated approach to determining bond and currency allocations explored later in this chapter illustrates how a more explicit accounting of the risk and expected return due to currency can result in superior investment performance.

---

[1] Indices are expressed in local currency, U.S. dollars (unhedged), and hedged U.S. dollars. However the local currency index, which expresses market returns in each of the 16 or so currencies in the index, is not investable but is provided as a reference for comparing bond market vs. currency performance.

[2] For an excellent overview of currency management practices, including a detailed review of historical data, see Roger G. Clarke and Mark P. Kritzman *Currency Management: Concepts and Practices*, (Charlottesville, VA: The Research Foundation of the Institute of Chartered Financial Analysts, 1996).

[3] See Philippe Jorion, "Mean/Variance Analysis of Currency Overlays," *Financial Analysts Journal* (May/June 1994), pp. 48-56. Jorion argues that currency overlays, although they can add value, are inferior to an integrated approach to currency management.

Exhibit 1: Returns and Standard Deviation of Returns of the Salomon Non-U.S. Government Bond Index and Lehman Aggregate Index (Monthly Data, Unhedged, and Hedged Basis)

	1985-96	1985-88	1989-92	1993-96	1989-96
Annualized Total Return					
Unhedged Index	14.45%	25.15%	7.91%	11.00%	9.45%
Hedged Index	8.75	10.23	6.60	9.45	8.02
50% Hedged	11.26	16.93	7.00	10.09	8.53
U.S. Aggregate Index	10.10	11.76	11.66	6.94	9.28
Standard Deviation of Returns					
Unhedged Index	10.97%	13.34%	11.21%	6.89%	9.31%
Hedged Index	3.77	4.23	3.39	3.56	3.50
50% Hedged	6.65	8.28	6.57	4.17	5.52
U.S. Aggregate Index	4.86	5.90	4.12	4.24	4.22
Sharpe Ratio					
Unhedged Index	0.77	1.37	0.12	0.93	0.42
Hedged Index	0.73	0.80	0.00	1.37	0.70
50% Hedged	0.79	1.22	0.60	1.33	0.54
U.S. Aggregate Index	0.84	0.84	1.23	0.56	0.87

Most of the academic research on currency hedging for U.S. dollar-based investors suggests that a partially hedged benchmark offers superior risk-adjusted returns as compared with either a fully hedged or unhedged benchmark.[4] This research has led some to recommend a 50% hedged benchmark for either a passively managed currency strategy, or as a good initial hedged position for an active currency manager. In addition to selecting an appropriate benchmark, a suitable currency hedge position, or benchmark hedge ratio, needs to be determined. For example, a U.S. dollar-based fixed income investor whose primary goal is risk reduction might adopt a hedged or mostly hedged benchmark as the diversification benefit has historically been greater from hedged international bonds. Despite a higher correlation with the U.S. bond market than unhedged international bonds, hedged international bonds offer better risk reduction due to a lower standard deviation of return than even the U.S. market. In addition, this lesser volatility of hedged international bonds results in more predictable returns. Conversely, an investor who has a total return objective, and a greater risk tolerance, would be more likely to adopt an unhedged, or mostly unhedged benchmark and allow more latitude for active currency management.

International bonds have historically provided higher returns than U.S. bonds. As seen in Exhibit 1, over the 12 years through 1996, the Salomon Non-

[4] See Gary L. Gastineau, "The Currency Hedging Decision: A Search for Synthesis in Asset Allocation," *Financial Analysts Journal* (May-June 1995), pp. 8-17 for a broad overview of the currency hedging debate.

U.S. Government Bond Index has outperformed the Lehman Aggregate Bond Index by an average of 435 basis points per annum. When looked at on a hedged basis, however, the non-U.S. index lagged the U.S. performance by 135 basis points. The standard deviation of returns for the non-U.S. unhedged index is substantially higher than the standard deviation of U.S. returns. However, the standard deviation of returns for the hedged index is lower than the standard deviation of U.S. returns during all periods. Using Sharpe ratios to compare returns on a risk-adjusted basis,[5] both the hedged and unhedged non-U.S. index underperformed the U.S. over the 12-year period. However, the results for each of the three 4-year periods are too variable to draw a firm conclusion about which provides the better risk-adjusted return.

Although the unhedged non-U.S. bond index often provided higher returns than the hedged index, the nearly 15 percentage points in annualized outperformance of the unhedged over the hedged index from 1985 through 1988 was extremely unusual. This was due to the dollar's rapid decline from its 1984 peak. If instead only the eight years from 1989 through 1996 are analyzed, the picture changes dramatically with the unhedged index outperforming the hedged index by 143 basis points. The Sharpe ratios for this period are 0.42 for the unhedged index and 0.70 for the hedged index, compared with 0.87 for the Lehman Aggregate index. According to the data in Exhibit 1 the argument for international bonds as an asset class for U.S dollar-based investors hardly seems compelling. However, it is the correlations of different asset classes that provide the diversification benefit, and when international bonds are included as a component of a U.S. dollar-based fixed income portfolio, the analysis provides dramatically different results.

Exhibit 2 shows that when the same analysis used in Exhibit 1 is applied to a portfolio composed of a 30% allocation to international bonds, the risk-adjusted returns improve substantially. Over the 12-year period, the portfolio with an allocation to unhedged bonds provided 130 basis points of added return over a domestic-only portfolio while slightly lowering overall portfolio volatility. Although the portfolio including hedged international bonds returned 41 basis points less than the domestic-only portfolio, its Sharpe ratio was higher than the domestic-only portfolio because its standard deviation was 25% lower than that of the domestic-only portfolio. In fact, the domestic-only portfolio had the highest standard deviation of any of the four portfolios, giving it the lowest Sharpe ratio.

As shown above, returns from currency have been highly variable depending on the time period chosen. The academic literature, and the data in Exhibits 1 and 2, support adopting a partially hedged currency benchmark. A benchmark currency position should be established in accordance with careful consideration for risk tolerances and return objectives.

---

[5] The Sharpe ratio measures returns in excess of the risk-free rate, per unit of standard deviation. The formula is $(R_p - RFR)/\sigma_p$ where R_p is the return on the portfolio, RFR is the risk-free rate, and σ_p is the portfolio standard deviation. The U.S. Treasury bill component of the Salomon Brothers World Money Market Performance Index was used as the risk-free rate.

Exhibit 2: Returns and Standard Deviation of Returns of a Portfolio with 30% International Bonds and 70% Domestic Bonds (Monthly Data)

	1985-96	1985-88	1989-92	1993-96	1989-96
Annualized Total Return					
Unhedged Index	11.40%	15.78%	10.54%	8.16%	9.33%
Hedged Index	9.69	11.30	10.14	7.70	8.90
50% Hedged	10.45	13.31	10.26	7.89	9.05
U.S. Aggregate Index	10.10	11.76	11.66	6.94	9.28
Standard Deviation of Returns					
Unhedged Index	4.79	5.82	4.51	3.63	4.12
Hedged Index	3.64	4.38	3.10	3.20	3.18
50% Hedged	4.00	4.89	3.56	3.25	3.44
U.S. Aggregate Index	4.86	5.90	4.12	4.24	4.22
Sharpe Ratio					
Unhedged Index	1.13	1.54	0.87	0.43	0.91
Hedged Index	1.02	1.02	1.14	0.98	1.04
50% Hedged	1.11	1.33	1.03	1.02	1.01
U.S. Aggregate Index	0.84	0.84	1.23	0.56	0.87

Returns of those portfolios with a 30% international bond allocation over the 1989 to 1996 period are lower than the full 12-year performance figures, but the risk-adjusted performance of each of these portfolios remains higher than the domestic-only portfolio. The return on the portfolio including a 30% allocation to unhedged international bonds of 9.33 was five basis points higher than the domestic-only portfolio, and its standard deviation of 4.12% was ten basis points lower than the domestic-only portfolio, giving it a Sharpe ratio of 0.91 compared to the domestic portfolio's 0.87. The Sharpe ratios for the other two portfolios that include hedged and 50% hedged international bonds are even higher at 1.04 and 1.01 respectively.

Risk Limits

Many investment guidelines will include explicit risk limits on bond and currency positions as well as duration and credit risk. Exposure limits can be either expressed as absolute percentages, or portfolio weights relative to the benchmark. Expressing limits in terms of trading blocs, which exhibit a high degree of correlation, allows the portfolio manager more scope for shifting exposures without adding significantly to overall portfolio risk. Bond markets can be divided into five trading blocs: the *dollar bloc* (the U.S., Canada, Australia, and New Zealand), *core Europe* (Germany, France, Holland, and Belgium), *peripheral Europe* (Italy, Spain, the U.K., Denmark, Sweden, Finland, and Portugal), Japan, and the *emerg-*

ing markets. These dividing lines, however, are somewhat subjective. For example, the U.K. often trades more closely with dollar bloc than European markets, and many might place Denmark with the core European countries. Limits on investment in countries outside the benchmark should also be specified at the outset. Despite the pitfalls of using duration to measure interest rate risk across countries, risk limits on duration are nonetheless useful and should be established.

The risk limits in Exhibit 3 might be appropriate for a moderately risk averse investor. Note that in Exhibit 3 the range of allowable exposures is wider for bond exposures than currency exposures and that the minimum U.S. dollar exposure is 20%.

Credit risk limits, usually a minimum average credit weighting from the two major credit rating agencies, and limits on the absolute amount of low or non-investment grade credits, should also be included. Apart from default risk, the illiquidity of lower rated securities poses another type of credit risk as international fixed income portfolio managers tend to shift funds in and out of markets frequently. Due to the lack of a liquid corporate bond market in most countries, and the relative illiquidity of Eurobonds compared to domestic government bond markets, most credit risk in international bond portfolios is concentrated in U.S. and emerging market bonds.

Exhibit 3: Examples of Bond and Currency Risk Limits for an International Bond Portfolio

Bond Exposures

Currency Bloc	Benchmark	Minimum	Maximum
Yen	32%	15%	45%
U.S.	0%	0%	15%
Dollar Bloc	6%	0%	18%
Core Europe	47%	30%	65%
Peripheral Europe	16%	0%	35%
Other Markets	0%	0%	15%
Total Duration as a % of Index	100%	80%	120%

Currency Exposures

Currency Bloc	Benchmark	Minimum	Maximum
Yen	32%	10%	40%
U.S.	0%	20%	95%
Dollar Bloc	6%	0%	20%
Core Europe	47%	15%	55%
Peripheral Europe	16%	0%	25%
Other Markets	0%	0%	10%
Total Foreign Currency Exposure	100%	5%	80%

Derivatives

Investment guidelines should specify the permitted use of derivatives in the portfolio. Although derivatives are required to hedge currency exposures, they are a useful, but not necessary, tool for duration management. Guidelines will usually place limitations on the leverage[6] that can be obtained through use of derivatives, for example by requiring cash to be set aside equal to the notional amount of a long futures position, or by prohibiting the writing of uncovered put or call options. Structured notes, which combine derivatives, such as swaps and options, with a certificate of deposit or medium-term note to create a specific exposure to interest rates or currencies, should be subject to the same limitations on leverage. Many structured notes were engineered to have risks commensurate with, or less than, plain vanilla bonds. The separation of coupon and principal payments in most structures notes gives them a similar appearance to fixed income securities. However, structured notes, like the derivatives of which they are composed, can also be highly levered. The risk to capital incorporated in some of these securities, if poorly understood, can result in substantial losses. Thus, the use of structured notes need not be prohibited, but guidelines for their use should contain criteria consistent with those applied to the derivatives of which they are composed.

Custodian Banks

Other housekeeping issues include setting up an account with a global custodian bank, usually a large international bank with branches or correspondent banks in each of the countries in which the portfolio will invest.[7] Although the ultimate responsibility for all aspects of the investment process rests with the portfolio manager, the custodian bank will be responsible for the settlement and delivery of any securities and foreign exchange transactions, collection of coupon income, and maintenance of cash balances. The custodian bank will also provide portfolio and trading reports, although the portfolio manager should have internal portfolio account systems for a variety of reasons including identification of trading errors and risk management.

PORTFOLIO STRATEGY

Once the investment guidelines have been established, the portfolio manager needs to develop a portfolio strategy appropriate to the investor's objectives and risk tolerances. Just as in many other areas of investment management, portfolio managers often subscribe to different management styles, or investment disciplines. As the performance of most portfolio managers is judged against the benchmark return,

---

[6] Implicit in most derivatives, both fixed income and currency derivatives, is an exposure to shifts in short-term interest rates.

[7] See Robert Binney "Implementation Issues: Global Custody," pp. 78-83, from *Global Portfolio Management* (Charlottesville, VA: AIMR, 1996).

they are constantly seeking opportunities to outperform the benchmark. There are a number of means by which portfolio managers can add to returns, however, the bulk of excess returns relative to the benchmark come from broad bond market and currency allocation decisions. A disciplined investment approach, based upon fundamental economic factors and market indicators of value, can facilitate the market and currency selection process. Because of the historically high volatility of currency returns, the approach to currency management should be of primary concern.

Styles of International Bond Portfolio Management

The image that many people have of international bond managers is that of a jet fighter pilot: well seasoned, cool under fire, and ready to pit his nerve and skill against the market. However, the metaphor that best describes the international bond manager is not that of the fighter pilot, but the captain of a 747. Rather than "pushing the envelope" of his machine's performance, the jumbo jet pilot relies more on checklists and management of computer flight and navigation systems than piloting skill. The modern jetliner is an extremely complicated piece of machinery that requires a depth of experience and skill in managing the wealth of resources available on the flight deck. The pilot, in addition to drawing from his own years of experience, relies on other inputs as well; some from other members of the crew, and some from talking to controllers and meteorologists on the ground. Like managing a portfolio, piloting a jetliner involves managing risks, and a safe arrival is better achieved by avoiding dangerous situations than by deft manipulation of the controls in an emergency.

The complexity of the international fixed income markets is more akin to the complexity of the U.S. equity market than the U.S. bond market. First, the global fixed income portfolio manager must operate in the U.S. bond market *plus* 10 to 20 other markets, each with their own market dynamics. Second, changes in interest rates generally affect all sectors of the U.S. bond market in the same way (with the exception of mortgage-backed securities), although the magnitude of the changes may vary. Like the equity market, where it is not unusual to have some industries or market sectors move in opposite directions, international bond markets may also move in different directions depending upon economic conditions and investor risk tolerances.

Equity managers use a variety of investment disciplines, such as value, growth, or small capitalization, to try to create some sense of order out of the chaos of the market. Equity investors also use a variety of indicators, such as price-to-earnings ratios, earnings momentum, and technical analysis, to help identify attractive opportunities. As different as each of these approaches are, they are all designed to provide superior market returns. International bond managers also utilize one or more different management styles. These can be divided into four general categories:

- *The Experienced Trader.* These managers use experience and intuition to identify market opportunities. They tend to be active traders, trying to anticipate the next market shift by international fixed income and hedge fund managers. The basis for these trades is derived from estimates of competitors' positions and risk tolerances bolstered by observation of market price movements and flow information obtained from brokerage houses. The experienced trader is often a contrarian, looking to profit from situations where many investors may be forced to stop themselves out of losing positions.

- *The Fundamentalist.* This management style rests upon a belief that bonds and currencies trade according to the economic cycle, and that the cycle is forecastable. These managers rely mostly upon economic analysis and forecasts in selecting bond markets and currencies. These managers tend to have less portfolio turnover as the economic fundamentals have little impact on short-term price movements.
- *The Black Box.* The quantitative manager believes that computer models can identify market relationships that human beings cannot. These models can rely exclusively on economic data, price data, or some combination of the two. Quantitative managers believe that use of computer models can create a more disciplined investment approach which, either because of other managers' emotional attachment to positions, their lack of trading disciplines, or their inability to process more than a few variables simultaneously, will provide superior investment results.
- *The Chartist.* Some investors may rely primarily on technical analysis to determine which assets to buy or sell. Chartists will look at daily, weekly, and monthly charts to try to ascertain the strength of market trends, or to identify potential turning points in markets. Trend following approaches, such as moving averages and stochastics aim to allow the portfolio manager to exploit market momentum. Counter-trend approaches, such as relative strength indices and oscillators try to identify when recent price trends are likely to reverse.

Very few international bond portfolio managers rely on only one of these management styles, but instead use some combination of each. Investment managers that rely on forecasts of the economic cycle to drive their investment process will from time to time take positions contrary to their medium-term strategy to take advantage of temporary under or overvaluation of markets identified by technical analysis, or estimates of market positions. Even "quant shops" that rely heavily on computer models for driving investment decisions will sometimes look to other management styles to add incremental returns. Regardless of the manager's investment style, investment decisions must be consistent with the investor's return objectives and risk tolerances, and within the investment guidelines.

International bond portfolio managers would do well to emulate equity investors in maintaining a disciplined approach to buy and sell decisions. This would require each allocation away from the benchmark to have a specified price target (or more often yield spread or exchange rate level), and stated underlying rationale. As long as the investment rationale that supported the initial decision remained unchanged, the position would be held, or potentially increased if the market moves in the opposite direction. Each trade should be designed with consideration for the relevant bond yield or exchange rate's behavior through time. For example, an exchange rate that exhibits a tendency to trend will require a different buy and sell discipline than an asset that is mean reverting.[8]

Sources of Excess Return

The baseline for any international bond portfolio is the benchmark. However, in order to earn returns in excess of the benchmark, after management fees, the portfolio manager must find ways to augment returns. These excess returns can be generated through a combination of five broad strategies: bond market selection, currency selection, duration management/yield curve plays, sector/credit/security selection, and, if permitted, investing in markets outside the benchmark. Each of these strategies can add to returns, however, currency and bond market selections generally provide the lion's share of returns.

Bond Market Selection

Incremental returns from overweighting the best performing bond markets can be extremely large. Annual local currency return differentials between the best and worst performing bond markets ranged from 7% to 39%, with an average difference of 17 percentage points according to the 18 years of annual return data from the Salomon Brothers World Government Bond and Bond Performance Indices which include only developed markets.[9] When currency movements are added, the return differentials nearly double. As shown in Exhibit 4, in U.S. dollar terms, the smallest range between the best and worst performing market was 14% and the widest was 65% with an average differential of 31 percentage points. Thus, international bond portfolio managers can significantly enhance returns by overweighting the better performing bond markets, and currencies, in the index.[10]

---

[8] For example, if the widening of a yield spread to an all-time wide level causes a portfolio position to suffer losses, the temptation may be to increase the size of the position. This would be rational if the spread has historically shown mean reverting patterns and is expected to continue to do so. Then profits could be made as the spread converges towards its mean. If, however, the yield spread tended to follow long-term tightening and widening trends then a discipline applying stop-loss limits would be more appropriate.

[9] The Salomon World Government Bond Index began in December of 1984, and presently contains 15 markets. The Salomon Bond Performance Index began in 1978 and was discontinued in 1995. The Bond Performance Index contained 10 markets, and included Euro and Foreign issues as well as Government bonds. Exhibit 4 uses the Bond Performance Index from 1978 through 1984, and the World Government Bond Index thereafter.

[10] As of this writing, it appears likely that at least several countries will adopt the Euro as a common currency when European Monetary Union is scheduled to commence in January 1999. Although the impact of this event is a matter of some debate, the bond markets in the countries which have adopted the single currency will trade much more closely than before.

Exhibit 4: U.S. Bonds and Non-U.S. World Index versus Best and Worst Performing Markets

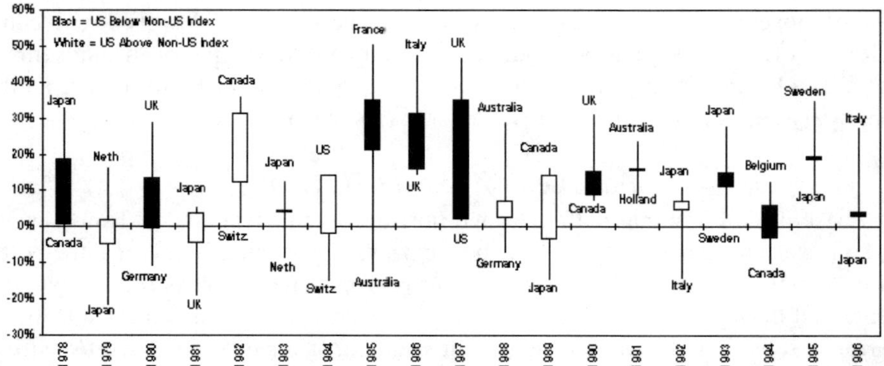

Currency Selection

Regardless of the initial portfolio hedge ratio, most guidelines will allow for some active management of currency exposures. The attraction of active currency management is strong because the potential gains are so large. However, as the volatility of currency returns is generally higher than that of bond market returns, the incremental returns gained from currency exposures must be evaluated relative to the additional risk incurred. For an active currency management strategy to consistently provide superior risk-adjusted performance, a currency forecasting method is required that can predict future spot rates better than forward foreign exchange rates. As shown later, forward foreign exchange rates are not forecasts of future spot foreign exchange rates, but are determined by short interest rate differentials.

Academic studies have shown that several strategies have been successful in generating consistent profits through active currency management. The fact that forward foreign exchange rates are poor predictors of future spot exchange rates is well known. Historically, discount currencies (i.e., those with higher interest rates than the base currency) have depreciated less than the amount implied by the forward rates, providing superior returns from holding unhedged positions in currencies with higher interest rates. Overweighting of currencies with high real interest rates versus those with lower real interest rates has also been shown to provide incremental returns.[11] In addition, currency movements are not a random walk, but exhibit serial correlation, or a tendency to trend.[12] Thus, simple technical trading rules, such as the crossover of a short and long

[11] See Gastineau, "The Currency Hedging Decision," pp 13-14.

[12] One suggestion as to why currency markets trend is that central banks attempt to smooth foreign exchange rate movements through intervention. Thus, because central bank participation in the foreign exchange market is not motivated by profit, their actions keep the market from being truly efficient. See Robert D. Arnott and Tan K. Pham, "Tactical Currency Allocation," *Financial Analysts Journal*, (May/June 1993) pp. 47-52.

moving average, can provide opportunities for incremental currency returns.[13] These findings, demonstrating that excess currency returns can be generated consistently, provide a powerful incentive for active currency management.

Duration Management

Although closely aligned with the bond market selection decision, duration management can also enhance returns. Bullet versus barbell strategies in a curve steepening or flattening environment can enhance yield and total return. In addition to these strategies that are also available to domestic portfolio managers, the international fixed income portfolio manager has the option of shifting duration between markets while leaving the portfolio's overall duration unchanged. Likewise, duration-neutral positions across markets can be achieved by targeting preferred sectors of the yield curve.[14]

Duration management, however, is more difficult in international bond investing as very few foreign bond markets have liquid bond issues with an original maturity longer than 10 years. Most foreign bond markets also lack the broad range of instruments, such as strips and repos, that allow for low-cost, active management of duration. Recent progress on these fronts is being made in the U.K., Italy, and Germany. Interest rate futures, available in most markets, offer a very liquid and low cost vehicle for changing duration or market exposure quickly. The interest rate swaps market is generally very liquid across international bond markets; however, counterparty credit, technical, and operational barriers limit effective participation in this market to large institutional investors.

Sector Selection

Investing in non-government bonds can also enhance returns as most indices include only government bonds. However, options are more limited as government and government-guaranteed issues account for 62% of all bond issues outstanding[15] compared with 12.7% for the corporate bonds. If the U.S. is excluded, where corporate bonds account for one third of all U.S. dollar-denominated bonds outstanding, the figure drops to only 4.2%. Corporate bonds account for less than 15% of the market capitalization in all other bond markets — except for a 26% share in the Netherlands. In several large countries, such as Germany and Italy, non-financial corporate bonds are virtually nonexistent. This scarcity of corporate bond markets outside the U.S. is due to a policy of discouraging the raising of capital through bond issuance in favor of bank financing and equity issuance in many countries. Other instruments are also available in selected markets including Eurobonds, mortgage bonds, and inflation indexed bonds.

---

[13] See Richard M. Levich and Lee R. Thomas, "The Merits of Active Currency Risk Management: Evidence from International Bond Portfolios," *Financial Analysts Journal*, (September/October 1993) pp. 63-70.

[14] As discussed later, a duration-neutral position to the benchmark would mean having the same contribution to duration from each country as the benchmark. Contribution to duration, measured as the weight times duration of a given market can be achieved with a large market weight of short duration bonds or a small market weight of long duration bonds.

[15] Data from Salomon Brothers, "How Big is the World Bond Market? — 1996 Update," (August 1996).

Investing in Markets Outside the Index

If allowed by portfolio guidelines, allocating assets to markets outside the index can significantly enhance returns without dramatically altering the risk profile of the portfolio. For example, Finland was one of the best performing bond markets during 1995, but, because of its small size, was not included in the Salomon Brothers World Government Bond Index (WGBI) until June 1996. Similarly, New Zealand's very attractive U.S. dollar return of 18% during 1996 would have ranked it as the fourth best performing market in the WGBI. For those investors with a higher risk tolerance, exposure to emerging markets can significantly add to returns. For example, a portfolio composed of 80% exposure to the Salomon Non-U.S. Government Bond Index and 20% exposure to the Salomon Brady Bond Index from 1991 through 1996 would have added 186 basis points to the return of the international index and *reduced* the standard deviation of returns by 13%.

A Fundamental-Based Approach to Investing

The portfolio strategy is often composed of both a medium term *strategic* allocation, and a shorter term *tactical* allocation. The strategic allocation is composed of positions designed to take advantage of longer term economic trends designed to be held for one to three months, or longer. The tactical allocation generally relies on technical analysis or flow information to identify shifts in market prices that are likely to occur within a few days to several weeks. Tactical allocations are often contrarian in nature, driven by expectations of a reversal in a recent price trends; however, tactical allocations can also be momentum following, especially if a breakout of a technical range appears likely. The strategic allocation can be compared to the course set by a sailing ship. The tactical allocation may result in substantial divergence from the course setting at times, much as a ship must tack when sailing into the wind. The trick, however, is to be able to identify when changing conditions warrant a change in the set course, or only a small detour.

The strategic decision of which bond markets and currencies to overweight usually begins with an outlook for the economic cycle and bond and currency forecasts in each of the markets to be considered for investment. As shown in Exhibit 5, the long-run economic cycle is closely correlated with changes in bond yields, and trends in both the economic cycle and bond yields tend to persist for a year or longer. The millions of dollars spent each year by money management firms, banks, and brokerage houses in forecasting economic trends is testimony to the potential returns that can be achieved by correctly forecasting economic growth, especially turning points in the economic cycle. Forecasting interest rates, however, is extremely difficult and the academic literature generally holds that interest rate forecasts are unable to generate consistent risk-adjusted excess returns. This is partly because market prices can deviate substantially over the short term from the level consistent with the economic fundamentals which only impact bond and currency prices over the medium to long term. Also, the volatile nature of certain economic data series may result in an exaggerated market reaction to an individual data release that may be at odds with the actual trend in the economy. These deviations may persist for several months until either the initial figure is revised, or several subsequent data releases reveal the error in the initial interpretation.

The creation of an independent economic outlook can be useful in several ways. It can help identify when market interpretations of the economic data are too extreme, or add value through correctly anticipating economic shifts not reflected in the market consensus. Also, as it is often not absolute changes in interest rates, but changes in interest rates relative to other markets that determines the margin of performance in international fixed income investing, an independent economic outlook does not require accurate growth forecasts for each individual market, but only economic growth differentials to be able to add value. Whether the portfolio will invest in U.S. bonds or not, the large influence of the U.S. dollar and the Treasury market on foreign markets underlines the importance of an independent outlook on the U.S. economy.

Thus, the economic outlook forms the foundation for the *strategic* allocation for bonds and currencies. The economic outlook should also include an indication of the relative conviction regarding the economic view for each country to assist in ranking the relative attractiveness of markets. However, even though economic fundamentals in a particular country may be extremely bond supportive, bond prices may be too high to make it an attractive investment. Likewise, bonds are sometimes excessively cheap in countries with poor economic fundamentals thus providing an attractive investment opportunity. Thus, the economic outlook must be compared with either consensus economic forecasts, or some measure of market value to identify attractive investment opportunities. In addition, the volatilities and correlations of the various bond and currency markets should be used to assess the incremental impact of any position on overall portfolio risk compared with its expected return.

Exhibit 5: G7 Industrial Production and Change in Bond Yields

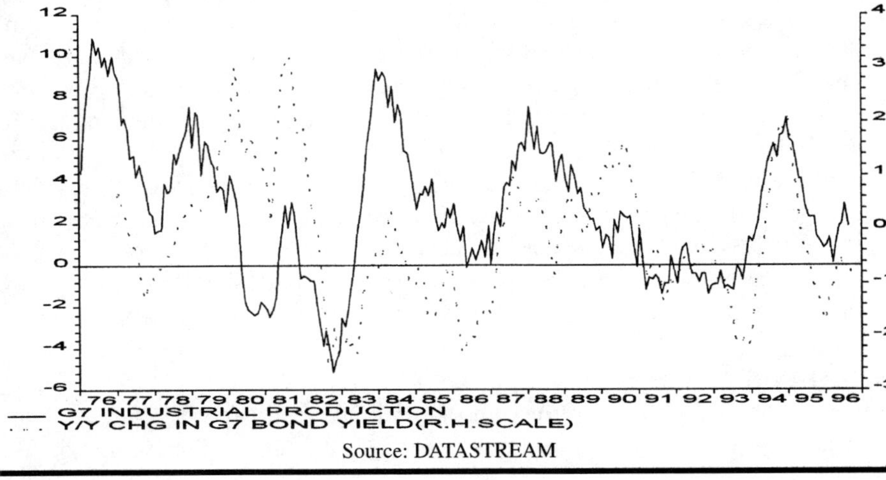

Source: DATASTREAM

The strategic allocation decision of which markets to over or underweight relative to the benchmark is thus a complex interaction of expected returns derived from assessments of economic trends, technical and value factors, and risk factors, estimated from historical volatilities and cross-market correlations. Each set of variables is defined and explored below, beginning with the fundamental factors used to create the economic outlook.

Fundamental Economic Factors

The seven main categories of fundamental economic influences are: cyclicals, inflation, monetary policy, fiscal policy, debt, the balance of payments, and politics. Each factor needs to be evaluated against market expectations to determine its likely impact on bond and currency prices. For example, a drop in inflation in a country such as Germany which has a history of low inflation may have a much lesser impact on bond prices than a drop in Italian inflation.

Cyclicals

As shown above, bond and currency valuations are heavily influenced by the economic cycle. A strong economy raises fears of higher inflation which erodes the value of fixed income securities and the purchasing power of the currency. In assessing the potential inflationary impact of stronger growth, analysts examine both the pace and composition of growth. One measure of inflationary pressures caused by economic growth, used by both academics and market participants, is the output gap. The output gap is a measure of the difference between present growth rates and the long-term potential growth rate of the economy. The economy's potential growth rate can be estimated using either a long-run historical average growth rate or a projection based on such factors as estimated growth in the labor force and productivity growth rates. If an economy is growing below its potential growth rate, it has excess labor and manufacturing capacity that should act as a constraint on wage and price increases. Conversely, if the economy is growing above its potential growth rate, bottlenecks should soon appear prompting business to bid up wages and the cost of raw materials to meet demand, and eventually pass these increased costs onto consumers.

The composition of growth also has a direct bearing on the potential for fueling inflation. Growth that is driven by capital investment rather than consumer demand is less likely to be inflationary (unless investment spending results in a competition for raw materials that drives up producer price inflation.) Likewise, strong export growth, is less likely to be inflationary, unless it is driven by a currency depreciation that raises the cost of imported goods. Thus, the outlook for economic growth and its composition will have a strong impact on inflation expectations.

Inflation

Inflation expectations have a direct impact on financial asset prices. As the future purchasing power parity of a country's currency is eroded by higher inflation, this prompts investors to demand a higher return for their savings (which represents deferred consumption) as they come to believe that their money will purchase less in the future. In its impact on the financial markets, it is the direction and magnitude of changes in the inflation rate *relative to market expectations* that counts. Bonds may rally on an increase in the rate of inflation which falls below market expectations while unanticipated increases in inflation usually cause bond yields to rise reflecting an increase in the inflation risk premium. The required rate of return demanded by the market may also change over time as risk appetites change. The required rate of return has become more uniform across markets as capital controls and other barriers to cross-border investment have been removed. The role that real yields play in market valuation is explored below.

A change in the rate of inflation can have a very different impact on currencies over the short and long run. Over the short run, an unexpected rise in inflation may lead to currency strength as the market anticipates a hike in managed interest rates to combat the inflation pressure. Over the long run, if the higher inflation persists, the erosion of purchasing power due to higher inflation leads to a depreciation of the currency relative to lower inflation countries. The chart below shows that there has been a strong correlation between the change in exchange rates relative to the dollar since the demise of fixed exchange rates in the early 1970s, and changes in the price level. For example, the price level in Australia grew more than six times from 1972 levels, about half again as much as the nearly fourfold increase in U.S. prices. Thus, the U.S. dollar now buys about 50% more Australian dollars than it did 25 years ago. The currencies of Japan, Germany, Switzerland, and the Netherlands, whose price levels grew only 60% to 80% as much as in the U.S., all appreciated significantly against the U.S. dollar, which could purchase only one third to one half as much of these currencies as in 1972.

Exhibit 6: U.S. $ versus Foreign Currencies and Change in Price Level 1972-1996

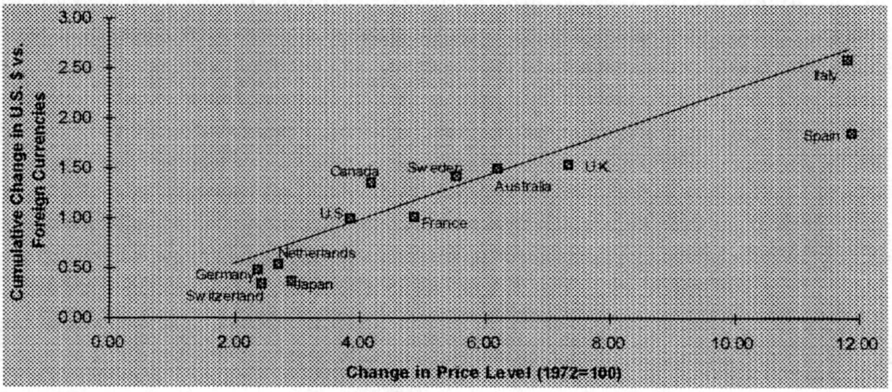

Source: OECD

Monetary Policy

Central Banks throughout the developed world place great importance on price stability. In recent years, nearly all central banks have accepted price stability as their primary goal. Central banks in eight countries (Australia, Britain, Canada, Finland, Italy, New Zealand, Spain, and Sweden) have adopted, at least temporary, explicit inflation targets. An additional four (France, Germany, Switzerland, and Denmark) have medium term inflation objectives. Some central banks, such as the Bank of England, the Bank of Canada, and Sweden's Riksbank, also publish regular reports on the inflationary outlook. Other central banks (such as the Bank of Canada with its Monetary Conditions Index) also take explicit account of the impact of exchange rate movements in assessing the overall tightness of monetary policy.

Monetary policy is effective in allowing central banks to control short term interest rates but has only an indirect influence on bond yields. Nevertheless, short interest rate movements, especially changes in the direction of monetary policy, do have a significant impact on rates across the yield curve. Changes in short term interest rates have a direct impact on currencies as they impact both the returns to investors and hedge costs. Because the gains from effectively forecasting changes in official rates can be substantial, many in the financial markets devote resources to examining the personalities and decision making process at the Federal Reserve and other central banks. Some also use models to predict the direction of monetary policy, such as the Taylor Rule,[16] which utilizes the output gap, and a stated or implied inflation target, to measure the relative monetary policy stance.

Fiscal Policy

Although fiscal policy is more long term in nature, it can have a significant impact on financial asset prices, especially when fiscal policy is in the process of being tightened or loosened. A higher fiscal deficit will result in higher rates through the "crowding out" of private borrowers and increased demand for capital. The greater a country's dependence upon the capital market for funding, the more its long term interest rates will tend to fluctuate over the business cycle. The following chart shows the increase in 10 year bond yields during 1994, a severe bear market for global bonds, plotted against deficit to GDP. Clearly, fiscal policy can have a large influence on bond prices, especially during a period when investors are becoming more risk averse.

Debt

The national debt is simply the accumulation of past deficits. Debt levels are normally analyzed in relation to GDP both for ease of comparison internationally, and because economic growth facilitates the servicing of debt. Debt service costs are a function of the size of the debt and the average interest rate paid on that debt. Countries such as Italy where nearly two thirds of their government bonds are either floating rate or less than one year in maturity, find that their debt service

---

[16] John B. Taylor, *Discretion versus Policy Rules in Practice*, Policy Paper No. 327 (Stanford, CA: The Center for Economic Policy and Research at Stanford University, 1992).

costs can fluctuate substantially from year to year with interest rate changes. If a country's debt levels rise to the point where investors are reluctant to hold its bonds, then it could fall into a debt trap. As investors demand a higher risk premium for holding the highly indebted country's bonds, interest rates on new debt issues are driven up adding further to debt service costs, until credit concerns prompt the market to halt lending altogether and default or debt restructuring becomes inevitable.[17] However, debt levels can have an impact on bond prices well before reaching levels where the debt trap becomes a concern.

In addition to the size of the debt, the amount held by foreigners is also important. Some countries, such as New Zealand issue little in other currencies, yet have more than half of their government bonds held by foreign investors. Canada and the U.S. have approximately one quarter of their government bonds held offshore. Interest rates in countries that depend on foreign capital to finance local spending, usually because local savings have already been tapped, can be particularly sensitive to changes in foreigner's willingness to lend. For emerging market countries the debt to exports ratio is commonly used as a measure of the country's ability to generate foreign exchange to service its foreign currency debt.

The Balance of Payments

Capital flows have a much greater impact on international markets than on U.S. asset prices as the sizes of foreign capital markets are smaller, and the dependence of their economies on foreign trade is often much larger than in the United States. Shifts in the balance of trade, however, often take years to work their way through the economy. These shifts may be obscured by noise in the data or other factors such as the "J-curve" effect. The impact of a shift in the balance of payments on financial asset prices, although long term in nature, can still offer opportunities for investment outperformance by identifying longer term secular shifts that will affect the long term growth potential of a country and the underlying demand and supply situation for its currency represented by its current account position.

Exhibit 7: Budget Deficit and 1994 10-Year Yield Change

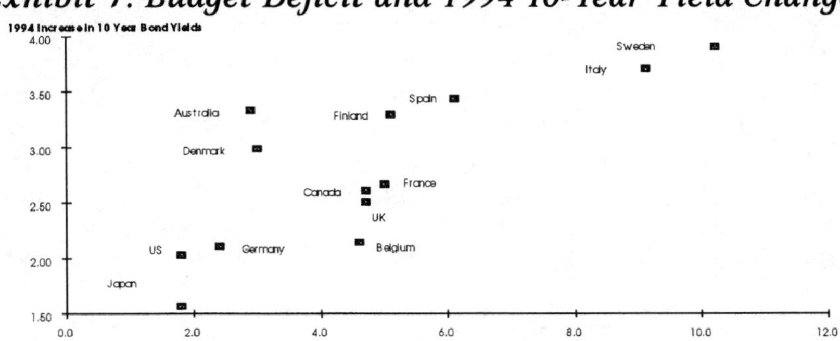

Source: OECD

[17] For a more complete discussion of the dynamics of the debt trap see *OECD Economic Outlook,* No. 58, (Paris: OECD, 1995), pp. 19-23.

Exhibit 8: Yen/Dollar Exchange Rate and Bilateral Trade Balance

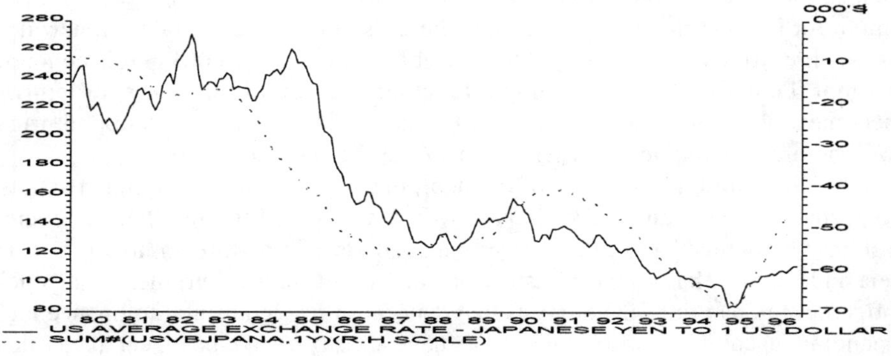

Source: DATASTREAM

For example, much of the strengthening of the U.S. dollar against the yen during 1996 can be attributed to a steep drop in the size of the U.S./Japanese bilateral trade deficit as shown in Exhibit 8. The U.S. dollar/Japanese yen exchange rate is heavily influenced by the cumulative current account deficit of the U.S. with Japan. The current account, which measures the flows of goods from one country to another, is offset by the capital account. The capital account represents the investment of the trade surplus in either direct investment (the building of physical plant), or portfolio investment (the purchase of debt or equity securities). Hence, the cumulative current account represents the transfer of wealth from one country to another.

Politics

While they may be the most difficult of the factors to quantify, there is no denying that, at times, political events can have a profound impact on financial asset prices. Elections, changes of government, parliamentary votes, and political scandals all have the power to move bond and currency prices. Perhaps the best illustration of the impact of a political event on the financial markets is the case of European Monetary Union, or EMU. Although EMU has far-reaching economic consequences, the entire undertaking is essentially political, including deciding which countries will be allowed to participate and when the switch from national currencies to a single currency will take place. In financial markets, unforeseen political events more often have the consequence of precipitating drops in asset prices, thus monitoring of the political environment and events can be instrumental in controlling portfolio risk.

Value and Technical Indicators

Identification of trends in economic fundamentals can help identify attractive investment opportunities in markets, but without some yardstick with which to measure value, we are like Archimedes with his lever but with no fulcrum on which to rest it. The determination of relative value is highly subjective. Most investors have preferred measures for assessing market over or undervalution, however, even the most respected market strategists often get it wrong. Some more objective measures of value, including real yields, technical analysis, and market sentiment surveys are explored below.

Real Yields

A real yield is the inflation-adjusted rate of return demanded by the market for holding long-term fixed income securities whose value can be quickly eroded by sustained increases in inflation. Real yields are impacted by supply and demand for capital as well as inflation expectations. Real yields are nominal bond yields minus *expected* inflation, however, expected inflation is often difficult to quantify. A few countries, such as the U.K., Canada, and Australia, and, as of January 1997, the U.S., have inflation-indexed bonds that pay a real rate of interest above the inflation rate. These bonds not only provide investors with protection against a surge in inflation but also offer a means of gauging investor inflation expectations.[18] Surveys often include inflation expectations, but these have a relatively short history .

Nominal bond yields deflated by *current* inflation, although not a precise measure of the market's real interest rate premium, are easily measurable and can still provide some useful insight into bond valuation. Real yields can be compared across markets or against their long run averages, such as 5 or 10 years, in each market. As shown in Exhibit 9, a strong correlation exists between nominal 10 year bond yields and the average inflation rate over the last 10 years. This relationship tends to be stable over time despite changes in the absolute level of yields. This suggests that the market has a long memory and will need to be convinced of a fundamental change in a country's inflation prospects before reducing the inflation risk premium on its debt. Thus the early recognition of such a change creates the potential for substantial profit.

Technicals

Technical analysis can be as simple as drawing a trend line on a chart or as complicated as calculating the target of the third impluse wave of an Elliott wave analysis. In addition to bonds and currencies, technical analysis is applied to everything from stocks, to gold, to pork bellies. What all technical analysis has in common, is that it tries to predict future prices solely from examining past price movements. Most technical analysis models fall into one of two camps: trend following and counter trend. The former try to identify trends that should persist for some period of time, and the latter attempt to predict when a recent trend is likely to change. Trend following models include: simple or exponential moving averages, stochastics, and MACDs. Counter trend technical models include: relative strength indices and oscillators.

---

[18] Nominal yield to maturity is composed of a real yield and an inflation expectations component (Yield to Maturity = Real Yield to Maturity + Expected Inflation to Maturity). In these markets the nominal government bond yield and the real yield offered by inflation-indexed debt of the same maturity can be used to calculate the expected inflation rate to the maturity, sometimes called the breakeven inflation rate.

Exhibit 9: Nominal 10-Year Bond Yields and 10-Year Average Inflation

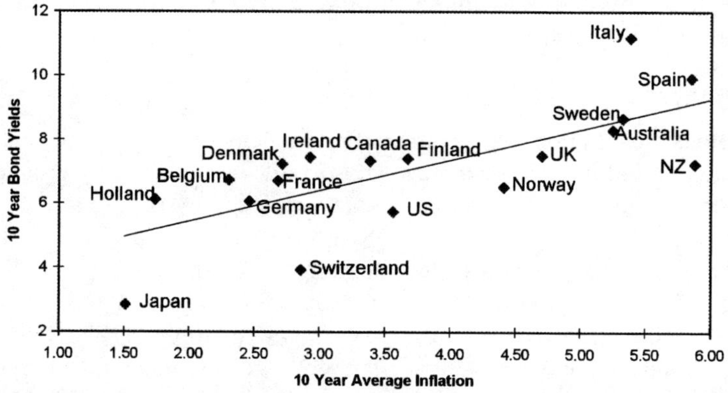

Market Sentiment

Market sentiment can be used as a contra-indicator of value as a heavy overweight of a particular market implies that fewer managers are likely to add to that market, and more managers, at least eventually, are likely to sell. Several surveys of investor sentiment are available including a quarterly Merrill Lynch survey of money managers, and a monthly Lehman Brothers survey, among others. Historic trends, as well as the overall levels should be taken into account when assessing market sentiment. For example, an indication that the market is underweight Japanese bonds might lead some to conclude that they are due for a rally, when historically, international fixed income managers have consistently underweighted the Japanese market, in part due to its low nominal yields. Sentiment surveys, however, do not tell the whole story as buying and selling by domestic investors, who are often not included in sentiment surveys, can also move markets.

PORTFOLIO CONSTRUCTION

Translating the strategic outlook into a portfolio allocation requires a framework for assessing expected returns against incremental portfolio risk. The following discussion on sources of return illustrates how returns can be separated into three components: excess returns on bonds, excess returns on currencies, and the risk-free rate. This methodology can assist in identifying where market prices are most out of line with the strategic outlook and whether bond market exposures should be hedged or left unhedged. However, the potential for higher returns is often associated with greater risk, and reference to market correlations can help estimate the incremental risk posed to the portfolio by any change in allocation. A brief discussion of other tools for portfolio construction, such as breakeven analysis and forward curves, closes this section.

Components of Return

The total return of an unhedged international bond portfolio for a U.S. dollar based investor can be expressed in the following equation:[19]

$$R_\$ \approx \sum w_i(r_i + \varepsilon_{\$,i}) \quad (1)$$

where

$R_\$$ = total portfolio return in U.S. dollars
r_i = bond market return for country i in local currency
$\varepsilon_{\$,i}$ = percentage change of the dollar exchange rate with country i
w_i = weight of the bonds of country i in the overall portfolio

Thus, the expected return on the portfolio is a function of the expected returns on the bonds and currencies in each market and their weights in the portfolio. However, in order to fully comprehend the impact of currency exposures on returns, the mechanics of currency hedging must first be understood.

Mechanics of Currency Hedging

Hedge costs are driven by short-term interest rate differentials. The covered interest rate parity theorem, associated with Keynes and Fisher, states that the forward foreign exchange rate for a fixed period must be equal to the interest rate differential between the two countries, otherwise riskless arbitrage would occur to bring the two back into equilibrium.[20] The formula is:

$$F = S_0\left(\frac{1 + c_d}{1 + c_f}\right) \quad (2)$$

where F is the forward foreign exchange rate, S_0 is the spot foreign exchange rate, and c_d and c_f are the domestic and foreign cash returns, or short-term (risk-free) interest rates, which match the maturity of the forward contract. By rearranging equation (2), the forward discount or premium f (or the percentage change of the forward rate from the spot exchange rate), becomes approximately the differential between the risk-free rates.[21]

$$f = F - S_0 \approx c_d - c_f \quad (3)$$

---

[19] The structure of this discussion is taken from Brian D. Singer and Denis S. Karnosky, *The General Framework for Global Investment Management and Performance Attribution* (Charlottesville, VA: The Research Foundation of the Institute of Chartered Financial Analysts, 1994). An abridged version also appeared in *The Journal of Portfolio Management* (Winter 1995), pp. 84-92. The relationship in equation (1) is approximate because bond market and currency returns of a foreign investment is more accurately expressed as the compounded gain of the two components: $(1 + r_i) \times (1 + \varepsilon_{\$,i}) - 1$.

[20] Uncovered interest rate parity would hold if the forward rates were an unbiased indicator of future foreign exchange rates, which was shown to be false in the portfolio strategy section. For an excellent introduction to currency terminology and the calculation of forward exchange rates see Chapter 1 of Clarke and Kritzman, *Currency Management: Concepts and Practices.*

The forward rate can also be expressed in "points" or the difference between the forward and spot rate, $F - S_0$. When interest rates are lower in the foreign country (i.e., the forward points are positive), the forward foreign exchange rate trades at a premium. That is, for the return on cash deposits to be equal in both currencies, the lower interest rate currency must appreciate to the forward foreign exchange rate. For example, as German rates are presently lower than U.S. rates, the forward points are positive for the U.S. dollar against the German mark. Thus, if cash returns are to be the same in both currencies, the percent appreciation of the German mark against the U.S. dollar would have to be exactly equal to the forward premium.

The Currency Hedge Decision

If the possibility of hedging using currency forwards is allowed, the portfolio return of equation (1) changes. The currency term would be left unhedged if the percentage return from currency is expected to be greater than the forward discount or premium, $\varepsilon_{\$i} > f_{\$,i}$, or hedged with forwards if the expected currency return is expected to be less than the forward discount or premium $\varepsilon_{\$i} < f_{\$,i}$. Thus the equation for a hedged portfolio becomes:

$$HR_{\$} = \sum w_i(r_i + f_{\$,i}) \tag{4}$$

As equation (3) showed, the forward premium or discount is effectively equal to the short-term interest rate differential; thus, $f_{\$,i} = c_{\$} - c_i$. By substituting this identity for the forward hedge, the equations for individual country unhedged and hedged returns become:

$$R_{\$i} = r_i + \varepsilon_{\$,i} \qquad \text{(unhedged return)} \tag{5}$$

$$HR_{\$i} = r_i + f_{\$,i} = r_i + (c_{\$} - c_i) \qquad \text{(hedged return)} \tag{6}$$

where $R_{\$i}$ is the unhedged returns from country *i* for a U.S. dollar-based investor and $HR_{\$i}$ is the hedged return. There remain, however, two further options: cross hedging and proxy hedging. Cross hedging replaces the currency exposure to country *i* with currency exposure in country *j*, ($\varepsilon_{\$,j}$), through a cross forward rate, ($f_{j,i}$). Proxy hedging keeps the currency exposure in country *i*, but creates a hedge by establishing a short position in country *j*'s currency ($-\varepsilon_{\$,j}$). These strategies would normally be considered only where the currencies of country *i* and *j* are highly correlated, and the hedge costs in country *j*, are lower than in country *i*.

---

[21] Equation (2) assumes that exchange rates are quoted in "direct terms," i.e., the U.S. dollar value of one foreign currency unit, though quote conventions vary by market. Futures and options on currencies traded on the Chicago Mercantile Exchange are all quoted in direct terms; however, over-the-counter forward contracts use market convention, most of which are in indirect terms (foreign currency units per U.S. dollar). Using indirect terms, the forward discount *or* premium in equation (3) becomes $f = c_f - c_d$. To avoid the complexities of compounding, the time period is assumed to be one year.

$$CR_{\$i} = r_i + (f_{j,i} + \varepsilon_{\$,j}) \quad \text{(cross-hedged return)} \quad (7)$$

$$PR_{\$i} = r_i + \varepsilon_{\$,i} + (f_{\$,j} - \varepsilon_{\$,j}) \quad \text{(proxy-hedged return)} \quad (8)$$

By substituting short term interest rate differentials for the forward returns and rearranging equations (5), (6), (7), and (8), it becomes apparent that the difference in return among the three strategies is entirely due to short term interest rates and currency exposure. The bond component of returns thus becomes the bond return minus the domestic short term interest rate, rather than the full measure of return.

$$R_{\$i} = (r_i - c_i) + (c_i + \varepsilon_{\$,i}) \quad \text{(unhedged return)} \quad (9)$$

$$HR_{\$i} = (r_i - c_i) + c_{\$} \quad \text{(hedged return)} \quad (10)$$

$$CR_{\$i} = (r_i - c_i) + (c_j + \varepsilon_{\$,j}) \quad \text{(cross-hedged return)} \quad (11)$$

$$PR_{\$i} = (r_i - c_i) + (c_i + \varepsilon_{\$,i}) + [(c_{\$} - c_j) - \varepsilon_{\$,j}] \quad \text{(proxy-hedged return)} \quad (12)$$

Equations (9), (10), (11), and (12) show how integral the short-term interest rate differential is to the currency hedge decision. Hence, the short-rate differential should be attributed to the currency decision, and bond market returns should be calculated minus the domestic short-term interest rate. This can be made explicit by adding and subtracting the U.S. cash rate from each of the four equations above. This allows the forward premium ($f_{\$,i} = c_{\$} - c_i$) to be inserted into the currency term creating three distinct components of return: the risk free rate ($c_{\$}$), the excess bond return ($r_i - c_i$), and the excess currency return, either hedged, unhedged, cross-hedged, or proxy hedged.

$$R_{\$i} = c_{\$} + (r_i - c_i) + (\varepsilon_{\$,i} - f_{\$,i}) \quad \text{(unhedged return)} \quad (13)$$

$$HR_{\$\mathrm{i}} = c_{\$} + (r_i - c_i) \quad \text{(hedged return)} \quad (14)$$

$$CR_{\$\mathrm{i}} = c_{\$} + (r_i - c_i) + (\varepsilon_{\$,j} - f_{\$,j}) \quad \text{(cross-hedged return)} \quad (15)$$

$$PR_{\$\mathrm{i}} = c_{\$} + (r_i - c_i) + [(\varepsilon_{\$,i} - \varepsilon_{\$,j}) - f_{j,i}] \quad \text{(proxy-hedged return)} \quad (16)$$

Thus, the excess currency return becomes the currency return in excess of the forward premium (or discount). It can be seen that the bond decision is purely a matter of selecting the markets which offer the best expected excess return and that the bond and currency allocation decisions are entirely independent. This method of analyzing sources of return in effect treats bond and currency returns as if they were synthetic futures or forward positions. Equations (13) through (16) could be applied to a purely leveraged investor, such as a hedge fund, by simply omitting the risk free rate term. Cash investors with limited ability to take currency exposures independently of bond positions may find equations (9) through (12) more useful where the risk free rate is treated as an integral part of the currency hedge decision.

This methodology of attributing cash returns to the currency decision, and the excess return over cash to bonds, has implications for how allocation decisions are made. The returns of higher yielding markets, or those with inverted yield curves, will look somewhat less attractive when analyzed net of the cash interest rate. For example, at the beginning of 1996, Italian 10-year bond yields were 10.70% and 1-year Italian interest rates were 10.10%, thus the running yield that could be attributed to bond performance was only 60 basis points. In order to gain the additional 10.10% in running yield, the position would have to be run unhedged. One-year interest rates in the U.S. were 6% resulting in 410 basis point differential with Italy. Thus, it would have cost a U.S. dollar-based investor 4.1% to hedge exposure to the Italian lira over 12 months using currency forwards. In other words, hedging the Italian lira exposure in essence would have substituted the U.S. cash yield (or risk-free rate) of 6% for the Italian cash yield of 10.10%. Thus, if the Italian lira depreciated by less than the 4.1% against the U.S. dollar implied by the forward rate over 1996, the unhedged lira position would have added value over a hedged position.

In actuality, the Italian lira appreciated by 4.3% against the dollar during 1996, and the Italian bond component of the Salomon Brothers World Government Bond Index returned 27.2% in U.S. dollar terms. Thus, it might seem that 4.3% of the return from holding unhedged Italian bonds should be attributed to currency gain, and 22.9% to bond returns. However, following the methodology laid out in equations (13) and (14), the 4.1% Italian/U.S. 1-year interest rate differential should be added to the currency component of return because it was the decision not to hedge that allowed the manager to earn that full measure of return. The Italian 1-year interest rate should then also be subtracted from the Salomon Index's Italian bond market return of 21.9% in local currency terms. Thus, less than half of the gain from holding unhedged Italian bonds, 8.4%, came from excess currency returns, and 11.8% came from excess bond returns. The hedged return would have been only 17.8%, calculated from the Italian bond excess return of 11.8% plus the U.S. 1-year cash return of 6%.[22]

Market Correlations

Two factors that aid in assessing the incremental risk of changes to a portfolio are the volatility of returns and the correlation (or covariance) of returns with the portfolio as a whole. Normally when a decision is made to overweight a market, a less attractive market will be identified to be reduced by the same amount. Otherwise the trading costs associated with keeping all other markets in the same relative proportion to each other would be excessively high.[23] Thus, two risks, rather

[22] Due to compounding of the bond and currency returns, the sum of the currency and local bond market return figures is 1% less than the U.S. dollar-based total return figure (i.e., 4.3% currency gain × 21.9% local currency bond return = 1%). The Salomon U.S. dollar-hedged index return for Italian lira bonds, based on a rolling 1-month hedge, was 17.5%.

[23] In other words, if a particular market is selected for a 1% overweighting relative to the benchmark, it is often too costly to reduce all other markets by an equal fraction of that 1% to raise the money for the new purchase.

than one, need to be evaluated: the portfolio risk incurred from the overweight position, and that from the underweight position. A more rigorous approach involves an estimate of the impact on total portfolio risk from each hypothetical change in allocation. A model that utilizes the variance/covariance matrix of portfolio assets can be used to explicitly calculate the incremental impact on portfolio volatility (value at risk and similar models are examined in the final section). Nonetheless, a reasonable estimate of the impact on portfolio risk can be obtained by taking account of the historical volatility and correlations of the two markets to each other through the use of a correlation matrix like the one in Exhibit 10.

Market correlations for both bonds and currencies within trading blocs are much higher than across trading blocs. For example, correlations for the core European bond markets of Belgium, France and the Netherlands with Germany are an extremely high 89%, 80%, and 93%, respectively. Currency correlations among these four markets are all close to 100%. Bond market correlations with Germany for the peripheral European markets of Italy, Spain, Sweden, and Denmark are not quite as high, but still significant, ranging from 46% to 64%. Correlations of peripheral European currencies with the German mark range from 83% to 99%. At the same time, standard deviation of return in European bond and currency markets are fairly similar. Thus, shifting exposure from one of these markets to another to take advantage of tactical trading opportunities should have a minimal impact on a portfolio's overall risk or variance profile, especially within the core European markets.

As seen in Exhibits 11 and 12, 10 year bond yield correlations among the G3 (the U.S., Germany, and Japan) are highly variable, sometimes hovering near zero or even showing negative correlation. However, within trading blocs correlations tend to be much more stable, generally staying above 75% for the past several years, and only dropping below 60% during periods of great stress, such as the breakup of the Exchange Rate Mechanism in 1992 and 1993. This allows portfolio managers to actively over or underweight countries within a trading bloc while only modestly altering a portfolio's risk profile. Although the correlation of bond yields within trading blocs may be high, differences in magnitude of yield changes between markets offer significant opportunities for profit.

Forward Rates and Breakeven Analysis

In the previous section, various methods of evaluating value were explored. Before these can be translated into a market allocation, the strategic outlook needs to be compared with that which is already priced into the market. This can be accomplished by either converting the economic outlook into point forecasts for bond and currency levels, or looking at the forward rates implied by current market conditions and comparing them with the economic outlook. Bond and currency breakeven rates, those which make two investments produce identical total returns, are usually calculated versus the benchmark market (e.g., against German bunds for all European markets) over a specific time horizon. A large yield spread between two markets implies a larger "cushion" (the required spread widening to equate total returns in both markets, or the breakeven rate) the longer the investment time horizon.

Exhibit 10: Bond and Currency Correlation Matrix

	AUD	BEF	CAD	DEM	DKK	ESP	FRF	GBP	ITL	JPY	NLG	SEK	AUD Bond	BEF Bond	CAD Bond	DEM Bond	DKK Bond	ESP Bond	FRF Bond	GBP Bond	ITL Bond	JPY Bond	NLG Bond	SEK Bond	USD Bond
AUD	1.00																								
BEF	0.10	1.00																							
CAD	0.06	−0.32	1.00																						
DEM	0.12	0.99	−0.33	1.00																					
DKK	0.14	0.99	−0.33	0.99	1.00																				
ESP	0.14	0.98	−0.34	0.98	0.98	1.00																			
FRF	0.04	0.97	−0.34	0.97	0.97	0.96	1.00																		
GBP	0.43	0.37	0.00	0.39	0.41	0.36	0.31	1.00																	
ITL	0.30	0.84	−0.34	0.84	0.85	0.85	0.84	0.48	1.00																
JPY	−0.25	0.45	−0.20	0.45	0.43	0.45	0.42	−0.09	0.25	1.00															
NLG	0.11	0.99	−0.34	1.00	0.99	0.98	0.97	0.38	0.84	0.45	1.00														
SEK	0.20	0.82	−0.26	0.83	0.84	0.84	0.83	0.33	0.77	0.28	0.83	1.00													
AUD Bond	−0.20	−0.18	−0.03	−0.16	−0.15	−0.14	−0.18	−0.11	−0.17	0.08	−0.17	−0.06	1.00												
BEF Bond	0.22	−0.56	0.22	−0.54	−0.52	−0.53	−0.56	−0.04	−0.39	−0.29	−0.54	−0.37	0.09	1.00											
CAD Bond	0.16	−0.27	0.59	−0.27	−0.26	−0.30	−0.30	0.20	−0.21	−0.33	−0.28	−0.11	−0.04	0.46	1.00										
DEM Bond	0.20	−0.53	0.35	−0.50	−0.50	−0.50	−0.55	0.00	−0.39	−0.27	−0.51	−0.36	0.03	0.89	0.58	1.00									
DKK Bond	−0.04	−0.62	0.19	−0.60	−0.59	−0.56	−0.62	−0.27	−0.53	−0.20	−0.60	−0.40	0.29	0.70	0.17	0.64	1.00								
ESP Bond	0.06	−0.50	0.27	−0.51	−0.49	−0.47	−0.47	−0.09	−0.37	−0.29	−0.51	−0.30	0.08	0.66	0.35	0.62	0.49	1.00							
FRF Bond	0.08	−0.65	0.30	−0.63	−0.63	−0.60	−0.64	−0.18	−0.54	−0.26	−0.63	−0.46	0.21	0.82	0.37	0.80	0.82	0.62	1.00						
GBP Bond	0.28	−0.28	0.13	−0.29	−0.28	−0.26	−0.31	−0.01	−0.15	−0.37	−0.29	−0.09	0.04	0.64	0.50	0.63	0.34	0.59	0.53	1.00					
ITL Bond	0.10	−0.45	0.11	−0.44	−0.43	−0.37	−0.42	−0.18	−0.32	−0.13	−0.45	−0.25	0.33	0.62	0.18	0.55	0.58	0.65	0.62	0.47	1.00				
JPY Bond	0.13	−0.25	−0.13	−0.22	−0.21	−0.22	−0.22	0.07	−0.17	−0.30	−0.22	−0.19	0.26	0.33	0.06	0.24	0.32	0.04	0.32	0.14	0.30	1.00			
NLG Bond	0.21	−0.56	0.28	−0.55	−0.54	−0.53	−0.58	−0.08	−0.41	−0.36	−0.56	−0.36	0.06	0.92	0.52	0.93	0.69	0.66	0.81	0.67	0.60	0.29	1.00		
SEK Bond	0.00	−0.56	0.18	−0.56	−0.55	−0.54	−0.55	−0.16	−0.47	−0.33	−0.56	−0.36	0.03	0.51	0.17	0.46	0.65	0.55	0.64	0.33	0.48	0.19	0.55	1.00	
USD Bond	0.16	−0.22	0.31	−0.21	−0.21	−0.21	−0.21	−0.03	−0.14	−0.20	−0.22	−0.12	−0.13	0.52	0.71	0.59	0.16	0.43	0.39	0.54	0.36	0.02	0.55	0.10	1.00

Source: JP Morgan Riskmetrics as of 12/19/96. Bond markets are estimated using 5-year government zero-coupon bond equivalents in each market.

Exhibit 11: G3 10-Year Bond Yield Correlations

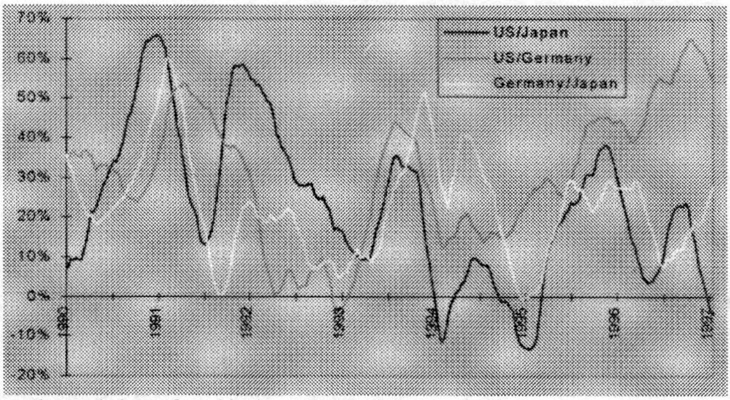

Rolling 6-month correlations of weekly data (smoothed).

Exhibit 12: Correlation of Core Eropean 10-Year Bond Yields

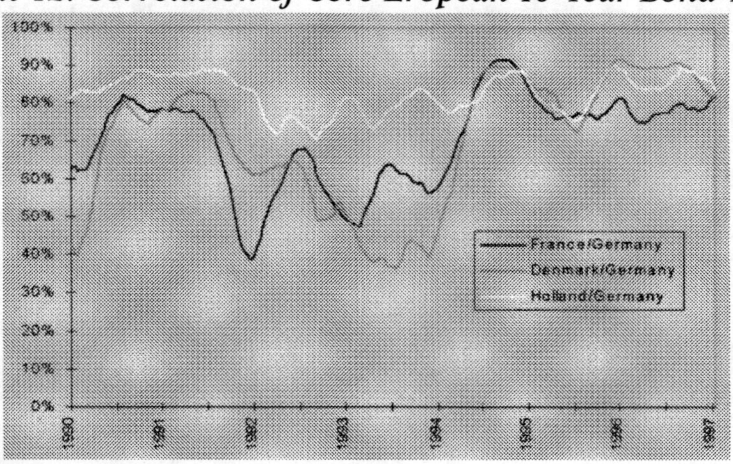

Rolling 6-month correlations of weekly data (smoothed).

Comparisons of forward interest rates can be instrumental in identifying where differences between the strategic outlook and market prices may present investment opportunities. Forward interest rates, which use the shape of the yield curve to calculate implied future bond yields, allow a quick comparison of what is required in terms of yield shifts for bonds in each market to provide a return equal to the risk free rate (a zero excess return). This would correspond to a bond excess return of zero in equations (9) through (16), or $(r_i - c_i) = 0$. Forward interest rates represent a breakeven rate, not across markets necessarily, but within markets. The strategic bond allocation can then be derived by increasing exposure to markets where the expected return of bonds over the cash rate is most positive, that is where the expected bond yield is furthest below the forward yield. Forward rate calculators are also available on systems such as Bloomberg as can be seen in the graph of German forward rates in Exhibit 13.

The forward foreign exchange rate represents a breakeven rate between hedged and unhedged currency returns as shown above in the analysis on components of return. In terms of equations (11) through (14), currency excess return is zero when the percentage change in the currency equals the forward premium or discount. As forward foreign exchange rates are determined by short term interest rate differentials, they can be estimated from Eurodeposit rates as in equations (2) and (3), or obtained from market data services such as Bloomberg and Reuters.

Breakeven analysis provides another tool for estimating relative value between markets. Because the prices of benchmark bonds are influenced by coupon effects and changes in the benchmark, many international fixed income traders and portfolio managers find it easier to keep pace with changes in yield relationships than price changes in each market. Exhibit 14 displays page MEUR from Reuters' market information service which provides 10-year conventional yields and yield spreads to both the U.S. and Germany expressed on an annual-pay basis.[24] A constant spread between markets when yield levels are shifting, however, may result in a variation in returns as differing maturities and coupons of benchmark bonds result in a wide spread of interest rate sensitivity across markets. For example, of the benchmark 10-year bonds listed in Exhibit 13, the modified duration ranges from a low of 6.13 in Spain to 8.56 in Japan where yields are less than half that of the next lowest yielding market. Thus, market duration must be taken into account in determining breakeven spread movements.

Exhibit 13: Forward Yield Curve Analysis

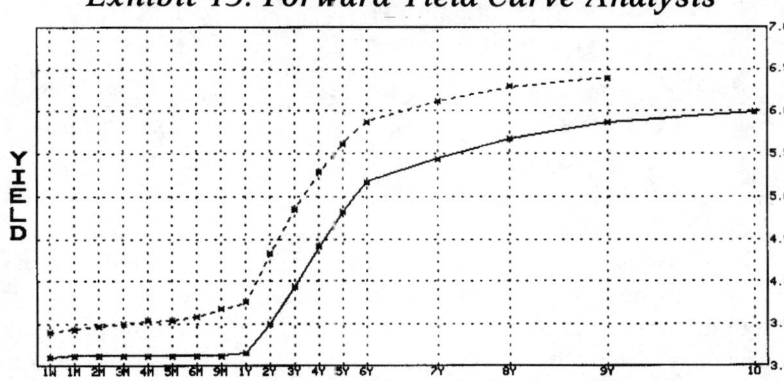

Source: BLOOMBERG Financial Markets

[24] U.S. bonds, and most other dollar bloc bonds, pay coupons semiannually, whereas in Japan, and the European markets (except for the U.K.) bonds pay interest annually. This difference in market convention understates the yield of dollar bloc bonds when compared to Japanese or European bonds, so when calculating the yield spread, semiannual yields are converted to annual yields using the formula:

$$\text{Annual yield} = (1 + \text{Semiannual yield}/2)^2 - 1$$

Exhibit 14: 10-Year Benchmark Bond Yield Spreads

0000	JP MORGAN		BENCHMARKS				JP MORGAN	MEUR
	COUNTRY		ISSUE		PRICE	CNV YLD	O/UST	O/GER
1154	US	6.50	15-10-06	T	98.95-99	6.64		
1154	JAPAN	2.90	20-12-06	JGB	102.28-28	2.61	-410	-326
1154	GERMANY	6.00	04-01-07	BUND	100.60-66	5.91	-84	
1154	FRANCE	5.50	25-04-07	OAT	97.04-18	5.88	-87	-3
1154	UK	7.50	07-12-06	GILT	99.02-02	7.64	+103	+187
1154	ECU	7.00	25-04-06	ECU	105.61-71	6.17	-58	+26
1154	ITALY	8.75	01-07-06	BTP	108.73-93	7.57	+82	+166
1154	SPAIN	8.80	30-04-06	BONO	112.99-14	6.84	+9	+93
1151	BELGIUM	6.25	28-03-07	OLO	101.53-63	6.03	-72	+12
1151	HOLLAND	6.00	15-01-06	DSL	101.71-79	5.75	-101	-17
1151	SWEDEN	6.50	25-10-06	SGB	98.22-42	6.74	-2	+82
1154	DENMARK	8.00	15-03-06	DGB	109.52-62	6.57	-18	+82

For example, calculation of the breakeven yield spread of Italy to Germany over a 3-month time horizon, requires an analysis of the price changes in both bond markets, as well as the difference in yield earned over the period. The spread differential of 166 basis points equates to 41 basis points of additional income over a three month period. The modified duration of the Italian 10-year benchmark bond of 6.21 implies that this yield "cushion" provided by the higher yield of Italian bonds over German bunds translates to less than 7 basis points of spread widening over a 3-month period (6.21 times – 0.07 is approximately equal to 41 basis points). This is not much of a cushion given that 7 basis points is far less than the average weekly volatility of Italian bond yields. The breakeven spreads of Spain and Sweden to Germany are even tighter at 4 and 3 basis points. Thus, the anticipated direction of bond market movements is of paramount importance in the portfolio allocation decision.

Security Selection

Once the bond market allocation decisions have been made and the optimal duration and yield curve profile selected for each market, this overall portfolio structure needs to be constructed through the purchase or sale of individual securities. Many international bond investors prefer to trade only benchmark issues as they offer more liquidity than other bonds of a similar maturity. This can sometimes lead to a "hump" in the yield curve as investors prefer a certain issue or maturity sector. The same phenomenon can result from a squeeze of certain issues in the repo market, or short-term demand imbalances for bonds deliverable into short bond futures positions. As mentioned earlier, few foreign markets have a developed corporate bond market, however, other instruments are available such as mortgage bonds, Eurobonds, and inflation-indexed bonds.

Taxation issues also need to be taken into account when selecting individual bonds for purchase. For example, several markets have tax systems that encourage investors to hold lower coupon bonds, hence certain bonds will tend to trade rich or cheap to the curve depending on their coupon. In markets that impose withholding taxes on coupon payments, international fixed income portfolio managers often minimize their tax liability by replacing a bond that is near its coupon date with another bond of similar maturity. Market anomalies can also arise from differing tax treatment within markets. For example, Italian Eurobond issued before 1988 are exempt of withholding tax for Italian investors, hence they tend to trade at a lower yield than similar maturity bonds issued after 1988.

MEASURING RISK AND EVALUATING PERFORMANCE

Once the portfolio has been created, it must be monitored to assess how changing market conditions affect the portfolio's performance and risk profile; hence, a system for tracking portfolio positions and measuring returns is needed. One of the most basic portfolio monitoring tools is the *position report*, which breaks down the interest rate and currency risk market by market. More technically demanding is a portfolio variance approach such as value-at-risk, which estimates potential losses based upon statistical analysis of historical volatilities and correlations. The value-at-risk approach can also be translated into a *tracking error report* that evaluates portfolio risks against the benchmark. These risk models can be used together with performance attribution to assist the portfolio manager in identifying the strengths or weaknesses of his portfolio strategy.

Portfolio Profile

A portfolio profile is usually designed to monitor exposures to the two major sources of risk in international bond portfolios: currency risk and interest rate risk. These market-by-market breakdowns are also useful in estimating how positions will affect portfolio performance versus the benchmark. A sample portfolio profile versus the Salomon Brothers Non-U.S. Government Bond Index is provided in Exhibit 15. The profile shows the percentage allocation to bonds and currencies for each country, as well as the duration, relative to the index. A breakdown by duration cell of each bond market allocation is provided to highlight any yield curve positions. (The country breakdown by duration cell for the index, which has been excluded for simplicity of presentation, would be extremely helpful in identifying where yield curve positions differ from the index.) Finally, the portfolio profile provides a measure of duration weighted exposure (from equation (17)), and currency exposure net of hedges, relative to the index. Summary exposure figures for each of these categories, broken down by trading bloc, are provided at the bottom of the report.

The measure of portfolio interest rate risk in each individual market is a combination of its weight in the portfolio and its duration relative to the duration of the index for that country. For example, the U.K.'s contribution to duration is neutral to the index (i.e., a relative weight of zero percent) despite the higher percentage allocation to U.K. due to the portfolio's shorter U.K. duration. The larger-than-index market weighting in the U.K. is unhedged as indicated by the equivalence of the market weight and the currency exposure, 11.9%, and represents a nearly 4% portfolio overweight position in pound sterling relative to the index.

Exhibit 15: Sample Portfolio Profile
Portfolio Profile versus Salomon Non-U.S. Government Bond Index

	Market Weight (%)		Average Duration (Yrs)		Currency Exposure (%)	Portfolio MV% by Duration Cell					Relative Weights (%)	
Market	Index	Portfolio	Index	Portfolio	Potfolio	0-2	2-4	4-6	6-9	9+	Duration	Currency
Austria	1.3		4.1								−1.1	−1.3
Australia	1.5		4.3								−1.3	−1.5
Belgium	3.9	3.0	4.8	6.0	3.0				3.0		−0.2	−0.9
Canada	4.6	4.6	5.2	11.7	4.6					4.6	6.1	0.0
Switzerland	0.7		5.2								−0.7	−0.7
Germany	14.9	18.0	4.2	6.6	15.0				18.0		11.4	0.1
Denmark	2.6	8.0	4.3	6.0	8.0				8.0		7.5	5.4
Spain	3.7		3.8								−2.9	−3.7
Finland	0.7		4.3								−0.6	−0.7
France	11.4	5.0	5.1	2.7	5.0		5.0				−9.1	−6.4
U.K.	8.1	11.9	5.9	4.0	11.9			11.9			0.0	3.8
Italy	9.5	15.0	3.3	2.	15.0	15.0					−0.4	5.5
Japan	29.1	30.0	5.7	3.4	24.0		30.0				−13.2	−5.1
Netherlands	5.2	2.0	5.0	3.2	2.0		2.0				−4.0	−3.2
Sweden	2.6	2.5	4.2	2.9	2.5		2.5				−0.8	−0.1
Other												
Total	1.0	1.0	4.9	4.4	91.0	15.0	39.5	11.9	29.0	4.6	−9.5	−9.0
Currency Bloc	Index	Portfolio	Index	Portfolio	Potfolio	0-2	2-4	4-6	6-9	9+	Duration	Currency
Japan	29.1	30.0	3.3	2.0	24.0	15.0					−0.4	5.5
Dollar Bloc	6.1	4.6	5.0	11.7	4.6					4.6	4.7	−1.5
Core Euro	38.1	28.0	4.7	5.6	25.0		30.0		29.0		3.0	−3.2
Periph Euro	26.7	37.4	4.4	3.5	37.4		9.5	11.9			−16.8	−9.7
Other												
Total	100.0	100.0	4.2	4.0	91.0	15.0	39.5	11.9	29.0	4.6	−9.5	−9.0

The summary figures in the bottom right hand corner of the portfolio profile suggest that the sample portfolio's greatest bond market underweight is in peripheral Europe. The 16.8% underweight position there is larger than the sum of the overweight positions in the dollar bloc and core Europe, leaving the portfolio 9.5% underweight duration, or 90.5% of the 4.9 year benchmark duration or 4.4 years. In currencies also, the largest deviation from the benchmark is in peripheral Europe where exposures are 9.7% underweight the index. The overweighting in the yen, and underweighting in core Europe and dollar bloc are largely offsetting in this framework. The overall portfolio is 9% underweight currency exposure, or 9% hedged relative to the unhedged benchmark.

As helpful as they are in quantifying risk within individual markets, the traditional risk measures of duration and percent currency exposure have significant shortcomings when aggregated as a measure of portfolio risk. These shortcomings are explored in more detail below, along with some complimentary approaches to risk measurement that can be instrumental in addressing them.

Contribution to Duration

Many international fixed income portfolio managers measure their bond market exposures in terms of the simple percentage allocation to each particular market. However, a better measure of exposure to any individual bond market is one that combines the percentage of portfolio assets allocated to that market with the duration of that exposure. As seen in equation (17), contribution to overall portfolio duration for each market is the weighted duration in that market multiplied by the percentage weight of that market in the portfolio where D is the duration and w percentage weight of market i in the overall portfolio. Thus, the sum of the contribution to duration of each market will equal the portfolio's overall duration. The duration weighted exposure is calculated by dividing the contribution to duration in each market by the total benchmark duration, D_B as shown in equation (18). The duration weighted exposure figure can then be compared directly with the benchmark composition, providing a more useful gauge of market risk than percent allocation. The sum of the weighted duration figures may add up to more or less than 100%.

$$\text{Contribution to Duration: } CD_i = D_i \times w_i \qquad (17)$$

$$\text{Duration Weighted Exposure: } WD_i = CD_i / D_B \qquad (18)$$

Duration can be a helpful measure when comparing a portfolio's allocation relative to the index, however, its inability to capture the effect of non-parallel shifts in rates is compounded by further shortcomings when used as a measure of interest rate risk in a global setting. Portfolio interest rate exposure will not be equal to a simple sum of the duration weighted exposures from equation (18) in each market as interest rate movements in different countries are not perfectly correlated. Also the differing volatility across markets means that the contribution-to-duration from a given market is not entirely comparable to that of another market. The use of volatility-adjusted duration[25] is one means of addressing this impracticality. An additional compromise would be to compare volatility-adjusted contribution-to-duration only between the highly correlated markets within each trading bloc. Thus, a portfolio could have the same modified duration as the benchmark but show a different sensitivity to global bond market moves as a result of different weightings in especially low or high volatility markets or in markets with low correlation to other markets.

The shortcomings of duration as a measure of interest rate risk internationally can be reduced by accounting for differing volatilities and correlations across markets. This requires either a manual interpolation of portfolio risk from a volatility and correlation matrix or use of a risk measure that incorporates these relationships. One example would be a market risk measure that captures the relative volatility of markets and yield curve sectors as well as the correlation to the "market," which could be defined as a hedged, or unhedged, global or international bond index. One approach, suggested by Goldman Sachs & Co., is to make use of beta measures similar to those found in the capital asset pricing model.[26] A portfolio with a weighted average market risk of 1.12, for example, would be 12% more sensitive to bond price changes than the international bond index. This approach could be extended to currencies as well.

Currency Exposures

Portfolio currency exposures, examined separately from the bond exposures, suffer from some of the same shortcomings as duration as an overall risk measure. A simple aggregation of currency exposures across a portfolio ignores the sometimes substantial differences in currency volatilities across markets. For example, from 1987 to 1996 a U.S dollar-based investor would have experienced three times more volatility from movements in the value of the yen than in the Canadian dollar. Thus, offsetting short or long currency positions relative to the benchmark in the yen with the opposite positions in either the dollar bloc or core Europe could lead to a misunderstanding of the portfolio's true exposure to currency risk.

Direct comparison of currency and interest rate risk measures poses another difficulty. For example, a 5% duration-weighted position in a bond market and a 5% currency exposure can represent significantly different risks to the overall portfolio. Again, measures incorporating volatility and correlation measures allow these different sources of risk to be evaluated on an equal footing. The next section discusses the virtues of a value-at-risk approach that also incorporates volatility and correlation of interest rate and currency risk.

---

[25] For example, if interest rates were twice as volatile in Italy than in Germany, a factor of 2 could be applied to bond holdings in Italy when comparing them to the German bond holdings.

[26] Beta can be estimated by either regressing historical returns of the given market sector versus the market as a whole, or by using the following formula: Beta = Cov (R_i, R_m)/Var (R_m) where R_i and R_m represent the historical returns of the market sector and the entire market, respectively.

Derivatives

Because of their inherent leverage, futures and options can significantly change the risk profile of the portfolio with a minimal cash outlay. Hence, they present special difficulties in calculating their impact on the portfolio. Treatment of futures contracts are relatively straightforward. For currencies, the notional amount of the currency position in either futures or forwards, can be added and subtracted from the relevant currency pair. For bonds, the duration impact of a futures position in any country can be estimated by multiplying the duration of the cheapest-to-deliver bond for that contract by the notional amount of bonds represented by the contract. In any futures contract there is also a small short-term interest rate effect that is also to be considered. Options can be treated in a similar fashion, once a delta for the option is calculated. However, it must be kept in mind that option payouts are inherently asymmetric whereas the framework discussed so far assumes that returns are linear.

Tracking Error and Value at Risk

Each portfolio allocation decision should be evaluated on the basis of the expected return enhancement of the trade versus its impact on portfolio volatility, both in absolute terms and relative to the benchmark. Volatility is often expressed in standard deviations of returns, i.e., movements either up or down. On the assumption that most international bond investors are concerned about limiting downside volatility (i.e., losses) more than upside volatility, the value-at-risk concept, popularized by JP Morgan, serves as a constructive framework.[27] The value-at-risk approach uses historical volatility and correlations across bond and currency markets to arrive at an estimate of the likely loss, expressed either in dollars or as a percent of the portfolio, only in the case of an extreme shift in market prices against portfolio positions. For example a value-at-risk figure calculated with a 95% confidence interval (or a 1.65 standard deviation downward move in market prices) would estimate the magnitude of the loss that should be exceeded no more than 5% of the time.

Value-at-risk measures are especially useful for estimating the risks of assets with non-normally distributed returns, such as bond and currency options. Thus, a model that can capture the differences between the risks of a long (or purchased) option position which has a limited downside, and a short (or written) option position which has open-ended downside risk, will serve as an important risk management tool.

---

[27] The value-at-risk concept, known in prior academic papers as semi-variance or lower partial moment, is simply a transformation of the more traditionally used standard deviation measure of volatility, but expressed as a measure of downside risk only. Traditional mean-variance optimization will produce similar results when using either portfolio value-at-risk or volatility as the constraint if portfolio returns are assumed to be normally distributed. For a more detailed discussion, see JP Morgan Riskmetrics Technical Document, and W.V. Harlow, "Asset Allocation in a Downside-Risk Framework," *Financial Analysts Journal* (September-October 1991).

Exhibit 16: Tracking Error Report

	Portfolio Profile Summary Relative Weights		Contribution to Tracking Error (bp)		Contribution to Tracking Error (%)		Marginal Tracking Error (bp)	
Market	Bond (%)	Currency (%)	Bond	Currency	Bond	Currency	Bond	Currency
Austria	−1.1	−1.3	−0.2	10.8	0	7	0.0	−7.6
Australia	−1.3	−1.5	1.0	-2.4	1	−2	−1.0	1.5
Belgium	−0.2	−0.9	0.7	7.9	0	5	3.6	−7.6
Canada	6.1	0.0	27.2	0.5	17	0	7.1	2.6
Switzerland	−0.7	−0.7	0.1	6.8	0	4	0.7	−10.1
Germany	11.4	0.1	50.3	0.1	32	0	3.7	−7.6
Denmark	7.5	5.4	22.1	−43.2	14	−27	2.9	−6.9
Spain	−2.9	−3.7	−11.8	27.4	−8	17	4.2	−7.3
Finland	−0.6	−0.7	0.0	4.3	0	3	0.0	−6.2
France	−9.1	−6.4	−17.2	43.5	−11	28	2.1	−7.6
U.K.	0.0	3.8	−4.6	3.9	−3	2	3.0	1.2
Italy	−0.4	5.5	−3.4	−20.5	−2	−13	2.8	−4.1
Japan	−13.2	−5.1	6.6	28.3	4	18	−0.1	−5.8
Netherlands	−4.0	−3.2	−14.8	39.3	−9	25	−2.4	−7.8
Sweden	−0.8	−0.1	−0.4	−5.0	0	−3	2.7	−4.3
Other	0.0	0.0			0	0	2.8	0.0
Japan	−13.2	−5.1	6.6	28.3	4	18		
Dollar Bloc	4.7	−1.5	28.1	−1.9	18	−1		
Core Europe	3.7	−3.3	36.6	69.1	23	44		
Peripheral Europe	−4.7	0.9	−15.6	6.1	−10	4		
Other								
Total	−9.5	−9.0	55.7	101.5	35	65		

Total Portfolio Diversified Tracking Error	Fully Diversified	Non-Diversified
	157.3	1267

Although portfolio tracking error has traditionally been defined as the historical variance of portfolio returns about the benchmark, it can be extremely useful in the portfolio management process when used as an estimate of future deviation from the index, or more specifically as the relative value at risk. The total value at risk of the sample portfolio in Exhibit 16 is 590 basis points at the 95% confidence level, while tracking error equals 157 basis points. In other words, the portfolio should, at worst, lose 5.90% in value in any year, or underperform the benchmark by 157 basis points, with 95% confidence. Which measure deserves more emphasis depends on the portfolio objectives and risk constraints. For example, an income-oriented investor with little tolerance for losses could set a portfolio constraint on value-at-risk equal to the expected income earned over a given time horizon. This could provide some assurance, with 95% confidence for example, that portfolio total return will remain positive. An investor more concerned with diversification, however, might find tracking error a more suitable risk measure as it better identifies large deviations from the benchmark which could alter the portfolio's correlation to other asset classes.

The value-at-risk framework may uncover risks to the portfolio not fully apparent in traditional measures while providing the portfolio manager a common yardstick to evaluate the risks of bond market and currency positions.

In Exhibit 16, the sample portfolio is shown to have 101.5 basis points of tracking error (65% of the total) due to currency positions away from the benchmark and 55.7 basis points (35% of the total) due to bond market positions. A manager could use these measures to ensure that the magnitude of risks taken relative to the benchmark are consistent with the level of conviction and the investment style relied upon to outperform. Presumably, this manager is comfortable taking a larger currency position than bond market position. The underweight bond and currency position in France, summarized in the left-hand column, is a net contributor to tracking error. However, the bond market position actually has the effect of reducing tracking error by 17.2 basis points. The 9.1% duration underweight in France constitutes a large allocation away from the benchmark, however, it offsets portfolio overweight in other core European bond markets; markets to which French bonds are highly correlated. The same could be said for the UK, Italy and Spain as the correlation between peripheral and core European bond markets is a high 0.76 (see Exhibit 18). As shown in the far right column of Exhibit 16, marginal tracking error (the portfolio impact from a 1% shift in assets) from a 1% shift into French government bonds results in an increase of 2.1 basis points in portfolio tracking error. Thus, the existing underweight in French bonds is a risk-reducing position and adding back French bond market exposure will increase tracking error. Almost all readings in the far right hand column are negative suggesting that adding foreign currency exposure will reduce tracking error to the benchmark. This is consistent with the estimated 65% of tracking error coming from currency positions, most of which are underweight or hedged back into U.S. dollars.

The Value at Risk report in Exhibit 17 provides a summary of the sources of absolute risk. For example, the profile summary at left shows that the portfolio has twice as much of its market value exposed to Japanese yen as it does British pound sterling. However, after adjusting for volatility and correlation differences the contribution to portfolio value at risk from the yen position is 30% more than that for sterling, 104.0 versus 79.9 basis points. Interestingly, the bond market contributions to risk total only 4% of total risk. This results from the low volatility estimates of bond market risks and negative correlation to currency risk that are input into the model. As can be seen in the right hand column of Exhibit 17, shifting 1% of portfolio assets to either Dutch or Swedish bond markets reduces portfolio value at risk by 1.9 and 1.0 basis points respectively.

A manager looking to maximize expected excess return per unit of risk would be able to compare return expectations to the contribution to value at risk or tracking error. A certain threshold of return per unit of risk may be required to meet a portfolio target. Model outputs in this context allow managers to weigh the risks against return potential for various portfolio assets and, using the marginal value at risk and tracking error numbers, have a reasonable estimate of how potential portfolio trades will impact, portfolio risk, both relative to the benchmark and on an absolute basis. Traditional mean-variance optimization, where portfolios exhibiting the most attractive Sharpe ratios are identified on the so-called efficient frontier between expected excess return over cash and volatility, can offer some insights about portfolio risk not captured by the framework presented above. However, the flexibility and detail offered by the careful break-down of portfolio risk above can offer significant advantages to managers seeking to better understand the sources of risk and fine-tune portfolios.

Exhibit 17: Value at Risk Report

	Portfolio Profile Summary		Contribution to Value at Risk (bp)		Contribution to Value at Risk (%)		Marginal Value at Risk (bp)	
Market	Contribution to Duration	Currency Weight (%)	Bond	Currency	Bond	Currency	Bond	Currency
Austria	—	0	0.0	0.0	0	0	0.0	8.7
Australia	—	0	0.0	0.0	0	0	0.0	3.8
Belgium	0.18	3	0.1	25.0	0	4	0.0	8.5
Canada	0.54	5	11.5	–2.7	2	0	1.4	–0.6
Switzerland	—	0	0.0	0.0	0	0	0.6	9.6
Germany	1.18	15	4.7	128.6	1	22	0.2	8.7
Denmark	0.48	8	–4.8	72.9	–1	12	–0.7	8.3
Spain	—	0	0.0	0.0	0	0	–0.5	8.2
Finland	—	0	0.0	0.0	0	0	0.0	7.0
France	0.14	5	–1.3	38.4	0	7	–0.7	7.8
U.K.	0.48	12	8.8	79.9	1	14	0.8	6.7
Italy	0.30	15	02	96.8	0	16	–0.2	6.6
Japan	1.01	24	7.9	104.0	1	18	0.0	4.3
Netherlands	0.06	2	0.0	0.0	0	0	–1.9	8.8
Sweden	0.07	3	–2.9	22.9	0	4	–1.0	6.0
Other	—	0					0.5	0.0
Japan	1.01	24	7.9	104.0	1	18		
Dollar Bloc	0.54	5	11.6	–2.7	2	0		
Core Euro	2.52	45	7.5	344.8	1	58		
Peripheral Europe	0.37	18	–2.7	119.7	0	20		
Other								
Total	4.44	91	24.2	565.8	4	96		

Total Portfolio Diversified Tracking Error	Fully Diversified	Non-Diversified
	590.0	1505

Exhibit 18: Bond Market and Currency Correlation by Currency Bloc

	Core Europe	Peripheral Europe	Japan	Dollar Bloc	Core Eur. Currency	Peripheral Currency	Japanese Yen	Dollar Bloc Currency
Core Europe	1.00							
Peripheral Europe	0.76	1.00						
Japan	0.40	0.19	1.00					
Dollar Bloc	0.65	0.44	0.43	1.00				
Core Eur. Currency	–0.39	–0.57	0.12	–0.18	1.00			
Peripheral Currency	–0.40	–0.16	–0.17	–0.28	0.51	1.00		
Japanese Yen	–0.19	–0.48	0.07	–0.14	0.64	0.24	1.00	
Dollar Bloc Currency	–0.08	0.04	0.09	0.17	–0.13	0.04	–0.26	1.00

The value-at-risk approach to calculating tracking error, however, is not a perfect measure of portfolio risk. For one thing, portfolio variance measures such as value-at-risk assume that market relationships do not change, which can be misleading. For example, it has been shown that correlations tend to rise during periods of above-average volatility which suggests that value at risk models will tend to underestimate risk during periods of extreme volatility.[28] Thus, many practitioners advocate the use of worst-day or disaster scenario measures to supplement the use of value-at-risk measures. Another approach compares the diversified value-at-risk measure (the traditional portfolio variance approach) with the non-diversified measure (which assumes no correlation among assets), as the ratio of diversified to non-diversified risk can be used as a proxy for the correlation risk inherent in the diversified risk measure.

Performance Attribution

A performance attribution analysis can assist in the portfolio management process by identifying the source of returns (and losses) versus the benchmark. The breakdown of components of return in equations (9) through (16) above provides a good foundation for a rigorous performance attribution analysis will analyze returns in terms of bond market weight, duration, yield curve position, and currency weight, both market by market and for the portfolio as a whole.[29] Performance attribution systems, however, are extremely data intensive, requiring daily updates of index returns and portfolio returns and allocation, including a separate accounting of each transaction. The performance report in Exhibit 19 offers a simplified version of attribution in that it identifies the sources of return from bond and currency allocations in each market. A majority of the returns in excess of the benchmark in the sample portfolio came from bond market allocations, while currency allocations added only marginally to the portfolio's excess return. In addition to identifying the sources of return, the performance attribution analysis can be combined with other risk reports to estimate the additional risk incurred to generate those returns. For example, the source of excess returns over the benchmark can be compared with the sources of risk identified by the tracking error report to assess the performance of the portfolio strategy on a risk-adjusted basis. Such an analysis can contribute to future returns by helping allocate resources toward areas that have added to returns, and identify areas that have tended to detract from performance.

---

[28] See Bruno Solnik, Cyril Boucrelle, and Yann Le Fur, "International Market Correlation and Volatility," *Financial Analysts Journal* (September/October 1996), pp. 17-34.
[29] See Karnosky and Singer, op.cit.

Exhibit 19: Performance Attribution

Nov-95	Hedged Bond Market Return						Currency Return			
	Relative Duration Weight	Salomon Index Return	Contrib. to Index Return	Portfolio Return	Contrib to Port Return	Relative Return	Relative Currency Rate	Currency Return	Relative Return	Total Outperf
Other	0.0	0.00	0.00	0.98	0.00	0.00	0.0	0.00	0.00	0.00
Cash	0.0	0.42	0.00	0.00	0.00	0.00	0.0	0.00	0.00	0.00
Japan	–6.1	0.56	0.16	0.55	0.14	–0.03	–5.4	–0.05	–0.03	–0.06
Germany	1.3	1.85	0.27	1.74	0.35	0.08	9.9	–1.56	–0.14	–0.07
France	–1.9	1.98	0.23	2.43	0.15	–0.07	–7.1	–2.21	0.15	0.08
U.K.	0.7	2.22	0.18	1.92	0.18	–0.01	0.6	3.18	–0.02	–0.02
Belgium	–3.7	1.85	0.07	0.00	0.00	–0.07	–3.9	–1.55	0.06	–0.01
Denmark	2.1	1.67	0.04	1.99	0.11	0.07	–3.9	–1.55	0.06	–0.01
Netherlands	–5.1	1.81	0.09	0.0	0.00	–0.09	–5.1	–1.68	0.09	–0.01
Austria	–1.1	1.56	0.02	0.0	0.00	–0.02	–1.4	–1.56	0.02	0.00
ECU	–0.6	1.41					–0.7			0.00
Italy	–1.1	2.82	0.27	1.56	0.25	–0.03	–0.4	0.09	–0.01	–0.03
Spain	0.3	3.55	0.13	3.44	0.14	0.00	0.3	–1.55	–0.01	0.00
Sweden	1.4	2.45	0.06	2.62	0.08	0.01	0.3	–2.24	0.01	0.01
Norway	4.2	1.19	0.00	1.46	0.04	0.04	3.5	–1.26	–0.04	–0.01
Canada	0.1	2.60	0.12	2.89	0.12	0.00	0.0	–0.48	0.00	0.0
Australia	2.3	1.30	0.02	1.50	0.04	0.02	–0.6	2.71	0.01	0.03
Totals	–2.6	Local	1.68	Local	1.84	0.16			0.02	0.18
		Ccy	–0.54	Ccy	–0.52					
Summaries		Total	1.15	Total	1.32					
U.S.	0.0		0.0		0.17	0.17	4.9		–0.02	0.15
Japan	–6.1		0.16		0.14	–0.03	–5.4		–0.03	–0.06
Europe-Core	–8.4		0.91		0.79	–0.13	–3.9		0.11	–0.02
Europe-Other	4.8		0.47		0.46	–0.01	3.7		–0.02	–0.03
Dollar Bloc	7.2		0.14		0.26	0.12	1.5		0.02	0.15
* Interest Rate Derivatives Value Added (incorporated above)										
Short German Bund Call Options						0.16				
Long Call Options Italian BTPs						0.10				

Exhibit 20: Expected Returns French/German Swap

	France	Germany	Cross Hedge
Expected Bond Market Return			
Expected Bond Return (A)	3.5%	3.0%	
c_i = Domestic Cash Rate (B)	–3.0%	–3.0%	
Bond Excess Return (C = A – B)	0.5%	0.0%	
Expected Currency Return			
$\varepsilon_{\$i}$ = Expected Currency Appreciation	2.3%	2.5%	2.5%
c_i = Domestic Cash Rate (B)	3.0%	3.0%	3.0%
Unhedged Currency Return (E = B + D)	5.3%	5.5%	5.5%
$c_\$$ = Hedged Return (F or U.S. Interest Rate)	5.5%	5.5%	
$\varepsilon_{\$i} + c_i - c_\$$ = Excess Currency Return (G = E – F)	–0.2%	0.0%	
Unhedged Expected Return (C + E)	5.8%	5.5%	
Hedged Expected Return (C + F)	6.0%	5.5%	

CONCLUSION: AN INTEGRATED INVESTMENT PROCESS

The objective of this chapter was to provide a broad overview of the issues facing international fixed income portfolio managers at each step of the portfolio management process. This process involves a continuous cycle of evaluating risks and returns, implementing portfolio strategy, and monitoring market movements and portfolio performance. The complexities of the international arena increase the value of a disciplined approach to investing, of which the fundamental-based approach outlined in this chapter is but one variation.

Exhibit 20 attempts to tie the themes of the portfolio construction and risk management sections together by showing how a portfolio manager might turn a market view into a portfolio allocation. The outlook is for the French bond market to outperform Germany's bond market, but for the French franc to provide a lower return than the German mark. The bond and currency return forecasts may have been generated by a fundamental economic approach, such as the one outlined in this chapter, or from one of the other management styles. The expected return from any allocation should be evaluated against the incremental risk it is likely to add to the portfolio.

An example comparing explicit return forecasts for 5-year duration bonds in the French and German government bond markets (i.e., duration neutral) is provided in Exhibit 19. Total returns are expressed as the sum of the excess bond market return plus the excess return due to currency, consistent with the approach explained in equations (13), (14), (15), and (16), which are restated below.

$$R_{\$i} = c_\$ + (r_i - c_i) + (\varepsilon_{\$,i} - f_{\$,i}) \qquad \text{(unhedged return)}$$

$$HR_{\$i} = c_\$ + (r_i - c_i) \qquad \text{(hedged return)}$$

$$CR_{\$i} = c_{\$} + (r_i - c_i) + (\varepsilon_{\$,i} - f_{\$,i}) \qquad \text{(cross-hedged return)}$$

$$PR_{\$i} = c_{\$} + (r_i - c_i) + [(\varepsilon_{\$,i} - \varepsilon_{\$,j}) - f_{j,i} \qquad \text{(proxy-hedged return)}$$

For example, the expected excess return from bonds $(r_i - c_i)$ of 0.5% in France, equal to the expected return on bonds (3.5%) less that on French cash (3.0%), is the same regardless of whether the currency is hedged, unhedged, or cross hedged. The currency hedge decision is based upon whether the expected currency appreciation is greater than the interest rate differential $\varepsilon_{\$,i} > (c_{\$} - c_i)$ or less than the interest rate differential $\varepsilon_{\$,i} < (c_{\$} - c_i)$ Thus, as the expected return on French francs of 2.3% is less than the interest rate differential of 2.5% over the 1-year horizon (5.5% in the U.S. – 3.0% in France), the position would offer a higher return when hedged back into U.S. dollars. Stated another way, the expected excess currency return component to a U.S. dollar-based investor from an unhedged holding of French bonds is –0.2%.

Cross hedging allows portfolio managers to create a currency exposure which can vary substantially from the underlying bond market exposure. A cross hedge replaces one foreign currency exposure with another that usually has a higher expected return. Using the currency (or far right hand) components of equations (8) and (10), a cross hedge will be attractive when $(c_j + \varepsilon_{\$,j}) > (c_i + \varepsilon_{\$,i})$; or the cash rate plus expected return in the cross currency is greater than the cash rate plus expected return in the exposure currency. Of course, if the U.S. dollar cash rate is greater than either of these two terms, a hedged, or proxy hedged, position is preferable to either foreign currency exposure. In terms of the present example, the expected excess currency return from the additional French franc exposure is a negative 20 basis points. Hence this currency exposure would probably be hedged back into the dollar. A cross hedge into German marks could also be used, however, the expected excess currency retrun from holding German marks is zero.

The next step is to estimate the incremental risk to the portfolio associated with the transaction. Exhibit 21 provides several risk measures for evaluating the proposed swap from Germany into France on overall portfolio risk. The historical volatilities of the bond and currency movements in each market can provide a rough approximation of incremental risk from the portfolio allocation (the volatility of a hedged bond market return would be approximately the same as the volatility of the local bond market return). The similar bond and currency volatilities in France and Germany,[30] and the high correlation between the markets, suggests that a shift of market exposure from one market to the other would be relatively risk neutral. However, some of the tools developed in the risk management discussion allow for a much more accurate estimation of risk. The two columns entitled marginal tracking error and marginal value at risk from Exhibits 16

[30] The variance formula treats the bond and currency components as separate assets in calculating the expected volatility for any country using the following equation: $\sigma_i^2 = \sigma_x^2 + h_y^2\,\sigma_y^2 + 2\,h_y\,\mathrm{Cov}_{xy}$, where subscript i represents a country, x represents bonds, y represents the currency and h represents the percent currency exposure (i.e., $1 - h$ = the hedge ratio), and Cov_{xy} is the covariance between the bonds and currencies.

and 17 provide estimates of the incremental addition to risk that would result from a 1% shift of the portfolio's market value into any individual bond market or currency. For example, on the basis of the figures from the Total column of Exhibit 21, the swap from German to French bonds reduces both value at risk and tracking error by 1.6 basis points. Risk can also be evaluated on a hedged basis, using the data in the bond market column. The risk reduction figures in this case are very similar on either a hedged or unhedged basis. However, the 50 basis points of incremental expected return from a hedged swap from Germany into France is greater than the 30 basis points of expected return on an unhedged basis. One possible conclusion from this example is that the expected return enhancement per unit of excess tracking error is most attractive when the swap is done on a hedged basis. If the differences between value at risk and tracking error were greater, a portfolio managed more for capital preservation might place more weight upon the value at risk measure perhaps leading to a different conclusion.

As the prior example shows, the implementation of portfolio strategy can clearly be a highly involved process of evaluating the risk and reward trade-off between different portfolio investment alternatives. However, the simplified example above did not address other types of decisions confronted by international fixed income portfolio managers including ongoing management of currency hedges, yield curve strategies, and using options to take views on the direction of actual or implied volatilities. In addition to conveying the complexities presented by international fixed income investing, hopefully this chapter has been able to convey some of the excitement that comes from meeting the challenges of investing in a dynamic global market.

Exhibit 21: Risk Analysis French/German Swap

	Bond Market	Currency	Total
Volatility			
France	6.7%	13.7%	4.8%
Germany	7.4%	14.2%	5.1%
Marginal Value at Risk			
France	–0.7	7.8	7.1
Germany	0.2	8.7	8.9
Marginal Tracking Error			
France	2.1	–7.6	–5.5
Germany	3.7	–7.6	–3.9
Net Impact on Portfolio – Germany into France			
Value at Risk	–0.9	–0.9	–1.8
Tracking Error	–1.6	0.0	–1.6

Correlations			
French to German Bonds:	0.80	French Bonds to French Francs:	–0.64
Francs to German marks:	0.97	German Bonds to German marks:	–0.50

Marginal Value at Risk and Tracking Error (from Exhibits 16 and 17) are estimates of the change, in basis points, to portfolio Value at Risk and Tracking Error for a 1% addition of the relevant bond of currency exposure to the portfolio profiled in Exhibit 15.

Chapter 3

Global Fixed Income Portfolio Investing: The Art of Decision Making

Chris P. Dialynas
Former Managing Director — Portfolio Management
Pacific Investment Management Company

Ellen Rachlin
Co-Head IBJI Agent Department
Aubrey G. Lanston & Co. Inc.

INTRODUCTION

Today's investment marketplace is a growing one. Existing capital markets are expanding and new capital markets are emerging. Lesser-developed countries whose main source of outside capital has been traditionally supra-national and corporate or private bank loans can now expect to tap many other sources of private capital. Global fixed income portfolio managers who select investments amongst all the worldwide financial markets provide a significant amount of this new capital. Consequently, well-developed countries find themselves competing with lesser-developed, higher yielding or riskier capital markets for capital from bond portfolio managers. So, for the bond portfolio manager, investing in today's worldwide open financial markets is a most complex task.

As the world's capital markets develop, the investment opportunities for bond portfolio managers increase in tandem with the possibilities for emerging countries to attract capital. These emerging market countries that make up an increasing proportion of the bond portfolio manager's investment opportunities are slowly moving from the environment of rolling short-term bank loans to the environment of long-term capital as provided by portfolio managers. Historically, the emerging market countries had to finance their growth through either supra or private bank loans most often collateralized with assets and therefore, being relatively limited, dependent on their own domestic savings, production, and natural

The authors would like to thank Stephen Hannah of IBJ International plc and David Jones of Aubrey G. Lanston & Co. Inc.

resource base. Now, these countries are in a position to compete worldwide for capital that can be allocated to any country that produces the highest expected risk-adjusted returns. Because most of this debt is issued without collateral support, the potential leverage in these emerging countries has increased substantially. Later in this chapter we will discuss these investment risks which include (1) market risk, (2) credit risk, (3) political risk, (4) liquidity risk, and (5) event risk. Bond portfolio managers have become one of the largest suppliers of capital for global economies.

THE BOND PORTFOLIO MANAGER

Because the portfolio manager is competing for capital against other portfolio managers over relatively short-time periods (general performance terms are expressed relative to an index) his investment choices are far less committed than the loans of supras or other banks. In spite of the fact that the initial term of the commitment (maturity of the bond) is greater than the typical term of a bank loan, the homogeneity of the bond markets, the competition among portfolio managers, and the organization of the bond markets, in general, serve to enhance liquidity. Turnover will occur and bond prices will change as the opinions of portfolio managers change.

Within the current global information and communication revolution, fresh information is readily available from which assessments of global credit risks can be determined. Yet, all of the hazards for the portfolio manager when considering investments in many of the world's developing countries still exist. He must assess the probability within his interest rate forecast that private capital might be suddenly withdrawn from a particular country or that the willingness of the country to honor its obligations may change. The sudden withdrawal of funds may have a significant destabilizing effect on the economies and prices of the securities and currencies of emerging capital markets or of other capital markets with comparatively high volatility rates. Or, the capital attracted to developing countries from global investment funds, at times, can lead to temporary excesses. These excesses may manifest in real GDP growth, inflation, increasing trade deficits, speculative or financial bubbles, bad loans, depreciating currency among other problems. But it is the portfolio manager's primary responsibility to determine, *a priori*, if a new country path is being established or if excesses are developing. A significant increase in capital to a given market may well tend to improve the financial and economic health of that economy assuming the debt burden (cash flow and currency) is manageable under most economic scenarios.

The bond portfolio manager must assess global economies and their market environments, and then predict levels of interest rates and future currency values to determine the performance characteristics, in totality and in context of his investment portfolio. A bond portfolio manager's task is to predict the optimal combination of fixed income securities and currencies to hold in the global portfolio that will allow him to outperform a particular market index and compare favorably in performance terms against his competitors. The bond portfolio manager selects, in his judgment, the optimal combination of securities from the pool of possible choices within his investment set; that is, a global fund manger will choose among various sovereign and corporate securities, currencies, and cash for what financial instruments to hold in his portfolio.

The professional skills required of bond portfolio managers are complex and challenging. The bond portfolio manager ultimately utilizes his skills to create a portfolio comprised of bonds representative of the set of interest rate and currency forecasts that he believes in. The main attributes of a bond portfolio include: (1) duration, (2) cash flow distribution on various yield curves, (3) convexity, (4) credit quality, and (5) non-dollar bond and currency exposure. Each selected attribute is the result of multiple and complex evaluation techniques. And, the overall risk of the portfolio can be derived through a variety of normalization techniques. Alternatively, that is to say, a skilled practitioner should be able to examine a bond portfolio and derive the portfolio's embedded forecasts for: (1) interest rates, (2) volatility, (3) changes in yield curve shape, (4) inter-market spreads, and (5) intra-market spreads and relative currency values. The portfolio manager must develop a multitude of forecasts and utilize these forecasts in a variety of ways throughout the investment process. We will elaborate on the process and occasionally, demonstrate the practical importance of some of the subtle forecasts. We will show how inferences about a particular bond will effectively convey the important attributes of a forecast as well as the clarity or confidence in the forecast. Ultimately, it is the quality of the political-macroeconomic analysis, integrated with the quantification of the asset universe that will yield a rewarding experience.

The creation of an interest rate forecast, which is the overall backdrop for the bond portfolio's construction, in and of itself requires a portfolio manager to call upon his knowledge of: (1) economics, (2) politics, (3) history, (4) psychology, and (5) statistics, in addition to other disciplines. A reliable interest rate forecast and an understanding of the differences between that forecast and the implicit forecast of the market are critical to professional bond portfolio management. The portfolio manager must compare his interest rate forecast to the forward market prices and seek investment opportunities wherever his forecast deviates from market expectations. Therefore, it is insufficient to merely implement an externally developed forecast. The portfolio manager must have an in-depth knowledge of the assumptions inherent to the forecast, understand the subsector economic analysis, such as trade account product distribution, monetary targets, non-economic objectives, cultural norms, tax policies, and the marketplace for which he intends to apply his forecast. Indeed, he must know the unknowable.

It is a miscalculation to assume that a good economic forecast alone allows the portfolio manager to construct a high performing portfolio. Global economic forecasts are merely an intermediate step in the portfolio manager's effort to devise global interest rate and currency forecasts. Economic forecasts are generally described in terms of real GDP, GDP deflators (inflation rates), and unemployment rates and, occasionally, productivity changes. Economists provide important general conclusions to their economic forecasts such as short- and long-term Libor rates and bond yields that they believe are consistent with their overall economic forecasts. Additionally, economists provide the intermediate forecasts of forthcoming global government economic statistics a week or two prior to release. While these projections may be valuable to traders, these projections are not of much value to the portfolio manager beyond their aggregate temporal validation or repudiation of the portfolio manager's own forecast. The portfolio manager must thoroughly consider all important assumptions and components of his own global interest rate/currency forecast, assigning a measure of confidence to his forecast. Moreover, he must consider for all possible outcomes, plan a strategy for the eventuality on the portfolio valuations particularly should his critical assumptions prove incorrect.

The previous point is illustrated in Exhibit 1. The exhibit illustrates the volume and the complexity of the information with which portfolio managers are bombarded. All this information must be considered for the construction of a high-performing bond portfolio. Within each graphic is a comment about the importance to a portfolio manager of the micro-elements of each macro-factor category. The micro-elements signal secular direction and potential macro/political policy changes. The portfolio manager must decide whether the micro-element information is merely cyclical or whether it signals the beginning of a long-term trend. To do so, he must look for clues in the numbers and discern seminal changes well before they are upon him. The task seems utterly impossible. However as decisions crystallize, the portfolio will take shape, reflecting those decisions.

In simpler terms, although hardly simple, Exhibit 2 outlines some of the broad macroeconomic issues in a closed economy. The exhibit illustrates the complexity of the linkages among policy variables, markets, and economic outcomes. Exhibit 3 illustrates the complexities of monetary macroeconomic issues while only tangentially providing for an open, global economy. The graphics themselves are substantial and complex, let alone understanding the interrelations delineated. This chapter will present the practical transition that must be made from global political economist to global portfolio manager. For practical considerations, most of our discussion will be oriented around domestically located global bond portfolio management in order to present an understanding and appreciation for the impact of subtle economic developments on the management of any fixed income portfolio. By comparison, Exhibit 4 provides a simple economic model of an open system with multiple trading partners. Readily observable from this exhibit is the point that decisions regarding foreign bonds and foreign currencies add multiple layers of complexity, particularly in a portfolio management context where many fixed income products (futures, forwards, swaps, etc.) are available for strategy implementation. Moreover, on some level, decisions must be made and constraints developed that relate international exposure to ultimate asset purpose. That important topic is philosophical as well as social and economic and is well beyond the scope of this chapter.

Exhibit 1: The Open System: Global Policies and Free Market Prices

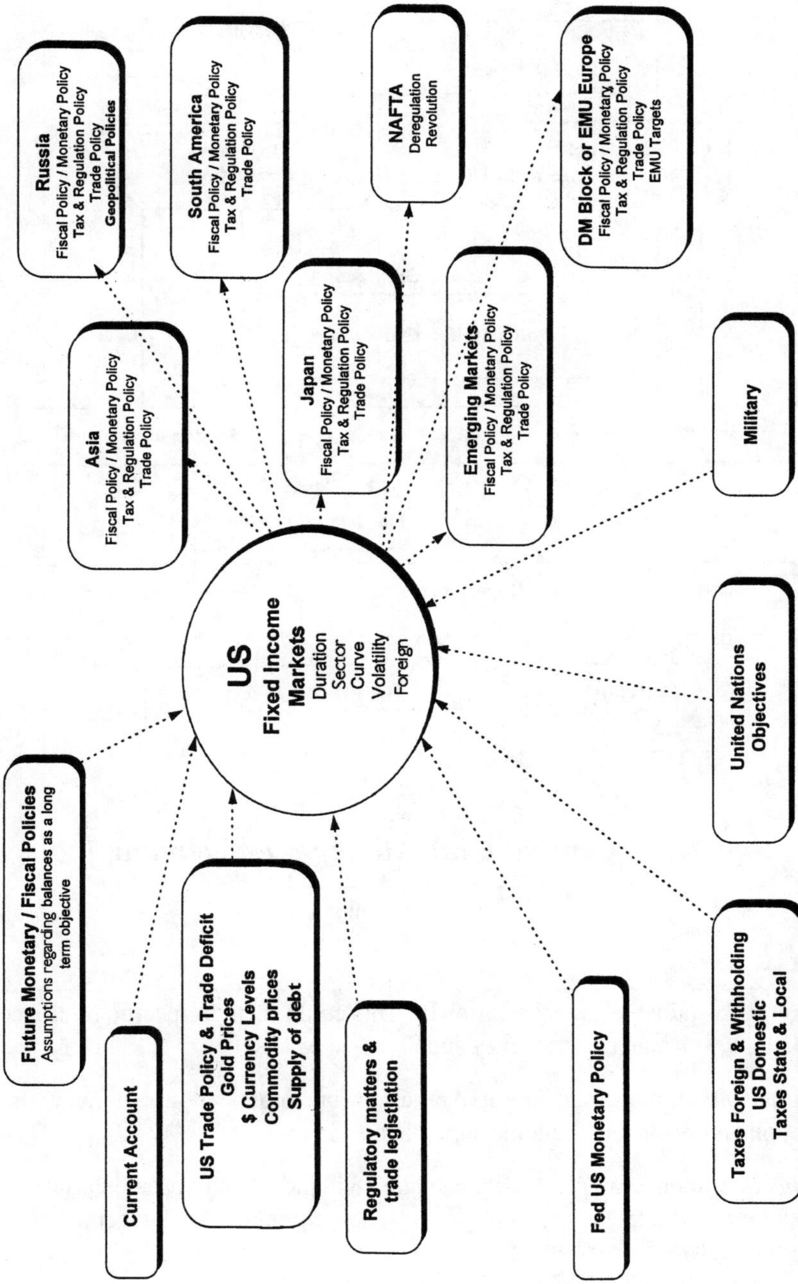

Design: Marie Sacheli

Exhibit 2: Closed Economy: Macroeconomic Issues

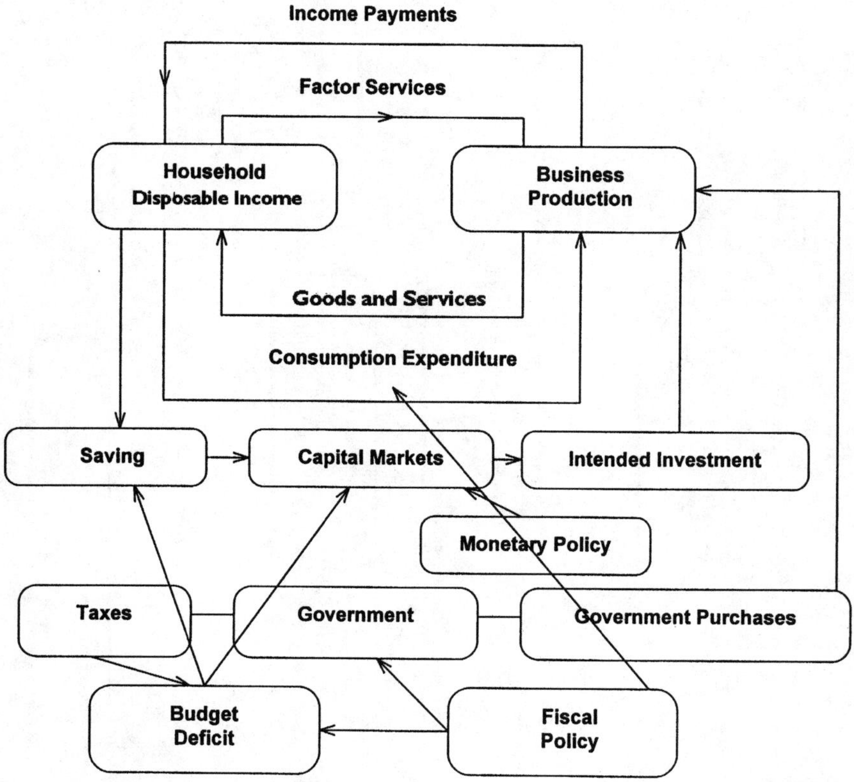

Exhibit 3: Central Bank Money Management Tools

Central Banks

Targets: sustainable economic growth. This could include specific reference to inflation, exchange rate or money supply objectives.

Instruments: Interest rates, reserve requirements, moral suasion, currency intervention and financial regulation/supervision.

Indicators: money supply,* exchange rate,* inflation,* activity, asset prices (e.g., equity prices, yield curves, credit spreads, house prices, etc.), budget deficit
* sometimes elevated to target status

Source: IBJ International plc

Exhibit 4: Global Bond Markets (Evaluating Impact of Global Monetary and Fiscal Policies

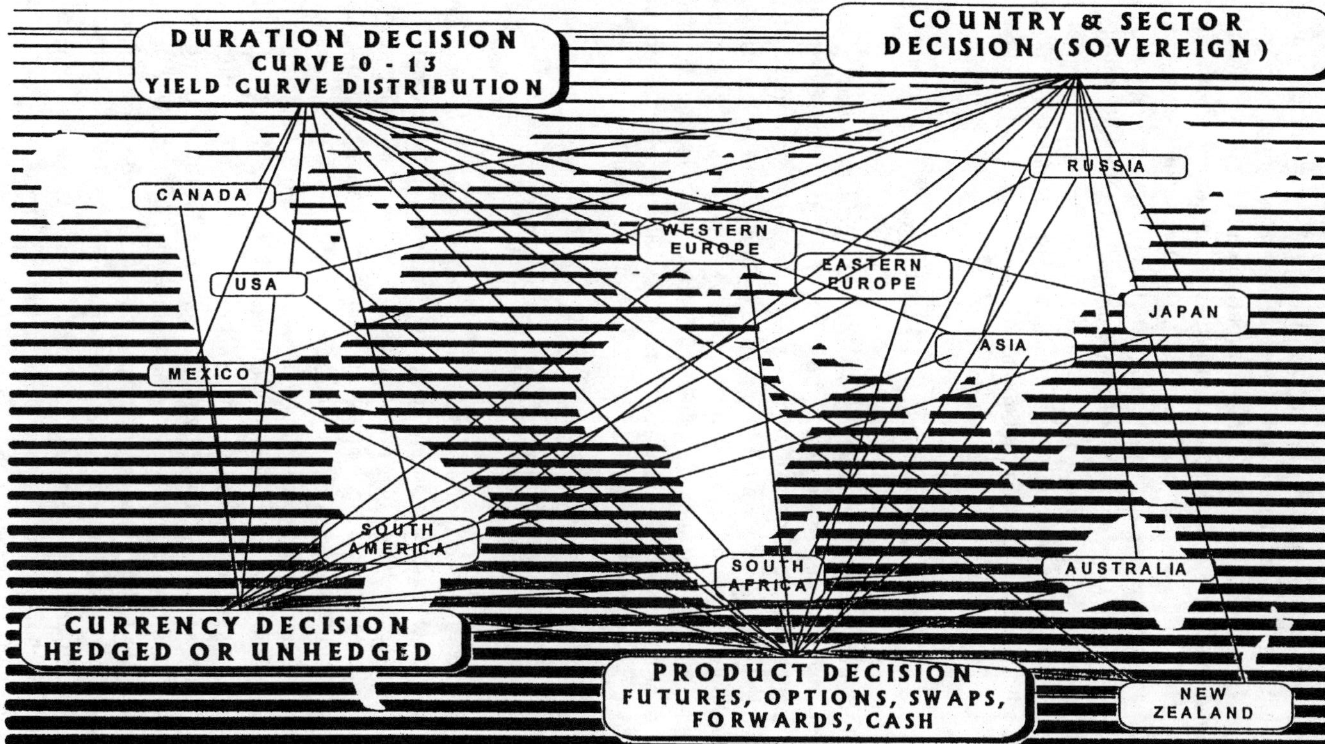

Design: Marie Sacheli

There are some practitioners who would argue that based upon the complexities of economic models and the volume of macro-information available, there is a strong case for technical analysis of the bond and currency markets. They argue that all this information, because of its sheer volume and potential unreliability, is noise and all-important information can be gleaned from global security and currency prices and patterns of prices. To technical practitioners, the prices themselves are the important clues to the future, so they apply technical analysis of market price levels of the various sectors of the market, from corporate spreads to foreign currencies, to structure a portfolio. We will not elaborate on this further other than to emphasize that the practice is prevalent and it is always useful to try to understand what other portfolio managers are doing and how their methods may impact the global markets.

THE GLOBAL CHALLENGE

The bond portfolio manager is generally posed with the challenge of outperforming a widely recognized, well-defined global index bogey. He is provided with a clear set of investment guidelines from which his investment pool of securities is derived. The guidelines should allow for a set of investment choices that is at least as great as the pre-ordained composition of the bogey and, preferably, substantially greater. The performance measurement period should be well defined and the commitment to the manager for a meaningful period of time such that a set of strategies can be implemented and the intended results achieved. The challenge is thus defined.

PORTFOLIO PARAMETERS

Ultimately, the portfolio manager must make investment decisions. In practice, this means buying and selling bonds and bond surrogates, and currencies and currency surrogates, to create a meaningful portfolio based on selected parameters. Among the most important parameters are the portfolio's country duration and expected cash flow distribution (yield curve exposure), currency positions, convexity, sector, and credit allocation. These parameters may be unique or so interrelated that the purity of their meanings may become obscured. Nevertheless, the portfolio's definition is discerned by its parameters. (In the abstract, however, a meaningful portfolio could be achieved, perhaps more efficiently, by merely placing allocations among the various market indices in combination with a macro currency allocation scheme.)

For example, the country-specific duration of a portfolio is the most potent source of forecast expression. Large relative positions in currencies can be equally important and, at times, dominate. Assuming a market-type bogey, extreme duration choices relative to the bogey represent expressions of the expectation for substantially higher or substantially lower interest rates in any given fixed income market. Implicit within an extreme duration-choice forecast is the expression of expectations for substantial changes in the volatility of interest rates. Similarly, extreme variation in currency composition relative to the bogey represents an expression about either (1) stable valuations among disparate yield, or (2) substantial changes in foreign exchange rates.

FORECAST CONFIDENCE AND RELATIVE RISK

One of the most important assessments that a portfolio manager must make is the degree of confidence he has in each part of his forecast. Forecast conviction also plays an important role in model usage. Highly confident forecasts may enable the portfolio manager to alter the model or the output of the model to reflect a "biased" distribution of outcomes. In essence, the manager is affecting the quantitative outcome in a way that is consistent with the qualitative forecast. Of course, the objective "fair value" determination will be distorted.

We previously elaborated upon the various forms of analysis that lead to the forecast. A strong conviction, high confidence forecast may result when the secular forecast is consistent with the cyclical forecast and both of those forecasts are consistent with the technical analysis. A weak conviction forecast may result when the conclusions the portfolio manager reaches are tentative when a potential major institutional change, for example, a G7-type meeting such as the Plaza Accord (1985), is within the forecast period. At this historic meeting, the seven most economically developed nations agreed to cooperate on strengthening the yen and the deutschemark. The forecast confidence is important because of its influence on the strength of the statement within the portfolio with respect to the portfolio parameters and character. Exhibit 5 illustrates the generalized statistical implication of forecast confidence.

Exhibit 5: Confidence Distributions

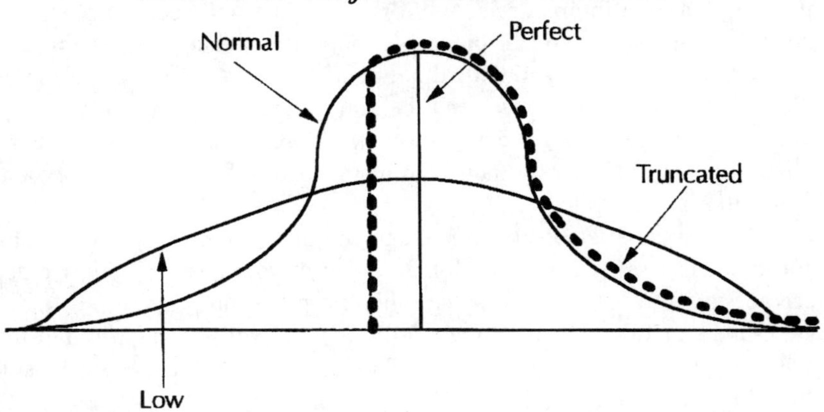

Low — Low Confidence, Normal — Moderate Confidence, Perfect, Truncated — High Confidence

A meticulous consideration of confidence levels may also help resolve potential portfolio contradictions. For example, a highly confident bullish country interest rate forecast in conjunction with a low confidence currency forecast would lead the portfolio manager to opt for high country duration and a neutral currency position whenever possible. Of course, in some local currency markets duration choices are limited to very short maturity bonds and money market instruments.

We will provide a few more examples to illustrate the role of forecast confidence in global bond management. However, in the abstract, differences in forecast confidence translates into:

Low confidence — insure
Moderate confidence — self-insure
High confidence — employ leverage, sell insurance

Practically speaking, the low confidence forecast would be insured via the strategic purchase of put options or by selling or buying assets in the portfolio to reduce the risk of the portfolio by moving closer to the global index bogey. Each strategy will render a different set of expected payoffs. The moderate confidence forecast normally results in a self-insure strategy with bets consistent with the forecast. The high confidence forecast translates into making extreme, leveraged bets consistent with the manager's forecast and selling assets whose returns would be derived from a forecast completely contrary to that of the manager. For example, in this latter case, the sale of put options on long bonds would reflect a highly confident forecast for lower yields on long bonds.

Consider a bond with the following characteristics: 30-year, non-callable Government of Spain bond, putable at par in five years. Let's look at how it may be used in two cases: the highly confident forecast and the weakly confident forecast. In both instances, assume that the volatility embedded within the bond's put option is lower than the volatility of conventional put options in the market.

If a portfolio manager with a global low-duration, 2.5-year assignment is highly confident that interest rates will drop, then he will seek ways to increase the portfolio's sensitivity to his forecast without dramatically increasing the risk. He may decide to use the hypothetical put bond. The bond provides for the upside of a 30-year bond if he is correct and the downside of a 5-year bond if he is not correct. In effect, he is long a 5-year bond with a call option on a 25-year bond and, therefore, has effectively increased his portfolio duration at the expense of yield, the alternative strategy.

Assume another portfolio manager holds a low confidence forecast for declining Spanish rates. He has a global market duration assignment. He decides to sacrifice yield to buy the insurance inherent in the put provision of the bond. He views his situation as being long a 30-year bond with the right to put the last 25 years back to the issuer. In this way he has decreased the "expected" cost to the portfolio of being wrong.

A much more powerful example of the importance of understanding forecast confidence to portfolio construction could be gleaned from an example involving the selection of foreign bonds in a political-economic context. Let's assume three portfolio managers hold a very strong conviction that interest rates in Europe will decline. One of the managers believes in a single tier complete European Monetary Union, another manager does not believe in a single tier European Monetary Union, and the third is very uncertain about the prospects for EMU. These beliefs may be expressed as follows:

Portfolio Manager	1	2	3
Bond Choice	Spanish	German	Putable Spanish bond (30/5)
Currency Choice	Spanish Peseta	DM	Basket of currencies or Call option on Spanish Pesetas

REGULATORY CHANGES, DEMOGRAPHIC TRENDS, AND INSTITUTIONAL BIAS

There are many important factors that are external to the economic system that may critically affect a bond portfolio's performance. These factors to varying degrees are difficult to anticipate. Topics such as demographics, mutual fund growth, and the multi-year plan for European integration are trending factors whose dynamics and influence may be discerned. However, sudden, meaningful changes — such as tax policy, pension plan allocation rules, guidelines, benefit payout rules, supply of bonds issued, types of bonds issued, Federal Reserve policy, and the implementation of credit controls, capital controls, trade treaties, IMF policies, and trade wars, among other issues — are more problematic to contemplate and incorporate. One step further is some abrupt aspects of life such as the outbreak of unanticipated wars or the formation of important economic cartels that are impossible to predict. All of these factors could induce dramatic changes in the following items: (1) direction of interest rates, (2) inter-market yield spreads, (3) shape of the yield curve, (4) volatility of the market and the pricing of expected volatility, (5) exchange rate values, and (6) intra-country yield spread, as well as other important financial valuations.

INFORMATION IN THE MARKETS

After considering the big picture, the global bond manager will consider regulatory issues, demographics, and institutional trends, in order to form an opinion about the more cyclical aspects of current macroeconomic fiscal and monetary policies. The global bond manager then examines the market for information. There are at least two types of information he will seek.

Exhibit 6: Global Economic Indicators

United States

- *Official surveys and reports:* Beige book, FOMC minutes
- *Domestic activity:* Industrial production, capacity utilisation, NAPM reports, quarterly GDP, retail sales (including weekly reports), auto sales, consumer confidence, durable goods orders, payrolls, initial claims, unemployment rate, housing starts, home sales, building permits
- *External activity:* goods and services balance, bilateral balances with Japan and China, quarterly current account
- *Inflation:* CPI, PPI, average hourly earnings
- *Special:* Budget documents, capital flows

Japan

- *Official surveys and reports:* the BoJ Tankan report, EPA monthly report, BoJ's quarterly economic assessment. Improve yen research by better co-ordination with Tokyo
- *Domestic activity:* Industrial production, quarterly GDP, Tokyo department store sales, overall retail sales, machinery orders (a proxy for investment), unemployment rate, job/applicants ratio, construction orders, housing starts
- *External activity:* trade balance, current account, bilateral Japan-U.S. surplus
- *Inflation:* CPI, WPI, M2+Cds, broad liquidity
- *Special:* land prices, banks' creditworthiness, fiscal balance

Europe

- *Official surveys and reports:* Bundesbank monthly report, Bank of England quarterly inflation report, other central bank reports
- *Domestic activity:* industrial production, quarterly GDP, retail sales/household consumption, car registrations, manufacturing orders, IFO/CBI/INSEE surveys, unemployment rate, construction/housing indicators, UK house prices
- *External activity:* trade balance, current account
- *Inflation:* CPI/RPI, PPI, WPI, import prices, wae inflation, money supply, credit growth
- *Special:* budget deficits and borrowing requirements, official reserves (especially during periods of exchange rate turbulence), land prices, banks' creditworthiness, fiscal balance

Emerging

- A variety of activity and inflation data are watched but much greater emphasis is given to measures of growth sustainability such as official reserves data, the balance of payments and capital flows.

Source: IBJ International plc

The first set, economic statistics, is readily available in a readable format. Some important global economic statistics are contained in Exhibit 6. This information is used in a historical business-cycle context to examine the present state of the economy and to derive inferences regarding the future. Pieces of economic statistical data are used to validate or repudiate a particular forecast or portfolio theme.

The second set of important information resides in the marketplace itself. This information is generally available in price form and its meaning or importance must be derived. Exhibit 7 provides a subset of this market information in the form of implied forward international government bond rates. These rates may be derived from current international government bond prices. The rates in Exhibit 7 result from inputting current international bond prices into complex computer valuation models (most of which are option pricing/contingent state models). For global bond managers, global yield curves, global money market and repo rates, global public and OTC options markets, global futures markets, global forward markets, global credit spread markets, and currency markets, among others, are rich sources of information. Obviously, to the extent models differ or other subjective inputs to the model differ, the inferences will differ. Today, too many practitioners rely on institutional models provided by external vendors. The vendors are reputable, but the portfolio manager has little knowledge of the theoretical foundations of the models provided. If institutional models are employed, the portfolio manager must be familiar with the theoretical foundation of the model and cognizant of any biases produced by the model or its inputs.

The importance of inferential market information cannot be overemphasized. This information provides the basis for the performance expectation during a specified period or base case returns for bonds. Therefore, it provides a benchmark from which the portfolio manager's forecast may be expressed. Consider the following scenario which is exaggerated for illustrative purposes.

Exhibit 7: Market Information: Implied Forward Government Rates

	1 yr	2 yr	3 yr	4 yr	5 yr	6 yr	7 yr	8 yr	9 yr	10 yr
Current										
U.S.	5.91	6.20	6.32	6.46	6.54	6.63	6.71	6.76	6.81	6.86
Germany	3.16	3.54	4.01	4.46	4.86	5.20	5.46	5.67	5.85	5.99
U.K.	6.78	6.87	7.05	7.17	7.27	7.34	7.40	7.45	7.51	7.56
Japan	0.60	0.84	1.19	1.54	1.84	2.12	2.36	2.56	2.71	2.84
1-Year Forward Rates										
U.S.	6.49	6.53	6.64	6.70	6.77	6.84	6.88	6.92	6.97	
Germany	3.93	4.44	4.90	5.29	5.61	5.85	6.03	6.19	6.31	
U.K.	6.96	7.19	7.30	7.39	7.45	7.50	7.55	7.60	7.65	
Japan	1.08	1.48	1.85	2.15	2.42	2.66	2.84	2.98	3.09	
2-Year Forward Rates										
U.S.	6.56	6.72	6.77	6.84	6.91	6.95	6.98	7.03		
Germany	4.96	5.39	5.75	6.04	6.24	6.39	6.52	6.61		
U.K.	7.41	7.47	7.54	7.57	7.61	7.65	7.69	7.73		
Japan	1.89	2.24	2.51	2.76	2.98	3.14	3.25	3.34		
3-Year Forward Rates										
U.S.	6.68	6.85	6.88	6.94	7.02	7.04	7.07			
Germany	5.43	5.86	6.20	6.46	6.63	6.75	6.86			
U.K.	7.59	7.62	7.67	7.69	7.72	7.75	7.78			
Japan	2.24	2.59	2.84	3.09	3.29	3.43	3.52			
4-Year Forward Rates										
U.S.	6.92	7.11	7.11	7.16	7.22					
Germany	6.39	6.80	7.10	7.31	7.42					
U.K.	7.95	7.92	7.94	7.92	7.93					
Japan	2.95	3.31	3.52	3.74	3.91					

Source: Bloomberg Financial Markets

Assume a portfolio manager is bearish on UK short-term interest rates. She expects a 25 basis point increase in the base rate and her most bearish case is for a 75 basis point increase in base rates funds. She has a very strong conviction that interest rates will subsequently fall. She has a bogey reflective of 2-year gilts. Based upon her forecast, she decides to reduce her duration by selling part of her 2-year securities position in the portfolio. Upon further reflection, she decides to consult with the market. She learns that the yield curve shape is reflective of a 150 basis point increase in short rates and the futures contracts for Eurosterling has a similar increase priced in for short rates. Paradoxically, although her expectations for interest rates are bearish, compared to the market's expectations her expectations are actually bullish. She decides that selling may not be a good idea and reflects further about the possibility of actually buying.

Discrepancies in inferential information gleaned from different markets regarding the same variable can be very profitable. Sometimes these discrepancies provide a clue to a portfolio manager about a systematic mispricing in a particular market. Unfortunately, most frequently, the discrepant information is a clue that the models are misformulated and that some other variables, such as liquidity differences or carry costs are not being accounted for properly. Other times, the dynamics among the variables are not properly modeled or perhaps, the dynamics inexplicably change over time. The point, of course, is that while market information is a rich input into evaluating bonds, currencies, and derivatives, the limitations of modeling reinforce the need for the portfolio manager to understand all parts of the process, including model development, and to think carefully about the meaning of the information considered. Uncertain truths are commonplace in the profession.

DURATION AND YIELD CURVE

The very extreme case of two assets, cash, and 30-year French OAT bonds, provides an example of the clean, unambiguous meaning of duration. Over the short term in this portfolio, the vast majority of return performance is determined by the change in long OAT rates and the percentage of the portfolio allocated to the long OAT. Exhibit 8 is a graphic expression of the recent yield history of 30-year OAT bonds and is indicative of the potential impact of good duration management on total return during this period. There are numerous significant changes in yield direction within the context of a period of a very significant reduction in the yield of long OAT bonds.

Ambiguities regarding intent and meaning increase with the number of investment choices. For example, merely adding a zero-coupon bond whose duration is similar to that of the long OAT bond complicates the decision process. The zero-coupon bond, although similar in duration to the 30-year OAT, has a unique set of performance characteristics. These include yield curve shape changes, volatility changes, as well as experiences duration decay with respect to time. It is unlikely, although possible, for a cross current of portfolio themes to prevail in this example. As the investment alternatives increase, the cross currents of decision making increase at a substantially greater rate, complicating the decision-making process. In Exhibit 9, the ambiguities of these choices and their impacts are noted by the double arrows (↔), indicating feedback effects. The exhibit attempts to include all of the possible investment choices available to the fixed income portfolio manager and to illustrate the volume of decisions that are constantly required to manage an international portfolio.

Forward curves (future yield curves predicted by current interest rates) are rarely, if ever, realized. The management of yield curve shape changes by capitalizing on any disagreements is a portfolio manager's potent source of superior return. Historically, short-term interest rates have been more volatile than long-term interest rates. Exhibit 10 provides some historical information from U. S. Treasury yield curves. An implication of these differentials on historical volatility is that yield curve shapes are unstable. In fact, during the past 15 years there have been numerous large swings in the shape of the yield curve. Beyond offering a rich arena of yield curve management, shape changes exert significant influences on inter-market and intra-market bond spreads. It is easy to imagine a number of potentially conflicting strategies arising from a given forecast of particular interest rates during a particular period. It is through changes such as those associated with the yield curve coupled with a comprehensive understanding of the various classes of bonds that enable the construction of a portfolio consistent with a manager's forecasts and convictions. Exhibit 11 is a partial representation of sets of bonds and the influences that cause their prices to change, the logical investment strategy per bond type from a given economic and price environment.

Exhibit 8: Yield History of 30-Year OAT Bonds: May 1991-August 1997

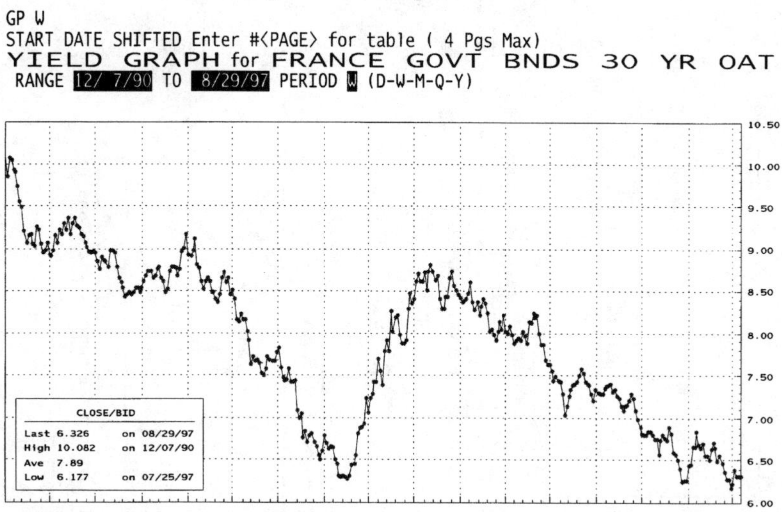

Source: Bloomberg Financial Markets

Exhibit 9: Guide to Bond Portfolio Management

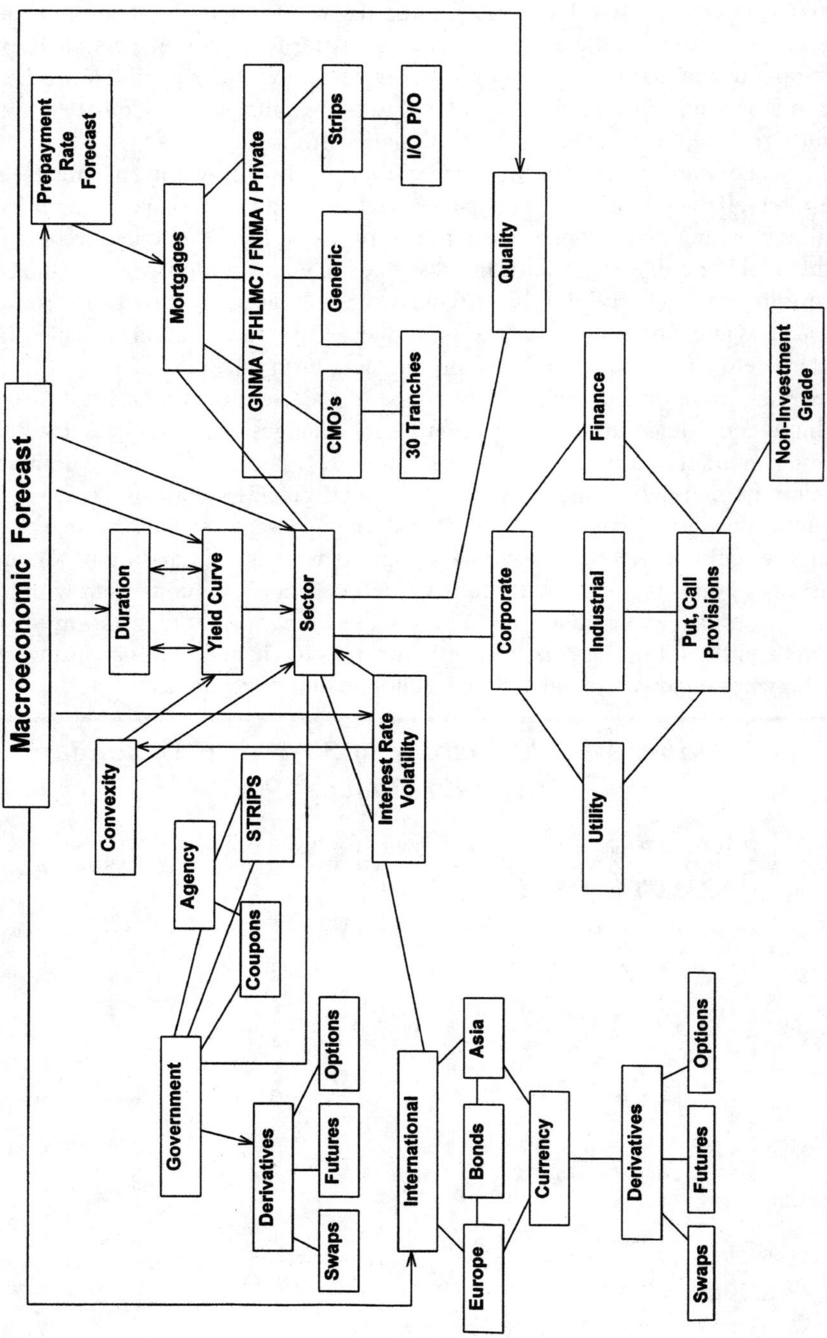

Exhibit 9 (Continued)

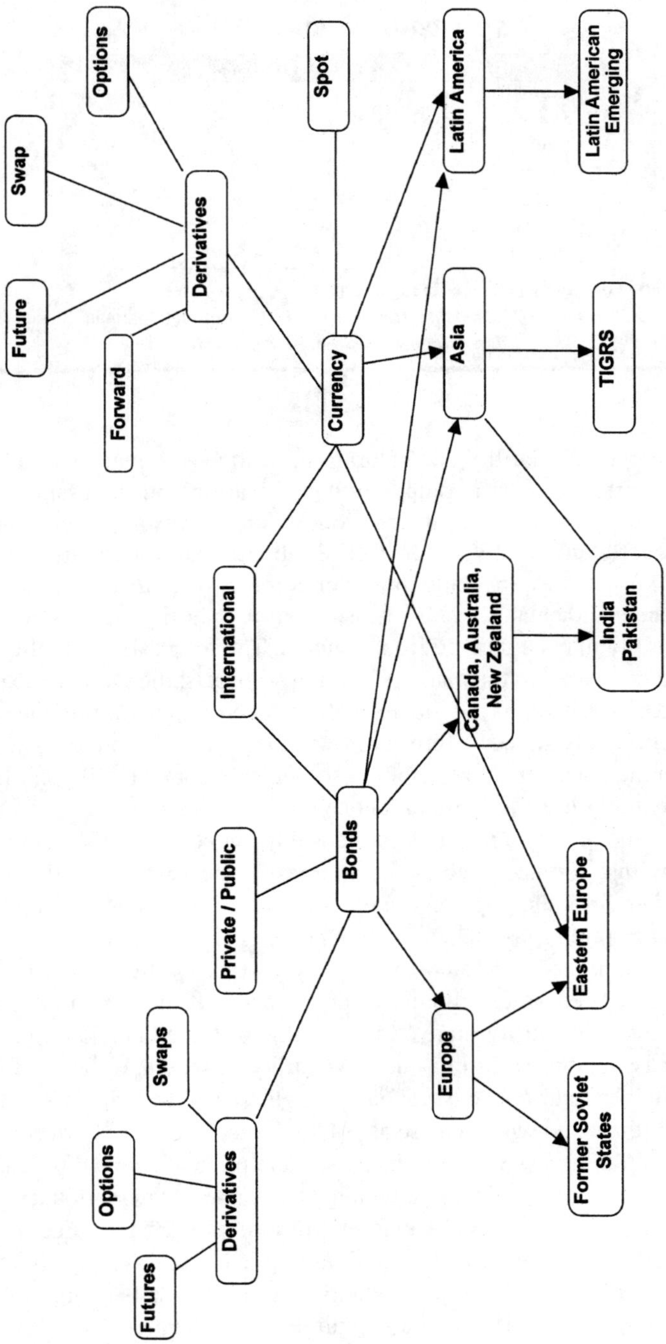

Exhibit 10: The Term Structure of Volatilities: Historical Evidence, 1950-1992

Term	Proportional Volatility (Expressed Monthly)
1 month	14.6%
3 month	11.3%
1 year	9.6%
2 year	7.5%
5 year	5.2%
10 year	4.0%
20 year	3.3%

Standard deviation of monthly changes in logarithms

Source: © *Historical U.S. Treasury Yield Curves 1993 Edition*, (Coleman, Fisher, Ibbotson).

VOLATILITY

If a high degree of volatility is a natural implication of a manager's global interest rate forecast, then the drift component specification and the assumptions for the correlation of volatility along international yield curves are important theoretical issues for quantitative analysis. (Inferences about volatility are difficult and model-dependent.) Practically speaking, however, a forecast for a substantial drop in rates implies change and change can be measured as a volatility factor. Once again, forecasted volatility may be derived from a model. The forecasted volatility expectation can then be compared to the market's pricing — that is, the market's expectation for volatility. The decision to buy or sell volatility in the portfolio is the result of this comparison. Simply stated, if forecasted volatility exceeds (is less than) market volatility, then the manager should employ strategies that buy (sell) volatility.

Volatility itself is an important characteristic that must be accounted for and managed by the portfolio manager in the following contexts. First is the hedging of positions with options. As volatility increases, the value of a given option will increase. Therefore, the popular strategy of covered writes, where a portfolio manager shorts an option against an underlying cash position to gain extra income for the portfolio, actually becomes a costly strategy when volatility increases. The second context involves securities with embedded options. If the portfolio manager holds putable bonds as volatility increases, the value of the embedded option to put the bond to the issuer increases in value as volatility increases. If the portfolio manager is long a callable security, the issuer has the right to call the bond at a particular price. The value of this bond will decrease as volatility increases. The third context involves credit spread trading. As volatility increases, the price of "spread products" — such as emerging market sovereign, international corporate or international mortgage debt — will decrease in value, as the market will assign a greater value to more liquid securities. The last context involves trading implied volatility. A global bond portfolio manager will assess the implied volatility in the markets along global the yield curves and may buy or sell different volatilities along the global yield curves depending on his relative assessment of the markets' valuation for these implied volatilities.

Exhibit 11: Guide to Strategy Selection Based on Forecasts

Sector/ Forecast	High Volatility	Low Volatility	Lower Rates Steeper Yield Curve	Lower Rates Flatter Yield Curve	Higher Rates Steeper Yield Curve	Higher Rates Flatter Yield Curve
Corporates						
Growth	Lower Quality Non-Callable	Lower Quality Callable	Lower Quality Non-Callable	Lower Quality Non-Callable Putable	Lower Quality Callable	Lower Quality Putable Callable
Recession	Avoid	High Quality Callable	Avoid	Avoid	Avoid	Avoid
Mortgages						
Growth	Convex P.O. Discount Mtgs PACS	Premium PACS Non-Agency Pass-thrus	Current Coupon PO Long Discount CMO	Current Coupon PO Long Z Tranches	Positively Convex IO Premium Pass-thrus	Avoid
Recession	Convex IO Discount Projects PACs	Negatively Convex Pass-thrus Neg Convex IO	Current Coupon Pass-thru Intermediate PACs	Long PACs	Positively Convex IO Premium Pass-thrus	Positively Convex IO Premium Pass-thrus
Governments						
Growth	Barbell	Bullet	Long Bullet	Long Barbell	Cash	Cash
Recession	Barbell	Bullet	Long Bullet	Long Barbell	Cash	Cash
Foreign Bonds						
Growth	Industrialized Markets Low Duration (Avoid)	Emerging Markets Low Duration				
Recession	Industrialized Markets High Duration	Industrialized Nations High Duration				
Foreign Currency						
Growth	Emerging Markets	Emerging Markets				
Recession	Industrialized Markets	Industrialized Markets				

Global interest rate volatilities are usually the result of a reversal of policies that have been maintained so long that adverse side effects develop. For example, initially, a generous monetary policy in a given country should reduce interest rates in that country and promote growth but will ultimately hinder growth as factor price volatility increases. A reversal of monetary policy in a given country to a "tight" mode raises interest rates and slows economic growth in that country. And sometimes, the monetary policies of one country can have a multi-country impact on interest rates. As observed during the 1990s, easier monetary policy in the United States has allowed for access to cheaper dollars globally and consequently, lowered global interest rates and changed global interest rate volatilities. Dramatic changes in fiscal and tax policies also induce volatility into the bond markets. Intra-bond/currency market correlations are an important input to the risk-adjustment analysis of global fixed income portfolios.

The volatility characteristic of the global bond portfolio is a very important decision. The expectation for a particular volatility factor is an input to the valuation of most bonds in the market. Forecasts for high volatility relative to the market normally imply that the embedded options in bonds, which investors are usually short, are of greater value thereby rendering the bonds less valuable. Mortgage securities and corporate bonds generally contain embedded options and are, as a class, substantially affected by volatility forecasts. In today's markets, within all sectors, there are bonds that perform well for a particular volatility forecast. One word of warning, it is usually difficult to separate and differentiate between the liquidity influence and the quality influence on intermarket spread changes coincident with volatility changes.

Exhibit 11 provides a guide for strategy selection based on volatility, yield curve change, and economic forecasts. Details are provided for each sector of the bond market.

In addition to product-related volatility which has dominated our discussion so far, let's introduce financial volatility and the macroeconomic effects of prolonged periods of either high or low volatility. Then, let's consider how that may feed back into the portfolio manager's forecasts for interest rates. In general, sustained levels of high volatility will retard economic growth and sustained levels of low volatility will promote economic growth. This truth is the basis for the monetarist's advocacy of low stable money supply growth to achieve sustained, non-inflationary economic growth.

The portfolio manager must define interest rate volatility, specifying it as a function of both maturity and term. Generally, volatility is a declining function of both maturity and term. Exhibit 12 provides historical data substantiating this proposition. The natural implication of this proposition is that for a given portfolio duration, the portfolio's shorter securities are expected to be more volatile in a yield sense or more risky than its longer bonds. (See Exhibit 13.) For substantiation of this point, the portfolio manager need only consider the over-the-counter market for options on U.S. Treasury securities to understand the market's pricing of yield curve volatilities.

Exhibit 12: Term Structure of Volatility

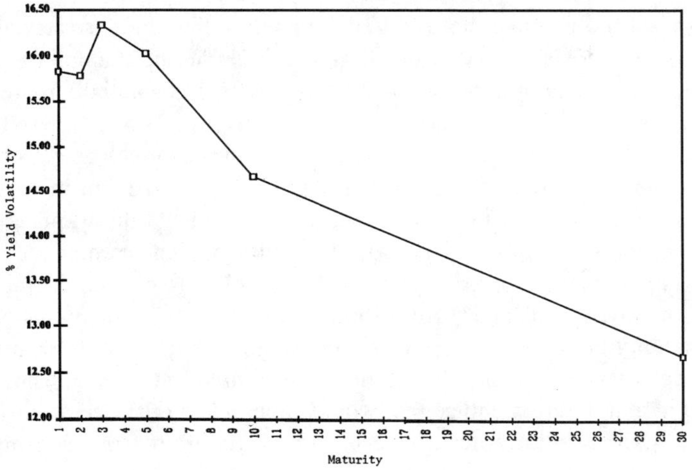

Exhibit 13: Volatility Adjusted Duration

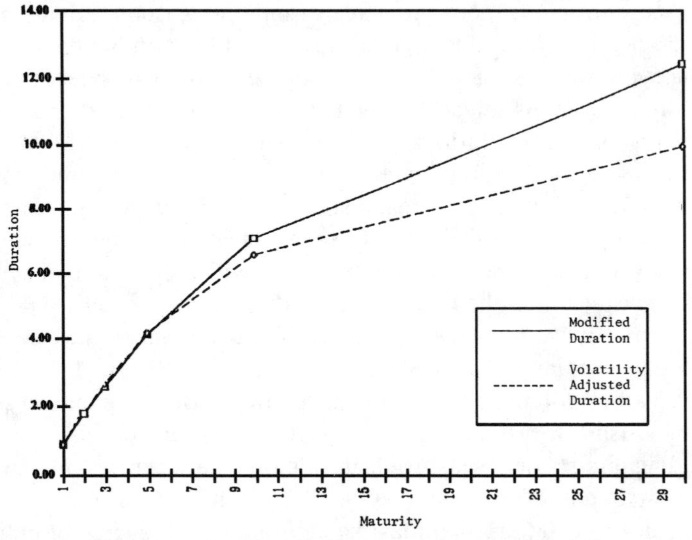

The assignment or selection of volatility along international yield curves is an important decision for the bond manager. It not only affects the valuation of embedded and actual call options, but it affects the overall risk adjustments of the portfolio. Risk-adjusted durations, risk-adjusted convexities, and risk-adjusted portfolio yield are partially a function of volatility. Therefore, strategically, the portfolio manager may want to "buy" volatility on a particular part of a yield curve and "sell" it at another part to secure the desired risk-adjusted factors.

LIMITATIONS OF SOVEREIGN ONLY BOND PORTFOLIOS

Assume a portfolio manager holds a high conviction that interest rates are going to drop across global yield curves. Furthermore, assume the manager believes that rates on the shorter end of the yield curves will decline substantially more than long-term interest rates. The implications of this forecast are (1) own a very high global duration, (2) weight the duration to shorter term bonds as much as possible, and (3) avoid bonds that will be called away to the portfolio's detriment in the markets in which he selects to invest (i.e., bonds whose call-adjusted durations are short). A thorough evaluation of global forward rates confirms that the manager is, in fact, more bullish and expects a greater steepening of yield curves than the market.

However, the manager will be bothered by his desire to be as short as possible on a given yield curve to capitalize on the greater relative drop in short rates when the yield curve steepens. He will have to weigh his choice against the potential return of a higher duration choice that would capitalize on the overall drop in global interest rates. The solution is less than satisfying, even if one considers higher yielding local currency emerging markets as forward currency rates may discount completely any global interest rate differentials. This point will be explored later in the chapter. In any case, it is understood that short bonds are inherently short duration.

A seasoned global portfolio manager initially reasons that absent leverage, the best that can be achieved is a portfolio of zero-coupon bonds at the targeted duration wherever such a market exists; if not, he is likely to select the maximum duration instrument in his selected market. This solution is less than satisfying and he may search for novel solutions such as found in the United States or Danish mortgage market, or by constructing a hybrid barbell solution in any global market. A portfolio of principal-only mortgage strips (POs) is an example of the former. The sole source of return for the PO is the prepayment of the underlying mortgages. The PO has a very high duration and very convex with respect to prepayment rates. It should be reasoned that the return on this long duration bond would be largely driven by the prepayment rates on mortgages. The prepayment rates are very sensitive to both the changing yield and the changing shape of the yield curve. In the latter case, the barbell solution, duration is added from elsewhere on the yield curve. In fact, the bullish forecast induces the global manager to sell his poor convexity, higher yielding, prepayment sensitive Danish mortgage securities in favor of longer duration zero-coupon Danish treasury bonds. The final choice, however, will be driven by return calculations that must be adjusted by the degree of belief in each particular scenario. Exhibit 14 illustrates the duration/yield curve shape trade off.

INTERNATIONAL CORPORATE BONDS

The yield spread of a corporate bond relative to a government bond is negatively correlated to the growth of the economy. Greater economic growth in the global economy generally provides greater profitability to corporations thereby reducing the probability of default. Therefore, yield spreads of corporate bonds over government bonds narrow as default risk diminishes. Exhibit 15 provides historical evidence of the cyclical influence on yield spreads in the Japanese market. Cursory empirical evidence indicates that the inflection points of the yield spreads are related to turning points of bond yields.

A portfolio manager who can confidently identify the transition from recession to growth and vice versa can add substantially to portfolio performance. Not only will he accurately forecast the change in the direction of interest rates and aid in currency selection, but he will also add tremendous value with his sector choices. As Exhibit 11 suggests, low quality corporate bonds satisfy the confident high growth forecast. Holding global government bond rates constant, the most potent returns would result from low quality, non-callable, long maturity corporate bonds in emerging markets. Alternatively, corporate bonds should be sold entirely if an economic slowdown or recession is forecast; emerging market corporate bonds should be sold first.

Exhibit 14: Yield Curve Total Return Analysis Hypothetical Par Securities (3-Month Horizon)

Coupon (%)	Maturity	Duration (Years)	Projected Terminal Yield (%)	Appreciation (%)	Income (%)	Total Return (%)
7.00	2/15/99	1.84	6.30	1.129	1.75	3.040
7.00	2/15/01	3.44	6.50	1.626	1.75	3.376
7.00	2/15/02	4.16	6.75	0.987	1.75	2.730
7.00	2/15/04	5.46	6.85	0.785	1.75	2.535
7.00	2/15/07	7.11	6.90	0.686	1.75	2.436

Exhibit 15: Benchmark JGB/AA Class Industrial Bonds

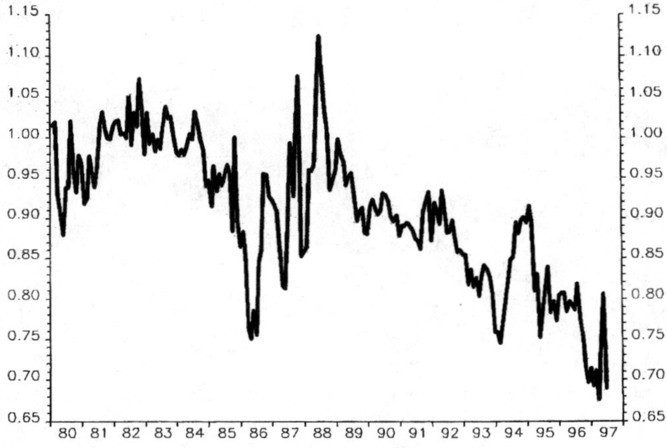

Source: Datastream

The fact that emerging market corporate bond spreads are variable and that part of their variability is related to the quality of the credit (issuer's credit rating) and part related to the country of domicile has important yet subtly complex implications. For example, corporate bond spread variability implies that these bonds may be more volatile than government bonds. They may even perform asymmetrically with respect to the direction of volatility changes. That is to say, the price of the corporate bond will change by varying amounts, conditional on the direction of the change in the spread even though rates on government bonds do not change at all. (This is the simplest case to explore.) Asymmetrical changes in value occur in a typical callable corporate bond for two reasons: the embedded call features and the normal asymmetry associated with quality spread term structures.

We will use an example to better illustrate these issues. Assume we have a corporate bond rated A with a 30-year maturity and callable in five years at 105. The prevailing generic quality term spreads for similar structures are as follows: AAA — 0.50%, AA — 0.65%, A — 1.00%, BAA — 1.65%, BA — 2.75%, B — 4.50%. Exhibit 16 illustrates the asymmetry feature. It shows the possible performance result as the bond spread narrows. Because its duration shrinks, its price does not change significantly relative to the downgrade. If there is a downgrade and the call option goes "out of the money," the price change is quite large. The asymmetry is quite apparent. The portfolio manager must determine how much yield is required to compensate for this risk. He must first assign a particular volatility assumption to each issuer so that the proper yield premium can be determined. He may simply choose to assign a probability to both scenarios to assist in his decision process.

Exhibit 16: Credit Spreads, Call Options, and Price Asymmetries

Consider the following hypothetical A rated international sovereign bond, denominated in U.S. dollars, 7.00% coupon, maturing 9/1/27 priced at 100, callable 9/1/02 at 102.5.*

<table>
<tr><th rowspan="2">Rating</th><th rowspan="2">Yield Spread (%)</th><th rowspan="2">Yield (%)</th><th rowspan="2">Price to Call</th><th rowspan="2">Price to Maturity</th><th colspan="2">Percent Price Change</th></tr>
<tr><th>to Call</th><th>to Maturity</th></tr>
<tr><td>AAA</td><td>0.50</td><td>6.50</td><td>103.921</td><td>106.563</td><td>3.92</td><td>6.56</td></tr>
<tr><td>AA</td><td>0.65</td><td>6.65</td><td>103.270</td><td>104.523</td><td>3.27</td><td>4.52</td></tr>
<tr><td>A</td><td>1.00</td><td>7.00</td><td>N/A</td><td>100.000</td><td colspan="2">0</td></tr>
<tr><td>Baa</td><td>1.65</td><td>7.65</td><td>N/A</td><td>92.396</td><td colspan="2">(7.6)</td></tr>
<tr><td>Ba</td><td>2.75</td><td>8.75</td><td>N/A</td><td>81.531</td><td colspan="2">(18.47)</td></tr>
<tr><td>B</td><td>4.50</td><td>10.50</td><td>N/A</td><td>68.213</td><td colspan="2">(31.79)</td></tr>
</table>

*For simplicity, we assume a flat term structure at 6.00%, constant credit spreads along the term structure, and a constant term structure volatility.

FOREIGN INVESTMENT SELECTION

The tasks confronting an international fixed income portfolio manager are increasingly complex as the global fixed income markets are presently expanding. New sovereign names are tapping the fixed income markets for capital and other existing sovereign names are expanding the list of security types they are offering. The world capital markets present a huge and broadly distributed set of investment considerations and choices. These issues will be simplified at the outset, then a few layers of complexity will be added. Exhibit 4 is illustrative of how complex matters can become.

The value inherent to a bond is the enforceability of the bond contract. In a very real way, with substantial historical precedent, investments in bonds of foreign issuers are void of enforceability powers. Investments in foreign bonds are perhaps more akin to equity-type investments. In this regard their political default risk as opposed to corporate default risk in equity investments, is extremely low but real. This risk should be considered in addition to the volatility risks implied by the options markets for foreign bonds and currencies and should be reflected in the portfolio risk adjustments.

A country consideration set for the international portfolio manager today includes: (1) Canada, (2) Europe, (3) Asia, (4) Australia and New Zealand, (5) Russia, (6) Latin America, (7) Middle East, and (8) Africa. Of course, depending on his appetite for global risk, a portfolio manager may wish to consider a more simplified country selection set representative of advanced capital markets, for example, considering only: (1) Canada, (2) Germany, and (3) Japan. In any of the above instances, the analytical focus would continue to be on specific country macroeconomics as in our one country example (both cyclical and secular), but the political analysis would take on greater importance. Additionally, currency valuations are introduced.

There are four major components of risk and reward in international bonds: (1) yield, (2) changes in interest rates, (3) changes in currency values, and (4) liquidity. The components are a function of market risk, credit risk, and political risk. The last component, liquidity, is particularly significant to the global bond portfolio manager when considering emerging market bonds. The less-liquid markets may provide extraordinary yields and performance opportunities, but provide genuine hazards during periods of rising interest rates or political/economic volatility. By contrast, because the cash, futures, forward, options, and swap markets in the larger international capital markets are fairly well developed, market inferences about volatility expectations and forward break-even rates and prices for both currencies and bonds are more easily discerned. Exhibit 17 provides examples of this information.

Exhibit 17: International Fixed Income Investing

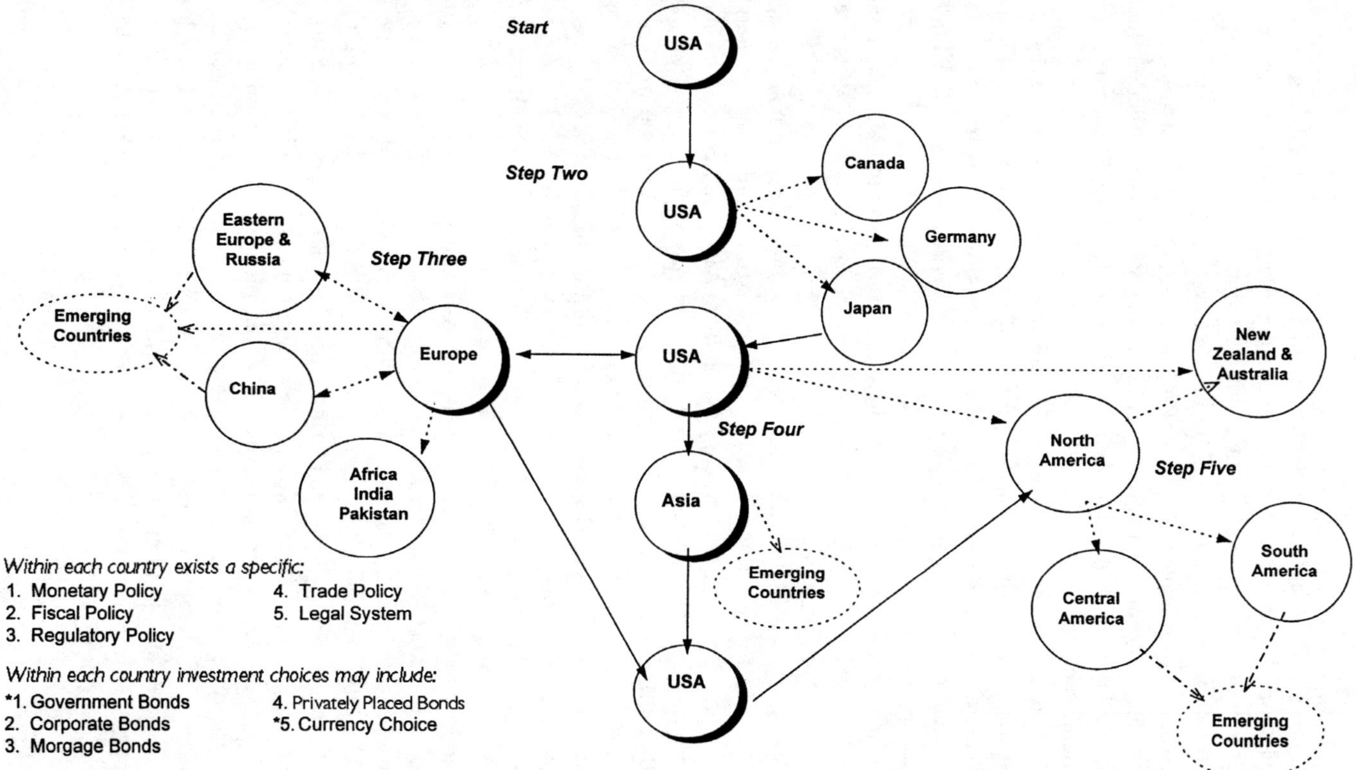

Within each country exists a specific:

1. Monetary Policy
2. Fiscal Policy
3. Regulatory Policy
4. Trade Policy
5. Legal System

Within each country investment choices may include:

*1. Government Bonds
2. Corporate Bonds
3. Morgage Bonds
4. Privately Placed Bonds
*5. Currency Choice

*Spot market, forward markets, option markets and in some cases, organinzed futures markets.

Design: Marie Sacheli

As mentioned above, the global portfolio manager's analysis of government bonds in foreign countries is similar across all bond markets. However, the portfolio manager must consider the currency risk as well. He must develop theoretical and technical models for currency analysis. The analysis must consider current accounts, trade accounts, monetary policy, fiscal policy, as well as, regulatory, institutional, and tax policies and more. The bond decision ought to be considered as a currency-hedged one (i.e., the bond stripped of the currency exposure versus a currency non-hedged one). Investment choices then can be viewed more easily relative to one another. More importantly, Exhibit 18 demonstrates the benefits of international diversification in a relatively stable-state world. (In this example this means moving beyond U.S. domestic security choices, even though the foreign currency exposures are hedged back into U.S. dollars.) Empirically, considering just the 5-year period 1991 to 1996, superior returns were achieved by the G-5 portfolio hedged back to U.S. dollars. By increasing the "dollar" investment choices, the bond portfolio manager will increase his chances for higher returns. By adding currency exposure, the bond portfolio manager will further increase his chances for higher returns, but he will have also taken on greater risk or variance of returns via his exposure to a variety of foreign currency price fluctuations.

The task of international investing is complicated as the universe of investment alternatives increase, perhaps including the emerging markets of (1) Eastern Europe and Russia, (2) Central and South America, (3) Asia, and (4) India and Pakistan. As Exhibit 18 illustrated, the investment universe can become almost unlimited, especially when bonds issued by global private companies are introduced.

CURRENCY SELECTION

There are many theories about currency-value determination. The most popular fundamental ones are based on (1) purchasing power parity (PPP), (2) trade balances, (3) real interest rate differentials, and (4) growth rates and growth prospects. None of these are very satisfying. Each has proved important but the importance of any one has varied over time. Therefore, technical analysis of the currency markets is quite prevalent.

The portfolio manager must decide upon the relative weights of each of the factors, in conjunction with technical analysis since, most often, the signals will be mixed. For example, PPP may be positive for the currency while the trade balance is negative. He must also consider the influence of cartels, such as European Monetary Union efforts and central bank intervention in the currency markets. A simplified analysis is provided below:

	PPP	Growth Rate	Balance of Trade	Real Interest Rate Differential
Correlation with currency valuation	+	+	+	+

Exhibit 18: Diversification Analysis for Dollar-Based Accounts

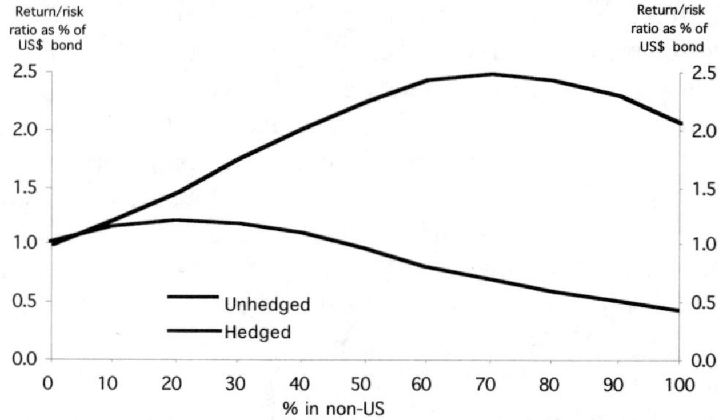

Total Returns Correlations — $, Unhedged, Latest 5 Years

	US	Jap	Ger	Fra	UK
US	1.00	0.13	0.30	0.31	0.32
Japan		1.00	0.57	0.48	0.21
Germany			1.00	0.91	0.56
France				1.00	0.63
UK					1.00

Total Returns Correlations —$, Hedged, Latest 5 Years

	US	Jap	Ger	Fra	UK
US	1.00	0.28	0.39	0.28	0.33
Japan		1.00	0.43	0.10	0.17
Germany			1.00	0.74	0.69
France				1.00	0.68
UK					1.00

Market Statistics for 5-Year Bonds (January 1992-December 1996, Monthly Data)

	US	Japan	Germany	France	UK
Local Currency					
Average Monthly Return (%)	0.5	0.7	0.8	0.8	0.8
Variance (%)	1.7	1.7	1.0	1.5	2.8
Return/Risk Ratio	0.3	0.4	0.8	0.5	0.3
Unhedged					
Average Monthly Return (%)	0.5	0.7	0.7	0.7	0.7
Variance (%)	1.7	11.8	8.4	6.6	6.7
Return/Risk Ratio	0.3	0.1	0.1	0.1	0.1
Fully Hedged					
Average Monthly Return (%)	0.5	0.8	0.6	0.6	0.6
Variance (%)	1.7	1.7	1.0	1.5	2.7
Return/Risk Ratio	0.3	0.5	0.6	0.4	0.2
Spot FX Rate					
Average Monthly Return (%)		-0.1	0.1	0.0	-0.1
Variance (%)		9.6	9.2	8.8	9.6
Return/Risk Ratio		0.0	0.0	0.0	0.0

Source: Steven Hannah, Chief Economist IBJ International

Exhibit 19: Forwad Yen Currency Rates

	Yen/Dollar Values
Spot	116.15
1 Month	115.65
1 Year	110.14
3 Years	98.83
5 Years	90.63

Note: The currency forward prices traded in the market are important to the management of foreign currencies. The prices indicate that the term of the currency investment is important as is the currency itself.
Source: IBJ London Branch

The yen/dollar forward values are derived from the prevailing interest rate term structure differentials between the two markets. For example, the approximate 5% difference between the 1-year rate in the United States and the 1-year rate in Japan yields an approximate 5% drop in currency values. However, we know that forward currency values are affected by other variables as well. So, we can express our conviction that the interest rate term structure differentials are not fully incorporating the influence of those other variables by being long or short the forward currency exchange rates. (See Exhibit 19.)

The following hypothetical example may help illustrate the point. Assume our secular forecast for the United States is dominated by demographic influences. The predominant aspect of this forecast is an aging of the baby boom generation and, as implied, the transformation from consumers to savers. Therefore, we conclude that the demand for imports will decline and the savings rate will increase. Both of these phenomena imply an improved current account balance. Moreover, we believe that the demographics in Japan are such that savings will decline substantially and a secular deterioration in the Japanese current account will result. Because of this secular forecast, we adopt a "strong dollar" forecast. We know that the interest rate differentials imply a weak dollar. We bet against the market's pricing by buying dollars forward five years and selling yen forward at an exchange rate of 90.635 dollars per yen. This is a 22% discount to the prevailing spot exchange rate of 116.15. The purchase of options on a 5-year forward dollar/yen is the weaker form of expression of the secular strong dollar forecast.

Global bond portfolio performance can be enhanced dramatically when the global bond portfolio manager considers as many potential factor changes as possible, deriving comparative rate forecasts that differ significantly from the current static snapshot of currency rates as evidenced in current forward currency markets. Then, of course, his conclusions will have an important impact on his global interest rate bets as well. These decisions are inseparable and provide many performance opportunities for the thorough global bond portfolio manager. For the leveraged global money manager, currency selection is critical for another reason. The leveraged money manager searches for the cheapest currency from which to borrow funds. The analysis involves comparing various term currencies rates as swapped into one baseline currency, say U.S. dollars, to identify the currency that trades cheapest to Libor for the desired term. The leveraged fund manager will borrow in the cheapest currency to finance all his global bond purchases in whatever country he selects.

The potential for very good or very bad results increases as one moves further from a domestic currency bond portfolio. Increases in one's investment universe such as those described in this chapter invite quick performance responses as multiple bond and currency markets fluctuate. Markets occasionally move in a step-function fashion rather than smoothly. The volatility in the Southeastern Asian countries as depicted in Exhibit 20 is illustrative of a step-function movement. The exhibit clearly illustrates the prior history of smooth foreign exchange value. This extreme change in movement is important for many reasons. We will illustrate the obvious performance implication importance last.

Exhibit 20: Volatility in the Southeastern Asian Countries

PAC Rim Short Rates— HK, Kor, Indo, Mal, Phil, Sing, Thai
Eq. Wts., Sep 30, 13.03%

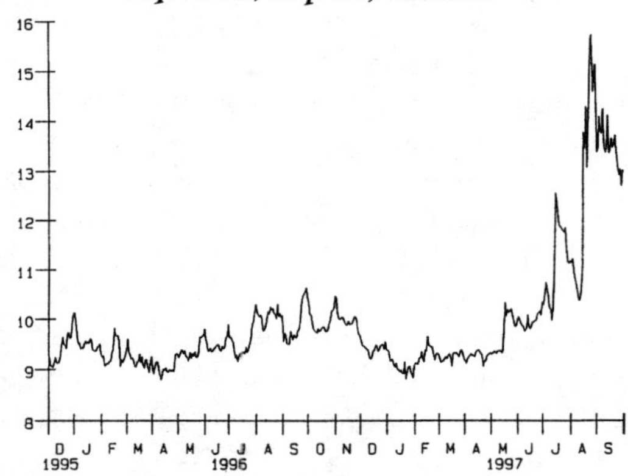

PAC Rim Currencies — HK, Kor, Indo, Mal, Phil, Sing, Tai, Thai
Eq. Wts., Oct. 2, 123.2

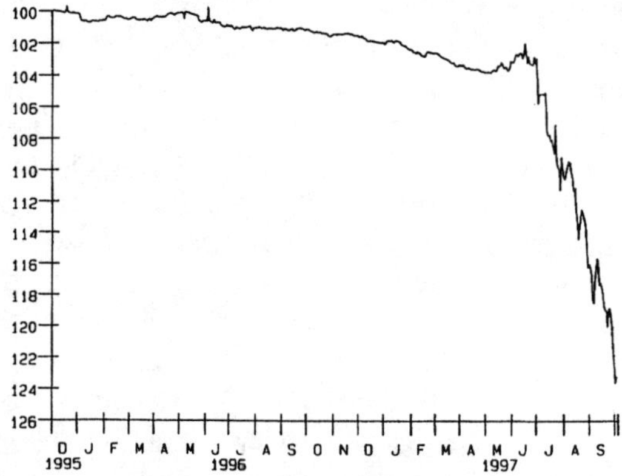

Source: International Strategy & Investment Group Inc.

The abnormality of a step-function movement in a market violates important assumptions regarding the distribution of returns commonly assumed for the formulation of state contingent pricing models. We have elaborated exhaustive about the importance of these models for portfolio management.

There is another important market phenomena, economic crisis measures, that occurs but is not captured in the exhibit in the emerging market countries (the so-called *Little Dragons*). The government will impose emergency economic measures such as capital flow restrictions. In response, short-term interest rates soar. Many investors can be effectively trapped with assets whose values plummet. Portfolios overweighted in these countries are exposed to this danger and experience greater volatility and reduced return, completely opposite of the presumed positive pattern of return touted with diversification. A similar episode can occur, but far less frequently, in well-developed economies. For example, as the initial attempt at EMU failed in 1992 and countries dropped out such as Great Britain, short-term interest rates across Europe soared as each of these countries attempted to protect their currency values. (See Exhibit 21.) Ultimately, despite state-of-the-art technology and information, only a keen analysis of the political-economic environment would have enabled a global portfolio manager to escape these episodes. (The politically savvy portfolio manager could have prospered nicely during these episodes through the effective construction of short positions.)

CONCLUSION

The global fixed-income portfolio manager has a significant role to play in benefiting not only the fixed-income investor, but the emerging and developing countries as well by providing more permanent capital to markets that will yield attractive returns. Global portfolio managers know that market consensus as reflected in current prices on a forward basis can be an incorrect predictor of future rates. A skillful portfolio manager will be able to assess all the germane bits of market information accessible to him and apply his knowledge in the form of market strategies that express his disagreement with current global forward prices. That is to say, in order to achieve effective results and reach responsible investment decisions the portfolio manager must be diligent in gathering information, and be able to interpret, understand, and process that information in an independent fashion. After he has gone through this process, he must create a global bond portfolio that reflects his beliefs in a cost and risk effective way in the context of current market prices of his investment set.

To review, the basic factors that the global fixed-income portfolio manager must examine include: worldwide economic, political, historic, psychological, monetary and fiscal policies, products available, risks associated in buying and selling these products, the impact on other investors on market movements, regulatory issues, and the competitive advantages of other competing portfolio managers. Once the portfolio manager has gathered all this global information, he must decide on short- and long-term interest rate and currency forecasts and the expected time frame for his investment decisions to perform as well as alternative strategies should market conditions alter his initial assumptions. Then the portfolio manager must create a global bond portfolio considering all the possible securities within his "bogey" set of investment possibilities, deciding on duration and how to achieve the duration goal, cash flows and distribution of cash flows on the yield curve, convexity, credit quality, country selection/hedged international exposure, and non-dollar or currency exposure. In doing so, the global fixed income portfolio manager, armed with his interest rate and currency forecasts, is faced with the eternal trade-off between expected returns or percentage total returns against risk or the variance of the percentage of total returns and liquidity parameters regardless of his set of investment or "bogey" alternatives. In essence, the portfolio manager must constantly decide when to place more chips on the table and when to take them off. The process of global fixed income portfolio management is, therefore, always an exercise in constrained optimization.

Exhibit 21: U.K. Rates

U.K. Pound — Dec 31, 1.5

Europe Short Rates G.F.I. UK — Dec. 31, 6.34%

Source: International Strategy & Investment Group Inc.

Chapter 4

International Fixed Income Investment: Philosophy and Process

Anthony L. Faillace
Vice President, International Product Manager
Pacific Investment Management Company

Lee R. Thomas, Ph.D.
Managing Director, Senior International Portfolio Manager
Pacific Investment Management Company

INTRODUCTION

In 1985, the U.S. bond market accounted for over 50% of the world's outstanding debt issues. Ten years later the U.S. share had shrunk to 42% of the world's debt market, as the total market increased nearly three and a half times to almost $23 trillion.[1] The U.S. share of the world fixed interest market will no doubt continue to shrink as more countries embrace economic reform and choose to finance governmental and corporate needs in the world's capital markets. Portfolio managers, driven by increasingly liberal investment restrictions, are reaching out for superior risk-adjusted return wherever in the world it can be found. This, combined with sophisticated financing techniques finding their way to a broader number of countries, makes debt issuance possible for an increasing number of international entities.

In light of its increasing size and return potential, investors can ill afford to ignore the opportunities available in international bond markets. Before describing these potential benefits, it will help to define exactly what we mean by an international bond.[2] This characterization can be based on the domicile of the issuer or principal buyers, primary trading market, or currency denomination of the instrument. For the purposes of this chapter, international bonds refer to issues denominated in a currency different from that of the investor. This — currency of denomination — is

[1] Merrill Lynch & Co., *Size and Structure of the World Bond Market: 1996.*

[2] The terms international and foreign bonds are often used interchangeably. Global bond portfolio or mandate typically refers to a portfolio managed against an index which includes all major government bond markets.

probably the single most important determinant of yield. U.S. dollar bond prices fluctuate in sympathy with the direction of U.S. interest rates, while other international fixed income markets are tied to their own interest rate cycles.

This chapter is divided into three sections. The first section describes how international bonds can be used, distinguishing between tactical and strategic uses. The second section describes an appropriate investment philosophy for harvesting the risk reduction and excess return potential of strategic international bond portfolios. The final section examines one effective portfolio management process — our firm's — which can be used to implement this investment philosophy.

USES OF INTERNATIONAL FIXED INCOME

There are two basic ways to use international bonds. The first is tactically (or opportunistically), as a substitute for domestic bonds. This in effect creates another sector of the bond market for the portfolio manager to use in outperforming a domestic benchmark like the Lehman Aggregate or Salomon Broad Indices. The second is strategically, as a separate asset class. This typically takes the form of a separate portfolio which is benchmarked to one of the major global indices such as the J.P. Morgan Government Bond or the Salomon World Government Bond Indices. This section reviews the arguments for both uses of international bonds, and updates empirical studies regarding these instruments' volatility properties.[3] The updated data support the consensus that international bonds can effect meaningful risk reduction by providing effective diversification. Recent arguments that the benefits of global bond diversification are declining are also examined.[4] The conclusion is that evidence for increased correlation between U.S. and foreign bond returns is weak.

The Case for Tactical Use of International Bonds

International bonds can be used sporadically, as a substitute for domestic bonds, just as mortgage-backed securities or corporate bonds are used as tactical substitutes for U.S. Treasuries by active domestic bond managers. Because economic and interest rate cycles are asynchronous, international bond markets often present substantial opportunities compared to an investor's domestic market. These markets expand the tool set with which to add value to a domestic bond portfolio.

---

[3] Andre Perold and Evan Schulman, "The Free Lunch in Currency Hedging: Implications for Investment Policy and Performance Standards," *Financial Analysts Journal* (May-June 1988); Lee Thomas, "The Performance of Currency-Hedged Foreign Bonds," *Financial Analysts Journal* (May-June 1989); Richard Levich and Lee Thomas, "The Merits of Active Currency Risk Management: Evidence from International Bond Portfolios," *Financial Analysts Journal* (September-October 1993).

[4] Michael Rosenberg, "International Fixed Income Investing: Theory and Practice," Chapter 55 in Frank J. Fabozzi (ed.), *The Handbook of Fixed Income Securities* (Burr Ridge, Il: Irwin Publishing, 1997).

Exhibit 1: Total Return of the World's Major Bond Markets

Year	Top Performer (Hedged Into U.S. Dollars – %)		U.S. Return (%)	Worst Performer (Hedged Into U.S. Dollars – %)	
1975	France	19.55	9.25	Canada	1.62
1976	Germany	30.19	14.82	Italy	–31.16
1977	U.K.	64.51	2.42	Canada	–2.96
1978	Japan	36.82	1.69	Canada	–4.48
1979	Italy	11.51	1.91	Japan	–18.89
1980	Japan	28.54	0.13	Italy	–14.17
1981	Japan	18.66	5.47	Italy	–26.84
1982	U.S.	33.92	33.92	Belgium	–1.50
1983	Japan	15.67	2.76	Netherlands	–4.29
1984	U.S.	14.35	14.35	U.K.	–11.63
1985	U.S.	20.94	20.94	Australia	–0.07
1986	U.S.	15.73	15.73	U.K.	8.13
1987	U.K.	12.75	1.93	U.S.	1.93
1988	France	15.04	7.07	Australia	3.59
1989	U.S.	14.40	14.40	Netherlands	2.84
1990	Australia	11.10	8.62	U.K.	2.23
1991	Australia	19.83	15.30	Netherlands	7.49
1992	U.K.	10.47	7.21	Spain	–2.24
1993	Italy	19.70	10.69	Belgium	6.90
1994	Japan	–0.91	–3.36	U.K.	–7.92
1995	Netherlands	20.54	18.30	Italy	12.58
1996	Spain	18.80	2.72	U.S.	2.72

Source: 1975-1984 Ibbotson/IMF and proprietary sources
1985-1996 Salomon WGBI hedged country returns (Datastream)

Exhibit 1 shows the best and worst market returns currency hedged into U.S. dollars, as well as U.S. market returns in each year. The average difference between the best performing market and the worst is 24.01%. From the U.S. investor's perspective, the average difference between domestic market returns and the best performing market was 11.17%. While the inflationary period of the 1970s produced large return discrepancies between markets, data from the last 10 years (1987-1996) also show a 10.83% difference between the highest and lowest returns, and a 5.35% difference between the best performing international market and the United States. This represents the potential for adding value — improbably if the manager had chosen the best market each year. Clearly, the key is timing. The manager must rotate into international bonds before they outperform domestic bonds, and then rotate back when international bonds are poised to underperform. Obviously, this requires effective active bond management.

Opportunistic use of international bonds can be effective, but has limits. International bonds create substantial tracking error. A 5% excess allocation to mortgages produces about 8 basis points in tracking error against a domestic benchmark. The corresponding figure for investment-grade corporate bonds is approximately 10 basis points. By comparison, a 5% position in international bonds adds about 16 basis points of tracking error against a domestic benchmark, even when the international bonds are currency hedged. This means that portfolio managers will ordinarily make only a small allocation to global bonds if they are evaluated against a domestic benchmark. To encourage a higher allocation, the manager must be given a global or mixed domestic/global benchmark. The high tracking error associated with international bonds is created by low correlations between U.S. Treasuries and international markets. To the extent that those correlations rise in future years, it will be easier to use international bonds as a tactical asset class. Accordingly, it is not clear that higher correlations would make international bonds less attractive for U.S. investors, as is frequently alleged. Lower correlation favors U.S. portfolio managers who use international bonds tactically, but reduces their attraction for strategic users.

Tactical use of international bonds only makes sense for active managers, but strategic users may choose passive or active management styles. In other words, the strategic benefits of international bonds do not depend on active management, though active management may enhance them. The strategic benefit offered by international bonds is risk reduction, and the mechanism is the classical gains from diversification. However, this depends on international and domestic bonds being imperfectly correlated.

The Case for Strategic Use of International Bonds

The strategic arguments for international bonds rest on two principles. First, as with tactical use, wide differences in returns among international markets create significant opportunities for enhancing investment results. As Exhibit 1 shows, the opportunity to construct a portfolio of global bonds clearly offers a manager an expanded opportunity for producing superior returns.

The second and more important principle recommending strategic use of international bonds is risk reduction. International bonds can help to reduce volatility for two reasons. First, certain individual international bond markets (hedged into U.S. dollars) are typically less volatile than the U.S. bond market. As a result, they are good raw material for creating a lower risk bond portfolio. To illustrate, Exhibit 2 shows volatilities of individual international bond markets from 1975-1996. U.S. market volatility is higher than the continental European countries influenced by the Bundesbank and Japan. This was especially marked in the 1970s and early 1980s. While whether past returns are a predictor of future volatility is open to question, for various historical reasons, there is likely still less institutional tolerance for inflation in continental Europe and Japan than in the United States.

Exhibit 2: International Bond Market Volatilities Hedged into U.S. Dollars (1975-1996)

Country	Volatility* (%)
U.K.	9.68
Italy	9.19
U.S.	7.53
Japan	5.85
Netherlands	5.83
Germany	5.48
France	5.19

* Annualized standard deviation of monthly returns

Second, aside from individual markets having less volatility than the U.S. market, a global index typically has lower risk than its components. This is because correlations between international and U.S. bond returns have historically been low. For example, for the 10-year period 1987 to 1996, the correlation between the J.P. Morgan U.S. Index and the J.P. Morgan Hedged Global Ex-U.S. Index was 54.3%. That means the U.S. market explained only 29.5% of the variations in international returns bond; 70.5% of international bond volatility was unrelated to the U.S. market.

That international bond markets are loosely correlated should not be surprising. Bond markets are primarily driven by economic cycles and central bank activity. Different economies have different economic growth and inflation patterns. Structural features of economies such as different factor endowments can mean asymmetric impacts to external shocks. This will naturally illicit different policy responses. The fiscal and monetary policy appropriate for one country may not be appropriate or politically feasible for another. These structural, political, and cultural differences are not likely to meaningfully decline in the near future. In fact, the scope to run independent monetary policies in different countries was one of the most important reasons cited for adopting a floating exchange rate system in the early 1970s. Asynchronous interest rate cycles should continue into the foreseeable future.

Because the returns to the U.S. and international indices are not highly related, substantial benefits can be realized by combining them. Using 22 years of historical data in Exhibit 3, if we start with a portfolio of U.S. bonds and add 10% international bonds, the volatility of the resulting portfolio falls from 7.52% to 7.00%. Increasing the international allocation to 30% reduces the volatility to 6.03%. In fact, the minimum variance portfolio, which consist of 90% international bonds and only 10% U.S. bonds, has a volatility of 4.36%, or almost half the volatility of a U.S. portfolio.[5] This reduction in volatility has not been associated with a

[5] These results use data from 1975 through 1996, or 22 years. After 1986 all data represent J.P. Morgan bond indices. The U.S. index is the J.P. Morgan U.S. Government Index; the foreign index is the J.P. Morgan Global-Ex U.S. Index, Currency Hedged. Prior to 1986 the data represent liquid, 10-year government bond issues constructed by the authors. These results are robust: if we reduce the sample period to 1989-96 (8 years), the volatility of a U.S. only portfolio was 4.19%; the volatility of a 50/50 foreign/U.S. portfolio was 3.45%, or 17.7% lower.

commensurate reduction in return. In fact a 90%/10% foreign/U.S. portfolio has returned 10.10% per year, or about 1.24% more than a U.S. portfolio.[6,7]

Why Use a Currency Hedged Benchmark?

International bonds provide risk reduction due to the low correlation that they have with U.S. bonds and with each other. This reduces a U.S. portfolio's volatility. Unfortunately, these bonds carry with them exchange rate risk which does not diversify away because it is in each instance risk versus the dollar. U.S. interest rates may go up or down completely independent of other market's interest rates but the U.S. dollar's appreciation or depreciation automatically means corresponding depreciation or appreciation on the part of other currencies.

The net result is that after adding about 15% international bonds to the portfolio, risk begins to increase. This results because additional foreign exchange rate risk overwhelms the benefits of reducing interest rate volatility by diversification. This can be seen in Exhibit 3. Notice that adding unhedged foreign bonds ultimately increases the volatility of the portfolio substantially. Adding hedged international bonds reduces the volatility until about 70% of U.S. Treasuries have been replaced by their foreign counterparts.

Foreign bond returns were higher in this sample either hedged or unhedged, but in examining these return data, one should be skeptical of differences in returns. Economic theory provides no convincing and empirically confirmed explanation as to why one industrialized country bond market should have statistically different expected returns from another similarly rated industrialized market.[8] Differences in returns in Exhibit 3 are not statistically significant and cannot be confidently expected to persist in the future. From the perspective of a passive investor, there should be no difference between the expected returns between major markets either on a hedged or unhedged basis. This ultimately gets to the "free lunch" from hedging. Numerous studies of currency risk premia have found that there is a zero expected return to foreign currency. Yet currency clearly imparts significant risk or volatility. It is incumbent on the portfolio manager to get the maximum amount of return for each unit of risk. To make an investment with a zero expected return but substantial volatility would be an investment management cardinal sin.

---

[6] Although foreign bond returns have historically been higher than U.S. returns during the past 22 years, you should be very cautious about exaggerating the importance of this historic performance. There is little reason to suspect they will be higher during the coming 22 years. The difference of 137bp between an all U.S. and all foreign hedged portfolio is not statistically significant. There is little reason to suspect that the 137bp represents a stable risk premium favoring foreign bonds. In fact, using a CAPM framework, using recent volatility and correlation data, the expected return to foreign bonds should be *less* than the expected return to U.S. bonds, largely to compensate for lower volatility of foreign bonds.

[7] You should not place too much faith in this estimate of the foreign bond risk premium either: applying the CAPM requires a number of simplifying restrictions that create a highly imprecise estimate of the future outperformance of foreign bonds. To be conservative you should discount both historical data and CAPM based forward looking projections. Realistically it is not possible to say if foreign bonds or U.S. bonds will have higher returns going forward.

[8] Variants of the international CAPM offer a theory of currency risk premia but empirical evidence supporting stable risk premia which conform to economic theory is weak.

Exhibit 3: Risk and Return 1975-1996

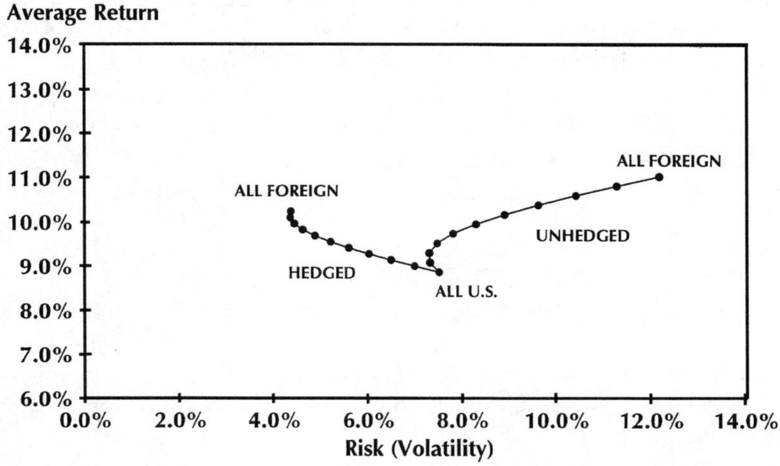

Source: U.S. government portfolio represented by the U.S. component of the J.P. Morgan Government Bond Index after 1986. Foreign bonds represented by the foreign component of the J.P. Morgan Hedged Bond Index after 1986. Prior to 1986, the data represent liquid, 10-year government bond issues.

Are the Benefits of Global Diversification Declining?

It has become commonplace to observe that global markets are becoming more integrated.[9] One apparent consequence of this is that the benefits from global bond diversification are declining. However, this is not necessarily so in principle, and does not appear to be the case in practice.

The first principle says that the risk reduction afforded by international bonds depends on two factors. The first is the correlation between international and domestic bonds: the smaller the better. The second is the volatility of international bond returns. Again, the smaller the better. Increasing correlation could be offset if international bond volatility was falling, compared to the volatility of domestic U.S. issues.

Second, the conclusion that increasing correlation has caused the benefits of diversification to decline rests on a crucial assumption, that bond market correlations are increasing. The basis for this assumption appears to be casual observation of the 1994-1995 period. Bond prices fell sharply during 1994, and recovered sharply during 1995, around the world. Inconveniently for the increasing integration thesis, bond

[9] Jeffrey Sachs and Andrew Warner, ("Economic Reform and the Process of Global Integration," *Brookings Papers on Economic Activity*, 1995) observe that economic and financial integration was probably greater at the end of the 19th century than it is today. The degree of integration declined during the interim, but is now rising again. While the future seems to offer more integration, at present most investors in most countries invest most of their wealth in domestic financial markets. It is unlikely that we can consider global investors to represent the marginal investor in most markets. This is one of the problems associated with applying an international CAPM framework to the problem of estimating equilibrium foreign and domestic expected returns.

returns substantially diverged again in 1996 with the U.S. market dramatically underperforming the European markets as well as Japan, on a currency hedged basis.

Exhibit 4 illustrates how G3 bond market correlations have evolved. It shows rolling 3-year correlations of German and Japanese bond returns with U.S. Treasuries from 1975-1996. Over this time period there have been periods of increasing and decreasing correlation, but there is no clear trend. In fact, recent data indicate declining correlation, which is not surprising given the asynchronous business cycles among the major three blocs in 1995 and 1996.

STRATEGIC INTERNATIONAL FIXED INCOME INVESTMENT PHILOSOPHY

Having determined that the risk reduction properties of hedged international bonds warrant a strategic allocation, the next question is whether to invest in a passive strategy or employ an active manager for the portfolio. While the majority of the global fixed income managers do not outperform their appropriate benchmark over relevant time periods, there are managers who have added value while producing volatility similar to that of the index. Crucial to consistent outperformance is the global fixed income manager's basic investment philosophy. Six basic areas are of critical importance. These include management of tracking error versus a benchmark, use of multiple sources of value added, separation of the bond and currency decision, effective country and currency allocations, and the use of analytical tools for both risk management and identification of return opportunities.

Exhibit 4: Rolling 3-Year Correlation with U.S. Treasuries

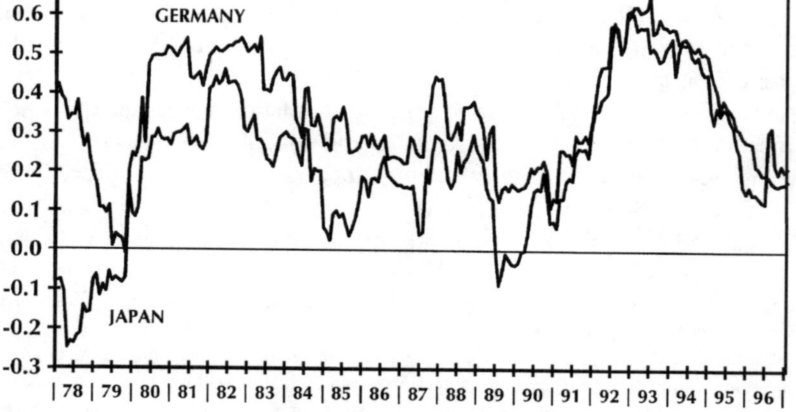

Source: U.S. government portfolio represented by the U.S. component of the J.P. Morgan Government Bond Index after 1986. Foreign bonds represented by the foreign component of the J.P. Morgan Hedged Bond Index after 1986. Prior to 1986, the data represent liquid, 10-year government bond issues.

Volatility, Tracking Error, and Correlation

Most institutional investors hold foreign bonds as a portion of a broader portfolio of securities. The allocation among different asset classes is based on assumptions about the risks and correlations of all the assets. Accordingly, it is important that the global bond manager produce a portfolio which has index-like volatility and modest tracking error. To ignore tracking error or to create a portfolio with very different volatility to the index and correlation with other asset classes would render the broader asset allocation decision meaningless. As a result, global bond managers must be extremely conscious of volatilities and correlations, both at the individual security and portfolio levels.

The goal of the manager should be to create additional return or alpha, but with similar to index volatility and correlations with other markets. Moreover, tracking error should be constrained to be consistent with the investor's risk tolerance. In essence, this defines the manager's tracking error, or "risk budget," which ensures that the mandate retains the essential characteristics of the asset class desired in the overall portfolio allocation. The manager's role is to decide how to best spend the risk budget across the major areas which impart tracking error versus the index, while also extracting as much additional return from relative value opportunities and market inefficiencies at the security selection level of the process.

Multiple Sources of Value Added

In the same way that diversification across countries helps reduce the total volatility of the overall portfolio, so too does diversification across sources of value added help to produce consistent results within the global bond allocation. Large exposures to a single type of risk which consume the entire "risk budget" should be avoided in favor of a number of small departures from the benchmark, all of which together should produce the acceptable level of tracking error.

Value added strategies can be divided into two groups — macro (or top down) strategies and relative value (or bottom up) strategies. (See Exhibit 5.) Macro strategies impart most of the tracking error versus the index. These include country and currency allocations — yield curve slope or curvature strategies, and overall portfolio duration management. Relative value strategies focus on sector allocation, rich/cheap analysis between particular bonds, use of futures and options, and cash management techniques. A prerequisite for extracting value at the security selection level is significant investment in analytical and credit research resources.

It is essential that a global bond manager have expertise in each of these areas when attempting to add value to its benchmark index. This is important because international markets will often offer substantial opportunities in one area and very few in another. The ability to use a variety of tools lessens the need to press any one area to produce the majority of the portfolio's outperformance. Unfortunately, global bond management is often performed by boutique investment managers whose expertise is in one particular top down area, often either currency or country selection. Consequently, a single dimension is favored at the expense of the others.

Exhibit 5: Value Added Strategies

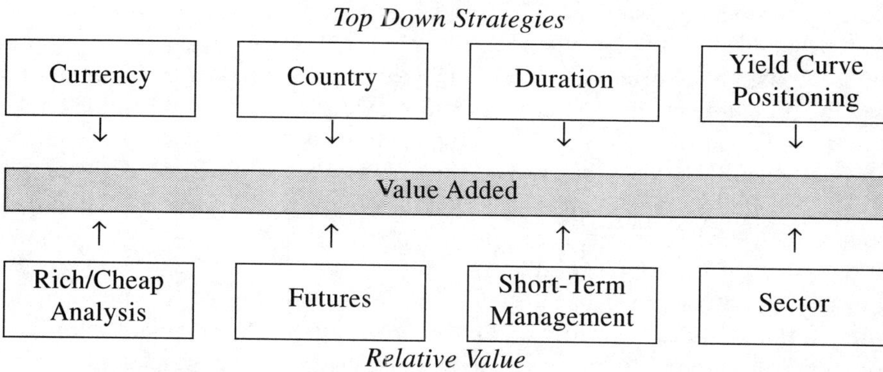

Separation of Country Bond and Currency Decisions

Global bond mandates entail the management of two entities, a bond portfolio and a currency portfolio. Bond and currency decisions should be analytically separated, aside from the few exceptions described below. The reason is that factors which influence bond markets often influence currencies differently. Specifically, bonds resonate to a business cycle, increasing in value as economic growth and inflation decline and decreasing as these indicators pick-up. Conversely, currencies show little correlation with the business cycle and tend to be more dominated by the fundamentals associated with their relative purchasing power, levels of short-term yields, and market trend or technical factors.

Given the number of efficient hedging tools, it is possible to have exposure to a bond, but not to the currency in which it is denominated. It is also possible to have exposure to a currency but not to the corresponding bond market. Or, exposure can be obtained to both bond and currency markets, or to neither. The key to making all these investments possible is using currency hedging devices, such as currency forwards and futures. To illustrate, if an investor wants bond market exposure only, he can purchase the bond, but sell the underlying currency forward to strip away the bond's currency risk.[10] If the investor wants currency exposure, but no interest rate exposure, he can buy the currency forward.[11] If the investor wants both currency and bond market exposure, he can buy the bond but not currency hedge. This is unlikely since it is only optimal whenever the currency exposure desired *exactly* corresponds to the desired bond exposure. In practice, the optimal bond and currency portfolios probably do not conform exactly in this way. If it does, it is entirely coincidental.

[10] Lee Thomas, "International Bonds: Stripping Away Currency Risk," 1988. It should be noted that bond repos will accomplish the same objective.

[11] Alternately you can purchase currency futures or short duration foreign currency investments, such as foreign Treasury bills or floating-rate notes. We exaggerate slightly when we say "no" interest rate exposure.

Since there is bond exposure independent of currency exposure in any market, the portfolio selection procedure chosen must recognize this independence by separately selecting the bonds from the currency exposures. However, even a correct principle can be exaggerated until it becomes incorrect. There are a number of senses in which bond and currency decisions should not be separated, or are not separable. First, separating the currency and bond decisions does not mean having separate macroeconomic forecasts for each. For example, it would be absurd to choose a German bond position based on a forecast of weak German GDP growth, but use a forecast of strong German growth for a deutschemark forecast. Instead, a single macroeconomic view must separately be applied to a forecast of German interest rates and exchange rates.

Second, interest rates influence exchange rates, and exchange rates influence interest rates. In other words, interest and exchange rate changes are correlated. Portfolio selection should not ignore this correlation. Indeed, recognizing and accounting for such correlations is one reason why Modern Portfolio Theory (MPT) improves upon naive portfolio selection rules in global bond portfolios.

Third, in practice, bond and currency decisions may interact through the constraints placed on the optimal portfolio solution. For example, if leveraging the portfolio is not permitted, then all positions have some degree of interdependence, since increasing the size of one position requires a reduction in the size of another. There are many other plausible examples of this, but one will suffice to illustrate how interdependence may arise from these types of investing constraints. Suppose an investor is not permitted to use currency forwards or futures to establish a currency position. Instead, forwards and futures can only be used for hedging an exposure which was created by an international bond position. (Restricting the use of forwards and futures to hedging only is common in practice.) Now suppose that the investor wants currency exposure in German marks. Since the investor cannot secure it with forwards or futures, he may have to buy German bonds. If he does, he has not completely separated his bond and currency positions. (In practice he will probably purchase German short-term bills or floating-rate notes, which have little interest rate risk.)

Country Bond Allocation

There exists no compelling evidence that bond prices are influenced by past price behavior, or so called technical trends. Accordingly, the country bond allocation process should focus on economic and credit fundamentals as the key determinants of value in fixed income markets. Analysis of economic data, real yields, and country risk modeling serve to identify in which countries a manager should invest. The overriding principle of country allocation process should be that the real yields of a particular market must be commensurate with the risk in that market.

The first step in the process is to determine the real yield of a particular security. While the nominal yield is simply the market interest rate, the relevant inflation rate to deduct in finding the real yield may involve subjective judgment, or it may be estimated using formal econometric techniques. Real yields must then be considered in light of the risk associated with each market.

In order to rank the markets by their relevant country risk, an investor must first ask just exactly what is risk when investing in a country's government bond market. Unlike with corporate debt, sovereign debt issued in a country's own currency has virtually no chance of defaulting. This is because the country's central bank may simply cover the Treasury's obligations through increases in money supply. As a result, the true risk to sovereign debt is that the investor will be paid back in devalued currency as a result of inflationary monetary policy. To an economist, it may seem obvious enough that money causes inflation. A fixed income manager, however, must ask what are the conditions which cause irresponsible monetary policy. Usually, this is the result of stresses on public budgets associated with low real growth. Poor economic growth reveals fissures in a government's finances which ultimately may be addressed through easy monetary policy and inflation. As a result, longer term investment analysis of sovereign debt must focus on the country's fundamental economic prospects and the ability to repay its debt in a strong currency.

Models which evaluate relative country risk must include in a rigorous fashion those factors which most influence economic growth and the state of a government's finances. These factors would include openness of the economy to international trade and capital, fiscal policy and its impact on deficits, debt and total government spending, as well as free and flexible labor markets. These country risk rankings are then compared to the real yields to determine which countries have the best risk-adjusted yield. The goal is to invest in countries which appear to strike the best balance between attractive real yields and low economic risk ratings.

Exhibit 6 shows a list of major industrialized market yields and their corresponding risk rankings. These real yields and rankings are longer term measures of a country's credit worthiness. This must be married with a cyclical analysis of exactly where this country is in its business cycle. Longer term and cyclical factors may be at odds, since over shorter periods of time country bond markets which outperform tend to be those which have weak economic growth and the potential for central bank policy rate cuts.

Currency Allocation

Whether the benchmark is hedged or unhedged, currency decisions are a powerful tool for increasing or decreasing returns. While academic literature is rich with theoretical models for forecasting exchange rates, there are three basic approaches which empirically are most useful for predicting currency returns. These are (1) fundamental analysis, focused on measures of relative purchasing power, (2) short-term yields, and (3) market trend or technical factors.

Relative purchasing power models serve as the principal source of fundamental analysis in the currency market. While purchasing power parity tests of currencies exhibit little predictive power of returns in the short run, recent academic evidence points to this as an effective tool over a longer time horizon.[12] When examined over three or more years, currencies seem to revert towards their underlying fundamental value, as defined by their purchasing power.

In principle, short-term yields should not be useful for predicting currency returns. The principle of uncovered interest rate partly holds that high interest rate currencies will, on average, depreciate at a rate just sufficient to counter their yield advantage. However, there is persistent evidence that currencies with high short-term yields have higher returns than those with lower yields.[13] Consequently, all other things equal, managers should avoid exposure to low yielding currencies and favor currencies with higher yields.

Another curious anomaly exists in the currency markets: successive exchange rate changes appear to trend. Explanations of this phenomena tend to focus on central bank intervention as the main source of this price action. As a result, past market trends should be included as a variable in a manager's currency analysis.[14]

Exhibit 6: Real Yields and Country Risk Rankings

Country	Real Yield (%)*	Risk Rank**
New Zealand	5.8	1
Sweden	5.6	10
Australia	5.3	5
Canada	4.7	3
Finland	4.3	8
U.K.	4.2	7
Denmark	4.0	4
Germany	3.9	11
France	3.9	12
U.S.	3.7	2
Netherlands	3.4	9
Japan	1.3	6

* 10-year bond yields as of March 31, 1997 minus PIMCO estimates of future inflation.

** Based on the risk model developed by Jeffrey Sachs, Harvard University. Lowest numbers correspond to lowest risk.

[12] See, for example, Nelson Mark, "Exchange Rates and Fundamentals: Evidence on Long Horizon Predictability," *American Economic Review* (March 1995).

[13] John Bilson, "The Speculative Efficiency Hypotheses," *Journal of Business* (July 1981), and John Bilson, "Technical Currency Trading," in Lee R. Thomas (ed.) *The Currency-Hedging Debate* (IFR Publishing Ltd., 1990).

[14] Trends are documented in Levich and Thomas, "The Merits of Active Currency Risk Management: Evidence from International Bond Portfolios." However, it should be noted that recent evidence indicates that currency trends are much less predictive than they were during the 1980s. In other words, whereas trend following behavior produced positive returns in the currency markets in the 1980s, it failed to do so in the 1990s. Interestingly, central banks lost significant sums by intervening in currency markets during the 1980s, but currency market interventions may have been profitable for central banks during the 1990s.

Use of Advanced Analytical Tools

Advanced quantitative tools are crucial in (1) monitoring the impact of specific positions on the total portfolio risk, (2) identifying relative value investment opportunities, and (3) analyzing performance to show which strategies have systematically added value and which have not. Fundamental to the process of risk control is the analytical tools which are available to measure and monitor volatility in the portfolio. These tools include (1) extensive summary information of portfolio holdings, (2) a risk optimizer which indicates, for a set of expected returns, volatilities, and correlations, an optimal portfolio structure, and (3) models of interest rate sensitivity which give a more accurate measure of individual security and portfolio risk than traditional duration and convexity analysis alone would allow.[15]

Extensive use of analytical models has the additional benefit of allowing the investor to better leverage his human capital and provide a dispassionate check on the various investment decisions made in the portfolio. It also provides the ability to do attribution analysis to determine which strategies are consistently adding value and which need to be altered in the future.

AN INTERNATIONAL INVESTMENT PROCESS

Along with an appropriate international investment philosophy, an effective international fixed income manager will also have a disciplined process from which investment decisions flow. This will include top down and bottom up decisions, but here we will focus on the more important top down decisions. In this section, we will describe how top down decisions are made at our own firm.

The first step is to get the long run right. We believe that analyzing secular economic and political influences is fundamental to sound portfolio decisions. Holding a firm long-term view helps guard against becoming caught up in the periodic bouts of euphoria and depression that often characterize financial markets. We are much more optimistic about our prospects for identifying long-run value through fundamental economic and credit analysis than our ability to time short-term market movements. We consider secular analysis to be so important that we devote one week each year to what we call our "Secular Forum." Selected members of the investment staff are assigned specific areas to monitor throughout the year, including monetary and fiscal policy, demographics, international trade and capital flow issues, inflation, and productivity trends. At the Secular Forum, these internal presenters join with outside speakers to address these issues for our firm's staff of investment professionals. This serves as a background for further discussion by all key investment decision makers. The purpose of the forum is to arrive at a 3- to 5-year outlook for the direction of U.S. and international interest rates and currencies.

[15] For an example of such a post-modern model of interest rate sensitivity see Ram Willner, "A New Tool for Portfolio Managers: Level, Slope and Curvature Durations," *Journal of Fixed Income* (June 1996).

Secular analysis must be combined with an analysis of cyclical or business cycle trends. We meet as a firm quarterly to evaluate growth and inflation at the business cycle horizon. At these sessions, our investment professionals focus on recent economic data in order to decide whether GDP growth and inflation in the world's major economic blocs will exceed or fall short of the market's consensus views. These views help refine and update our forecasts for shorter term (two to four quarters) trends in G-3 (U.S., Japan, and Germany) interest rates and currencies.

With the firm's secular and cyclical analysis as a foundation, our international portfolio management team meets weekly to discuss those issues uniquely relevant to adding value in our international portfolios. We examine opportunities in four key areas: overall portfolio duration and tracking error; country and currency allocations; relative value strategies; and, cash management. Within the group, particular individuals are assigned ongoing responsibilities for particular areas, but all are encouraged to contribute to the group's consensus. These decisions translate into portfolio statements versus our benchmark indices.

Tracking Error and Portfolio Duration

The most fundamental decision which our group makes each week is how much risk or total tracking error to benchmark indices we wish to take. Typically, we work within a range of 200-300 basis points of tracking error. When we recognize particularly attractive return possibilities, we position the portfolio near the top end of the range. When opportunities appear more limited, we move closer to 200 basis points of tracking error. Exceptional situations may cause a shift outside the range, though it would be very rare for this to be more than an additional 50 basis points in either direction.

Overall portfolio duration is primarily the result of our secular and cyclical forecasting processes described above. Within the international team, we exercise a ±0.5 year duration discretion around the firm's stated target. Broad portfolio duration targets are then set by geographic region, depending on our view for regional, long-term economic trends, coupled with local cyclical forecasts for economic activity and inflation. We draw on information from the firm wide process and then augment it with additional data and viewpoints within this smaller group. Weighted portfolio duration is maintained by policy within ±2.0 years of the benchmark, although practically we are rarely beyond ±1.0 year given our tracking error limitations. Our process ensures that tracking risk and portfolio duration is shifted in a measured fashion consistent with our long-term focus.

Country Bond Allocation

As mentioned previously, our philosophy mandates that we compare real yields to relative risk ranks in order to determine a baseline of long-term value for particular bond markets. Real yields are reviewed weekly to reflect recent market activity. Risk rankings, which are less dynamic given their longer term focus, are reviewed annually and on an *ad hoc* basis if there are unexpected political and economic changes which warrant examination.

Exhibit 7: Major Country Bond Positions

Country	DWE* Versus Index	Real Yield	Risk Rank
Overweights			
Australia	0.50	5.3	5
Canada	0.30	4.7	3
Sweden	0.25	5.6	10
Finland	0.15	4.3	8
Underweights			
Germany	–0.05	3.9	11
Japan	–0.20	1.3	6
U.S.	–0.20	3.7	2
France	–0.35	3.9	12

* Duration-weighted equivalent basis.

In addition to this long-term value assessment, our group examines recent economic data for each country in order to understand the specific cyclical underpinnings of each market. We compare our interpretation of recent data to that of the market's to find areas of clear disagreement. This might be in the form of our group having a fundamentally different view of a market's coming GDP growth or inflation than the consensus or more commonly when we find that the market is not adequately pricing in the consensus view (and our own) of these data to a particular bond market.

At the end of the discussion, we are left to allocate particular country underweights and overweights. We do this on a duration-weighted equivalent basis (DWE). This simply means that we multiply the country's index market value by its index duration to get the duration years that it represents in the total index portfolio. We then compare that country's market value multiplied by its duration in our portfolio to that of the index. Exhibit 7 shows how we spread our country risk versus the index on March 31, 1997. Our eight major country statements are highlighted. The exhibit shows how these positions rank based on real yield and country risk. While we still must be thoroughly comfortable with these positions on a cyclical basis, the clear bias is toward our longer term measures of value.

Yield Curve Exposures

Yield curve or slope exposures in particular countries often present outstanding opportunities. Our group's goal is to identify not only which countries to overweight or underweight but where on each country's yield curve we want to take our exposure. A particularly attractive yield curve opportunity can also prove the impetus for an overweighted country exposure. For example, Exhibit 7 shows we have significant overweights in Canada and Sweden. Each of these positions is focused in the 2-year government note. This is a clear statement on our part that we do not expect the same degree of central bank tightening as does the market. In Japan, our total underweighted position of 0.2 DWE is all focused on the 10-year Japanese government bond. We find 2.5% nominal and 1.3% real yields unattractive given that the market is implicitly making the statement that the Japanese economic growth and inflationary environment will not normalize in the next 10 years. This is in comparison to the short intermediate part of the yield curve where we find the market's view consistent with our own, namely that the Bank of Japan will not be raising interest rates during the next year.

Aside from outright underweight or overweight statements on one part of a country's yield curve, we also evaluate from a duration neutral perspective whether within a particular country we wish to be in a barbelled mix of long and short maturities or a bulleted intermediate maturity structure. These structures can produce dramatically different returns given changes in the shape of a country yield curve. Specifically, during the periods where short-term interest rates are falling relative to longer rates, a bullet portfolio provides superior total return. PIMCO uses the full spectrum of maturities to build portfolio structures that maximize returns given our expectation for relative changes in rates.

Currency Allocation

As mentioned previously, these allocations are separate and distinct from our bond positions. We apply the criteria of fundamental analysis (notions of purchasing power), short-term yields, and market trend. Given the three forces which impact exchange rates, underweights and overweights of particular currencies should be founded on at least two of the three forces recommending the position. Preferably, all three dimensions will point in the chosen direction. In situations with only one or perhaps two forces weakly suggesting the allocation, a neutral position is the preferred portfolio strategy.

These three factors determine our view of expected returns for the various world currencies. These views are then combined with volatilities and correlations to show the weighting in a portfolio context. Because currency movements tend to impart more volatility, careful management of currency risk is especially important. To get the fullest perspective of currency tracking error risk, we use both historical and implied market volatilities, using ⅓ and ⅔ weightings, respectively.

Relative Value Strategies

Analytical models and credit research are the foundation of our relative value strategies. These enter the portfolio process through analyst interface with portfolio managers on a day-to-day basis. Strategies tend to focus in the following four areas: sector allocation, rich/cheap analysis, futures, and cash management.

Sector Allocation

Sector strategies tend to be most important within the U.S. component of a global portfolio. This is because the U.S. fixed income market has by far the most developed corporate and mortgage markets. The non-dollar portion of our portfolios have largely been in government holdings, as most international non-government securities markets are relatively small and illiquid. There are however selected opportunities abroad in the corporate and mortgage area which require sector specific relative value analysis.

We rely on resources in other parts of our firm for analysis of these sectors. First, we rely on our macroeconomic analysis to set our broad view of particular sectors given that corporate bond outperformance tends to be linked to the improved corporate cash flows and profitability associated with stronger economic growth, while mortgages outperform in a more stable economic and interest rate environment. Estimates of economic growth and volatility as well as historical spread relationships determine the relative weights of these sectors compared to government securities.

Second, at the security selection level, bottoms up credit research which stresses fundamental analysis of company prospects is performed on all of the corporate credits that we own. Similarly, each mortgage security purchased is rigorously tested using our proprietary models in order to determine accurate duration and convexity characteristics. The call features and prepayment options in mortgage securities make these instruments extremely sensitive to changes in market volatility making their duration and convexity characteristics unstable.

Use of Futures Versus Cash Bonds

Often exposures to particular bond markets may be gained via the futures contract on that particular bond in a cheaper manner than buying the actual bond. Evaluation of whether the futures contract is fairly valued focuses on mechanics such as conversion factors, deliverability options, and the implied repo rate. Following the basis (difference between the cash bond price and the converted futures price) carefully in a number of country bond markets can often reveal futures mispricings. This is quite apart from the value which can be added by buying fairly priced futures and then outperforming the implied repo rate with an active cash portfolio.

Cash Management

Active cash management is an often overlooked avenue to adding value to an international fixed income portfolio. Cash strategies are used when exposure to a market is gained through the use of futures or options as well as when securities are lent out for specific periods of time. In each instance, cash is created with an interest rate which is close to and sometimes below a short-term risk-free rate. Within our portfolio management team, short-term specialists exploit opportunities in higher-yielding cash equivalents in the U.S. market by actively managing the underlying pool of assets used to back the futures, options, and repurchase obligations. In this manner, we also avoid leverage in the portfolio through the use of these derivative instruments.

This strategy has been highly effective in contributing substantial rates of return without adding material risk. This is due to the inherent term and liquidity premiums available by investing slightly further out the yield curve from these shortest assets. We are also able to exploit an expanded opportunity set which includes instruments such as adjustable-rate and high-coupon mortgages, floating-rate notes, commercial paper, and near maturity corporate bonds. Each of these offers substantial return relative to the financing rates embedded in futures, options, and repurchase agreements.

SUMMARY

International fixed income investing offers two significant benefits: risk reduction from diversification and increased return potential that results from having more investment choices. Only strategic allocations provide the full advantage of the risk reducing properties associated with international investing. Evidence strongly indicates that this investment should use a currency hedged benchmark. Currency hedging affords substantial risk reduction without reducing long-run expected returns.

To take advantage of this strategy's inherent risk reduction properties and create above index returns, fund managers of international fixed income portfolios will need an investment philosophy which stresses the following areas: management of tracking error and volatility versus a benchmark; using multiple sources of value added; separating the bond and currency decisions; effective country and currency allocations; and, use of analytical tools for both risk management and identification of return opportunities. In addition, a disciplined investment process is necessary to ensure adherence to appropriate philosophy and style. Our experience is that focus should be on both longer term secular forces as well as shorter term cyclical forces in making investment decisions. This analysis forms the basis of the top down or macro strategies which drive country and currency allocations as well as specific yield curve positioning and overall duration posture. The investment process must also promote relative value strategies through investment in analytical resources and credit research. This will help guarantee that maximum value is being harvested from areas such as sector and issue selection, use of futures and options, and active cash management.

Chapter 5

Global Bond Portfolio Management: A Disciplined Approach

Jonathan Reiss, CFA
Senior Portfolio Manager — Global Fixed Income
Sanford C. Bernstein & Co., Inc.

INTRODUCTION

Our approach to global fixed income management comprises three steps: (1) quantifying expected returns on a universe of securities; (2) identifying and assessing the risks of these securities; and, (3) constructing optimal portfolios to meet client objectives. While this process might seem fairly straightforward, in the world of global bond portfolio management it is anything but mainstream.

Our estimates of expected return represent all of the effects that we think will influence the price of the bond over the near term. While such evaluations would traditionally be driven by a macroeconomic forecast of global economies, interest rates and currencies, our process greatly reduces the importance of such a "top-down" assessment. We have found that there are a variety of factors, in addition to and apart from a macroeconomic forecast, which can be used to estimate the expected returns of bonds and currencies in the bond markets of developed countries around the world. [1]

Given the departure of this approach from traditional global fixed income portfolio management, it is not without controversy. How much should we depend on historical input when developing our models? To what extent should we open ourselves to more intuitive forecasts about the future? Peter Bernstein summa-

[1] Emerging market debt raises sovereign-credit questions and currency issues that we have just begun to address, and which are not covered in this chapter.

The author wishes to recognize the many people who over the years have contributed ideas and work appearing in this chapter. Among them are colleagues at Sanford Bernstein, including Frank Trainer, Mark Hamilton, Mark Gordon, Giulio Martini, Gary Gottlieb, David Levine, Leon Zhu, Sloane Lamb, Andrea Tasker, Mark Singer, Bob Putz, Richard Kaye, Jody Goldberg, and Gina Toth; as well as others, notably Bob Litterman, Lee Thomas, Michael Rosenberg, Ronald Kahn, and Antti Ilmanen.

rizes the issue nicely in *Against the Gods: The Remarkable Story of Risk*: "[There is] a persistent tension between those who assert that the best decisions are based on quantification and numbers, determined by the patterns of the past, and those who base their decisions on more subjective degrees of belief about the uncertain future. This is a controversy that has never been resolved."[2]

We do not believe that this debate ever will, or should, be resolved in favor of one side or the other, because we believe that the best solution lies in a combination of the two beliefs. We believe our quantitative, historical approach adds value because it allows us to exploit the opportunities that arise when investors apply flawed decision-making rules to financial forecasting.[3] But this approach requires good judgment. The structure of the models we build reflects our judgments about the fundamental factors important to the market. In addition, we recognize that the world changes, and so we are constantly vigilant should the models no longer be relevant, or should they need modification. Nonetheless, we do believe that most investors are too ready to believe that fundamental changes have occurred. As Alan Greenspan put it, "history is strewn with visions of such 'new eras' that, in the end, have proven to be a mirage."[4]

In relying heavily on historical data, our goal is not to supplant judgment, but to bring our best judgment to bear on all aspects of the investment management process. This manifests itself in the historical periods that we choose, the relative weightings that we apply to those periods, the modifications made to empirical results, and countless other decisions. In the final analysis, the framework that we have developed can only be valuable if the judgments that underlie it are valuable as well. But by securing our judgments in empirical models, we believe we have reduced our susceptibility to the flawed decision-making to which all investors are prone.

A fundamental building block of our investment process is *expected return*. Since our objective is to optimize the investor's return, subject to risk considerations, we assess each factor's expected impact on the bond's return. Clearly, such things as yield, and transaction and default costs, will translate directly into return. In other cases, such as with yield or spread levels, we estimate the expected change and then translate that into its return impact. Thus we arrive at a single measure of a bond's attractiveness that incorporates all of the effects that we believe are important.

A second step in our process is a systematic assessment of all of the risks we might take. This is a multidimensional problem encompassing many countries' interest rates and currencies, as well as credit and related risks. Once we

---

[2] Peter L. Bernstein, *Against the Gods: The Remarkable Story of Risk* (New York, NY: John Wiley & Sons, Inc., 1996), p. 6.

[3] These biases are discussed thoroughly in Daniel Kahneman, Paul Slovic, and Amos Tversky, *Judgment under Uncertainty: Heuristics and Biases* (Cambridge, England: Cambridge University Press, 1982); and, Richard H. Thaler, *The Winner's Curse: The Paradoxes and Anomalies of Economic Life* (Princeton, NJ: Princeton University Press, 1992).

[4] Alan Greenspan's testimony before the Senate Banking Committee, February 26, 1997.

have risk assessments, we can construct optimal portfolios. Our approach is general and flexible enough that it can be used to manage portfolios benchmarked to international or global fixed income benchmarks. We use the same process when investing opportunistically in foreign bonds for fixed income accounts with U.S. benchmarks. We also combine it with a similar equity process to manage global portfolios containing a mix of stocks and bonds from around the world. We use this process for all of the developed markets we cover, and the methodology can be applied from the perspective of any liquid base currency. To make the process concrete, in this chapter we illustrate our points with examples from the German market on June 30, 1997, from the perspective of an American investor.

CALCULATING EXPECTED RETURNS

The two most important decisions to be made in managing a global bond portfolio are: (1) how much interest-rate exposure should we take in each country? and (2) how much currency exposure should we take, and where?

These questions may seem to be closely related, since interest rate and currency movements are affected by many of the same factors, including GDP growth, inflation, and trade. However, those factors often affect a country's interest rate movements and currency in different ways. In fact, interest rate changes in a country are typically *not* highly correlated with that country's currency. As shown in Exhibit 1, the correlation between the British pound and British interest rates has been only 0.10. Similarly, the correlations of the major countries' bond markets to their currencies have been close to zero. As a result, we can separate the bond market decision from the currency choice.

Exhibit 1: Correlation Between Interest Rate and Currency Movements: January 1985 - December 1996

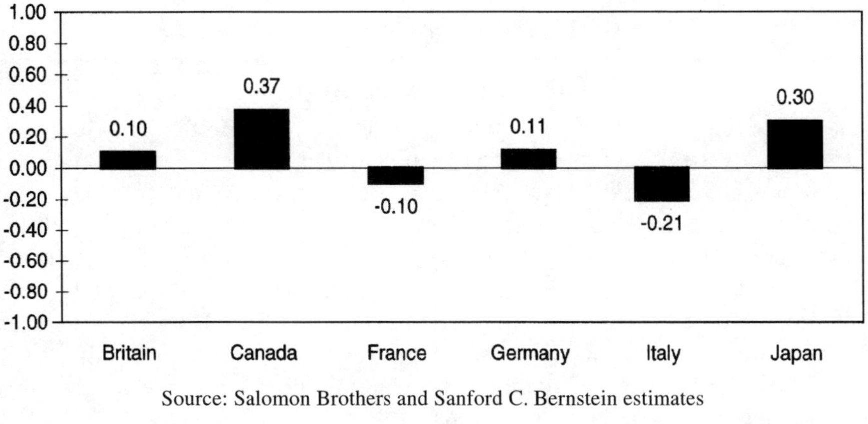

Source: Salomon Brothers and Sanford C. Bernstein estimates

Exhibit 2: U.S. and German Yield Curves: June 30, 1997

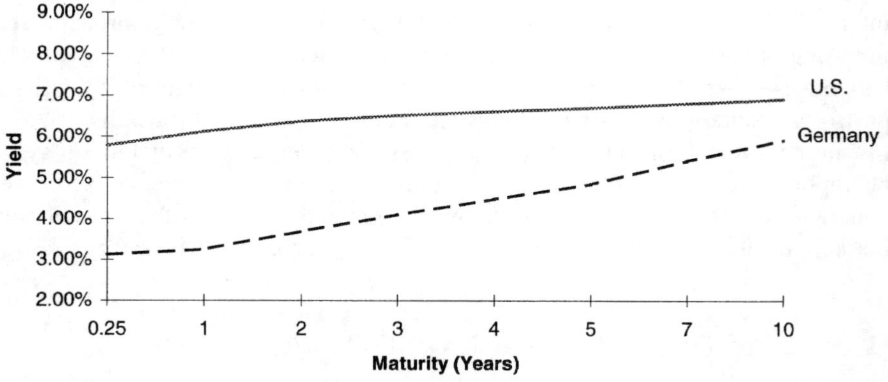

Source: Bloomberg Financial Markets

Exhibit 3: Hedged and Unhedged German Yield Curves: June 30, 1997

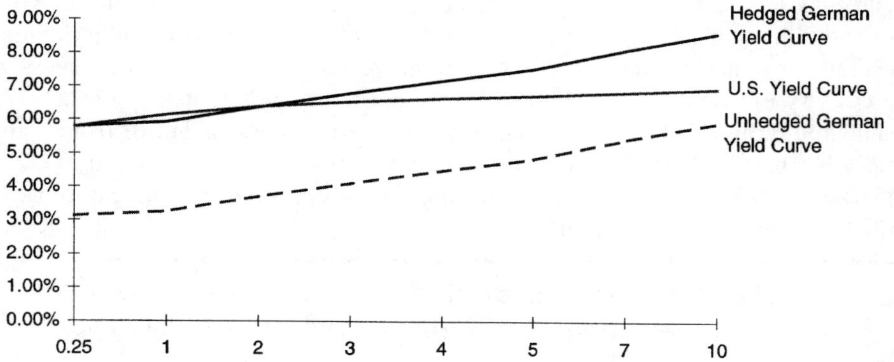

Source: Bloomberg Financial Markets and Sanford C. Bernstein estimates.

Country Decisions

To separate the interest rate decision in each country from the question of currency attractiveness, we assess the attractiveness of each country on a currency-hedged basis. We quickly discover that it is the steepness of a country's yield curve that determines the "yield" on the investment. For example, Exhibit 2 shows a comparison of (unhedged) German and U.S. yield curves as of June 30, 1997. The German yields are clearly lower than those in the United States. However, when we hedge the German bonds into dollars by selling Deutschemarks three months forward, the relationship between the yield curves shifts to that shown in Exhibit 3. Clearly, there is a substantial difference, with German yields much higher on a currency-hedged basis.

These examples allow us to make a couple of interesting points about hedged yields.[5] First, the hedged yield will be equal to the domestic yield where the maturity matches the life of the hedge, in this case three months. This is assured to be true to within a very close approximation by arbitrage between the global money markets and currency markets. For instance, in mid-1997 the difference between the U.S. 3-month interest rate of 5.78% and the German 3-month rate of 3.12% was 2.66%. The mark sold at a 3-month forward premium of 0.67%, which is 2.68% at an annual rate. Thus, the gain from the forward almost exactly offsets the yield given up.

Second, the yields beyond the horizon of the hedge are determined by the relative *slopes* of the domestic and foreign yield curves. Thus, in our example, the German yields on a hedged basis are higher than those in the United States because the German yield curve has a much steeper slope — as you extend maturity in German bonds, you pick up more yield. Because the gain locked in on the hedge remains the same, you wind up with a higher hedged yield.

Our research has found that high hedged yields are good forecasters of high hedged returns. Why is this true? Traditional financial theory argues that steep yield curves reflect investors' forecasts of rising yields. If yields do rise, there will be capital losses that offset the higher yield. But, it turns out that yields tend not to actually rise. We believe that there are two reasons for this. Sometimes the extra steepness reflects an unusually large market risk premium. In this case, by investing in steep curves, we are taking the large risk premia offered. At other times, the yield curve reflects market forecasts of short-term rates, but the market, on average, overpredicts — that is, interest rates do not rise as much as the market has forecast. The result is that intermediate and longer-term rates decline. In either case, the returns are, on average, significantly better in countries with steep yield curves.

Our second finding is that there is momentum in bond markets — that is, markets that have been strong tend to continue to be strong. We attribute this to two related phenomena. First, economic cycles take some time to play out. Periods of strong or weak growth tend to persist for a while. Because investors react to this information incrementally, the market has some tendency to move in trends. Partly for the same reason, central banks tend to move glacially. They do not change interest rates suddenly and by large amounts, but make repeated smaller moves in one direction. A prime example of this has been the Bundesbank, which lowered the repo rate 22 consecutive weeks by an average of 5 basis points a week during 1994. Again, the market is aware of this behavior, but appears not to take it fully into account.

We have validated both the yield curve and the momentum effects on a database of a dozen developed countries. While we tested the model country by

[5] By hedged yield, we mean currency-hedged yield — that is, a bond hedged by a short-term currency forward. The "hedged yield" is the return on the position assuming that the yield on the bond does not change. The investment is insulated from currency movements for the period of the hedge. At the end of the hedge period, the position can be re-evaluated and the hedge rolled over or the position closed.

country, in practice we use a single global model, for two reasons. First, the estimation is more robust when a broader data set is used. Models tailored to individual countries surely would have worked better over the estimation period; however, they would be more likely to break down in the future. Even more importantly, a single model enables us to make more consistent comparisons between countries.

These models provide our baseline estimates of expected returns from taking interest rate risk in each country. These estimates are reviewed by our Global Investment Policy Group, which includes our international economists, and modifications are made as appropriate. For example, we have modified the expected returns for Japan to account for the exceptionally low level of interest rates. Conversely, we have reviewed the assumptions for European countries in light of the prospect of European Economic and Monetary Union (EMU), but we have not considered it necessary to modify the model. We continue to monitor this situation and will almost certainly make modifications as EMU progresses (or breaks apart).

When we applied our model to 5-year German bonds on June 30, 1997, we noted the high hedged yield of 7.50% — one of the highest in the world. Historically, the returns of markets with high hedged yields have exceeded their yields, for two reasons. First, since the yield curve is extremely steep, the bond's yield declines more than usual as the bond shortens with the passage of time. This results in extra return that we call "roll." Second, steep yield curves tend to revert towards a normal shape. Typically, much of this reversion occurs as short-term interest rates rise, but a portion occurs as longer-term rates fall. This decline in rates adds to the return of intermediate and long bonds. While history suggests that the expected return should exceed the hedged yield on this bond, we apply our models cautiously to the future. As a result, we translated the 7.50% hedged yield into an expected return of 7.39%. Momentum was also somewhat positive. The market had rallied moderately leading up to this date, so we added 0.27% to the expected return due to momentum to bring us to a total expected return of 7.66%. The momentum effect we used was also a conservative estimate, relative to our past empirical results.

The German economic backdrop was quite favorable to bondholders. The German economy had substantial excess capacity (as reflected in an 11.4% unemployment rate), and inflation was running at 1.6%. The economy had been expected to accelerate for some time but, due in part to fiscal tightening, it had not done so. The only clouds on the horizon, from a bondholder's perspective, were currency related. The first was EMU — if it goes according to plan, German bonds will be redeemed in a currency called the "euro," which will be an amalgam of Deustchemarks, French francs, Italian lire, Spanish pesetas, and other European currencies. This is certainly of some concern. However, the countries to be included in EMU had similar economic circumstances. For example, Italy's inflation rate was actually lower than Germany's. Thus, the risk of interest rates rising after monetary union occurred was not very great. The other cloud was that the mark had recently been weak enough that there was a possibility of the Bundesbank raising rates to fend off continued currency weakness and resulting inflation. However, on balance, we considered that German bonds warranted the 7.66% expected return that our models indicated, which made them very attractive relative to other bond markets.

Currency Attractiveness

We use four factors in assessing the expected returns of currencies: current account surplus, purchasing power, interest rate differential, and momentum. Again, we use a single model for all currencies because we believe it is more consistent and reliable to do so.

When a country is running a current account surplus, it is exporting more goods and services than it imports. This puts upward pressure on the value of its currency. Germany's current account surplus in the late 1980s was a factor in the mark's strength relative to the dollar at that time. Since German unification, Germany's balance of payments has turned negative. However, because Germany's current account deficit was smaller (as a percentage of GDP) than that of the United States, this was still a favorable factor for the mark versus the dollar, adding 1.16% to the expected return of the mark (Exhibit 4).

The second factor we use in evaluating currencies is relative purchasing power. This is an attempt to assess the "fair value" of a currency by measuring how much of a standard basket of goods it can buy. While purchasing power parity is somewhat controversial because it is not very effective in the short run, we find that currencies do move toward their fair values eventually. In fact, it is because the currencies diverge substantially from their parities that there are opportunities for this factor to add value. As of June 30, 1997, the Deutschemark was quite overvalued, as was tangibly reflected in Germany's extremely high labor costs compared to other countries. This reduced the mark's expected return by 0.86%.

Exhibit 4: Expected Return of the Deutschemark as of 6/30/97

	Impact on Expected Return (%)
Current Account	1.16
Purchasing Power	–0.86
Interest-Rate Differential	–1.34
Momentum	–1.27
EMU Adjustment	1.34
Total Expected Return*	–0.97

* This is the expected return on a deutschemark currency forward. We use it to determine the effect of hedging the mark on expected return It is the difference in expected return between hedged and unhedged German bonds.

The final two factors — interest rates and momentum — are analogous to those in our country model. Higher yielding currencies tend to outperform. Again, traditional financial theory predicts that higher yielding currencies would depreciate, offsetting the excess yield. As in the case of yield curves, empirically this does not prove true, either because higher yielding currencies have higher risk premia, or because market forecasts are poor. In our country analysis, the slope of a country's yield curve, not the level of the interest rates, is important, but here the absolute level of yields comes into play. Thus we reduced the expected return of the mark by 1.34% due to Germany's low level of short rates (relative to the United States).

We believe that momentum in currency movements is due primarily to two related phenomena. First, trade adjustments occur slowly. A corporation's initial reaction to an adverse currency move is to absorb the losses to preserve market share, rather than to raise prices and lose customers. Since prices are not adjusted, trade does not react to small moves, and so the economic forces that would be expected to cause a reversal do not come into play and the currency trend persists. Only after a substantial move do pricing adjustments (and therefore trade adjustments) occur, causing the market to reverse. Second, government intervention accentuates this process. Central bankers and finance ministers try to avoid major changes in currency values over short periods because they hinder growth and boost inflation. Thus, these officials tend to smooth out the necessary adjustment over a longer period of time. Since the mark had been quite weak during the first half of 1997, we reduced the currency's expected return by 1.27% for this factor.

Here, too, the output of our models is reviewed by the Global Investment Policy Group, which includes our international economists, and adjustments are made where necessary. In the case of currencies, we have modified the model to reflect the likelihood that EMU will proceed and that the mark, French franc, and quite possibly the lira and peseta will become a single currency. We treat each of these currencies in part independently of one another, based on their own fundamentals, and in part as a single currency based on the collective fundamentals of all of the countries likely to combine into the Euro. Since the other European currencies expected to enter EMU had, on average, better fundamentals than the mark, this had the effect of increasing the mark's expected return by 1.34%.

Exhibit 4 displays the components of the mark's expected return on June 30, 1997. As its expected return was slightly negative, we were somewhat underexposed to the Deutschemark.

Yield Curve Analysis

Having assessed the expected return of exposure to interest rates and currency for each of the countries in our investment universe, we optimize each (we will discuss optimization at greater length later in this chapter). This identifies the ideal country and currency exposures based on their attractiveness, our assessments of risk, and transaction costs. The next question is, How best do we achieve those exposures? For example, we may want German bonds to contribute 1.0 year of duration to the account and want 15% of the account to be exposed to Deutschemarks. The most straightforward way to accomplish this is to invest 15% of the account in German bonds with an average duration of 6.7 years.[6] On the other hand, we could also put a larger portion of the account into shorter-term bonds and hedge a portion of the position.

We address the maturity distribution question by analyzing the German government yield curve. We begin with the yield. To this we add expected price changes due to "roll," convexity, and the reshaping of the yield curve. As time passes and a bond approaches maturity, it typically decreases in yield — and increases in price — as it "rolls" down the yield curve. We refer to this change in price associated with the passage of time as the value of "roll." In addition, although we assume that, overall, the interest rate level will not change, we do allow for interest rate volatility. Volatility has a positive price effect on non-callable bonds called convexity.[7]

The final component is the price gain/loss due to the reshaping of the yield curve. Again, many managers derive a forecast for the change in yield curve shape from their economic outlook. We do not rely on an economic forecast but instead count on a reversion toward normality. Normally, the yield curve is upward sloping, more so at first, then leveling off. At any particular time, however, the yield curve can look considerably different.[8] The main causes of variations in the shape of the curve are market participants' expectations for future short-term interest rates (primarily central bank actions). If the yield curve is distorted because market participants are forecasting changes in short rates, this distortion will tend to dissipate over time, either because the expected change occurs and no further shifts are expected or because it does not occur and the forecast is abandoned. Either way, the yield curve should eventually revert to a more normal shape. We assume that the yield curve will move part way towards normal over our forecast period and we calculate the price change associated with that move.

In Exhibit 5, we have plotted the German government yield curve as of June 30, 1997, beside our estimate of a normally shaped curve. Exhibit 6 displays the calculation of expected returns for a 5-year and a 10-year German bond. Earlier we noted that the German yield curve was much steeper than normal. In this context the important question is, Where does the extra steepness occur? At that time, most of the extra steepness occurred between two and five years to maturity. As a result, the expected return due to roll was most positive in this section of the

---

[6] 6.7 years × 15% of the account will provide 1.0 years of weighted duration.

[7] Non-callable bonds have positive convexity, which reflects the favorable shifts in duration as interest rates change (duration lengthens when rates decline) as well as the non-linear effects of compounding.

[8] Earlier we used the yield curve to assess the overall attractiveness of investing in the country. At this point we are looking in more detail at the shape of the curve to determine what maturity structure to hold within the country.

yield curve. In addition, much of the yield benefit from extending maturity could be gained by investing in the 5-year area. Since convexity is most important for long bonds, and because the German government yield curve does not extend beyond ten years, convexity is not a significant consideration in this case. The expected normalization of the curve was close to zero for the 5-year bond, but quite beneficial to the 10-year bond.

Exhibit 7 displays the results of applying this analysis to the rest of the German market. The expected return curve rises steeply, but the important point here is that it is fairly linear, with a modest bulge around five years — this means that we had a slight preference for the 5-year area.

Exhibit 5: Actual versus Normal German Yield Curves: June 30, 1997

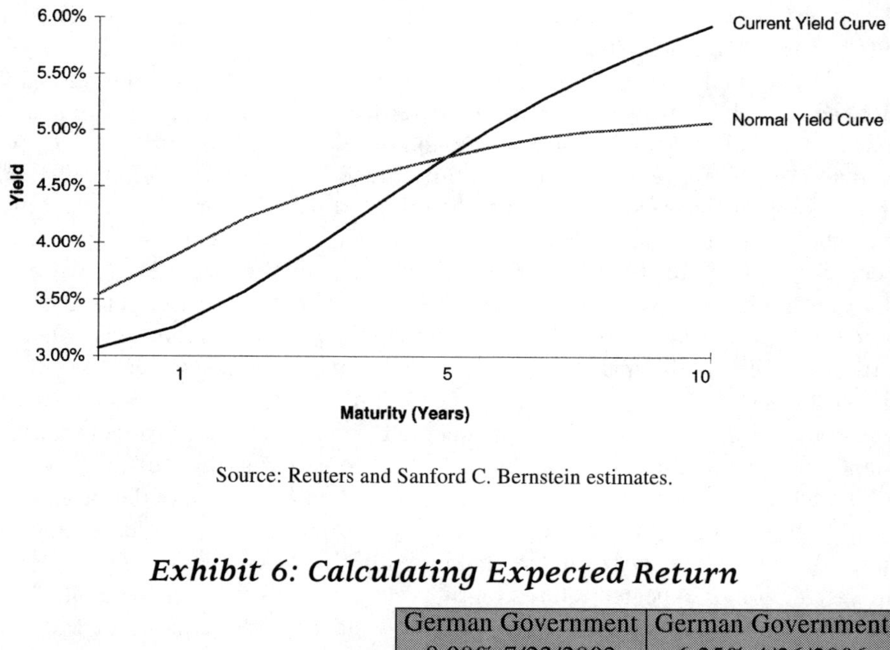

Source: Reuters and Sanford C. Bernstein estimates.

Exhibit 6: Calculating Expected Return

	German Government 8.00% 7/22/2002	German Government 6.25% 4/26/2006
Yield	4.72%	5.62%
+/- Expected Price Changes from:		
Roll	1.52	1.18
Convexity	0.07	0.18
Yield Curve Shift	−0.01	0.41
Expected Return	6.30%	7.39%

Source: Reuters and Sanford C. Bernstein estimates.

Exhibit 7: German Government Expected Return Curve: June 30, 1997

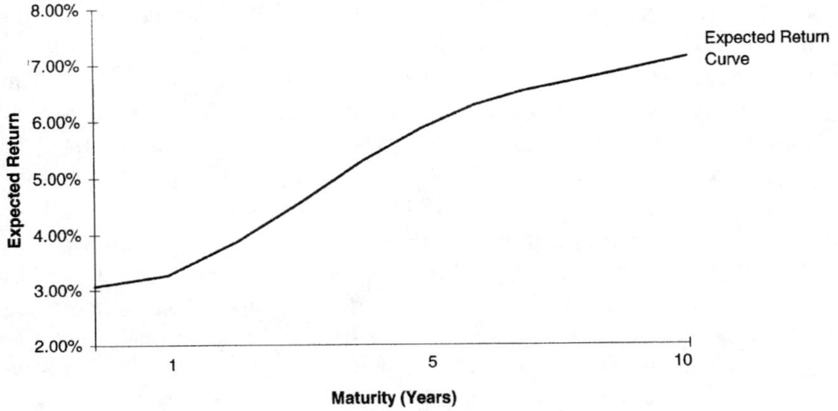

Source: Sanford C. Bernstein estimates.

If we could invest only in government bonds, we would determine our maturity distribution based on the government yield curve. Since we consider opportunities in other sectors, we may be influenced by the attractiveness of particular securities even if they are at less desirable points on the curve. Nonetheless, we use governments as a basis for our analysis of all other sectors.

Corporates, Eurobonds, Etc.

When we move to analysis of non-sovereign issuers, we take into account additional considerations. To arrive at corporate expected returns, we assess the expected values of default costs, event (e.g., takeover or restructuring) risks, and estimates of rating changes and spread movements, in addition to the factors used for governments.[9] We rely on our security analysts, who cover companies globally, as well as on rating agencies, to make the individual credit assessments for rating and event risk.

Our estimate of spread movements is based on global norms. The major issuers in these markets are large companies and institutions with a global financial presence. For example, the issuers we see in a typical survey of mark-denominated offerings included Abbey National, Deutsche Bank, the European Investment Bank, FNMA, General Electric, Kredit fuer Wiederaufbau, L-Bank, Province of Ontario (Canada), and Siemens. The important point is that all of these issuers also have U.S. dollar-denominated debt, and most of them also have debt outstanding in British pounds, Japanese yen, French francs, Australian dollars, and other currencies. When they are looking to borrow, they issue bonds in

[9] If the bonds are callable, we assess the option value. However, callable bonds are much less common overseas than in the United States.

whatever currency offers the lowest cost in terms of the credit spread. They then hedge the currency risk using the swap market. As a result, when an issuer's borrowing cost — its credit spread — is lower in one market than in others, that issuer will concentrate its borrowing in the market offering the lowest spread. This increased issuance should bring the spread back towards global levels.

We combine the various factors to arrive at an expected return estimate. The example in Exhibit 8 is for a Siemens Financial 5.50% bond due March 12, 2007, which was denominated in marks.

The Siemens bonds were rated Aaa by Moody's (on watchlist for downgrade) and AAA by S&P on June 30, 1997. Their yield on that date was 12 basis points above a comparable German government; of that yield advantage, we estimate 1 basis point in expected default costs. The roll, convexity, and yield curve effects were all identical for each bond. Our internal analysis of Siemens was negative — we estimated a cost of 25 basis points. However, the bonds were already trading somewhat cheaper than typical for their rating, so some of the downgrade was already reflected in the price (specific security misvaluation). Event risk is our assessment of the risk of a takeover, restructuring or leveraged buyout that would be adverse to the issuer. These events are less frequent outside the United States, but we still assess a penalty in some cases, though not for Siemens. The really significant negative for this bond (as for all corporates on this date) was the expected deterioration in price — 96 basis points — from a general widening of corporate spreads since spreads were well below historical averages. Finally, the bid/asked spread on this bond was wider than on the comparable government. Since we are likely to want to sell the bond before maturity, we also debit the Siemens expected return more than the bund for the incremental trading costs (liquidity).

Exhibit 8: Expected Return for Siemens Financial 5.50% due 3/12/2007 Versus a Comparable German Government (Bund)

	Siemens Financial	Comparable Bund	Difference
Yield	5.82%	5.70%	0.12%
Default costs	(0.01)	0.00	(0.01)
+/– Expected Price Changes from:			
Roll	1.07	1.07	0.00
Convexity	0.22	0.22	0.00
Yield Curve Shift	0.53	0.53	0.00
Ratings Changes	(0.25)	0.00	(0.25)
Specific Security Misvaluation	0.05	0.00	0.05
Event Risk	0.00	0.00	0.00
Sector Spread Changes	(0.96)	0.00	(0.96)
Liquidity Penalty	(0.25)	(0.12)	(0.13)
Expected Return	6.22%	7.40%	(1.18)%

When all of the adjustments are complete, the *yield* spread of 12 basis points turns into an *expected return* deficit of 118 basis points. This represents our best judgment of how this bond will perform. Because corporate spreads were generally extremely narrow on this date, we were largely invested in sovereign issuers.

Another factor taken into account in security selection is the impact of taxes. A few countries withhold a portion of the interest payments on bonds. One effective way to avoid these costs is to purchase so-called "Eurobonds" denominated in the currencies of these countries. For example, U.S. investors in Japanese domestically-issued bonds (such as Japanese government bonds) are subject to a 10% withholding tax on interest. On the other hand, there are Euroyen issues of major issuers that pay in Japanese yen (and therefore allow investors to get exposure to the Japanese bond market), but are not subject to withholding. While these Euroyen bonds typically trade at a slightly lower yield as a result, they are often one of the best means for American investors to access this market.[10]

This illustrates how the expected return methodology allows the comparison of numerous considerations — yield, default, spread changes, yield curve movements, and taxation are all quantified in terms of their expected value (cost) to the return of the bond, which allows the investor to make the best bond selection considering all of these factors simultaneously.

Futures

As noted above, we make our interest rate exposure decisions separately from our currency decisions. Sometimes a country's bond market is attractive, but its currency is not. In such circumstances, we would like to hold bonds in that market but avoid the currency exposure. We can accomplish this by buying bonds in that country and then selling currency forwards to hedge against the expected adverse currency movements, and we often do. However, there is another — and frequently better — way to implement a currency-hedged position, and that is to purchase bond futures.

The price of a German bond future is not directly affected by fluctuations in the value of the mark. When we hold bond futures we keep the underlying market value in short-term securities, to avoid being leveraged. But, because we do not want exposure to the Deutschemark, we keep the money in *U.S. dollar-denominated* short-term securities.[11] This position has the same economic exposures as a German government bond that is hedged by currency forwards. Investing in the futures contract incurs less in transactions cost and so it is often advantageous. At other times, there are specific bonds whose attractiveness more than offsets the greater costs of purchasing them. These considerations are all measured in terms of their impact on the expected return of the position.

---

[10] Futures, which are another vehicle that serves this purpose, are discussed below.

[11] For some futures contracts, the initial margin must be in the local currency. However, this only represents a small fraction of the market value of the position and can, if desired, be hedged with currency forwards.

RISK MEASUREMENT

Expected return is only half of the equation; we also need to measure risk. The calculation of risk begins at the security level. For each bond, we need to assess its exposure to all of the significant factors that directly affect the value of each bond. For example, the Siemens bond we analyzed above will be subject to fluctuations in the Deutschemark, German interest rates, and corporate spreads.[12] The exposure of a portfolio is the sum of the security exposures weighted by their portfolio weights.

To translate these exposures into risks, we need to estimate the volatility of each of the factors and their correlations with each other. A common way to do this is to employ historical relationships over a representative period, perhaps with judgmental modifications. While we do this in some cases, when performed globally, there are a great many correlations to be estimated, and these estimates are subject to error. In addition, relationships may be unstable over time. This means we must make a tradeoff — using a longer period will not capture evolution in the markets, but a short period will be subject to more error. Overall, the result tends to be an underestimation of the risk of optimal portfolios.[13]

We prefer, where possible, to reduce the structure to fewer, more fundamental factors using a process that combines our understanding of the markets with empirical analysis. For example, our investment universe includes 15 bond markets. Including currency risks, we have 406 different pairs of markets for which we need correlations (even before we get to factors within markets). We have reduced this complicated structure into a simpler one based on six factors for bond market risk and five for currencies. The bond factors include a global factor (markets tend to move together), regional factors, and some market-based factors — yield and the bond risk premium. The market-based factors capture the dynamic nature of market relationships. For instance, the "high yield" markets tend to move, to a degree, in sympathy, but which countries have high yields varies over time. Because we have explicitly modelled this, our risk estimates change in response. We then translate these basic factors into a correlation matrix for the countries and currencies. The result is a simpler matrix to estimate and one that reflects current market conditions.

To estimate the correlation between German and Australian bonds, we consider how each market is affected by basic factors. Both are influenced by global yield levels. Their regional exposures act in different ways, because they are, literally, a world apart. These are the static parts of the risk model and result in an estimate of the correlation between German and Australian interest rates of 0.31.

---

[12] Depending on the context, these may well be refined further. Sensitivity to German interest rates can be decomposed into sensitivity to changes in the level, slope, and curvature of the German yield curve. Corporate risk can be divided by rating and sector.

[13] Among randomly selected portfolios, you overestimate the risk of some and underestimate others. However, the optimization process tends to select portfolios whose risk you have underestimated.

On June 30, 1997, however, the fundamentals of the two markets were actually fairly similar. Therefore, the market-related factors raised our estimate of the correlation of those two markets to 0.40. At other times, when the fundamentals of the two markets differ, the estimate would be lower than our static estimate of 0.31.

Another element of risk control is to bring a degree of humility to the process. None of our estimates of risk and return will be perfect, and some will be more subject to error than others. To account for this we try to build conservatism into the process; where we feel the greatest uncertainty, we are the most conservative. Thus, models that are newer or more variable require more conservatism than those that have been estimated over long periods of time and have been very stable.

Once we have a complete specification of the expected returns and risks of all the securities in our investment universe, we are in a position to select optimal portfolios.[14] First, we need to decide what the objective is: Clearly, higher returns are better, but how do you define risk? Risk can be defined either in absolute terms (simply how variable the returns will be) or relative to a benchmark (how much the returns will differ from a market index). Sometimes it is appropriate to use both — that is, to include penalties for both absolute and relative risk in the objective function. If risk is defined as relative to a benchmark, then the exposures are measured as differences from the benchmark — if you have either more or less exposure to German bonds than the benchmark, that constitutes a risk.

PORTFOLIO CONSTRUCTION

Having defined risk, we can identify optimal portfolios. For each level of risk, we can find the portfolio with the highest expected return. These portfolios will typically be very well diversified in terms of active strategies. They will not reflect simply one or two themes, but will be taking risk along each dimension — each of the identified risk factors — in proportion to the opportunities available in that respect. This process also allows us to incorporate all portfolio guidelines and constraints.

Graphing the expected returns against the variance, we observe the "efficient frontier." The shape of this curve varies over time, reflecting the amount of mispricing in the marketplace. When there is not much return to be picked up for taking risk, the efficient frontier will be relatively shallow. Conversely, when the market is rich with opportunities, the frontier is steep — a good time to make significant bets (see Exhibit 9).[15]

---

[14] There is actually one additional consideration: transactions costs. We debit these from the expected returns of securities we are considering purchasing.

[15] The horizontal axis is labeled in standard deviations, but it is graphed linearly with the variance. This was done so that the indifference lines (discussed below) would actually be linear.

Exhibit 9: Efficient Frontiers

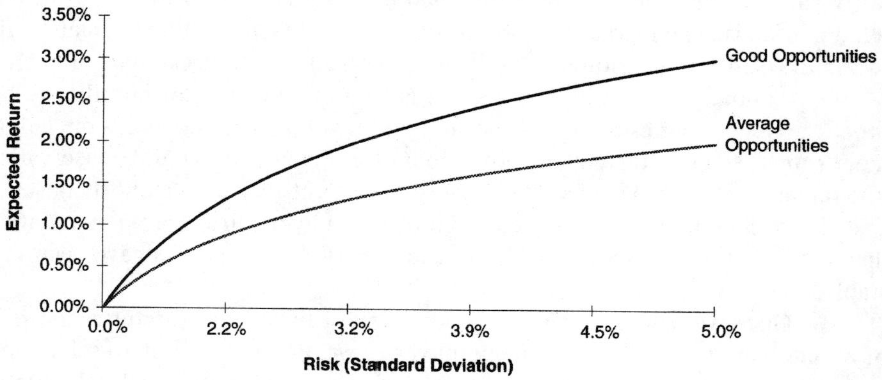

Exhibit 10: Efficient Frontiers

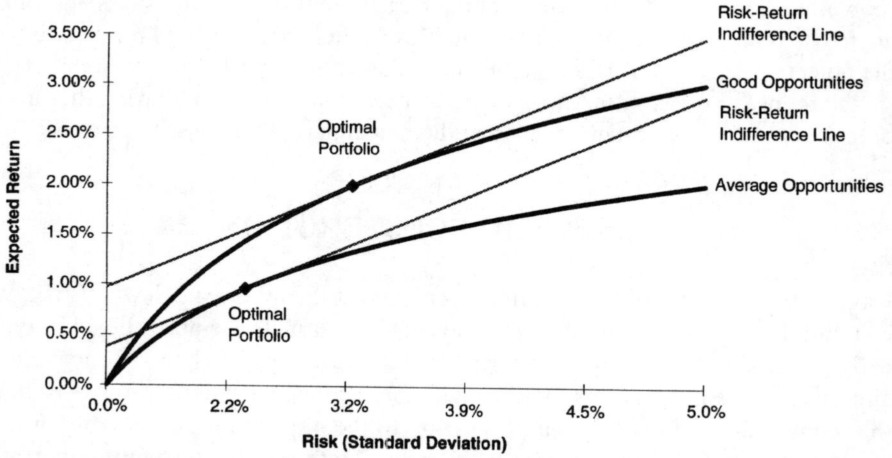

The final question is, Where on the frontier do you want to be? For each account we assess the appropriate risk/return tradeoff — the amount of added return necessary to take an additional increment of risk. For more risk-averse mandates, we demand more added return. This risk/return tradeoff for a particular account is pictured as the diagonal lines labeled "indifference lines" on Exhibit 10. As you move up and to the right along one of the indifference lines, the return is rising just enough for the added risk, so this account would be indifferent between any return/risk combination on those lines. The actual opportunities are shown as the efficient frontiers. At low levels of risk, the efficient frontiers are steeper than the indifference lines, so it pays to take more risk. But eventually, the efficient frontier flattens off to the point that it no longer pays enough to increase risk. The optimal portfolio is at the point that the slope of the efficient frontier is equal to the indiferrence line — the two are tangent.

As you can see in Exhibit 10, when there are better opportunities for each level of risk — that is, when the efficient frontier is steeper — the optimal portfolio is at a higher level of risk and return. In the average case, we would select a portfolio with an expected premium over the benchmark of 1.0%, with 2.5% relative risk. Given the "good opportunities" curve, we would pick up 2.0% in expected return for 3.2% in risk. The better level of opportunities justifies taking a greater amount of risk. This procedure optimally calibrates the amount of risk taken to the opportunities available. We will assume a more defensive posture when opportunities are not great, and we will take risk when it is warranted.

SUMMARY

Global investment management is a difficult undertaking. It is implicitly assumed that the market is inefficient. The task is to predict the future better than the market does. At the same time, the world is changing in ways that are often transitory, but are occasionally fundamental. We make our best effort, but foresight is never perfect. Our philosophy in approaching this task is well summed up by Paul Krugman in a similar context: "Guesswork is all we have to go on and those who discipline their guesses with models are more reliable than those who fly by the seat of their pants, no matter how well tailored."[16]

Accordingly, we have designed a process to discipline our subjective judgments with models. The investment management process we have described entails the estimation of expected returns and risks of bonds in a largely quantitative manner. The expected return measure enables us to integrate judgments about many factors into a single measure that we can apply consistently across time and market sectors. Rather than being based on a global economic forecast, this process relies largely on measures of value that have historically been good forecasters of return globally. We believe that this insulates us from decision-making biases and allows us to take advantage of opportunities created by other investors who are more subject to those biases. The portfolio construction process is intended to provide risk control. Just as importantly, it ensures that we only take risks for which we believe we are being more than adequately compensated. Thus we believe that this process will avoid undue risks, while producing superior returns.

---

[16] Paul Krugman, *Currencies and Crises* (Cambridge, Mass: MIT Press, 1992).

Chapter 6

An Integrated Framework for Valuation and Risk Analysis of International Bonds

Roveen Bhansali
Associate Director
Global Fixed Income Services
BARRA, Inc.

Lisa Goldberg, Ph.D.
Senior Consultant
Fixed Income Research
BARRA, Inc.

INTRODUCTION

International bonds now represent more than half of the market value of the world's fixed-income markets. In 1985 they comprised less than a third. Recent years have seen a tremendous growth in the international fixed-income markets and a corresponding growth in international bonds under management for U.S.-based mutual fund families and institutional investors. There are now over 200 mutual funds devoted to international bonds, more than double the number available just three years ago.

Part of this increased interest in international bonds stems from the more than 390 basis points of out-performance of international bonds as a group over the U.S. bond market over the last decade. Exhibit 1 displays the year by year performance comparison of the J.P. Morgan Government Bond Index ex-U.S. with the J.P. Morgan U.S. Government Bond Index. Another reason is the case made for diversification benefits that international bonds can offer in any fixed-income portfolio.

Investing in international bond presents substantial challenges for global investors. There exist idiosyncrasies within individual markets that result in widely differing market structures and trading patterns. When managing an international bond portfolio, one needs to understand not only the diverse types of assets within a market, but also to develop a complete understanding of the institutions that regulate the market. In addition, investors need to be cognizant of the dynamics between markets in order to identify global trends and trading opportunities.

Exhibit 1: Comparison of Bond Returns

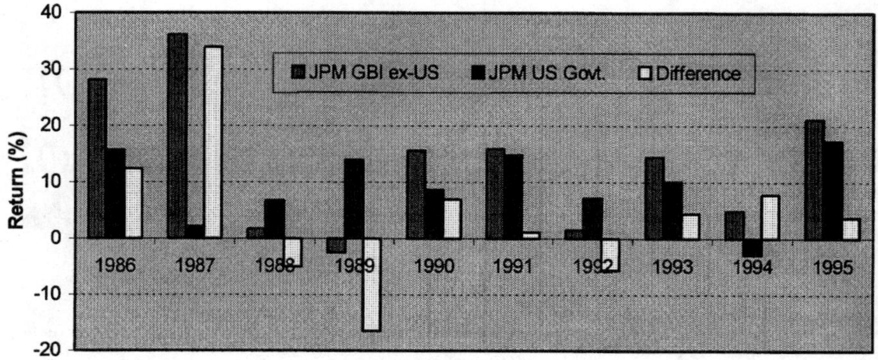

Bond values are driven by macroeconomic variables such as real interest rates, inflation expectations, GDP growth rates, employment outlook, budget deficit and monetary policy. Within each market, these variables determine the relative supply and demand for government securities, which in turn drives the prices. In addition, bond values also depend on the structural features and institutional characteristics within markets, such as liquidity, tax considerations, default risk, cash flow structures, and intra-market spreads. Any asset or market feature that changes investors' willingness to pay for a bond should be considered. We will elaborate on some of these below.

Although most government bond markets are fairly liquid, there clearly are differences across markets. Executing a \$500 million trade in the U.S. is very different from executing that trade in Norway. Additionally, different markets exhibit varying levels of liquidity along the yield curve. As an example, consider the Portuguese bond market. Even though the government bond issuance is well balanced across the long end of the curve (5-10 year maturity range).[1] In Japan, lack of an active repo market combined with high demand for KGBs for end-of-March year-end balance sheet purposes has historically resulted in the cash JGBs being relatively illiquid.

Differences in tax treatment across markets should be taken into account as that determines the net real returns to the international investor. Typically, bonds are not taxed when held by international investors, but this may not always be the case. For example, Italy has a 12.5% withholding tax on bonds issued after August 31, 1987[2] and a withholding tax levied at maturity on the difference between the face value and issue price. The withholding tax in principle is refundable for international investors. However, due to procedural issues and delays involved in this

---

[1] As of 1995, 33.8% of outstanding amount of government debt was in the 1-3 year range, whereas 27.3% was in the 5-10 year range.

[2] Bonds issued before August 31, 1987, mostly floating-rate *Certificati di Credito del Tesoro* (CCTs), are either tax-exempt or taxed at a 6.25% withholding rate.

process, an investor in Italian government bonds may treat the yields on a non-refundable basis. Similarly, tax issues in Japan may make investing in the Euro-yen market preferable to the international investor over the JGB market.

Investors also need to understand default risk of international bond issuers. Even two industrialized sovereign issuers of similarly rated local currency debt, may trade at differential spread in the Eurobond market. This would indicate default risk premium attached to the credit worthiness of one sovereign issuer relative to the other. The magnitude of the default risk premia becomes a more important element of a bond's value when analyzing emerging market debt or for Eurobonds issued by non-investment grade, non-sovereign issuers.

International investors also need to discern between the distinguishing attributes of different bond types. One such feature that needs to be analyzed is an embedded option. For example, in the Italian market the CTOs are putable — so they should trade at a lower yield than the equivalent BTPs.[3] In the U.S. market, some of the long maturity Treasuries have embedded call options — so their yields should be adjusted higher compared to equivalent straight bonds. The UK gilt market has bonds with special features, e.g., perpetuals.[4]

There are other subtleties within markets that merit consideration. Historically, callable bonds in the domestic Japanese market have never been called ñ therefore they trade as straight bonds. Some markets such as the UK gilt market and Danish government bond market use a "tap" issuance system where the issuer adjusts the offering price of the bond to regulate the amount of sales. Hence, there is more issuance when market prices go up than when prices drop.

Market knowledge is also essential in understanding the intricacies of intra-market dynamics. Consider the Pfandbriefe sector in the German market which accounts for over 30% of the domestic market value. Despite this large market share, the Pfandbriefe spread over the sovereign curve has historically been wide due to lack of liquidity in the secondary market. However, the recent establishment of standard indexes in the Pfanbriefe market together with the issuance of "Jumbo Pfandbriefes" targeted to the global investors has increased its appeal overseas. As a result, this market is more liquid and the intra-market spread has tightened.

Clearly, bond valuation has a market-specific component that requires substantial knowledge about each individual market. Before devising a global investment strategy, one must understand the elements that define the value of assets traded in each market. Although there exist differences between bond markets, it is nonetheless important to create a consistent and integrated framework from which to analyze international bonds.

---

[3] *Certificati del Tesoro con Opzione* (CTOs) are fixed-rate notes with a put option at par after three years. *Buoni del Tesoro Poliennali* (BTPs) are fixed-coupon bullet maturity bonds with recent issuances of maturity of 3-, 5-, 10-, and 30-years. For the bulk of CTOs though the option is now expired, hence they are identical to BTPs.

[4] Perpetuals, also called Undated or Irredeemable gilts are low-coupon bonds that have no final maturity date.

Exhibit 2: Currency Risk as a Percentage of Total Portfolio Risk for the Major Global Bond Indexes (February 29, 1996)

Numeraire	JPM GBI* (%)	SAL WGI** (%)
U.S. dollar	63.3	65.7
ECU	65.3	65.8
French franc	70.9	70.5
German deutschemarks	71.8	71.9
British pound	70.8	73.1
Canadian dollar	75.7	76.9
Japanese yen	82.8	81.9
Australian dollar	87.7	87.9
Italian lira	86.3	88.3
Mexican peso	92.9	93.5
South African rand	97.7	96.1

* J.P. Morgan Government Bond Index.
** Salomon Brothers World Government Index.
Source: The BARRA Cosmos™ Model

The various factors that contribute to a bond's value also provide insight into its risk. The volatile bond markets, particularly in 1994, exposed the shortcomings of traditional measures of bond risk, namely duration and convexity. Within a single market, duration as a risk measure proved inadequate in predicting the interest rate risk due to non-parallel movements of the yield curve. Additionally, duration — which represents sensitivity to small parallel movement in the yield curve within a particular market — loses its meaning when aggregated across markets. For example, the meaning of a 4.2-year duration for a portfolio consisting of U.S. Treasuries, JGBs, and German Bunds is dubious. Duration would only be a meaningful measure in the context of this portfolio if we were to assume that the all the markets in the portfolio would undergo identical parallel interest rate changes *simultaneously*.

Another major source of volatility in a portfolio that contains international bonds is currency movement. The higher return earned on an international bond can be neutralized if that bond's currency loses value. Typically, in an unhedged international fixed-income portfolio, currency movements can account for almost two thirds of the return and risk. Exhibit 2 shows the percentage of total portfolio risk[5] explained by currency movements in the major global risk indexes for various numeraire perspectives. Additionally, correlations between local market interest rate movements and foreign currency movements can also contribute to currency risk. A currency hedging strategy is required to take an interest rate view in a particular local market without incurring incidental cur-

5 Portfolio risk is defined as variance of excess return.

rency exposure. In developing a strategy for investing in international bonds, managers must assess carefully the currency aspects of their portfolio.

The purpose of this chapter is to describe, in the context of today's marketplace, approaches for constructing valuation models for international fixed income securities. These valuation models will assist investors in making trading decisions, marking portfolios to market, identifying relative value in securities, etc.

After developing a framework for accurate valuation of fixed-income securities, we address the issues pertaining to forecasting the risk of a portfolio of these securities. A successful global fixed-income strategy involves making the right bond and currency choices and managing the risk inherent in those choices. We identify the risk factors, namely interest rate risk and credit risk, that describe risk within an individual market. Using these factors, we develop a local market risk model for each individual market, that is applicable to all the securities in that market. In addition, we develop a security-specific risk model that explains the risk not explained by the market-wide factors. We then add to the risk model the dimension inherent in international portfolios, namely, currency risk. We then describe a model that accounts for correlations existing across local markets and currencies.

This multi-factor risk modeling approach lends itself to identifying the exposures of each security in an international portfolio to the various risk factors and quantifying the volatility and correlations of the different markets within the portfolio. This enables calculation of aggregate portfolio risk measures such as value-at-risk (VAR) and tracking error. At the same time, this approach allows a portfolio manager to decompose and better understand the various sources of risk. Local market interest rate strategies can be separated from currency strategies, facilitating formulation and analysis of alternative investment strategies.

VALUATION ANALYSIS

Technically speaking, a bond is a collection of promised future cash flows subject to a set of terms and conditions. The simplest and most familiar bonds are *straight bonds* for which the cash flow dates and amounts are fixed at the time of issue. As we will see below, bond characteristics can be quite complicated. In particular, they may cause the cash flow stream to be uncertain.

As mentioned in the introduction, a bond's value is affected by the credibility of the "promise" of its cash flows. In other words, the value of a bond is influenced by the likelihood that the issuer may default. Generally, sovereign bonds are considered to be default free while corporate bonds are somewhat riskier.[6] Hence, the price of a corporate bond typically should be less than the price of an otherwise identical sovereign bond.

The considerations above indicate that any model used to value bonds in a given market must have at least three components. The first is a term structure

[6] There are exceptions such as Italy where sovereign bonds are considered riskier than corporate bonds.

of interest rates which determines the time value of money. The second is a spread model which captures default risk. The final component is a stochastic interest rate model which describe how interest rates evolve. This is used to value bonds whose future stream of cash flows is uncertain. These components are discussed below in more detail.

Our strategy is to devise a uniform implementation of these three components for each market covered by our model. Then the components are enhanced to reflect the individual characteristics of the market. One of the challenges in designing a model of this type is to strike a balance between tailoring the components to the different markets and having consistency across markets.

Term Structure Model

The *term structure* is a curve that specifies a discount rate for every future time to maturity. For a straight sovereign bond, this is all that is needed to come up with the present value of a bond

$$PM(t) = \sum_{T} cf(T)e^{-s(t,T)(T-t)} + \varepsilon(t) = PF(t) + \varepsilon(t) \tag{1}$$

$PM(t)$ = Bond market price at time t
$cf(T)$ = Time T expected ash flow
$s(t,T)$ = Time t (continuously compounded) spot interest rate at maturity T
$Pf(t)$ = Bond model or fitted price at time t
$\varepsilon(t)$ = Time t pricing error

The term structure is a theoretical construct which is inferred from bond prices and other economic factors. One possible estimation procedure is as follows. First, determine the horizon of the market from the time to maturity of the longest bond. Divide the horizon into intervals that reflect the natural maturity sectors in the market. The forward rates can be assumed constant across these intervals. Finally, choose the rates which most closely match market prices, possibly subject to constraints.

The term structure is not uniquely determined. Rather, it depends on its inputs: the choice of bond universe and relative weightings of the bonds, economic factors used, variable constraints, and the precise form of the objective function. The number of parameters in the model depends on the quantity and reliability of the data as well as the way in which bonds are distributed across the maturity spectrum.

Once a term structure is determined, it can be used to compute fair value of bonds not in the estimation universe. Fair value of a bond can be used for the purposes of identifying trading opportunities, performing rich/cheap analysis by comparing fair value against the market price, or for marking portfolios of untraded assets to market. Of course, the results have to be interpreted with caution. The parameters estimated for each of the market are only as good as the data used in estimating them. Ideally, all the prices used should reflect trades occurring at approximately the same time. In practice, this is rarely the case. The source of a price is often a trader's assessment of a fair market value rather than a report of an actual traded price.

Yield Spread Model

Equation (1) can be enhanced to value straight non-sovereign bonds with the addition of a *yield spread model.* To construct a simple spread model, divide the universe of bonds into sectors based on industry, rating, liquidity, tax features, or other factors relating to the bond issuer or to the bond itself. Each sector is assigned a value or *spread* which affects a bond's model value according to a normalized quantity called an exposure. In some models, an exposure is either 0 or 1. For example, a financial bond has exposure 0 to the industrial spread, while an industrial bond has exposure 1. The total spread of a bond is calculated by multiplying the bond's exposure to each sector spread by the sector spread and summing over sectors:

$$\kappa(t) = \sum_i x_i(t) s_i(t) \tag{2}$$

$\kappa(t)$ = Bond spread at time t
$x_i(t)$ = Bond exposure to i-th sector spread at time t
$s_i(t)$ = i-th sector spread at time t

As we will see in the next section, the spread captures the level of credit risk associated with the rating and sector of the bond.

The bond is valued as in equation (1) with the term structure adjusted by the total spread. In mathematical terms, this is

$$\begin{aligned} PM(t) &= \sum_T cf(T) e^{-[s(t,T) + \kappa(t)](T-t)} + \varepsilon(t) \\ &= (PF(t) + \varepsilon(t)) \end{aligned} \tag{3}$$

Stochastic Interest Rate Model

The third ingredient needed for bond valuation is a *stochastic interest rate model.* This is a probabilistic view of how the term structure will evolve in the future and it is used to value bonds with uncertain future cash flows. A taxonomy of interest models is found elsewhere in this book. There are many standard interest rate models in the literature and the choice of model may have a large impact on the model value of a bond.

Customizing the Model

As mentioned previously, it is important to customize each of the model components to the institutional characteristics of the specific market. Features such as trading conventions vary from market to market. For example, the buyer of a German bund or a U.S. Treasury bond begins to accrue interest as of settlement date. However, a buyer of a French OAT accrues interest as of the trade date and the buyer of an Italian BTP for domestic settlement accrues interest as of the trade date plus three market days plus one calendar day. Similarly, the custody of the coupon goes to the buyer as of settlement date for a Japanese JGB, but as of trade date for a Swiss SGB.[7] Further, the settlement rules differ between markets and bond types. An Australian CGS settles at trade date plus three market days. In the United States, Treasury bonds settle at trade date plus one market day while corporate bonds settle at trade date plus three market days. Details such as these need to be handled in the local implementations of valuation formulas.

Markets differ in obvious ways such as size, distribution of bonds across the maturity spectrum, and investor willingness to substitute bonds of different maturities for one another. These considerations may render it necessary to vary the number of rates calculated. In the same spirit, it may be important to incorporate liquidity properties into the valuation model, since benchmark bonds generally trade at a premium and illiquid bonds generally trade at a discount. In markets where this is a nontrivial effect, extra parameters in the form of "valuation spreads" can be added to the term structure objective function. However, this may have undesirable consequences since adding parameters may over-determine the model in some markets.

Exhibit 3 lists the G7 countries together with the time to maturity of the longest bond, and the total number of traded, actively traded and benchmark bonds as defined by J.P. Morgan as of March 1996. Notice that Japan is an extreme example in that there is a single benchmark bond which typically accounts for over 50% of the total trading volume. This fact alone may have a subtle but important impact on model design. Suppose a benchmark spread is included in the objective function for the Japanese term structure. The benchmark bond will then be priced exactly by the model, but it will have no impact on the estimated forward rates.

Exhibit 3: Horizon and Liquidity Breakdown of Estimation Universe (March 1, 1996)

Market	Maturity of the Longest Bond (Years)	Traded	Active	Benchmark
Canada	29.25	11	16	5
France	29.65	6	18	4
Germany	27.84	14	52	5
Italy	27.67	11	14	4
Japan	19.56	43	17	3
United Kingdom	25.27	8	21	4
United States	29.96	139	10	5

Source: JP Morgan

[7] In particular, a Swiss SGB can have accrued interest that exceeds a coupon.

Valuation equations (1) and (3) must be modified to account for complicated bond characteristics such as embedded call and put options, optional extensions of maturity date, coupons which float according to an index, and sinking funds. In fact, the category of sinking funds incorporates many variants. In some cases the principal of individual bonds are repaid (sunk) according to a predetermined schedule. In other cases, a certain fraction of the total issue is sunk according to schedule; bonds to be sunk are selected by lottery. Sinking funds can have purchase options, which means that the issuer can redeem bonds by open market purchases, or they can have acceleration factors, where the fraction of the issue to be sunk can be increased by the issuer. Particular types of bonds are characteristic of certain markets during certain periods of time, and they contribute to the "personality" of their markets. As an example, there are many sovereign sinking funds in Denmark and Netherlands but none in Sweden. Historically, U.S. Treasury bonds are never sinkable but U.S corporate bonds frequently are.

Assessing the Proposed Valuation Model

We will now describe an approach to assess the proposed valuation model. A natural measure is the root mean square of the pricing errors of the bonds.

$$RMSE(t) = \left[\frac{1}{nbonds}\sum_i (PM_i(t) - PF_i(t))^2\right]^{1/2} \tag{4}$$

$RMSE(t)$ = Root mean square error at time t
$nbonds$ = Number of bonds in the universe at time t
$PM_i(t)$ = Market price of bond i at time t
$PF_i(t)$ = Model or fitted price of bond i at time t

However, equation (4) has to be used with care. The model will price all bonds perfectly if the number of rates is at least equal to the number of bonds. On the other hand, if there are fewer rates than bonds, a single data error might cause the root mean square error to be very large when in fact, most bonds are being priced very well. More seriously, a large data error can have significant impact on rates and skew the entire model. One way to handle this is to rerun the term structure estimation repeatedly, discarding outliers between iterations, until no outliers above a certain threshold remain. Then the model is reasonable if typically, the root mean square pricing error is small, the fraction of bonds discarded is small, and the number of bonds is much higher than the number of rates. Exhibit 4 shows these values for the G7 countries for term structures estimated by BARRA for March 1, 1996.

RISK ANALYSIS

As mentioned in the introduction, the dominant source of the total risk to a portfolio of international bonds is currency risk.[8] Other substantial risks come from

[8] This statement applies to a portfolio of sovereign and investment-grade corporate bonds. If "junk" bonds are part of the portfolio, credit risk may become the dominant source of risk.

within individual markets. These include fluctuations in the term structure of interest rates and credit risk. In precise terms, the *risk* or *volatility* of a portfolio can be defined as the standard deviation of excess returns to the portfolio. Here, *excess return* means the return over and above the return on a riskless investment.

An important related concept is the *active risk* or *tracking error* of a portfolio with respect to a benchmark. This is the standard deviation of the difference between the return to the benchmark and the return to the portfolio. Here, large sources of risk such as currency risk and risk due to parallel shift are typically hedged away. What dominates are higher order sources of local market risk and idiosyncratic or *specific risk*. These concepts will be discussed in more detail below.

Implicit in these definitions is a time horizon over which the return is calculated. In the discussion below, the horizon is taken to be one month. Note that, under the hypothesis that returns over any horizon are independent, the risk of a portfolio scales with the square root of the time horizon. Consequently, a 1-month horizon model can be scaled to give risk estimates over different horizons.

This section outlines the construction of a multi-factor global risk model. The model expresses excess portfolio return as a linear combination of basic variables whose covariance matrix is estimated within the model.

$$EPR = \sum_i x_i(EPR) \cdot r_i + \varepsilon \quad (5)$$

EPR = excess portfolio return
$x_i(EPR)$ = exposure of excess portfolio return to i-th factor
r_i = return to i-th factor
ε = error

Hence, the total risk of a portfolio is given by:

$$\sigma_p = sd(EPR) = (h^T[X^TFX + D]h)^{1/2} \quad (6)$$

Exhibit 4: Term Structure Estimation Diagnostics (March 1, 1996)

	RMSE	Fraction of Bonds Discarded	Number of Bonds	Number of Rates
Canada	0.11	0	32	8
France	0.24	0	28	8
Germany	0.22	0	71	8
Italy	0.22	0	29	8
Japan	0.32	1⁄64	63	7
United Kingdom	0.25	0	33	8
United States	0.33	0	154	8

Source: BARRA

σ_p = portfolio risk
h = portfolio holdings
X = bond exposures to factors
F = covariance matrix of factor returns
D = diagonal matrix of bond specific variances

The active risk of a portfolio with respect to a benchmark is obtained by replacing the portfolio holdings h with the difference $h_P - h_B$ between the portfolio holdings and the benchmark holdings in equation (6).

Also, given the above calculation for risk, a portfolio's value-at-risk (VAR) can be computed.

$$VAR = s_p \cdot \text{portfolio value} \tag{7}$$

Assuming normal distributions, the probability of losing VAR is 16%.

The strategy for estimating the global risk model is to construct a consistent family of local market risk models as well as a currency risk model. These components are pieced together into a global covariance matrix that accounts for linkages existing across markets and currencies. This covariance matrix is used as in equation (6) to forecast portfolio risk.

Local Market Risk: Variation in Term Structure

In any given market, changes in the term structure of interest rates account for most of the risk of sovereign and highly rated corporate bonds. In fact, in the U.S. bond market, interest rate fluctuations account for approximately 90% of the total portfolio risk. The remaining 10% is attributable to risks due to sector membership, quality rating, relative coupon, liquidity, and covariance factors. Exhibit 5 shows the decomposition of variance of return for a portfolio consisting of all U.S. corporate bonds with a minimum maturity of one year as of March 1, 1996. This exhibit illustrates the fact that interest rate factor is the dominant element of risk *within* a market.

Exhibit 5: Decomposition of Variance of Return
(BARRA All Corporate Index, March 1, 1996)

Source of Risk	Variance (%)
Interest rate effects	45.36
Quality and sector factors	7.23
Liquidity and maturity-dependent factors	2.80
Covariance terms	–5.36
Issue specific	0.01
Total	50.04

Source: BARRA

Exhibit 6: Monthly Standard Deviation/Correlation Matrix for the Japanese Market (January 1, 1988 - March 1, 1996)

	1 year	2 years	3 years	4 years	5 years	7 years	10 years	20 years
1 year	0.003053	0.706883	0.774184	0.740236	0.710354	0.605757	0.635143	0.550866
2 years		0.003098	0.963059	0.937033	0.900919	0.808655	0.77927	0.683171
3 years			0.003159	0.973894	0.943082	0.844661	0.842492	0.711944
4 years				0.003107	0.969274	0.895337	0.877645	0.724096
5 years					0.003129	0.895042	0.875251	0.753634
7 years						0.002743	0.914243	0.757892
10 years							0.002425	0.796097
20 years								0.00224

Source: BARRA

Theoretically, the term structure is a 1-dimensional curve specifying a discount rate for each time to maturity. To describe the change in term structure, it is convenient to use the discrete approximation outlined in the previous section of this chapter. Hence, for the purposes of this discussion, a term structure is given by a set of distinguished vertices and a discount or spot rate at each of the vertices. Discount rates between vertices are obtained by interpolation. Earlier in this chapter, interpolation based on the assumption of constant forward rates between vertices was mentioned. Other schemes such as piecewise linear interpolation or cubic splines could be used.

An intuitively appealing local market risk model is based on changes in interest rates at the vertices. A local market covariance matrix can be estimated from a time series over a particular data history. The dimension of the matrix is given by the number of vertices used to determine the term structure. Of course, the estimate obtained depends on the time window used, and whether or not the data are weighted to give more importance to recent observations. Assume for the purpose of discussion that these finer points of model structure have been settled.

Exhibit 6 shows a standard deviation/correlation matrix[9] for changes in spot rates for the Japanese market during the period January 1, 1988 through March 1, 1996. Eight vertices at times to maturity 1, 2, 3, 4, 5, 7, 10, and 20 years are used. A glance at the matrix diagonal illustrates the well known assertion that short rates are more volatile than long rates. It is also immediate from this exhibit that there is more to risk than a parallel shift. For if interest rates moved in parallel, the diagonal elements would have the same value and the off-diagonal elements would be equal to 1. This illustrates a point emphasized in the introduction. Duration, the sensitivity of returns to parallel shifts in the yield curve, is an inadequate measure of risk.

Further inspection of Exhibit 6 shows that while interest rates may not move in parallel, changes in interest rates at different times to maturity are highly correlated. This suggests that there may be a more concise way to capture the information held in an 8×8 covariance matrix of interest rate changes.

---

[9] This is an upper triangular matrix with standard deviations on the diagonal and correlations in the upper triangle. This matrix determines and is determined by the corresponding covariance matrix.

Exhibit 7: Percentage of Variance Explained by Principal Components in the Japanese Market

Number of Principal Components	Percentage of Variance Explained
1	84.98
2	91.48
3	95.40
4	97.58
5	98.62
6	99.44
7	99.78
8	100.00

Source: BARRA

Exhibit 8: Percentage of Variance Explained by Three Principal Components in the G7 Countries

Country	Percentage of variance explained by three principal components (%)
Canada	95.65
France	97.10
Germany	96.05
Italy	94.15
Japan	95.40
United Kingdom	97.21
United States	98.60

Source: BARRA

One way to pursue this is to convert from changes in interest rates to distinguished linear combinations of changes in interest rates. This can be done by a *principal components analysis*[10] which captures the largest percentage of variance possible. Exhibit 7 shows the cumulative percentage of variance explained by the 8 principal components of the Japanese covariance matrix. Evidently, by taking the first three principal components, in excess of 95% of the variance can be captured. This phenomenon is not isolated to the Japanese market. Exhibit 8 shows the percentage of variance captured by 3 principal components in each of the G7 countries.

It is an empirical fact, related to the high correlations among changes in interest rates, that the first principal component of a covariance matrix of changes

[10] A principal components analysis decomposes N×N covariance matrix (or more generally, any symmetric matrix) into a sum of N rank 1 matrices generated by the normalized eigenvectors of the original matrix. See Richard A. Johnson and Dean W. Wichern, *Applied Multivariate Statistical Analysis* (Prentice Hall, 1992), pp. 356-395 for more details.

in term structures looks roughly, though not exactly, like a parallel shift. This movement is termed *shift* and is viewed as the generalized movement whereby all rates move in the same direction. The shift factor shape for most markets is observed to be downward sloping with maturity, supporting the empirical evidence that short rates are more volatile than long rates. The shift factor has the highest explanatory power of all principal components for each market.

The second factor is a *twist* in the term structure. The twist shape reflects the short and long ends of the curve moving in opposite directions and gives rise to a steepening or flattening of the yield curve. The third factor is called a *butterfly*. The butterfly shape corresponds to the short and long ends moving in the opposite direction from intermediate rates.

The first three principal components of the German, Japanese, and U.S. markets are depicted in Exhibit 9. These principal components are similar in shape across all markets, but vary only in magnitude and the pivot points.

It is interesting to contrast the three factor model with the more traditional risk models given by duration or duration and convexity. A duration model is a one factor model with the single factor given by a parallel shift of the term structure. This is directly comparable to a one factor model given by a shift. But a shift is optimized to capture the maximum variance possible by a single factor and hence accounts for more risk than duration. That is, the shift factor can be viewed as a more generalized form of duration, hence it is expected to explain more local market risk than duration.

Exhibit 10 illustrates the difference in fraction of variance captured by the traditional duration and duration/convexity models along with the shift/twist/butterfly model.

The consistency of the shapes of the first three principal components along with the high fraction of variance they explain in each market support the premise that a reasonable way to build a global risk model is to use three empirical principal components as risk factors in each market. This approach has the added advantage of lowering the dimension of the global covariance matrix. This is important insofar as the data histories of some markets are not long enough to support a global matrix with 8 or 9 factors per country.

Once the factors are determined, the change in term structure over each period is approximated as closely as possible by a linear combination of the factors. The coefficients of the factors are the factor returns, and the history of these returns form the data series on which the 3×3 local market covariance matrix is based.

Local Market Risk: Credit

Unlike sovereign bonds, corporate bonds are exposed to default risk. Within our framework, this can be handled with the addition of one or more risk factors to each local market. Only corporate bonds will have a nonzero exposure to this factor.

Exhibit 9: First Three Principal Components: U.S.A., Germany, and Japan

U.S.A.

Basis Points/Year

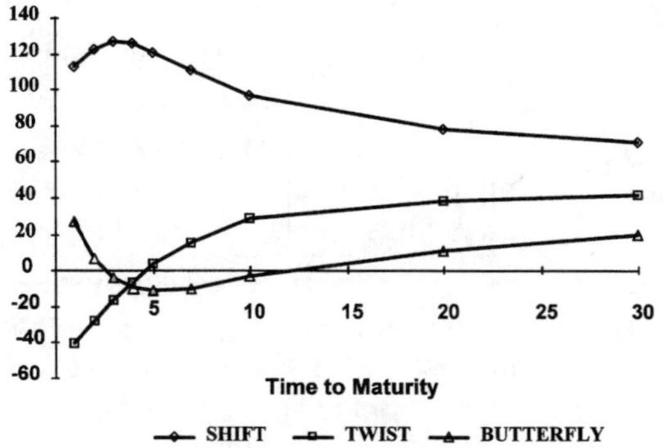

Germany

Basis Points/Year

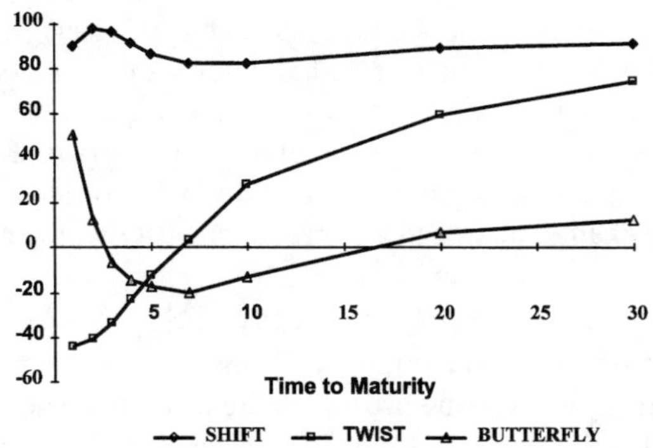

Japan

Basis Points/Year

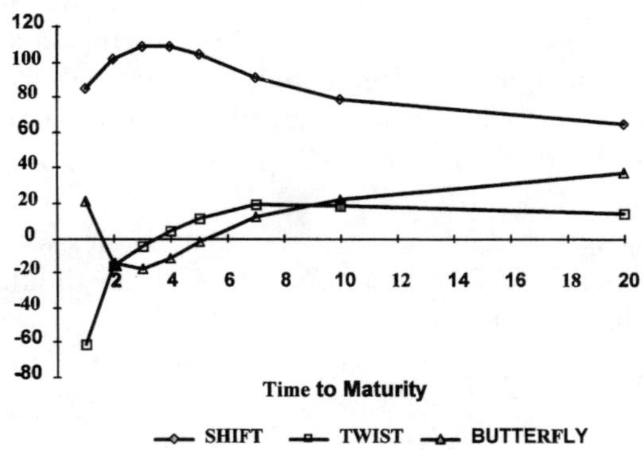

Exhibit 10: Comparison of Percentage of variance Captured by Duration, Duration/Convexity, and Shift/Twist/Butterfly

Country	STB	DC	D
Canada	95.6	88.9	76.7
France	97.1	90.1	81.4
Germany	96.0	90.9	76.7
Italy	94.1	81.7	72.7
Japan	95.4	88.2	79.9
United Kingdom	97.2	88.7	72.9
United States	98.6	94.8	87.8

A natural way to proceed within each market is to segregate the bonds into sectors based on rating, estimate a constant spread for each sector, and add the history of changes in spread to the collection of data series used to generate the covariance matrix. Unsurprisingly, this intuitive approach presents difficulties. The first is that there are many sectors in each market so the size of the matrix will be vastly increased, possibly beyond the natural bounds imposed by the length of the data history. The second issue is one of robustness. The size of a sector can be quite variable over time and at certain times, the spread may be determined by little data. This introduces excessive noise into the estimation.

An alternative is to add a single factor per market, given by the change in spread of the swap curve (approximately a double A rating curve) over the sovereign curve. The change in spread is a robust quantity which captures credit risk.

Currency Risk

In an unhedged portfolio, fluctuations in currency exchange rates are the dominant source of risk. At the same time, they are also the most challenging to model. Currency return series are highly non-stationary. In other words, it is not possible to postulate a single distribution with constant variance to which all the observations in a given time series of currency returns belong. For example, many European currencies were linked together until 1993 when internal economic pressures in many countries caused the ERM[11] crisis. During this period, currencies became unlinked and a period of high volatility followed. Another example is the dramatic fall of the Mexican peso in December 1994 when it lost over 50% of its value with respect to the U.S. dollar. This led to a period of high volatility for the peso-dollar exchange rate.

The discussion above suggests three principles which may be useful in forecasting currency risk. The first is that recent data should be weighted much more heavily than older data. The second is an inertia type principle that exchange rates which are volatile tend to stay volatile while exchange rates that

[11] ERM stands for European Rate Mechanism.

are stable tend to stay stable. Finally, the model must account for external shocks. An econometric strategy to handle this type of behavior is a GARCH (Generalized Auto Regressive Conditional Heteroskedasticity) model.

A typical[12] GARCH model is specified by the following set of equations.

$$r_t = \text{realized return from time } t \text{ to } t+1 = u + \varepsilon_t \qquad (8)$$

$$\begin{aligned}
u &= \text{expected return} \\
\varepsilon_t &= \sqrt{h_t} \cdot Z_t \\
Z_t &\sim N(0,1) \\
h_t &= \text{variance forecast at time } t \text{ for period } t \text{ to } t+1 \\
&= c + ah_{t-1}(Z_{t-1}^2 - 1) + b(h_{t-1} - c) \\
&= c + a(\varepsilon_{t-1}^2 - h_{t-1}) + b(h_{t-1} - c)
\end{aligned}$$

As can be seen in equation (8), the parameters a, b, and c represent the shock[13] effect, the persistence,[14] and the long-term average respectively. GARCH models are especially suited to currency risk forecasts since they take shocks or regime shifts into consideration.

Exhibit 11 shows a graph of GARCH volatility forecasts along with the $/Yen exchange rate. The GARCH volatility forecast stays close to its long-term predicted average during periods of stable exchange rates. But during periods of large fluctuations in the $/Yen exchange rates, the model quickly adapts as is evident from the increased volatility.

Integrating the Model

As explained at the beginning of this section, the risk model takes the form of a covariance matrix of factor returns. The discussion above describes local market factors, namely term structure and credit risk, and currency factors that facilitate the analysis of an international bond portfolio from the perspective of a single numeraire or base currency.

The two types of factor returns have rather different statistical properties. While the currency returns are highly non-stationary, empirical studies carried out at BARRA show that the local market returns tend to be roughly normal. As a consequence, it is plausible to estimate the local market block using a maximum likelihood estimate based on a normal distribution. As described in the section above, GARCH models are used to estimate the currency block.

---

[12] The formula here is a GARCH (1,1) model. There are many types of GARCH models, a general reference is Tim Bollerslev, "Generalized Autoregressive Conditional Heteroskedasticity," *Journal of Econometrics*, 31 (1986), pp. 307-327.

[13] The shock is determined by the impact of a two sigma event on a GARCH model at its long term average.

[14] The persistence determines the number of periods it takes to get halfway back to the log term average.

Exhibit 11: GARCH Model Volatility, U.S.$/Yen Exchange Rate, 1/94-6/96

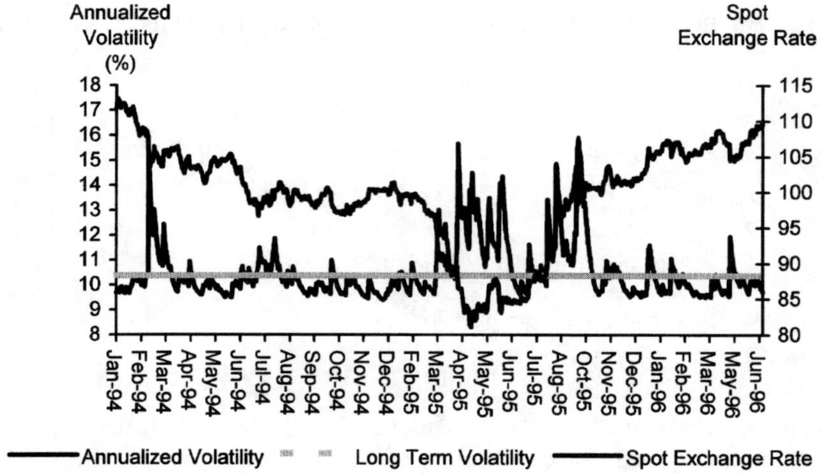

Finally, historical estimates are used to estimate covariances between local market factors and currency factors.

The final covariance matrix supports risk analysis. Additionally, it can provide return forecasts for countries outside the model by making use of correlations between markets.

Factor Exposures

To complete the analysis of equation (6), it remains to explain how to compute exposures. The *exposure* or *sensitivity* of portfolio return to a risk factor is simply the change in portfolio return with respect to a small, or infinitesimal change in the factor return.

Consider first the case of a single bond. Its exposure to a currency risk factor is 1 or 0 depending on whether or not the bond is denominated in the currency associated to the factor. Similarly, the bond's exposure to a local market factor will be 0 if the bond does not belong the local market. For a bond's exposure to the local factors in its own market, simple formulas can be used to compute the exposure. For example, the exposure of a straight German bond to the German shift is given by

$$x = \frac{1}{P}\frac{\Delta P}{\Delta shift} = \frac{1}{P}\sum_{j} cf_j T_j e^{-s_j T_j} \cdot shift_j$$

x = exposure of German bond to German shift

P = price of German bond

cf_j = j-th cash flow
T_j = time to maturity of j-th cash of flow
s_j = spot rate at time to maturity T_j
$shift_j$ = weight of shift factor at time to maturity T

Note that if the shift were parallel, the shift weights ($shift_j$) would all be 1. In this case, the shift exposure is simply the duration.

Once the bond exposures are known, portfolio exposures are simply weighted averages of bond exposures. To be precise, the exposure of a portfolio to a factor is given by

$$x(P) = h \cdot X = \sum_i h_i x(B_i)$$

$x(P)$ = portfolio exposure
B_i = i-th bond
h_i = portfolio market weight of B_i
$x(B_i)$ = exposure of i-th bond
h = vector of portfolio holdings
X = matrix of bond exposures

With this calculation complete, it is possible to derive portfolio risk estimates using equation (6).

The factor exposure as explained above measures the sensitivity of a bond to the underlying factor. For example, a shift exposure will measure the sensitivity of the bond to a shift event. That is, the shift exposure would be the return on the bond if the underlying term structure were to move by the shift movement in that market. This approach allows a manager to compare various bonds in the portfolio based on their sensitivities and target their portfolio exposure profile according to their risk/return expectations. This is a similar, yet richer, approach to adjusting the duration of the portfolio to a certain target. It encompasses the major factors that contribute to the variability of portfolio returns. Portfolios that are more highly exposed to these factors than the benchmark, even if duration-matched, can exhibit substantially different returns from the benchmark.

SUMMARY

This chapter has presented a framework for constructing valuation models for international fixed income securities. The valuation approach presented is based on the estimation of interest rates (or term structures) and spreads in each market. Interest rates are the primary determinant in computing the value of a security. The valuation model is further refined by taking into account the market specific factors that distinguish assets from one another.

A multi-factor risk model is developed that quantifies various sources of risk. It takes into account factors, namely, interest rates, currencies and spreads, that contribute to risk in a multi-currency fixed income portfolio. A covariance matrix that embodies the volatilities and correlations of the various factors is constructed using observed returns to these factors. Portfolio risk is calculated by measuring the exposure of each of the asset in the portfolio to these risk factors and mapping the factor exposures into the covariance matrix.

These factors provide more explanatory power than a simple duration based model or a duration and convexity based model. These factors provide further intuition into interest rate risk due to non-parallel term structure movements, such as steepening and flattening or reshaping. Particular emphasis is placed on outlining a currency model since currency risk is the major source of risk in an international bond portfolio.

This approach enables portfolio managers to formulate their strategies by separating out the local market or bond decisions from currency decisions. At the same time it also enables calculation of aggregate portfolio statistics like value-at-risk and identifying, monitoring, and controlling the bets in a portfolio.

Chapter 7

The Real Yield Approach to Global Investing

Steven I. Dym
Steven I. Dym & Associates

INTRODUCTION

Among the many approaches to global fixed income investment management, arguably the most theoretically justifiable is the search for real yield advantage. The real yield approach is applicable over an entire interest rate cycle, and is relevant to countries large and small. Buying and selling bonds in anticipation of changes either in foreign bond prices or exchange rates (i.e., market timing) is by nature a volatile procedure, as it calls for liquidating the investment when the anticipated change is realized — should it be realized at all — and instituting a new position in anticipation of the next change. By contrast, the real yield approach does not require changes in economic variables in order to be operative. Much like corporate bond investors, who search for borrowers with the ability to service their promised cash flows for long periods of time, international investors searching for real yield advantage largely follow buy-and-hold strategy, preferring countries able to maintain their promised bond coupon payments. The result is improved total return performance along with relatively stable country allocations over time.

THEORETICAL BACKGROUND

Components of Rate of Return

For simplicity, assume the investor has a horizon of one year, bonds pay annual coupons, and the investment takes place on coupon payment dates so that there is no accrued interest. We use the following notation:

P = price of bond on purchase date

e = exchange rate, in units of foreign currency per U.S. dollar, on purchase date

C = bond coupon

P^* = expected price of bond on horizon date

e^* = expected exchange rate on horizon date
y = yield to maturity of bond
Dur = duration of bond
ROR = expected rate of return
Δ = change

In the presence of possible foreign exchange rate fluctuations, the rate of return for a one year horizon is calculated as:

$$P/e = \frac{(C + P^*)/e^*}{1 + \text{ROR}} \tag{1}$$

so that

$$\text{ROR} = C/P + (P^* - P)/P - (e^* - e)/e \tag{2}$$

In words, the foreign investment's expected rate of return has three components: (1) current yield, (2) capital gain or loss, and (3) currency depreciation or appreciation. Again, for simplicity assume the bond is trading at par, so that we can replace the bond's current yield with its yield to maturity. Then, using the familiar relationship between yield and price changes via duration, equation (2) can be rewritten as:

$$\text{ROR} = y - \text{Dur} \cdot \Delta y - \Delta e/e \tag{3}$$

The contrast between possible investment styles is seen clearly here. Market timers look to Δy and Δe as their primary sources of return. Real yield investors look to y as the primary source of income. Of course, countries offering high yields are often those with the weakest currencies, so that y and Δe are intimately related. Hence, the real yield investor must be mindful of the currency factor even if he is not looking to currency movements as a direct source of earnings. The next section deals with this relationship.

Purchasing Power Parity

In a perfect world, with trade among countries free, tradable goods and services which are equivalent except for their country of origin should command the same prices regardless of where they are purchased, net of currency exchange rates. This is termed the *law of one price*. When applied to the aggregate of output of goods and services between a pair of countries, it is called *purchasing power parity*. This notion of purchasing power parity (PPP), to the extent it holds, has major implications for country asset allocation.

In reality trade is often not free, transportation costs are significant, goods differ by point of manufacture, and most services are not easily, if at all, tradable. So purchasing power parity may be a poor description of reality. However, if these other determinants are stable, PPP is relevant as a dynamic equilibrium measure, providing a "base case" against which to compare currency movements. That is, once exchange rates have equilibrated to reflect changing tastes, business cycle developments, and other "real" economic variables (as well as interest rate differentials, to be discussed below), the *path* of currency movements may well be described by PPP. This is the notion of *relative PPP* which can be written as:

$$\Delta e/e = \pi_a - \pi_b \tag{4}$$

where π_a and π_b are the inflation rates of country *a* and *b*, respectively, and $\Delta e/e$ is the path of the exchange rate in units of currency *a* for currency *b*. Since our analysis takes the perspective of a U.S. investor, we can write:

$$\Delta e/e = \pi_f - \pi_{us} \tag{5}$$

where *f* and *us* refer to the inflation rates of the foreign country and the United States, respectively. The rate of a currency's depreciation (or appreciation, if Δe is negative) equals the excess of the country's inflation rate relative to that of the United States.

Suppose interest rates in the foreign country rise to reflect, say, a stronger level of economic activity, apart from any inflation premium. All else the same, demand for the country's financial assets will likely rise, putting upward pressure on the currency. Once the exchange rate has adjusted to its higher level to reflect this "real" phenomenon its succeeding path will follow that described by relative PPP.

What does this mean for global investment management? Return to the general rate of return formula in equation (3). Assume the investor is targeting yield, so that his expectations are neutral with respect to a yield change (i.e., $\Delta y = 0$). Recognizing that the foreign country's nominal yield equals a real rate, *r*, plus an expected inflation premium, we have:

$$y = r_f + \pi_f \tag{6}$$

Substituting equation (6) plus the PPP result given by equation (5) into equation (3) produces:

$$\text{ROR} = r_f + \pi_{us} \tag{7}$$

In other words, the return to a U.S. investor from a foreign currency denominated bond equals the real rate in that foreign country plus the U.S. inflation rate. From the perspective of the U.S. investor, PPP has added the U.S. inflation premium to the real yield of foreign countries. Note that these relationships are now forward looking; that is, we are dealing with *expected* rate of return.

Since the π_{us} term is common to all foreign bonds, we conclude the following: an investor targeting yields from foreign bonds, and believing that purchasing power parity governs the long-term relationship among currencies, should seek to invest in assets denominated in the currencies of countries paying the highest real rates of interest. While this rule seems straightforward enough, it is easier said than done. The next subsection explains why.

Exhibit 1: Reasons For High Real Yields

Positive	Negative
Expansion stage of business cycle	Protecting currency to avoid imminent devaluation
Developing country borrowing for future growth	High debt/GDP ratio presenting sovereign risk

Practical Investment Considerations

We have shown that the return to an investor holding a foreign currency denominated bond — at least in the base case where PPP holds — depends on the real interest rate paid by the country. All else the same, therefore, the investor should choose foreign bonds with the highest real yields. But "all else" is not always the same. The real yield investor is interested in countries who are paying a high yield on their borrowings, but only those who can afford to continue doing so. If yields are high because of a crisis situation, then the benefits of the real yield advantage will be quickly wiped out by falling bond prices and/or a drop in the currency in excess of the amount predicted by PPP.

A comparison to corporate bonds is appropriate. Clearly, a firm will be in a position to service high yielding debt if its investment opportunities, which the bond issuance funded, are earning a high rate of return. But if the firm's prospects have dimmed, forcing the market to impose a high risk premium on the bonds, its ability to continue paying is suspect. The corporate bond investor prefers the former firm (paying a high real yield because of high returning investments) to the latter firm (forced by the market to pay a high yield due to its precarious financial situation), the higher stated yield of the latter notwithstanding. In short, a high yield payer is attractive if the reason for the high yield is positive, not negative. Indeed, ferreting out the first group of high yield corporate borrowers from the second is precisely what corporate bond credit analysts are paid to do.

The real yield driven international investor has a job similar to that of the corporate bond analyst, but applied to countries rather than corporations. Only those countries whose high yields reflect strength, not weakness, belong in the portfolio. Exhibit 1 summarizes positive and negative sources of high yields paid by countries.

A foreign government bond offering a high real interest rate due to one of the positive reasons in Exhibit 1 is the perfect candidate for inclusion in a global portfolio. For in that case the investor can be reasonably sure that the yield advantage will not be consumed by a fall in the currency and/or the price of the bond. Real interest rates are typically high in a country experiencing a business cycle expansion since firms, finding profitable investment opportunities, enter the capital markets and bid up rates. Similarly, a country in the early stage of economic development, when returns to investment tend to be strong, will attract outside capital, being able to pay high rates as it grows. By contrast, if a country's central bank is struggling to maintain the currency's value and raises interest rates in defense, chances are a devaluation is imminent. A high debt/GDP ratio, or other sovereign risk source, as the catalyst for high real yields, is also likely a precursor to a further increase in yield, which will hurt the portfolio's return.

As if discerning between negative and positive sources of real yield advantage is not difficult enough, the investor must also be aware that the impediments to PPP discussed earlier can cause a currency's path to diverge from its PPP implied value. While this is as likely to cause an appreciation as a depreciation, the portfolio manager's job becomes more complicated, since the elementary rule — invest in the country with the greatest real yield advantage — is no longer operative. The next section proposes a relatively simple method to take advantage of high real yields, but at the same time to reduce the chances of being caught by these negative surprises.

THE ALGORITHM

Given the above discussion, what we need is an investment procedure with the following features:

1. Increases allocation to countries with high real yields, that is, those which are in excess of that available in the United States.
2. Offers diversification among countries with a yield advantage
3. Limits exposure to countries whose yields are high for negative reasons.
4. Remains relatively simple and constant over the investment period.

The first characteristic is obviously the goal of the whole approach. But, taken to an extreme, it would imply a complete allocation to one or two countries with the greatest real yield advantage. Because the investor can never be certain of the source of the real yield advantage, as explained earlier, this strategy would present significant risk to the portfolio, from both the currency aspect of total return as well as bond price risk. Instead, the investment algorithm should give some weight to countries with lower real yields than the maximum, which, while hurting yield, would provide the benefit of diversification.

Countries with extremely high real yields are often — but certainly not always — those that are forced to raise interest rates for the negative reasons cited in the previous section. Thus, the algorithm should reduce allocation to those countries, recognizing that it will unavoidably reduce allocation to those offering very high yields for positive reasons. Finally, in order to demonstrate the benefits of the real yield approach using historical data, a fixed, simple algorithm must be applied, one that does not allow for any "massaging" during the period.

The algorithms proposed are applied to the Salomon Brothers World Government Bond Index (WGBI). WGBI is a weighted total rate of return index comprising the major industrialized countries, including the United States. The index is updated monthly, reflecting changes in bond issuance and currency values of component countries, as well as admission of new countries. The first algorithm, presented in Exhibit 2, uses the WGBI as a base. According to the algorithm, a country's weight in the portfolio will be a simple integer multiple of its weight in the index, starting from zero. The multiple increases as the country's real yield advantage over the United States increases. In order to reduce risk via diversification, even if a country has a real yield *dis*advantage, but no worse than 2%, it still has a representation in the portfolio. If the weights add up to less than 100%, the difference is allocated to U.S. Treasuries. Leverage is precluded, which means that should the algorithm sum to more than 100%, each country's weight must be scaled down accordingly. Importantly, a country's weight in the portfolio begins to decline for real yields in excess of 2%. In this context, real yields are calculated as the difference between the nominal yield on a 7-year government bond (a maturity which all countries in the index issue) and the year-over-year percentage change in the local consumer price index. The portfolio is updated monthly, using end-of-month data.

Notice in Exhibit 2 that the weight distribution of this algorithm is symmetric around the maximum multiple of three. That is, as the real yield differential moves away from one percent in either direction, the weights decline at the same rate. A more defensive approach, shown in Exhibit 3, calls for a more rapid decrease in weights for countries with dramatically higher real yields than the decrease for lower yields, for fear of the negative causes of high real yields. It also contains a lower overall maximum weight. Otherwise the algorithm is the same.

Exhibit 2: Index Multiples Based on Real Yield Differential
Symmetric Posture

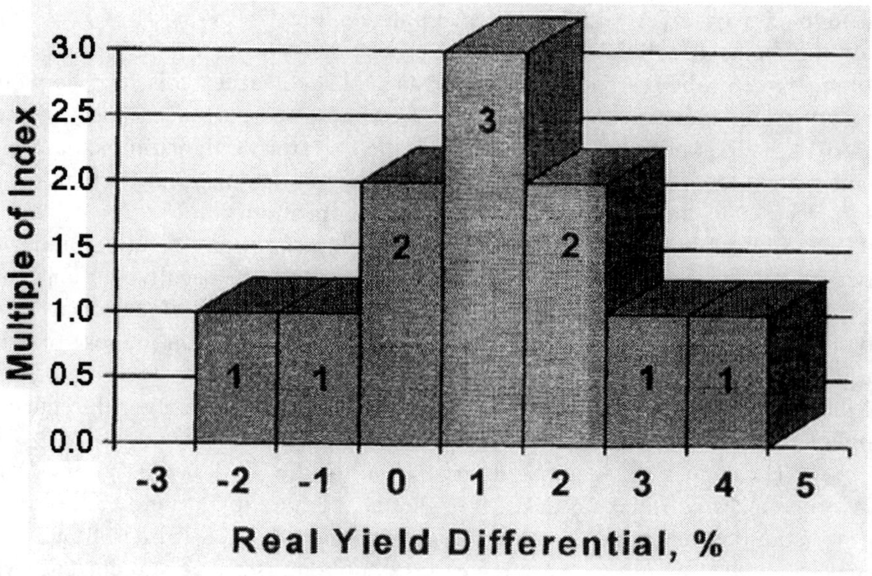

Exhibit 3: Index Multiples Based on Real Yield Differential

Defensive Posture

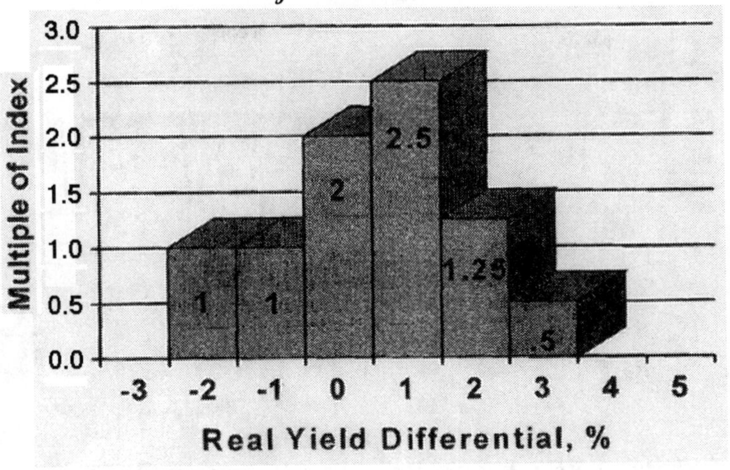

Exhibit 4: Symmetric Weights

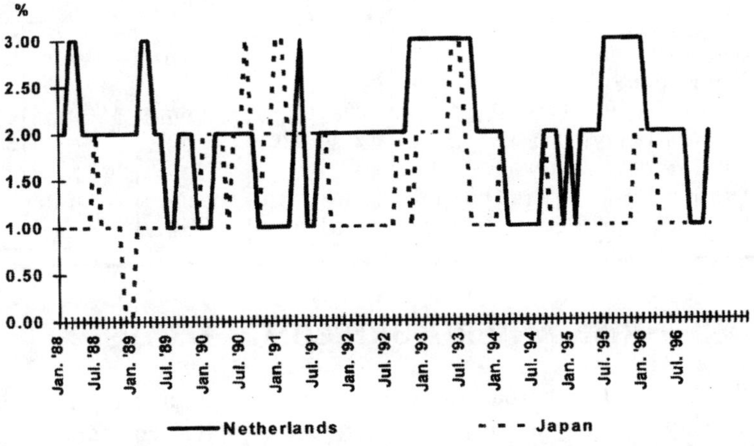

Before presenting the simulation results in the next section, it is worthwhile examining the stability of the portfolio allocation. Exhibits 4 and 5 present the multiples for both algorithms applied to Japan and the Netherlands. After the United States, Japan has the largest representation in the index. Thus, changes in its weight will cause a large degree of portfolio shifting. The Netherlands belongs to a diverse group of small countries in the WGBI. As is clear from the predominance of horizontal lines in Exhibits 4 and 5 for both countries, the algorithms produce a relatively stable allocation of weights over time. This is as it should be — the real yield approach seeks to "stay" with a country as long as it offers superior real interest rates and is deemed capable of doing so.

Exhibit 5: Defensive Weights

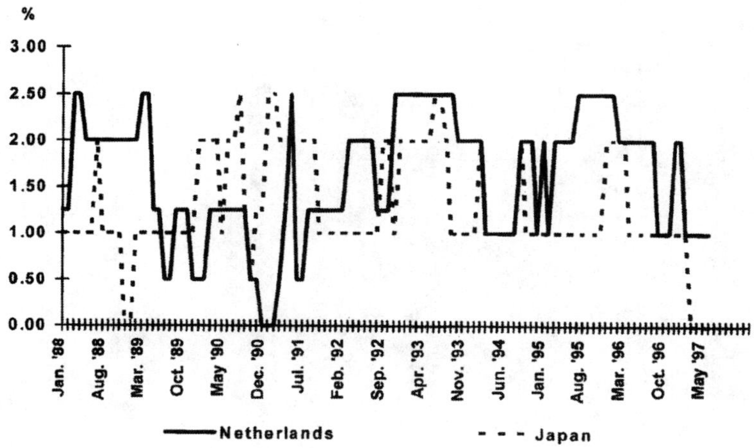

Exhibit 6: Risk and Return: Summary Measures

	U.S.	WGBI	Real Yield/ Defensive	Real Yield/ Symmetric	Non-Dollar WGBI
Monthly average returns (%, non-compounded) 1985- 1996	0.790	0.979	1.085	1.105	1.178
Monthly average returns (%, non-compounded) 1988- 1996	0.718	0.719	0.798	0.822	0.727
Volatility of returns (%) 1985- 1996	1.488	2.047	2.472	2.557	3.215
Volatility of returns (%) 1988- 1996	1.328	1.798	2.244	2.350	2.810
Average foreign exchange weighs (%) 1985-1996	0	0.545	0.749	0.818	1.000
Average foreign exchange weighs (%) 1988-1996	0	0.559	0.819	0.905	1.000

RISK AND RETURN COMPARISONS

Would the "real yield" approach have been successful in the past? Exhibit 6 presents the results of the two real yield algorithms, as well as comparative statistics for U.S. government bonds, the WGBI, and non-dollar WGBI. The last excludes the United States from the WGBI. The goal of the algorithms is to improve the returns of a global portfolio through its selection of foreign bonds, but limiting the foreign exchange risk by targeting high real interest rates relative to the United States. Two periods are examined. The first, 1985 through 1996, begins with the inception of the global indices (roughly coinciding with U.S. institutional investors entering the global fixed income markets in a meaningful way). Because the concerted efforts on the parts of central bank to bring down the U.S. dollar's value during the early part of the period caused an outsized return advantage for foreign bonds, and may bias the results in favor of the real yield approach, a second period, beginning in 1988, was examined.

Exhibit 7: Compounded Yearly Rates of Return

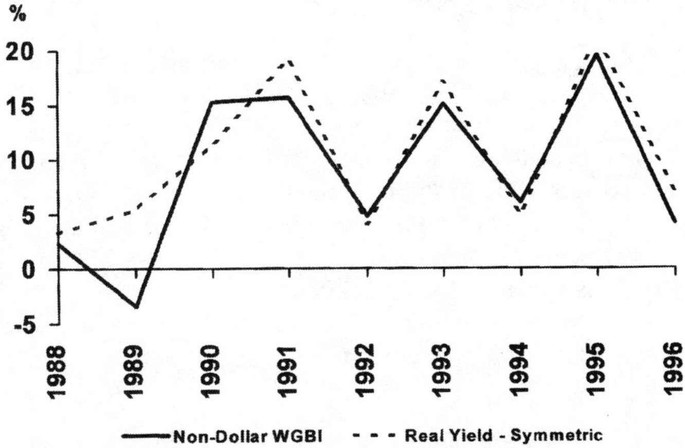

Consider first the longer period. While the non-dollar WGBI had the best performance, returns produced by the two real yield approaches provided a substantial pickup over U.S. Treasuries and over the WGBI. Indeed, the defensive and symmetric algorithms gave the investor 76% and 81%, respectively, of the excess of the non-dollar WGBI over U.S. Treasuries, but with only 57% and 62%, respectively, of the volatility, as measured by the standard deviation of return. Compared to the pickup of the non-dollar WGBI over the WGBI, the defensive and symmetric algorithms provided 53% and 63%, respectively, of the excess return, but with only 36% and 44% of the extra volatility.

These results are even more pronounced over the shorter period, where the stronger dollar in the later years hurt the performance of the non-dollar WGBI, and which excludes the 1985-1987 years of strong foreign returns. Both real yield algorithms handily beat the non-dollar WGBI, but with only 62% and 69%, respectively, of the extra volatility compared to U.S. Treasuries, and 44% and 55%, respectively, of the extra volatility compared to the WGBI. In short, the simple real yield based algorithms achieve the majority of the excess return provided by the foreign currency denominated bonds, but with significantly less volatility. What is perhaps more surprising is that this substantial improvement in risk-return tradeoff is reached with considerably less foreign exchange exposure, as seen in the last two lines of the exhibit.

These subdued volatilities, along with higher average returns, are illustrated in Exhibits 7 and 8, which track compounded rates of return by year. The results are only partly due to the substantially reduced foreign exchange weighting in the portfolios compared to the non-dollar WGBI, as the added foreign exchange weightings compared to the United States and WGBI *exceed* the volatility pickups. They are also due to higher weightings allocated to countries with high real interest rates (and backing off when their rates jump *too* high), which will typically have stronger currencies, as well as the mitigating effect on volatility of higher yields. In short, the real yield approach was able to pick the "right" periods to be outside the U.S. bond market.

THE NEXT LEVEL

The algorithms proposed above are elementary, as they revolve around one variable — the excess real yield of the foreign country relative to that of the United States. A host of enhancements to this basic approach are possible. One involves hedging the foreign currency exposure using forward contracts.

It is well known that "covered interest rate arbitrage" produces the following relationship between the spread of the forward exchange rate (fwd) and the spot rate, and relative interest rate differentials.

$$\frac{\text{fwd} - e}{e} = i_f - i_{us} \tag{8}$$

where i_f and i_{us} are the foreign and U.S. one year nominal interest rates, respectively. Compare equation (8) with equation (5), bearing in mind that, as in equation (6), nominal interest rates equal real rates plus an expected inflation premium. The *expected future* exchange rate will exceed the *forward* rate if the foreign real one year interest rate is above that of the United States. This immediately suggests a hedging strategy: sell the currency forward if the foreign country presents a real interest rate disadvantage. Note that this is a natural extension of the above algorithms, which decrease country exposure as the real yield advantage declines. Whether this enhancement actually improves returns must await empirical testing. It should be clear from the earlier results, however, that even a simple strategy capitalizing on real yielld differentials improves portfolio performance.

Exhibit 8: Compounded Yearly Rates of Return

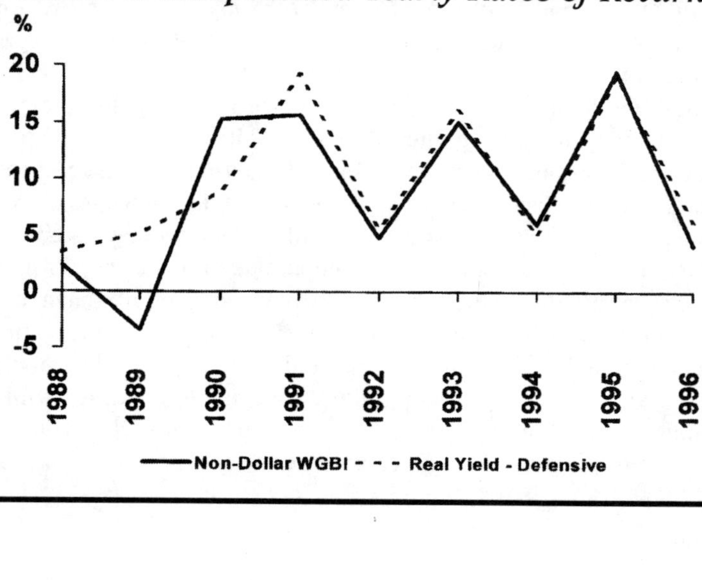

Chapter 8

Improved Measurement of Duration Contributions of Foreign Bonds in Domestic Portfolios

Ram Willner, Ph.D.
International Market Strategist and Risk Control Manager
Pacific Investment Management Company

INTRODUCTION

Managers of domestic bond portfolios are facing increasing opportunities for investments in non-benchmark foreign securities. This brings into question the tool of *domestic* duration as the primary instrument of portfolio management. It was Macaulay who first pointed out that matching the duration of one portfolio to another would, for small yield changes, ensure that the relative values of the portfolios would not change much. His idea has been applied as a general tool for managing any portfolio against a benchmark portfolio. However, implicit in that application is that both portfolios be exposed to the same source of interest rate risk. This is not true in the case of foreign versus domestic bonds. Moreover, as portfolio management becomes increasingly sophisticated, we recognize that Macaulay's concept of duration is only sufficient at an aggregate level. We can gain precision by considering duration or sensitivity of portfolios to changes in rates along the whole yield curve rather than just to the aggregate portfolio yield. Consequently, today's domestically benchmarked bond portfolio manager who is tempted to include attractive non-benchmark foreign bonds must face the somewhat inscrutable sensitivity of those bonds to the entire domestic yield curve.

In other research, Lee Thomas and I discuss the calculation of a portfolio's duration when bonds of a foreign nation are included in a domestic portfolio.[1] To the domestic portfolio manager, duration measures the sensitivity of the portfolio to domestic interest rate changes. For a conventional government bond,

[1] L.R. Thomas and R. Willner, "Measuring the Duration of an Internationally Diversified Portfolio," *Journal of Portfolio Management* (Fall 1997).

its duration can be calculated directly by assuming a yield change for the relevant local yield. The change in yield for a bond issued by another government may or may not have any effect on the original government bond and vice versa. In fact, without a theory that links the two economies, there is no reason to presuppose any coincident effect at all. Lee Thomas and I show that there generally is an empirical linkage and a relationship between yield changes in one country and another. However, these changes certainly are not one-to-one as is often assumed, and if so assumed can cause significant miscalculation of the portfolio's duration with respect to domestic interest rates. Consequently the exposures and risk experienced by the portfolio manager can be significantly different than what was anticipated. We propose a methodology for calculating the contribution to the domestic duration of the portfolio by the foreign bonds, as well as providing some guidelines and estimations for the degree of error in that methodology. Our recommendation is that the inclusion of foreign bonds in a domestically benchmarked portfolio be in reverse proportion to the anticipated degree of error.

Now let's turn to the other issue of the need for more precision in duration estimates altogether. In previously published research, I describe how conventional duration alone cannot explain the complete sensitivity of a portfolio to changes in the entire yield curve.[2] A functional representation of the yield curve based on three parameters — level, slope, and curvature — is employed. The conventional duration can be extended to duration with respect to each of the three parameters. This extension allows for a much more comprehensive description of the relationship between yield curve changes and changes in portfolio value. Conventional duration essentially relates only to changes in yield curve level. Other researchers have confirmed the significance of these first three moments or principal components of the yield curve in the determination of changes in portfolio value due to yield curve changes.[3]

In this chapter, we marry the concept of adjusting the duration contribution of a foreign bond to a domestic portfolio to the notion that a level, slope, and curvature representation of the yield curve is a more accurate way to measure the exposure of a portfolio to yield curve changes. We investigate the use of level, slope, and curvature duration contributions of foreign bonds within a domestic portfolio. The approach is a fairly straightforward extension of the basis analysis performed in my previous research.[4] The next section presents a review of that analysis and of the level, slope, and curvature duration model I developed in order to familiarize the reader with the two components of the married system pre-

[2] R. Willner, "A New Tool for Portfolio Managers: Level, Slope, and Curvature Durations," *Journal of Fixed Income* (June 1996), pp.48-59.

[3] See F.J. Jones, "Yield Curve Strategies," *Journal of Fixed Income* (September 1991), pp. 43-51; W.T. Golub and L.M. Tilman, "Measuring Yield Curve Risk Using Principal Components Analysis, Value at Risk, and Key Rate Durations," *Journal of Portfolio Management* (Summer 1997), pp. 72-84; and, R. Litterman and J. Scheinkman, "Common Factors Affecting Bond Returns," *Journal of Fixed Income* (June 1991), pp. 54-61.

[4] Thomas and Willner, "Measuring the Duration of an Internationally Diversified Portfolio."

sented in this chapter. The third section presents the methodology for combining the two. The fourth section presents the results of calculating the foreign adjusted level, slope, and curvature durations for 15 countries. The concluding section reviews the results of the analysis and provides some guidelines and cautions for the practical application of the methodology.

THE FOREIGN DURATION BASIS APPROACH

The problem of including foreign bonds in a domestic portfolio is essentially a basis problem with respect to duration due to the imperfect correspondence of domestic and foreign interest rate changes. Knowing the duration of the foreign bond and knowing the change in domestic interest rates is not sufficient to know the new value of the bond. We will focus the analysis on investigating this relationship. Assuming that duration alone explains capital appreciation or depreciation of a bond, that change in value can be written:

$$\text{Change in value} = \text{Duration} \times \text{Change in yield} \qquad (1)$$

The "Change in yield" refers to a change in yield due to a change in *domestic* interest rates. If the bond in question is a foreign bond, then the change in value can be written:

$$\text{Change in value} = \text{Duration} \times \text{Change in foreign yield}$$

But if we are interested in the change in foreign bond value given a change in *domestic* yield, we must explicitly recognize an interrelationship between domestic yield changes and foreign yield changes. This results in the relationship:

$$\text{Change in value} = \text{Duration} \times (\text{Change in foreign yield given a change in domestic yield} + \text{Other unrelated changes in foreign yield}) \qquad (2)$$

Note that we must include other unrelated (to domestic interest rate changes) but coincident effects on the foreign yield since these will also affect the value of the foreign bond — and since the portfolio manager will be subject to them. Such unrelated effects need not be unexplainable "noise" but can be due to persistent factors which are measurable but are not related to domestic interest rates. Since such factors can introduce variability into the portfolio, the portfolio manager must consider their impact. We shall discuss these factors later in this chapter.

The Thomas-Willner methodology considers the "Change in foreign yield given a change in domestic yield" in equation (2) as a basis problem in which one tries to calculate the optimal hedge ratio minimizing the variance between changes in foreign yields and domestic yields. This hedge ratio adjusts the duration of a foreign bond for its related but imperfect sensitivity to domestic interest rates. The adjustment is given by a beta coefficient which can be calculated through a regression of foreign yield changes on domestic yield changes. We also use the regression to get a sense of the impact of the other factors which might cause coincident but unrelated changes in bond value. We review this approach below.

We formulated the foreign to domestic bond relationship [applying equation (1)] as the following regression relationship:

$$d\Delta y_{\text{foreign}} = \alpha + \beta d\Delta y_{\text{domestic}}$$

where

d = duration
y = yield

Or since the durations are essentially the same for both foreign and domestic bonds, they are dropped from the equation giving:

$$\Delta y_{\text{foreign}} = \alpha + \beta\Delta y_{\text{domestic}} \tag{3}$$

The β is termed a "country beta." Duration attributed to a foreign bond in the domestic portfolio is calculated as $\beta \times d$. This means that the measured relationship between changes in domestic and foreign interest rates are incorporated into the assessment of a foreign bond's sensitivity to domestic interest rates.

Further, β can be decomposed into:

$$\beta = \text{correlation }(\Delta y_{\text{foreign}}, \Delta y_{\text{domestic}}) \times \sigma_{\text{foreign}} / \sigma_{\text{domestic}}$$

In general, the higher is the correlation component of beta, the greater the amount of the foreign bond which can be included in the domestic portfolio with the expectation that the beta adjusted duration will accurately represent the duration contribution of the foreign bond. However as stated previously, the alpha in the regression also plays a role in the accuracy of the estimated beta adjusted duration contribution. The alpha term represents the average contribution of all factors unrelated to domestic interest rates, but still affecting the change in foreign bond value. The smaller is this value relative to the standard variation (deviation), the better will be the accuracy of the beta adjusted duration estimate.[5] Exhibit 1 gives such betas measured over the period July 1992 to July 1997.

---

[5] R^2 measures a similar phenomenon: the degree of variation explained by the regression. The distinction here is that the measure of interest is not the degree of variation but its economic significance. For instance, if only 50% of the variation was explained, but overall that variation was quite small, that may be preferable to explaining 90% of a very large variation

Exhibit 1: Country Betas

Country	β	(t-stats)	R^2
Australia	1.04	(8.68)	0.49
Austria	0.23	(3.61)	0.13
Belgium	0.29	(3.00)	0.09
Canada	0.89	(8.67)	0.49
Denmark	0.48	(3.68)	0.14
France	0.51	(4.95)	0.23
Germany	0.42	(5.32)	0.26
Holland	0.45	(5.51)	0.27
Ireland	0.55	(4.65)	0.21
Italy	0.43	(2.53)	0.06
Japan	0.30	(2.75)	0.08
Spain	0.47	(2.82)	0.08
Sweden	0.49	(2.95)	0.09
Switzerland	0.25	(2.59)	0.07
UK	0.51	(4.30)	0.18

The Level, Slope & Curvature Model

The level, slope, and curvature (LS&C) duration model I developed represents the change in bond value as dependent on the sum of changes of each one of the yield curve parameters times the sensitivity of the bond to changes in the particular parameter.[6] The Nelson and Siegel mathematical function for representing the yield curve is employed.[7] Their function, dependent on three parameters which represent the level, slope, and curvature of virtually any yield curve, can be used to estimate every discount rate along the yield curve. Since the value of a bond is given as a sum of discounted cash flows, knowing the three parameters for the function, means knowing the discount rate estimates at every maturity along the yield curve, and thus the bond's value. A change in any parameter induces a change in discount rates and therefore a change in the bond's value. The sensitivity of the bond's value to a change in any parameter is its duration with respect to that parameter. In theory, the three parameters comprehensively describe the yield curve so that the complete sensitivity of the bond to the yield curve can be known by knowing the function and the changes in the parameters. In practice the description is generally not completely comprehensive but very close, so that the amount of noise introduced is small.

The LS&C model's extension to the simple formulation of change in a bond's value given by equation (1) is:

[6] Willner, "A New Tool for Portfolio Managers: Level, Slope, and Curvature Durations."

[7] C. Nelson and A. Siegel, "Parsimonious Modeling of Yield Curves," *Journal of Business* (1987).

Exhibit 2: An Example of LS&C Bond Change Valuation*

	Level	Slope	Curvature	Total
A. Duration	7.0	1.6	1.0	—
B. Start month value	5.5	2.5	0.5	—
C. End month value	5.3	2.0	0.5	—
D. Parameter Change (Line C – Line B)	–0.2	0.5	0.0	—
E. Value Change (Line A × – Line D)	1.4	–0.8	0.0	0.6

* Based on equation (4).

$$\text{Change in value} = d_L\,\Delta L + d_S\,\Delta S + d_C\,\Delta C \tag{4}$$

where d_X refers to the bond's duration with respect to parameter X and ΔX refers to the change in parameter X. If we assume that our portfolio starts at an initial value of 100, then "Change in value" gives the percent return of the portfolio.

Consider the following application of equation (4). Suppose that a French bond has level, slope, and curvature durations of 7.0, 1.6, and 1.0, respectively. Now suppose that the French yield curve was fit at the beginning of the month with best fit values for the level, slope, and curvature parameters of 5.5, 2.5, and 0.5, respectively, and at the end of the month the best fit parameters were 5.3, 2.0, and 0.5, respectively. Then the corresponding changes in level, slope, and curvature are –0.2, 0.5, and 0.0, respectively. This means that the level of the yield curve went down, the slope of the yield curve diminished (i.e., the short end of the yield curve came up somewhat) and the curvature remained unchanged. Given the assumed durations, the net effect was a gain in value of 0.6% (= 1.4 – 0.8 + 0.0). Exhibit 2 presents this example.

COMBINING THE LEVEL, SLOPE, AND CURVATURE MODEL AND THE FOREIGN DURATION BASIS APPROACH

Equation (4) gives us the starting point to extend the Thomas-Willner methodology to the LS&C model representation of the yield curve and its characterization of three durations. The problem is essentially the same: find the hedge ratio for each of the three durations (jointly) which provide the historically minimizing variance between the return of the foreign bond and the hedged (adjusted) exposure to the level, slope, and curvature durations of the domestic bond. This is a problem which is solved by conventional multiple regression[8] — an extension of the simple regression case previously presented. There is one caveat. Notice that in equation (4),

[8] A sketch of the proof that this is a multiple regression problem is to formulate the problem as: Minimize Variance $(R - H_L\, d_L\, \Delta L - H_S\, d_S\, \Delta S - H_C\, d_C\, \Delta C)$ where each term is a time series vector, yielding $\{H^*_L, H^*_S, H^*_C\}$. The problem is solved using matrix algebra and differential calculus, and thereby also considers the cross correlations between the durations. The solution is $\{H^*_L, H^*_S, H^*_C\} = \{\beta_L', \beta_S', \beta_C''\}$.

unlike in the conventional duration case, the duration itself does not drop out. We estimate the beta coefficients, three in this case, by performing the following time series regression which includes the duration factor, monthly over five years:

$$R_{\text{foreign}} = \alpha + \beta_L' d_L \Delta L + \beta_S' d_S \Delta S + \beta_C' d_C \Delta C \tag{5}$$

where R_{foreign} is the return of the foreign bond. Once we have estimated $\{\beta_L', \beta_S', \beta_C'\}$ we might notice that over the time period estimated, the duration values $\{d_L, d_S, d_C\}$are virtually constant. We will consider them as constant at their average value over the time period we studied. We can then define the three values $\{\beta_L, \beta_S, \beta_C\}$ as $\beta_L', \beta_S', \beta_C'$ divided by the average values of d_L, d_S, d_C, respectively. The resulting values $\{\beta_L, \beta_S, \beta_C\}$ can then be compared to the beta parameter described and calculated by Lee Thomas and me. We shall term the values $\{\beta_L, \beta_S, \beta_C\}$ "country level, slope, and curvature betas."

Exhibit 3 presents the results of regressions for the period July 1992 to July 1997 for 15 countries versus the United States (as well as including the conventional duration country betas (Exhibit 1) for comparison). The exhibit presents (1) the beta coefficients for level, slope, and curvature durations (equation (5)), (2) the adjusted R^2 for the regression, and (3) the beta associated with a regression of conventional duration (equation (3)) and its R^2. To use the exhibit in practice we would *multiply the foreign measured duration(s) by the corresponding beta coefficient* in the exhibit.

For example, suppose a Canadian bond has foreign (i.e., local) level, slope, and curvature durations of 7.34, 2.13, and 1.87, respectively. If that bond was to be included in a U.S. domestic portfolio we would assign it — multiplying by the corresponding beta — domestic (U.S.) level, slope, and curvature durations of 6.98, 2.07, and 1.76, respectively. According to the Exhibit 3, if the bond had a *conventional* foreign duration of 7.20, we would assign it a domestic duration of 6.41. Consider the performance of these approximate duration measures over July 1997. During this month there was a rally in the Canadian bond market. The yield on this bond dropped by 55 basis points which corresponded to a gain in value of about \$4.00 per \$100 bond (ignoring any currency effects). The yield on a U.S. bond of equivalent duration dropped by 50 basis points, suggesting an increase in value for the Canadian bond of \$3.20 (= 0.5 × 0.89 × 7.2). Using the LS&C model, for the month of July 1997, we would have measured a change in level, slope, and curvature of –0.43, 0.29, and –0.61, respectively. Multiplying those changes in U.S. yield curve parameters by the *adjusted* level, slope, and curvature durations and summing — that is, equation (5) — we get an anticipated change of \$3.50 (= 0.43 × 6.98 - 0.29 × 2.07 + 0.61 × 1.76), which is closer to the actual value of \$4.00. Exhibit 4 summarizes this situation.

We see in Exhibit 3 that for most countries the adjusted R^2 for the LS&C durations regression is greater than that for conventional duration. We also notice that for most countries the beta coefficient for level duration is closer to one than the corresponding beta coefficient for conventional duration. Note that a beta of 1.0 means that the durational effect of a foreign bond is equivalent to that of a domestic bond.

Exhibit 3: Duration Betas (July 1992 - July 1997)

Country	β_L (t-stat)	β_S	β_C	R^2	β	R^2
Australia	1.08	1.14	1.20	0.47	1.04	0.49
	(5.97)	(3.00)	(5.77)		(8.68)	
Austria	0.35	0.54	0.07	0.16	0.23	0.13
	(3.87)	(2.90)	(0.71)		(3.61)	
Belgium	0.48	0.82	0.04	0.13	0.29	0.09
	(3.58)	(2.91)	(0.24)		(3.00)	
Canada	0.95	0.97	0.94	0.47	0.89	0.49
	(6.30)	(3.07)	(5.44)		(8.67)	
Denmark	0.74	1.04	0.18	0.16	0.48	0.14
	(3.99)	(2.65)	(0.83)		(3.68)	
France	0.73	0.99	0.24	0.26	0.51	0.23
	(5.13)	(3.32)	(1.48)		(4.95)	
Germany	0.64	1.04	0.11	0.35	0.42	0.26
	(6.17)	(4.81)	(0.93)		(5.32)	
Holland	0.62	0.93	0.19	0.32	0.45	0.27
	(5.74)	(4.09)	(1.56)		(5.51)	
Ireland	0.72	0.84	0.40	0.20	0.55	0.21
	(4.18)	(2.33)	(2.02)		(4.65)	
Italy	0.83	0.74	0.16	0.07	0.43	0.06
	(2.92)	(1.24)	(0.48)		(2.53)	
Japan	0.22	0.03	0.36	0.07	0.30	0.08
	(1.66)	(0.12)	(2.38)		(2.75)	
Spain	0.79	0.70	0.26	0.08	0.47	0.08
	(2.99)	(1.26)	(0.86)		(2.82)	
Sweden	0.91	0.81	0.12	0.12	0.49	0.09
	(3.64)	(1.54)	(0.43)		(2.95)	
Switzerland	0.31	0.14	0.17	0.06	0.25	0.07
	(2.51)	(0.54)	(1.19)		(2.59)	
UK	0.77	1.00	0.24	0.20	0.51	0.18
	(4.49)	(2.77)	(1.23)		(4.30)	

Exhibit 4: Predicted Performance from Linking U.S. to Canadian Yield Curve Changes by Beta Adjusting Duration

	Actual	Expected from Adjusted Conventional Duration	Expected from Adjusted LS&C Durations
Canada	$0.40	—	—
U.S.	—	$0.32	$0.35

UNDERSTANDING THE SIGNIFICANCE OF THE LS&C DURATION BETA: EXAMINING SPECIFIC COUNTRIES

By examining the results presented in Exhibit 3, we can get a sense of the extra information provided by the disaggregation of duration into the components described by the LS&C model. We will examine the results presented with respect to explanatory power and statistical validity so that we can be more confident of our conclusions regarding the relationship between interest rates in different countries.

R^2 and *t*-Statistics for the LS&C and the Conventional Duration Models

Exhibit 3 indicates that in most cases the R^2 statistic, which indicates the degree of variation in foreign versus domestic interest rates explained by the model factor(s), is greater for the LS&C representation of duration(s) than for conventional duration. This is even after having adjusted for the two extra factors in the LS&C representation. In those cases, when the conventional duration approach provides a higher R^2, the numbers are very close and could be explained by the somewhat arbitrary approaches used to adjust R^2 for having two additional factors.[9] It is also interesting to note that this condition occurs only when the *t*-statistic for the conventional duration beta is greater than the *t*-statistic for the level duration beta. In general however, the LS&C model beta regressions are more explanatory. This should give the portfolio manager more confidence in applying this model and its associated betas.

Examining the *t*-statistics carefully, we observe a reassuring phenomena. In every case where the *t*-statistic is insignificant, the corresponding beta coefficient is close to zero. An example is the coefficient for the slope of Switzerland which has a *t*-statistic of 0.54, which is not at all significant, and a beta of 0.14. This indicates that there is no truly reliable (low *t*-statistic), nor measurable relationship (beta close to zero) between changes in the slope of the U.S. yield curve and the Swiss yield curve. In that case, the portfolio manager should be aware that there may be lots of unrelated fluctuation in Swiss bonds due to changes in the Swiss yield curve slope that will affect the value of Swiss bonds in the portfolio but will not be associated (correlated) to U.S. slope variations. However, Swiss changes in yield curve *level* can be more confidently attributed (*t*-statistic = 2.51) to be about one third of the contemporaneous change (β = 0.31) in U.S. level changes. Changes in curvature (*t*-statistic = 1.19), like those for slope, are less reliable than for those of level. This might suggest to the portfolio manager trying to manage risk and seeking confidence in domestic duration to hold *long maturity* Swiss bonds. Such bonds have the least exposure to slope and curvature variations.

---

[9] In all cases the actual (unadjusted) R^2 was higher for the LS&C case versus the conventional duration case.

Examining the Relationship Between the Beta for Level Changes and Yield Changes

The conventional duration model relies on changes in the overall yield of the bond to arrive at a country beta (equation (3)), and the overall yield must incorporate the net effect on yield of changes in the whole yield curve. If that is indeed the case, and if there is correlation between the factors of slope and curvature, then there is spurious noise introduced into the estimate of the country beta. In general, the correspondence between foreign and domestic level changes in the yield curve will be closer than that estimated by a (conventional duration) country beta — implying that the country beta should be closer to 1.0. The LS&C model would be expected to better segregate the effect of level changes in the yield curve when estimating the country level beta. We would expect the country level beta, which after all corresponds quite closely to the country beta,[10] to be closer to 1.0. In our sample this is true for all countries except Australia and Japan. We will examine the typical case using Canada as the example, and then Australia and Japan as two exceptional cases.

The Canadian country level beta is 0.95 and the country beta is 0.89. Both are highly statistically significant. In this case, the country level beta is closer to 1.0 as predicted. In fact for Canada, the country slope and curvature betas are also close to 1.0; they are 0.97 and 0.94, respectively. This indicates that Canada can be used as a fairly close substitute for the United States along all three dimensions of yield curve movements. Further, Canadian bonds can be included to a greater degree than, say, Dutch bonds (see Exhibit 3), while maintaining a higher degree of confidence that portfolio performance will be close to that of a purely domestic portfolio. Exhibit 5 presents the correlations between level, slope, and curvature in Canada over the 5-year period we consider. We notice that all correlations are fairly low, but not negligible. This explains why the country beta, albeit farther from 1.0 than the country level beta, is still quite close to 1.0. This also reaffirms that the LS&C model better sorts out the noise inherent in the slope and curvature correlations; that noise is only summarized in the conventional duration approach.

Exhibit 5: Canada: Correlations of Changes in Level, Slope, and Curvature Parameters

Correlation	Level	Slope	Curvature
Level	1.00		
Slope	–0.03	1.00	
Curvature	–0.12	–0.16	1.00

[10] For a discussion of this issue, see Willner, "A New Tool for Portfolio Managers: Level, Slope, and Curvature Duration."

Exhibit 6: Australia: Correlations of Changes in Level, Slope, and Curvature Parameters

Correlation	Level	Slope	Curvature
Level	1.00		
Slope	–0.45	1.00	
Curvature	–0.27	0.24	1.00

Exhibit 7: Japan: Correlations of Changes in Level, Slope, and Curvature Parameters

Correlation	Level	Slope	Curvature
Level	1.00		
Slope	–0.50	1.00	
Curvature	–0.52	0.22	1.00

The Australia country level beta is 1.08 and the country beta is 1.04. In this case the country beta is closer to 1.0. This result may appear to be puzzling at first since we would expect in general (for the reasons stated earlier) that that relationship would be reversed. However, Exhibit 6 may give us some insight into what is causing this condition. The exhibit shows us that there is significant negative correlation between level changes and slope and curvature changes (for instance, compare Exhibit 6 to Exhibit 5). The negative correlations may be creating a mitigating effect. Recall that the country beta is proportional to the covariance of changes in Australian versus U.S. yields. The offsetting effects of intra-Australian yield curve large negative correlations can depress the size of the overall covariance with the United States. Therefore, the volatility adjustment inherent in the country beta may be biased lower. We also note that the *t*-statistics for the level, slope, and curvature beta are all highly significant. This makes us comfortable that the non-level changes are significant so that their movement and its associated correlations are not spurious but a persistent part of the yield curve dynamics of Australian interest rates. These effects are therefore likely to be represented in the country beta.

The Japanese country level beta is 0.22 and the country beta is 0.30. In this case the country beta is closer to 1.0. However, the correlations in Exhibit 7 reveal an even more onerous situation. The correlations of level changes to slope and curvature changes are particularly high (in absolute value), suggesting that the single point estimation inherent in the conventional duration, yield-oriented model, can be misleading. Moreover, only the country curvature beta (representing the weakest yield curve change effect) is statistically significant. The conclusion drawn from these statistics is that Japan can be considered as fairly independent from the United States. Perhaps the best conclusion to be drawn is that no (or not much of a) relationship exists between U.S. and Japanese yield curves. The portfolio manager that hazards including Japanese government bonds (JGBs) in the portfolio is adding close to pure tracking error. Of course, lack of correlation with U.S. securities affords valuable diversification. However, this is not the issue we are addressing. Our research indicates that if a JGB is included in a domestic portfolio, its contribution to the domestic duration of the portfolio cannot be calculated reliably.

This analysis for Canada, Australia, and Japan indicates how every country should be analyzed and evaluated on its own merit. Clearly, LS&C durations are more elucidating than country betas alone since they present the marginal contribution of sensitivity of each type of yield curve movement rather than an aggregate which necessarily obfuscates the individual contributions. Exhibit 3 is easily revised for successive five year or other periods. The portfolio manager can then adjust the duration using the betas presented in Exhibit 3 and be more confident of a reasonable representation of the domestic duration contribution engendered by the inclusion of foreign bonds. The *degree* of confidence is the topic of the next section which concludes this chapter.

CONCLUSION

Previous analysis indicates the potential for basis risk engendered by including foreign bonds in a domestically benchmarked portfolio. Considering this issue as a hedge problem provides a way to quantify the indirect durational response of the foreign bonds to domestic interest rates and a methodology to adjust for it. The question we have addressed so far is: given the inclusion of a foreign bond in a domestic portfolio, how can its domestic duration be reasonably calculated? The conclusion is that the use of a hedge approach with derived country betas is good, while the use of a hedged approach with level, slope, and curvature betas is better. What we have not yet addressed is how good is it. How much of the differential reaction to domestic interest changes have we explained? And consequently, how much of the foreign bond can be included in a domestic portfolio?

The conclusive answer would require a comprehensive model of interest rate changes across and within the nations of the world. Then we could describe the performance of foreign bonds in total since all the effects on their interest rates would be modeled. Our hedge approach only picks up that movement of interest rates co-varying with domestic interest rates. If domestic interest rate change was the only factor necessary to explain interest rate changes in all countries (i.e., all other non-correlated foreign interest rate movement was simply noise), then our model could be comprehensive. In that case a well diversified holding of foreign bonds would substantially reduce risk and the durational behavior of bonds would very much be captured by this hedge approach. The danger comes about when the unexplained component of variation has covariance between two countries represented in our domestic portfolio, but not with the domestic country itself. An example might be two European countries vying to be members of the European Monetary Union (EMU) and having this affect their interest rates, while being represented in a U.S. domestic portfolio — whereas the U.S. interest rates are generally independent of EMU considerations.

Nontheless, a portfolio manager is interested in whether or not to include foreign bonds and how much of them to include. Elsewhere this issue is discussed at some length and the reader is referred to that more extensive discussion.[11] We shall only review some of the points here.

Recall that a beta can be dissected into a correlation term times a relative volatility term. A beta of 1.0, which generally indicates close correspondence between foreign and domestic interest rates, can be misleading. It may be close to 1.0 if the foreign and domestic interest rate performance is similar. But it may also be close to 1.0 if relatively high foreign volatility offsets low correlation of performance. For instance, when the correlation is 0.5 and relative volatility of interest rates is 2.0, $0.5 \times 2.0 = 1.0$. Therefore it is not sufficient to know the beta when trying to identify close substitute bonds. What is desirable is that foreign interest rates be highly correlated with local interest rates. Unfortunately, there is no single comprehensive correlation number when we extend country betas to the county level, slope, and curvature beta framework. However, for the purpose of determining the general correlation between interest rates as a guide to the inclusion of foreign bonds in a domestic portfolio, the conventional duration country beta is probably sufficient. The higher is the correlation, the more of the foreign bond which can be safely included. Exhibit 8 presents correlations for the 15 countries. The actual amount of the foreign bond to include is a topic of managerial discretion which we will not address here. Obviously, the more of the foreign bond, the more domestic benchmark tracking error introduced. The expected return is the reward for taking on such risk and the allowable tradeoff is a decision for the portfolio manager.

Exhibit 8: Correlations to U.S. Interest Rate Changes

Country	Correlation	Country	Correlation
Australia	0.70	Ireland	0.47
Austria	0.38	Italy	0.28
Belgium	0.32	Japan	0.30
Canada	0.70	Spain	0.31
Denmark	0.39	Sweden	0.32
France	0.49	Switzerland	0.28
Germany	0.52	UK	0.44
Holland	0.53		

[11] Thomas and Willner, "Measuring the Duration of an Internationally Diversified Portfolio."

Exhibit 9: UNFIRM Statistics Measured Against U.S. Interest Rate Changes

Country	%	Country	%
Canada	18	Holland	29
Ireland	19	Italy	29
UK	19	France	29
Australia	20	Switzerland	32
Germany	24	Spain	35
Sweden	24	Belgium	39
Denmark	24	Japan	41
Austria	28		

In the Thomas-Willner study, a statistic called "Unrelated foreign interest rate movement" or UNFIRM was also introduced. This statistic is measured as $2|\alpha|/\sigma$ where α is from the regression given in equation (5) and σ is the standard deviation of the return term (left hand side) of equation (5). We explain that this statistic is a proxy for the economic value of potential factors not included in the regression. The statistic attempts to measure the economic significance of these factors by comparing their average contribution to the typical value change. The UNFIRM statistics for the same 15 countries are presented in Exhibit 9.

Exhibit 9 is presented in ascending UNFIRM order, which reflects the closest substitutes for the United States first. It is interesting to note that the ordering occurs by block! First is the Anglo-block, with Canada the closest substitute, next is the European block, and finally there is Japan. This appeals to our intuition about the natural substitutes for the United States, at least, block by block. For instance, we would expect that more of Canada than Switzerland can be included in a U.S. portfolio for the same degree of tracking error of U.S. interest rates.

Our discussion has presented tools and approaches for careful inclusion of foreign bonds in domestic portfolios. We note the need for caution and a case-by-case approach for the bonds of each country. The domestic portfolio manager wishing to include foreign bonds may find it wise to apply the country level, slope, and curvature beta adjustments to their corresponding durations (or at least the country beta adjustment to conventional duration). Further, the manager should examine the betas' associated statistics, the corresponding country correlations and the UNFIRM statistics, to gauge the accuracy of such adjustments. This approach will assist in maintaining the usefulness of domestic duration as a guide for managing such portfolios. In the absence of a comprehensive trans-national interest rate model, such an approach may be the best alternative.

Chapter 9

Emerging Fixed Income and Local Currency: An Investment Management View

Luis R. Luis, Ph. D.
Managing Director
Scudder, Stevens & Clark

INTRODUCTION

Investment managers had an early and important role in the development of emerging markets fixed income as an asset class following the developing country debt crisis of the 1980s. Investment companies were created to take advantage of opportunities for excess return from investing in emerging bonds and defaulted bank loans to developing countries. Some of these initial investment vehicles were established as offshore entities, beginning in 1989, to facilitate access to the market by global retail investors who often resided in emerging countries themselves.[1] Thereafter, investment companies registered in the United States provided diversified emerging market portfolios for investors in developed countries. These dedicated funds generally aimed at providing high income with substantial potential for capital appreciation.

A second stage in the development of investment management involved the use of emerging market instruments as part of broader portfolios, often global and international bond portfolios. Emerging bonds also found their way to accounts and investment vehicles focused on U.S. bond markets. At the same time, dedicated accounts were established for institutional clients, mainly in the United States, and more recently in Europe, Japan, and other developed areas.

A third stage, evolving alongside deepening capital markets in emerging countries, is the management of local currency fixed income. The initial development of emerging fixed income was centered primarily in bonds and defaulted bank loans largely denominated in dollars and, to a lesser extent, other currencies of industrial countries. Although some use was made of instruments issued in the

[1] The first offshore vehicle to invest in emerging bonds is generally acknowledged to be the Sovereign High Yield Investment Company registered in Curacao, Netherlands Antilles, in 1989. This investment company was designed to invest primarily in bearer bonds issued by governments in emerging countries.

currencies of emerging markets, these were complementary rather than central to the asset class. They mostly comprised Treasury bills and other money market securities of a handful of countries, most prominently Mexico and other Latin American nations.

Investment managers face multiple challenges in seeking value while managing risk in the asset class. Value is derived from analysis of credit quality, market risk, and pricing relationships within the asset class and in relation to established bond markets. Information gaps played a major role in the early evolution of the asset class. Long lags in the availability of data, large voids in the data, and, most importantly, partial understanding of economic and political variables determining sovereign credit quality created opportunities to add value while presenting substantial risks. Value is enhanced and risk reduced in direct relation to analysis, information, and investment discipline.

As countries and other emerging issuers have strived to improve the flow and transparency of information following the 1994 Mexican peso crisis, the limiting factor is analysis of variables that determine credit quality and vulnerability to random events or shocks, not the lack of basic data and qualitative information.

As the marginal issuers in global capital markets, emerging countries are highly exposed, as may be expected, to shifting financial patterns and liquidity effects derived from core bond markets. As analysis improves and average credit quality rises, these effects are likely to diminish in size but will not be eliminated. Because relationships are not easily predictable, portfolio shifts within the asset class and in relation to other investments will characterize this market in the foreseeable future. This means that investment managers, possibly more than in other fixed income classes, are expected to design and manage portfolios in ways that take advantage of these shifts.

INVESTMENT OBJECTIVES

Investment managers view emerging markets as capable of satisfying a broad set of objectives. In general, portfolios and investment vehicles are classified into two main categories: those primarily seeking high income and those principally aiming at obtaining total return. Because price appreciation is most often a secondary objective and sometimes the primary goal, emerging markets fixed income is sometimes viewed as a "quasi-equity" asset class in contrast with traditional investment-grade fixed income investments. A third type of investor views emerging markets as primarily a means to diversify global or domestic fixed income portfolios.

Emerging market bonds are expected to provide high yield, certainly compared to investment-grade securities and even when placed against speculative grade corporate bonds. Most emerging countries are rated below investment grade. In mid-1997, emerging markets sovereign bonds had an average credit quality approximately equivalent to a BB/Ba as rated by the major agencies. Moreover, emerging bonds denominated in dollars have historically traded at wider spreads to benchmark U.S. Treasury bonds than other bonds of similar credit rating. For example, at the end of May 1997 emerging market bonds yielded approximately 417 basis points (bps) (net of collateral) and 294 bps (collateral included) over similar maturity U.S. Treasuries while similarly BB-rated U.S. high yield bonds yielded 185 bps.[2]

Spread curves for emerging market bonds in relation to U.S. Treasury bonds are upward sloping with the slope increasing in proportion to duration. This relationship holds for both normal Eurobonds and non-collateralized Brady bonds, as well as for Brady bonds which have collateralized principal and partial interest payments. In this case, market price reflects the view of the major rating agencies that collateral does not significantly improve the credit quality of the bond. This apparent paradox, captured by market pricing as well as rating agency views (even when the percentage of present value composed of high grade U.S. Treasury collateral increases as average maturity declines) provides a source of excess return for investors.

Many investment vehicles seek to generate *steady* as well as high *current* income from a portfolio of emerging bonds. Portfolios can be designed to optimize current income at the expense of other objectives such as price appreciation or stability of net asset value. As emerging market bonds comprise a wide variety of fixed- and floating-rate securities, portfolio management strategies can be found that help optimize or stabilize current income throughout the interest rate cycle. Utilization of interest rate swaps or other derivatives can contribute substantially to achieving income objectives. As an illustration, during the period of low short-term interest rates from 1992-1993, swapping floating-rate Brady cash flows to fixed rates added over 200 bps in current yield.

Investment vehicles can also be designed to generate steady *dividends* composed of current income, realized capital gains, and, depending upon accounting conventions, accretion of discount. Exhibit 1 shows the historical cumulative dividends and total return in U.S. dollars per share of the Sovereign High Yield Investment Company. The main investment objective of this fund is to provide high income with a secondary objective of capital appreciation. A steady dollar dividend has been maintained for long periods since the inception of the fund.

Investment vehicles aiming at total return are managed differently from those that primarily seek high income. Among the many differences in management and orientation, vehicles seeking total return will often consider a wider set of potential investments, particularly highly discounted bonds and loans or high spread duration bonds. Collateralized Brady bonds are also favored for strategies involving higher interest duration as the U.S. Treasury zero-coupon bonds backing the principal value of the bonds supplies additional interest duration.

---

[2] These are the approximate yields of the Emerging Markets Bond Index (EMBI) of J. P. Morgan (sovereign yield and blended yield) and of the Lehman Brothers BB index (long) of U.S. high yield bonds.

Exhibit 1: SHYIC Returns

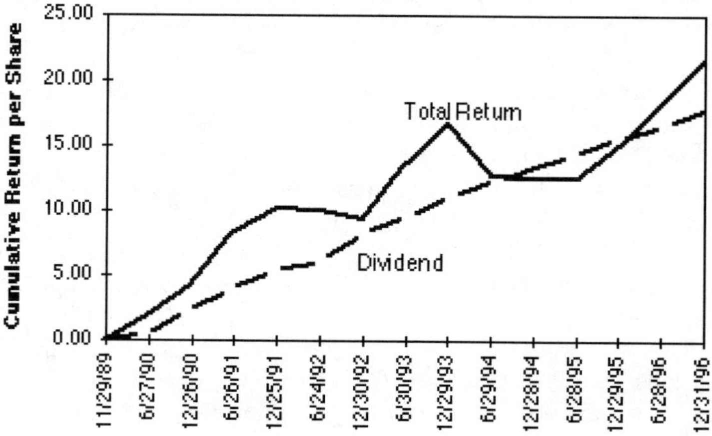

Source: Scudder, Stevens & Clark

A wide range of risk profiles is consistent with a total return orientation. Although discounts from par value — and the potential for above average price appreciation — are larger for issuers of lower credit quality, there are ample opportunities to invest in highly discounted securities of issuers with improving credit. Success in recent years in rapidly and effectively turning around countries involved in acute financial instability — Argentina, Brazil, Peru, and Poland, to name a few — provides evidence that even in cases of fragile credit quality framed in unstable macroeconomic conditions, successful turnaround can be produced within short periods of time. The record also shows that most of these major turnaround cases have led to sustained improvements in creditworthiness, breaking the cycle of stop-go progress that characterized major developing economies for most of the post-1945 years of the decade.

A number of portfolio management styles and techniques can be used to reach a total return objective. These range from long-term, research based portfolios which seek capital appreciation based on steady or improving fundamental conditions to trading-oriented vehicles which aim to take advantage of country- or issuer-specific events, U.S. bond market trends, or the global liquidity cycle. The deepening of emerging bond markets is providing increased liquidity, reducing the transaction costs of trading-oriented strategies. After the Mexican crisis at the end of 1994, a trend towards lower price volatilities lowered the cost of hedging and entering into derivative strategies which can enhance total return. Growing demand for hedging products will tend to lower transaction costs for derivatives as the markets mature.

Aggressive total return portfolios, as can be anticipated, are highly susceptible to conditions outside of the emerging markets, both of a fundamental nature and liquidity related. Brady bonds and long duration emerging Eurobonds are much more sensitive to fluctuations in the U.S. Treasury yield curve than implied by interest duration, spread duration, and other parameters that measure price sensitivity to yield or spread changes. While this sensitivity will tend to decline as discounts to par recede, markets mature, and the quality of information and analysis improves, emerging dollar bonds are likely to remain more exposed to shifts in Treasury bonds than other asset classes. Liquidity effects are another important consideration, particularly for portfolios that aim at boosting total return by employing a wide variety of trading strategies.

This pattern of sensitivity does not apply to local currency instruments, which have short duration and are segmented from global capital markets. Although the incipient development of local yield curves provides for only partial evidence, it appears that long duration bonds issued in local currencies have also reduced sensitivity to events in major global markets as compared to dollar pay issues. The segmentation of local fixed income markets from global markets results from the use of flexible exchange rates, restrictions or taxes on capital flows, and the lack of effective arbitrage between the local and international markets.

A third investment objective is asset diversification within a comprehensive investment program. It is not a distinct objective. Rather, it is achieved jointly with the other two objectives. Brady bonds and long-dated Eurobonds are sensitive to conditions in the U.S. bond market. Hence, these instruments are often not considered to provide much risk diversification for U.S. or dollar-based global bond investors. It is possible, however, to construct emerging bond portfolios which offer much greater potential for diversification by weighting more heavily emerging regions less associated with the U.S. bond market. Bonds of Asian, Central European, and Middle Eastern issuers historically have a lower correlation with the U.S. bond market than Latin American bonds. The latter account for about 80% of the mid-1997 capitalization of Brady and emerging Eurobonds.

Total return correlations of local currency markets with the U.S. and other developed country bond markets in recent years are generally not statistically different from zero at a high level of significance and as such can provide diversification advantages for U.S. and global bond investors. The substitution or addition of local currency instruments to U.S. or global portfolios can significantly reduce portfolio volatility and, sometimes, potentially increase returns. These results apply to local currency portfolios of short duration. The diversification benefits of local currencies are also enhanced because of the low correlation among the local currency markets themselves which helps explain the low volatility of local currency portfolios.

Asset diversification can be managed tactically or strategically to enhance returns during perceived favorable conditions in U.S. or global bond markets. Alternatively, diversification can be a primary defensive tool, for example by increasing the allocation to local currency investments. It too can help achieve interest duration objectives in diversified global portfolios.

ANALYTICAL ISSUES

The central principle behind a fundamental approach to emerging bond investments is that value, consistency, and risk control can be enhanced by systematic analysis. In a largely speculative asset class such as emerging markets fixed income, return optimization requires particular emphasis on risk control as the basis for portfolio construction and management. Analysis is needed as the centerpiece in gauging risks, determining relative value, and establishing potential arbitrage opportunities.

Although there are a number of ways to integrate analysis into the investment process, tilting research attention and resources towards particular aspects of the asset class, a fundamental approach, at a minimum, involves the following: sovereign risk, corporate credit, security analysis, market sensitivity, and for local currencies, currency or exchange rate risk.

Sovereign Risk

Sovereign risk encompasses several dimensions of risk. In its more general form, it measures transfer risk, sometimes denoted as *convertibility risk*. This is the probability that a government will not make foreign exchange available to meet foreign currency obligations. As such, sovereign credit quality will depend on the ability of the government to obtain foreign exchange and its willingness to maintain unimpeded flows of international capital to public and private borrowers.

The probability of default is a parameter that can be estimated either explicitly or implicitly. Ordinarily, however, the evaluation of sovereign risk involves more subtle differentiation among sovereign credits than just estimating a probability of default. Such probability tends to approach zero for periods of one year or less for investment-grade credits, but increases non-linearly as credits decline in quality below the investment-grade frontier. Nonetheless, markets are very sensitive to gradations in the perception of sovereign risk trends. Experience also indicates that markets tend to discount swiftly perceived improving trends in creditworthiness.

A key element for investment managers is the anticipation of changes in sovereign credit quality. A method to determine such changes is very useful as a guide to potential value and pricing of specific sovereign issues. This can be approached in a number of ways. The most desirable method is a thorough evaluation of macro, financial, and policy variables which will determine the government's ability and willingness to supply foreign exchange to entities operating within the country. Alternative approaches, which can be used as consistency checks, involve the use of quantitative models, indicators of creditworthiness, and check lists.

Among the key determinants of sovereign credit quality, to be assessed by thorough analysis, quantitative estimation, or other methods, are the following: the structure of the government's debt and debt service (external and internal), its international asset position, the fiscal position of the government, prospects for domestic output and demand, and a projection of dollar cash flows for the country derived from international trade and investment. The quality of economic policies in place, which can be quantified by indicators such as the status of International Monetary Fund programs, are also an important determinant. It is far more difficult to analyze and quantify institutional and political stability. Nonetheless, it is apparent that both markets and rating agencies devote considerable importance to this element which often helps to explain discrepancies in rating from that implied by more objective criteria.

Econometric analysis suggests that the structure of external debt is the central element involved in ratings of emerging markets by the major agencies. That this is the case should not be a surprise. After all, the probability of continuing to service external obligations will vary inversely with the burden of the debt. This is also the most readily quantifiable indicator of creditworthiness. It can be represented in simple form by the ratio of external debt to exports of goods and services. Other alternative ratios are also calculated, for example, the ratio of external debt to GDP. Likewise debt service ratios are often used to measure the current burden of servicing external debt.

Statistical analysis of sovereign debt ratings of the two major rating agencies, Moody's and Standard and Poor's, suggests that a small set of debt and economic indicators fits well the variation of ratings from a sample of 23 of the most important emerging countries. The results of two regressions, shown in Exhibit 2, indicate that the ratio of external debt to total exports, the ratio of total interest payments to exports, the trend growth of real GDP (average of the last three years) and the level of inflation for the last year account for 82% of the variance of Moody's ratings and 75% of the variance of ratings from Standard and Poor's. These results do not imply that the rating process used by the agencies is based solely or even primarily on these commonly used indicators. The standard errors of 0.39 rating and 0.53 rating, respectively, indicate that these equations are approximations of the process. Likewise, having 11 of 23 ratings split between the two agencies point out the important judgmental elements involved in the rating process. A statistical difference between the agencies appears to be that Standard and Poor's assigns somewhat greater weight to macroeconomic stability and growth than does Moody's as can be seen in the larger coefficients for trend growth and inflation in the regressions.

*Exhibit 2: Determinants of Sovereign Credit Ratings**

	Constant	Debt/Exports	Interest/Exports	Trend Growth	CPI Inflation	
Moody's	4.58	0.008	−0.027	−0.072	0.0084	R2 = 0.82
(t ratio)	19.2	2.85	−0.58	−2.88	2.2	s.e.= 0.39
Standard & Poor's	4.51	0.009	−0.049	−0.077	0.016	R2 = 0.75
(t ratio)	13.95	2.33	−0.79	−2.29	3.13	s.e. = 0.53

* Estimated from data in the Institute of International Finance, *Near Term Prospects for Emerging Market Economies* (Washington, D.C., April 1997). Ratings are those in effect as of June 1, 1997. For purposes of estimation, ratings were converted to a numerical equivalent where BBB/Baa is equal to 5.00 and BB/Ba equals 6.00 and so forth.

An evaluation of the mix of economic policies used by the government to attain financial and price stability and to help foster investment, growth, and financial deepening is essential in determining whether a country is on its way to achieving sustainable economic growth. Largely because of the diffusion of policy know-how and evidence that market-led policies instill confidence on investors and consumers, the quality of policies followed by developing countries has improved greatly in the 15 years since the debt crisis of 1982, the debacle which deeply set back development prospects for many middle-income countries. The lesson of the 1990s is that markets are rapid to acknowledge the benefits of stabilization based on a sound fiscal, monetary, and deregulatory policy mix. Likewise, selling state assets can rapidly provide signals to markets of a change in direction and an increase in the potential for solid fiscal policies.

A checklist can be a useful device to gauge the quality of the institutional and political environment in a country. The checklist may include factors such as the likelihood of a smooth transition of power, the stability of governing coalitions, and the chances for continuity of policies. Absent high political instability, which can lead to sharp reversal of policies, shifting coalition governments, and other non-violent signs of political change are not necessarily a huge negative in the evaluation of credit quality. It is when policies are affected negatively by either peaceful or violent political change that potential for a major reversal in credit trends exists.

Corporate Credit

Debt securities of emerging country corporations provide a means to enhance returns in emerging debt, high yield, or other fixed income portfolios. Credit research is essential in determining proper valuation and the identification of investment opportunities. Corporate credits can also be a source of diversification as a complement or an alternative to sovereign credits. On the other hand, corporate credits can be very sensitive to movements in sovereign credit quality in the country of corporate residence. It follows that corporate credits do not always provide much diversification to emerging debt portfolios.

Evaluation of corporate risk in emerging markets presents formidable challenges. Rapidly evolving operating environments, accounting and legal systems, and rapid shifts in financial variables compound uncertainty in assessing credit risk for corporations. Management quality is arguably even more of a determining variable in developing countries than in industrial ones. Because of these factors, financial outcomes for emerging country companies are often subject to greater error than is the case in developed economies.

The operating environment for companies in developing countries is deeply affected, almost by definition, by rapid structural change arising out of institutional development, liberalization of markets, the creation and transformation of regulatory systems, and the opening to competition from foreign companies. It is also characterized by greater cyclical variation in demand and output than in developed countries.

Accounting standards are shifting rapidly in many emerging countries and are converging gradually to U.S. GAAP. Some countries such as Chile and Argentina now use accounting standards which are close to those of the United States and other developed countries. The issuance of American Depository Receipts and international bonds by many emerging country corporations also forces these companies to restate their financial statements in harmony with either U.S. or commonly accepted international standards. Privatization is another force pressing for updating accounting standards as widening interest in state companies by potential strategic or portfolio investors requires a thorough restatement of financial data. The pace of change is strongest among many larger Latin American and East Asian companies which are now accessing the international capital market. Central European, South Asian, and African companies lag in these efforts.

There is a debate regarding the relative evaluation of corporate and sovereign credits. Traditionally, the sovereign ceiling, or the credit rating given to the government, has set a limit on the rating of corporations residing and largely operating in that country. In some cases, however, market prices signaled that investors viewed corporations as a better credit. For example, some Argentine corporate credits traded for substantial periods of time with spreads through sovereign bonds of comparable duration or maturity. Recently some credit agencies, among them Standard and Poor's and Fitch, have indicated conditions under which corporate credits could be subject to a higher hard currency credit rating than the sovereign.[3]

Historical price behavior gives some support to the view that corporate bonds may be more susceptible to systemic shocks than sovereign bonds. A shock is an unexpected shift in a financial or real variable that substantially alters the probabilities given by investors and consumers to normal economic outcomes. A sudden devaluation of the currency or a large drop in the price of a key commodity, such as copper for Chile or oil for Nigeria, can generate shocks. After the devaluation of the Mexican peso in December 1994, spreads of Eurobonds issued by Mexican and other Latin American companies widened significantly over comparable maturity sovereigns. In this case, the currency devaluation in one of the most prominent emerging debtors provided a systemic shock to the market which deeply hit corporate credits. A systemic shock affects a set of international investors and markets as opposed to a country-specific shock which disrupts only investors in a given country and its securities.

Banks and other financial companies in emerging countries are especially sensitive to the stress generated by structural change and to the dislocations provided by shocks. The combination of rapid credit growth, often prevalent in

---

[3] This refers mainly to "dollarized economies" where there is little or no difference between credit quality measured in local currency or in dollars. The limiting case of a dollarized economy is one where the dollar is legal and sole legal tender, such as Panama. Countries with a currency pegged to the dollar through a "currency board" system or other mechanism that maintains full backing of the monetary base by dollar reserves or equivalent assets can be considered dollarized. For a company operating in a fully dollarized economy, transfer risk approaches zero.

emerging economies during price stabilization and deregulation of the financial sector, and inadequate risk management and other controls at lending institutions, leads to a deterioration of loan portfolios. Shocks can exacerbate the situation by causing rapid downward shifts in economic activity or an increase in key prices and interest rates. Banking difficulties are common throughout the developing world and, paradoxically, in the more rapidly developing countries. Analyzing financial credits is one of the most challenging aspects of corporate credit evaluation in emerging markets.

Bonds issued by companies facing steady demand through the economic cycle and capable of reacting rapidly to shocks offer less risk and at times present opportunities for yield and yield-compression significantly over the sovereign. This is the case of some electric utilities and companies in the food processing sector. Transformation of energy pricing and regulation in emerging countries to systems based on fuel and capacity costs or, alternatively, on marginal cost pricing, such as in Argentina and Chile, are reducing uncertainty in evaluating company cash flows while increasing the likelihood that adequate interest coverage ratios can be maintained.

Investing in debt securities of all but the largest listed companies in emerging markets requires specialized credit work and wide access to local data and company management. Locally traded debt securities as well as private placements offer ample opportunities for excess return. However, this is a market segment which remains terra incognita for most investors located outside of the domestic market. The comments above regarding credit analysis, which pertain largely to the better capitalized corporations, are even more applicable to this much larger set of companies where the problems of risk evaluation are compounded by local operating environments, regulatory questions, and limitations of data and institutional understanding.

Security Analysis

Sovereign and corporate credit analysis provide essential inputs for security evaluation, country selection, and portfolio management. Additional evaluation is necessary to proceed with security selection in the investment process. Much like other debt securities, emerging bonds can be analyzed in terms of parameters determining yield and return, price sensitivity, and properties of the yield curve. The analytical issues are similar to those encountered in the evaluation of other debt securities. Analytical questions of special relevance for emerging market bonds concern collateral and unusual coupon structures in many Brady bonds, the abundance of floating-rate issues, and embedded options.

Collateral associated with Brady bonds requires calculation of stripped yields and spreads or, as alternatively called, sovereign yields and spreads, apart from the usual yield-to-maturity calculations. A stripped yield is derived from the cash flows net of collateral. This is straightforward when only the principal is collateralized, typically by a matching U.S. Treasury zero. It becomes more complex as two, or sometimes three, coupons are also collateralized. Such coupon collateralization can be evaluated by using alternative methodologies which incorporate the probability of default per coupon period.

Spread duration measures the sensitivity of price to changes in sovereign yield, as contrasted to ordinary yield-to-maturity (YTM) or "blended yield." This calculation is necessary for all Brady bonds except fixed-rate, non-collateralized bullets, where ordinary YTM calculations produce identical results. Spread duration is a central parameter in Brady bond evaluation and portfolio construction and management. It provides a measure of the sensitivity of total return of Brady bonds to changes in sovereign spreads over comparable U.S. Treasury bonds or other base yields.

Floating-rate bonds of intermediate and long-maturities were issued by the 15 countries that completed Brady debt restructurings in the 1989-1996 period.[4] Floating-rate syndicated loans of several countries, among them Russia and Morocco, trade actively in international markets. Several countries issued floating-rate Bradys and Eurobonds of varying maturities as part of their financing programs. These floaters have low or negative modified interest duration. Because of the discounts on most of these floating-rate bonds, interest duration provides a weak measure of the sensitivity of these bonds to shifts in the U.S. Treasury curve as well as to the sensitivity of the bonds to shifts in credit spreads. It is therefore essential to evaluate sovereign spread duration for these floaters as part of relative value, total return, and other portfolio summary statistics.

Call options to the issuer are embedded in most Brady bonds and in some sovereign Eurobonds. Corporate bonds are also issued in callable form. As long as call options on Brady bonds were deeply out-of-the-money, their value was safely ignored by investors. Brady bonds traded at deep discounts immediately after their issuance upon exchange of restructured loans. As Brady prices approach levels where the call options offer significant value, option-adjusted-spread (OAS) calculations become necessary as a means of establishing precise valuation, helping portfolio construction, and trading. OAS evaluation methodologies for Brady bonds are not yet standard and tend to produce substantial differences. This partly follows from Brady bonds' complex structures with one or two types of collateral and discrete coupon patterns. Furthermore, the probability distribution of Brady prices appears to differ appreciably from the lognormal distribution utilized widely to price options.

Market Sensitivity

Emerging market bond prices show, as a rule, high sensitivity to random events and to the impact of changes in international markets. For example, emerging bonds show more responsiveness to shifts in the U.S. yield curve than indicated by intrinsic measures of price sensitivity such as interest and spread duration. That this is so should not be a big surprise. Partly, it can be explained by the prevailing discount in most emerging bonds or other measures of risk premium.

[4] These countries are Albania, Argentina, Brazil, Bulgaria, Costa Rica, Dominican Republic, Ecuador, Jordan, Mexico, Panama, Peru, The Philippines, Poland, Uruguay, and Venezuela.

Exhibit 3: Sensitivity to Changes in U.S. Yield Curve (December 1990 to April 1996)

	Sensitivity	Interest Duration (years)
EMBI	−11.9	5.4
Fixed Rate Bonds	−15.0	10.7
Floaters	−8.7	0.4

Source: Calculated from J.P. Morgan's Emerging Markets Bond Index.

Brady bonds are highly sensitive to conditions in U.S. markets. Sensitivity of the Emerging Markets Bond Index of J.P. Morgan, which is composed mostly of Brady bonds, to changes in the U.S. yield curve in the period December 1990 to March 1996 is −11.9. This means that a change in U.S. rates on average produces a percentage change about −12 times larger in the EMBI index. This was calculated by regression of the EMBI on a U.S. yield curve (3 months to 30 years) weighted to produce interest duration equal to that of the EMBI plus a variable for emerging market shocks (such as the Real Plan in Brazil and the Mexican peso shock of December 1994).

Fixed-rate Bradys show a sensitivity of −15 compared, for example, to interest duration of 10.7 years. The data also show clearly that Brady floating-rate bonds are also very sensitive to shifts in U.S. interest rates. While the interest duration of floating Bradys (April 1996) is only 0.4 years, they show a statistical sensitivity of −8.7. Markets overshoot when U.S. rates fall as credit risk is perceived to decrease. Conversely, markets react negatively to rising interest rates partly because credit risk is negatively impacted. Vanishing liquidity, in turn, compounds these effects. This applies to both fixed- and floating-rate Bradys. Consequently, in periods of weakness in U.S. markets, Brady bonds will tend to overreact. Market sensitivity of Brady bonds to the U.S. yield curve may be presumed to fall as discounts recede.

There is an additional explanation for the sensitivity to the U.S. market. Emerging countries are the marginal issuers in international debt markets and they — and the holders of their debt securities — will be among the first to be affected or benefited by changing patterns of international capital flows. As risk is perceived to decrease, either because of changes in fundamental trend or improved information and analysis, sensitivity may tend to decline.

Can market sensitivity be measured in any systematic and reliable way? Usual calculations, including those implied by the capital asset pricing model, such as betas, or other statistical relationships, similar to those in Exhibit 3, are typically not very stable. Likewise, there are reservations about usual measures of variability, such as the standard deviation, since total return of individual emerging debt securities may show deviations from normality.

The heightened volatility of emerging debt securities appears to be related to the size of the risk premium. It may also be argued that often this risk premium may be larger than is implied by the excess volatility of emerging debt securities. While this is debatable, the risk premium is a potential source of excess returns and arbitrage opportunities.

Options on emerging bonds suggest as well that there is a premium paid for excess volatility, apart from premia caused by other factors such as liquidity and shortcomings in option modeling. Implied volatilities exceeded actual volatilities for the main Brady bonds in the two years to mid-June 1997. This is probably derived from a period of declining long-term volatility in the market. Nonetheless, the additional risk premia has probably hindered the use of hedging strategies.

Currency or Exchange Rate Risk

Investment in emerging debt securities issued and payable in local currencies presents separate analytical issues in addition to the topics covered above. The central issue presented by these local currency investments is the evaluation of currency risk. This is the risk of devaluation of the currency in terms of dollars. In most instances, devaluation risk could be narrowed further as the risk of a real devaluation of the exchange rate, or a devaluation in excess of the inflation differential with the United States. Measuring the risk of real devaluation enables comparisons among currencies of exchange rate risk.

Investing in local currency securities can provide excess returns over those of securities of similar duration in developed markets. Part of this return arises from prevailing local yields which in real terms are higher than required by underlying credit and currency risks. This could be the result of the need to maintain high positive real interest rates during financial stabilization and disinflation or derived from rigid expectations of policy or market behavior.

Evaluating the probability of a real devaluation enables the quantification and cross country comparison of currency risk. In most emerging countries, this requires the evaluation of the exchange rate regime and the policy rule followed. Most emerging currencies are managed according to preset rules, i.e., by pegging to the dollar or a basket of hard currencies, by keeping the currency within limits of a peg, or following a crawling peg. Quantification of the expected devaluation then involves evaluation of the policy rule and the ability of the central bank to follow it. Since most emerging currencies are managed against some central peg, as a rule they are more predictable and less volatile than developed currencies. In the 12 months to the end of May 1997, for example, the exchange rates of the deutsche mark and yen to the dollar were more volatile than the rates against the U.S. dollar of 15 of the more widely traded emerging currencies.

INVESTMENT PROCESS AND PORTFOLIO CONSTRUCTION

Portfolio construction and management are designed to reach the investment objectives within the risk tolerance indicated in the investment guidelines or prospectus. Alternative approaches to portfolio construction are determined by the investment process established to manage the portfolio. The investment process integrates all the elements needed to achieve investment objectives.

Investment Process

Emerging debt securities are generally in the lower segment of the credit quality spectrum. Investing in emerging debt consequently requires an especially rigorous process of country, security, and asset allocation as a means to control risk and provide for consistency of returns. It also requires comprehensive knowledge of trading conditions to provide for efficient timing of entry, exit, and hedging decisions.

While conceivably a variety of investment processes may produce superior and consistent performance, all of them require close integration of research and analysis on the one hand, and portfolio management and trading on the other. Likewise, a variety of investment styles will produce a number of investment processes, for example, very active, arbitrage-oriented portfolios or longer-term, value-oriented approaches.

Independent of the characteristics of the investment process, analytical support for the process involves a top-down component, centered on fundamental sovereign, sector, and market analysis and a bottom-up component that incorporates security, corporate, or sub-national analysis. This is then integrated with the timing decision, which requires a sharp understanding of trading conditions for specific securities.

Some investment processes emphasize security selection and the bottom-up aspect of the process. This may be akin to traditional corporate high yield investments. However, in emerging markets, companies operate within a wide variety of macroeconomic and institutional environments. So it is not easy to succeed with a pure bottom-up approach to the investment process, and a foundation of macro analysis is required to provide for differentiation across countries and interpretation of national and global events. Inasmuch as emerging markets become more integrated into the international economy through lifting of barriers to trade and capital, national operating conditions could become somewhat less important. The central premise in a bottom-up approach is security valuation.

A second type of process emphasizes the top-down component and the identification of potential gains from credit improvement or pricing divergence derived from analysis of fundamental country and macro trends. Just as the first approach requires integration with macro analysis, the top-down orientation must involve security analysis as an essential input in the determination of value. This said, since the majority of emerging countries are issuers of a few or even only one liquid security, country and security analysis often converge to the establishment of relative value in terms of individual securities.

In practice, disciplined investment processes involve both a top-down and a bottom-up component. The differentiation comes from the relative importance of each approach and the time dimension of investment decisions. Trading-oriented approaches may emphasize flow analysis, event appraisal, and global market effects, for instance, as the force driving investment decisions. These approaches can be viewed as complementary where they make most sense in managing global emerging market portfolios. For specialized portfolios, they can be considered stand-alone processes, for example, in managing country funds, where the investment process will largely be driven by security analysis.

Portfolio Construction

Construction of emerging market portfolios follows the same principles as other fixed income portfolios. Conceptually, this involves estimating, over the investment horizon, total return and its components for each security in the investable universe as well as estimation of risk characteristics. Research inputs are necessary in the estimation of total return. Risk characteristics could formally be projected from historical data on price and spread movements or from appropriate matrices of correlation coefficients. In practice, however, experience quickly teaches that such calculations have wide confidence intervals and are not stable enough to be interpreted without a great amount of care and sophistication. Quantitative analysis of risk and return and the use of optimization techniques can provide a rough and useful guide to the return and risk parameters for a portfolio.

One approach to portfolio construction involves having core and trading positions within the portfolio. Core positions will be driven by fundamental value to be realized within an intermediate investment horizon, say, three to six months, which in the dynamics of emerging countries can contain a sizable number of fundamental events. Core positions are adjusted as fundamental views change. They are changed in response to price action to realize price targets or implement a stop loss. Positions can also be altered as risk patterns change, for example, because of major deviations in volatility or security correlations. Nonetheless, the idea behind the core is that it should represent long-term views of credit direction, value, and relationship to the U.S. and other more developed bond markets.

Maintaining a core position requires much portfolio discipline and reliable inputs from analysis and research. By reason of the rapid change in emerging nations and the young stage of their financial institutions, governance, and markets, investors are continuously exposed to a substantial flow of information denoting the evidence of change and the resistance to and costs of change. Inevitably, this will be mixed news, often suggesting signals of some impending catastrophe. Exposed to this information flow and accompanying events, it helps to understand why turnover ratios in emerging debt portfolios are high.

A good example of the virtues of having core portfolios is provided by the massive correction and spectacular recovery that followed the devaluation of the Mexican peso in December 1994. The veritable collapse of the Brady bond market after the devaluation was followed with a sharp turnaround. Liquidity effects, including deleverage, rather than any sharp deterioration of fundamentals explained the market reaction, as well as the rapid recovery of prices. Sustaining core positions through this massive upheaval was no mean task, but it paid in terms of ultimately benefiting with the rapid recovery in prices. This would have required strong conviction derived from competent analysis. Instead, most investors tried timing the turning points in such rapid recovery, and a few succeeded.

Trading positions aim to take advantage of mispricing, event anticipation, and other elements which can give rise to temporary deviations from fundamental value. To be effective and to maintain overall control of risk, trading positions should be separate from the core. Of course, in a limiting case, the entire portfolio can be viewed as a collection of trades, subject to constant adjustment. This may work well, but strict accounting of trading and hedging costs must be made to ascertain the merits of the strategy.

Buy-and-hold portfolios are the other limiting case, when there is no adjustment of positions other than resulting from a change in core views. This could be derived from long-term fundamental views, or, in another limiting case, because the portfolio may be entirely passive, tracking a given benchmark. The latter are not used very widely, and it is not difficult to show that emerging market benchmarks are unlikely to be optimal from return or risk characteristics. Buy-and-hold portfolios may have limited room for flexibility when they are designed to match, directly or synthetically, certain desired characteristics such as maturity, duration, or current income. Specific purpose investment structures composed of emerging debt securities often fit well in the portfolios of insurance companies, banks, and other financial institutions.

Ordinarily, portfolio adjustments are made continuously as a result of changes in pricing or trading opportunities, and, less frequently, following the appreciation of shifts in fundamental value. Adjustments are also made when the portfolio profile no longer is within desired characteristics of spread and interest duration, currency exposure, or risk.

In a smoothly working investment process, initiative for portfolio changes may come from traders and portfolio managers, who are close to the price action, or from analysts who gauge credit or macro trends. In cases when fundamental variables drive adjustments, analysts can become involved in the process, even as origination may come from the portfolio management team. In practice, rapid events challenge the portfolio management process, as communication lags, for example, can lead to incomplete integration of the investment process and decisions which do not fully use the potential of the investment management team.

Failure to perform consistently up to expectations is usually the consequence of a failure in appraisal of fundamentals and not of errors in market timing. Of course, gauging the probability and impact of powerful positive or negative events adds value. It does and can provide for a large measure of success in managing emerging debt portfolios. Market and event related decisions, such as the timing of Brady buyback announcements, which have been made by several of the most prominent issuers of Brady bonds (Mexico, Argentina and Brazil), can be gauged by analysis of government finances and cash flows but equally require a keen understanding of capital market conditions.

One of the crucial aspects of managing emerging portfolios is the need to appraise the impact upon emerging borrowers of variables outside the investable universe, that is, financial and economic changes and expectations in advanced countries. This calls for an investment process integrated closely with fundamental and market analysis of U.S. and international bond markets. The flow of causality is almost exclusively from developed to emerging markets. Defensive or hedging strategies as well as strategies to take advantage of patterns in benchmark markets are a key part of the portfolio management process.

CONTROLLING RISK

Risk management is an essential ingredient in emerging markets fixed income. Risk management can be viewed in several ways, depending on the dimension of risk. In emerging markets, limiting credit risk, sovereign and corporate, is a central aim of the investment process and of portfolio management.

Risk control also involves mitigating market risk. This often involves reducing price or total return volatility. Investors will have widely differing levels of tolerance for volatility, depending on their ultimate aim. For an equity investor who views emerging debt as an equity alternative, maintaining low or moderate portfolio volatility may not be important or even highly desirable. On the other hand, a fixed income investor who aims at seeking excess return over U.S. bonds but maintaining volatility within some upper bound of the U.S. bond market will want to have a different portfolio profile than an equity-oriented investor.

Risk could also be viewed asymmetrically, for example, reducing downside risk. This can also be approached in a number of ways. The selected strategy to reduce downside risk will vary with the prospectus or guideline restrictions. At one end, it may require capping downside price movement by purchasing put options. Or, it may involve selling call options, matching assets and liabilities, or simply lowering interest duration. The cost of reducing downside risk will be gauged in the context of overall investment objectives and may not always be by itself a determining variable.

Another potential area for risk control would be to reduce the risk of underperformance versus a established benchmark or appropriate index. This can be thought of as aiming to keep tracking error within bounds from a benchmark. Tracking error is the standard deviation of the difference in performance (usually total return) between a portfolio and the benchmark. A portfolio guideline or constraint may be to maintain tracking error within ±2% of total return for a given benchmark or reference index. Since emerging market portfolios can have high volatility, there could be a sizable cost in potential return for keeping tracking error low, for example, at less than 1%. Limiting tracking error is probably best viewed as an exercise in performance management rather than risk management as it merely focuses on a narrow aspect of the risk dimension.

Comprehensive risk management can also be viewed from a value-at-risk perspective. This would involve ascertaining the potential loss resulting at a given level of confidence from a change in some variable. It could measure, for instance, the impact of a change in the price of the 10-year U.S. Treasury note on emerging Eurobonds in the portfolio at a 95% level of confidence.

Managing Credit Risk

Management of credit risk requires making sound judgments on sovereign and corporate credits. Fiduciary responsibilities usually require that investment managers make independent evaluation of credit risk and do not rely on the judgment of credit rating agencies, brokers, or other intermediaries. Credit agency ratings are an important guide to credit quality and have great bearing on security pricing and price movements. In many cases, investment guidelines impose a constraint based on agency credit ratings. This means that agency ratings have to be taken as a central reference point for investment managers, who, nonetheless, will have to form their own opinions regarding the quality of the credit.

Managing sovereign risk requires continuing assessment of factors that may imply or signal a deterioration of risk. Such monitoring can be done by research analysts or even by portfolio managers. Dependence on market information, made available by third parties such as banks, brokers, consultants, and the press does not relieve investment managers of their responsibilities versus clients.

The following steps are recommended as part of a continuing credit review process: (1) weekly, or at least monthly, review of all credits in a portfolio; (2) assessment of the impact on capacity to service debt of major changes in operating capability, government policies, external factors, or other exogenous changes; (3) analysis of interrelations among credits focusing on material impact that changes in one credit may have on other credits; (4) mitigation of elements that can lower the probability of serious impact upon the credit; and, (5) use of a value-at-risk or similar approach to quantify overall sensitivity to changes in key variables.

While quantitative techniques and management systems will enhance capabilities, management of credit risk involves a continuing assessment of fundamental variables that affect valuation. A review of technical, flow, or statistical associations that may affect market prices is very useful but not the central aspect. That is, managing credit risk involves making fundamental judgments about intrinsic risk that can potentially be expressed in fundamental value.

Managing Market Risk

Investors in emerging debt usually concern themselves with two types of market risk — volatility and pricing risk. The first is associated with variation of total return or prices as measured by traditional statistical measures such as the standard deviation or the standard error of estimate. In this section we will direct our comments mainly to the management of volatility and not to pricing risk.

Pricing risk is often a consequence of the lack of liquidity in issues with thin secondary markets. While a concern in portfolios that seek value and diversification by investing in minor sovereign and, especially, corporate issues, pricing risk is generally low in all the major Brady bonds and large sovereign issues. One obvious way to reduce pricing risk is to confine investments to major liquid issues.

Emerging debt is usually viewed as one of the most volatile fixed income asset classes. This is generally the case for long duration emerging bonds, particularly Brady bonds and long Eurobonds. On the other hand, as discussed in the next section, portfolios of local currency investments exhibit low volatility when properly diversified.

In the two years since the Mexican peso crisis, the volatility of Bradys and liquid Eurobonds declined steadily as indicated in Exhibit 4. By June 1997, the volatility of the Emerging Brady Bond Index Plus produced by J.P. Morgan (EMBI+), the most widely used benchmark, reached a little over 8% (26 week annualized volatility) from levels of around 25% at the beginning of 1995. Lower volatility is reflected in pricing of options on Brady bonds.

Investors assign variable degrees of importance to volatility. For some investors it is of secondary importance in the context of attaining investment objectives and no restrictions are desired to limit volatility beneath a given threshold. For others high volatility may be undesirable or must be kept within bounds to match liabilities, complement other assets, or to keep within a range of the benchmark.

The following approaches to managing volatility can be used in emerging debt portfolios: portfolio diversification, asset allocation, and sell disciplines. Option strategies are a fourth alternative, which can be used tactically or as an integral part of core portfolios.

Portfolio Diversification

One of the virtues of portfolio diversification is that it can dampen market risk as well as provide a mechanism for managing other types of risk (sovereign, credit, currency, event) over a set of securities. The capability of diversification to dampen market risk is a function of the interaction of price and return among emerging debt securities and with securities in other asset classes.

Exhibit 4: EMBI + Volatility

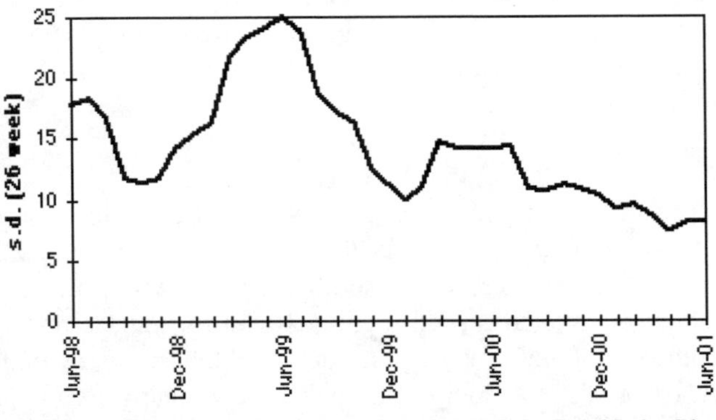

Source: Calculated from J.P. Morgan Emerging Markets Bond Index Plus.

Correlations and other statistical measures of association show that Brady bonds and Eurobonds are closely correlated. In addition, as mentioned before, volatility is not necessarily dampened in close proportion to the bonds' duration and other intrinsic properties. This means than when considering portfolios consisting mainly of Bradys and Eurobonds, there is only reduced scope for limiting low volatility by diversification within this asset class.

Other alternatives, such as strategies which imply use of options and other derivatives, can reduce volatility but their cost is generally high. This limits derivatives-based techniques to tactical and trading strategies, where they can add the most value. Ordinarily they do not provide an efficient approach to capping downside risk to the entire portfolio. As a comprehensive approach, extensive use of put options, covered calls, and other protective techniques is too costly for all but the most defensive strategies. Derivatives have an important role, when allowed by investment guidelines, in tactical positioning of portfolios or as a means of attaining implicit leverage. The growth of emerging debt derivatives trading in over-the-counter markets and in exchanges offers smooth execution and much more efficient pricing than was possible in the early stages of the evolution of the asset class.

One possible diversification strategy, blending Bradys and emerging Eurobonds on one side and local currency emerging debt on the other can often provide desirable risk-return characteristics and a substantial reduction in portfolio volatility.

Asset Allocation

Brady bonds and emerging market Eurobonds have lower correlation with other fixed income and equity securities than among themselves, providing for the possibility of constructing portfolios that will meet a wide range of desired objectives. The correlation matrix in Exhibit 5 illustrates correlations for 1993-1997 among the main emerging market debt indices — the EMBI and EMBI+ — and other fixed income and equity indices. In particular, it shows that whereas the EMBI+ and EMBI have moderate correlation with the U.S. bond and equity markets (Lehman G/C and S&P 500), correlation with global bonds (G. Govt) is essentially not statistically different from zero. This suggests that emerging bonds can be a useful complement to global and international bond portfolios. It implies also that adding global bonds to emerging market portfolios could be an efficient strategy in terms of risk-return trade-off for many investors who do not wish to have full exposure to emerging market risk.

Sell Disciplines

Emerging markets debt management requires strict sell disciplines in portfolios and trading strategies. There are several reasons for this emphasis on sell disciplines. Emerging countries are in the process of solidifying policies, institutions, and regulations aiming at providing a constructive environment for long-term investments and market development. But, unfortunately, setbacks and failures occur frequently, sometimes in difficult to predict conditions. This calls for continuing evaluation of positions and the taking of swift action to reduce, alter, or eliminate positions from the portfolio.

Exhibit 5: Emerging Markets Correlation Matrix
(Monthly data — December 1993 to March 1997)

Index*	Annualized Volatility	EMBI+	EMBI	ELMI	ELMI-EW	S&P 500	Lehm G/C	G. Govt.	MS EAFE
EMBI+	17.81	1							
EMBI	17.75	0.98	1						
ELMI	7.62	0.54	0.50	1					
ELMI-EW	3.74	0.42	0.34	0.82	1				
S&P 500	10.22	0.48	0.52	0.13	0.07	1			
Lehm G/C	4.89	0.45	0.47	0.02	0.07	0.60	1		
G. Govt.	5.14	0.03	-0.01	0.04	0.32	0.27	0.52	1	
MS EAFE	10.85	0.20	0.20	0.15	0.05	0.45	0.12	0.36	1

Source: Calculated on the basis of index data from J.P.Morgan, Lehman Brothers, and Morgan Stanley Capital International.

*Indices are as follows:
EMBI+: J.P. Morgan Emerging Market Bond Index Plus
EMBI: J.P. Morgan Emerging Market Bond Index
ELMI: J.P. Morgan Emerging Local Markets Index
ELMI - EW: Adjusted Equal-Weighted ELMI
S&P 500: Standard and Poor's 500 Stock Index
Lehm G/C: Lehman Brothers Government/Corporate Index
G. Govt: J.P. Morgan Global Government Index
MS EAFE: Morgan Stanley Capital International, Europe, Australia and the Far East Index

The high sensitivity of emerging bonds to conditions in global fixed income markets also calls for strict sell disciplines as a defensive posture when faced with potential setbacks in the U.S. bond market or, for many Asian issuers, in Japanese money or bond markets. Alternative management techniques can be used to complement sell disciplines such as careful management of interest and spread duration. As explained above, however, duration strategies do not always work well in emerging debt securities.

Trading-oriented investment processes likewise need to be based firmly on precise sell disciplines. This is, of course, critical in leveraged portfolios or those which employ short positions. Even in portfolios where leverage on short positions are not allowed by prospectus or investment guidelines, tactical positions must be controlled and gains taken or losses curtailed as price action surpasses set limits.

Derivatives can substitute for sell actions and can frequently be a superior alternative. As pricing efficiency increases, options can be employed at lower cost to cushion portfolios from adverse price movements. The fall in price volatility in Brady and Eurobonds in the two years to mid-1997 supports arguments that volatility is priced reasonably low compared to the historical trend in the market. The contrary argument is that implied volatilities remain higher than historical volatilities for most Brady bonds as of mid-1997.

LOCAL CURRENCY MARKETS

Local currency markets are the fastest growing component of the emerging debt asset class, driven by the explosive development of capital markets in developing nations. Three factors argue for an even more rapid development of liquid markets for local debt securities: (1) the deregulation of local capital markets; (2) the revolution in pension and savings systems in developing countries; and, (3) the swift advances in price and financial stability by nearly all large emerging nations.

Local debt markets are now the largest part of the emerging debt asset class. Money markets instruments and local bonds in 75 emerging countries by the end of 1996 exceeded $850 billion, according to estimates derived from International Monetary Fund, World Bank, and national data. By contrast, the market value of Brady bonds and other Eurobonds issued in international markets by governments and corporations in the same countries is estimated at $230 billion. Some $370 billion of local markets securities are located in Asia, $250 billion in Latin America, $90 billion in Africa south of the Sahara, and the rest in Central and Eastern Europe and the Middle East. These numbers exclude many government and corporate bond issues and commercial paper of lesser liquidity.

The bulk of liquid local assets are money market instruments, mainly government securities. Commercial paper is usually placed privately. A handful of countries have developed liquid bond markets, most importantly Argentina, South Africa, and, to a lesser extent, Chile and the Czech Republic. Government bills and notes are traded extensively in most countries, mainly in the interbank market but also in other active secondary markets. Clearing and custody are often sophisticated with book entry at the central bank or other central depository a common practice.

Local instruments are rarely traded offshore in direct form. However, liquid forward markets for local currencies are rapidly developing in major emerging countries and others that do not have strict capital controls. Offshore markets are also found in lesser currencies. By mid-1997, forwards and offshore notes were available in some 30 emerging currencies, most with reasonable liquidity. Banks are also active in designing offshore structures to capture the properties of local money market instruments when trading may be hindered by local operational practices such as lack of proper custody or certain types of exchange controls. These services are gradually becoming more competitive as international banks set up operations in new countries and local banks begin to enter the business through their offshore subsidiaries.

Exhibit 6 provides a sample of monthly money market returns in dollar terms comprising the ten emerging countries in J.P. Morgan's Emerging Local Markets Index (ELMI). The exhibit shows an average correlation of 0.11 from inception of the index in December 1993 to October 1996. Most coefficients in the exhibit are not statistically significant or negative among pairs of countries. Even among countries in some regions, the correlations are low. For example, the average correlation among the four Southeast Asian countries in the matrix is only 0.09.

Exhibit 6: Local Currency Correlation Matrix
(Monthly data — December 1993 to October 1996)

	Argen	Czech	Indon	Malay	Mexico	Philip	Poland	S.Afri	Thaild	Turkey
Argentina	1									
Czech Republic	−0.279	1								
Indonesia	0.200	−0.260	1							
Malaysia	0.239	0.240	−0.032	1						
Mexico	0.218	−0.219	0.384	0.145	1					
Philippines	0.218	−0.119	0.135	0.191	0.196	1				
Poland	0.098	0.564	0.030	0.183	−0.216	−0.086	1			
South Africa	−0.161	0.208	0.160	−0.204	−0.178	0.019	0.346	1		
Thailand	0.026	0.637	−0.046	0.375	0.106	−0.089	0.583	0.019	1	
Turkey	0.239	0.134	0.183	0.198	0.084	0.152	0.049	−0.023	0.154	1

* Based on portfolio of 90-day money market securities at market exchange rates.

Source: SS&C on the basis of data from J.P. Morgan.

Low correlations could well increase over time as currencies within a region may move together given an external shock or a change in external variables. Likewise, a successful speculative attack on one currency may well encourage speculators and investors to attack a neighboring currency or pull out massively from the currency. Recent evidence suggests that there may be links between attacks on currencies in separate regions, such as pressure on the Philippine peso following the Mexican peso 1994 devaluation and spillover effects from the Thai baht to neighboring currencies and the Czech koruny. Increased cooperation in Southeast Asia and other regions to share foreign assets and reserves should help reduce systemic currency risks. In effect, the Mexican peso devaluation of December 1994 had little impact on other Latin American currencies. Its impact was largely concentrated on bond and equity markets. Only Argentina experienced a sustained increase in money market rates resulting from the Mexico crisis.

As shown in Exhibit 5, the Emerging Markets Correlation Matrix in the previous section, ELMI had a correlation of 0.02 with the U.S. bond market as expressed by the Lehman Brothers Government/Corporate Index. The correlation with J.P. Morgan's Global Government Index was 0.04 and 0.15 with the EAFE index of Morgan Stanley Capital International. The correlation with the Emerging Markets Bond Index of J.P. Morgan was 0.50, reflecting the ELMI's nearly 25% average weight in Mexican pesos in most of the sample period of December 1993 to March 1997.

Greater diversification can reduce the volatility of local currency investments. This is shown by the use of an equally-weighted ELMI index or ELMI-EW, which could be considered as a potential alternative benchmark. This involves giving a 10% weight to each of the ten components of the standard J.P. Morgan index. Calculations were performed using a monthly sample for the period from the end of 1993 to March 31, 1997. As can be expected, this significantly improves the performance of the index in terms of portfolio volatility and lowers the correlation with the EMBI and EMBI+ index. Annualized monthly volatility of total return of the ELMI benchmark during the period was 7.62% as against 3.74% for the ELMI-EW. Correlation of the ELMI-EW with the EMBI was 0.34 compared with 0.50 for the ELMI. Comparisons with the EMBI+ are 0.54 and 0.42.

Aggressive investors may want to look at high yielding local currency investments such as those provided by countries in earlier stages of stabilization and reform than other emerging countries. In these cases also, diversification of local currency portfolios will help lower volatility as interest rates and currencies are determined principally by domestic factors and events.

The next stage in the development of local currency markets is the formation of full yield curves. In nearly all emerging countries, bonds with an average life longer than two years issued by governments and corporations are held to maturity by local banks, insurance companies, pension funds, and wealthy individuals. Thus there is no liquid secondary market. In some countries, there is limited liquidity of corporate and municipal bonds which can trade at the main security exchanges. Only in Argentina and South Africa is there extensive secondary trading of sovereign and corporate bonds issued in Argentine pesos and rands with ample participation by local and foreign investors. With the improvement in credit quality and the growth of financial savings in many emerging countries, issuance in local currency is likely to be transformed in coming years. Corporate and municipal issuers look at the local securities markets as a largely untapped and natural source of financing which could provide an alternative to bank financing as a source of long-term funds.

Chapter 10

Integrating Emerging Market Bonds into a Global Portfolio

Steven I. Dym, Ph.D.
President
Steven I. Dym & Associates

INTRODUCTION

The middle years of the 1990s witnessed a change in the attitudes of institutional investors towards bonds of developing countries. What once would not be considered part of "traditional" portfolios has now become an important ingredient in them. However, because of the newness of these instruments, the tools available to portfolio managers and analysts are just catching up to the need. The purpose of this chapter is to present a number of useful tools for analyzing emerging market bonds and a general approach for integrating them with bonds of industrialized countries into a global fixed income portfolio.

HISTORICAL MEASURES OF RETURN AND RISK

In this section, some historical measures of return and risk for emerging market bonds are presented. These statistics show why this asset class has become so popular. The next section summarizes the different types of emerging market fixed income assets. Then tools for analysis are presented, followed by the new "budget math" applicable to developing countries. Throughout these sections, the corresponding measures for bonds of industrialized countries are provided for comparison. The final section goes through the dynamics of decision making the investment manager must navigate in order to successfully integrate emerging market bonds in the portfolio.

Due to their significant risk of default, developing country bonds carry a high credit risk premium. This is particularly evident in their U.S. dollar-denominated issues. In principle, the risk of default should be relevant to any sovereign entity. But a government's theoretical ability to tax (and in some cases to require the central bank to purchase its debt) means that its ability to repay its *own* currency-denominated debt is not at risk — instead, the value of its currency is at risk. But servicing *foreign* currency-denominated debt requires the ability to convert its own currency into foreign exchange, something which may not always be possible for governments of relatively small, developing economies. This is why the rate of return requires a default risk premium. It is this variable which produces the distinct asset class, and raises the expected return from emerging market debt securities relative to those of industrialized countries. It follows that the absence of emerging market bonds from portfolios limited to industrialized country bonds means that adding emerging market debt must improve the portfolio's risk-return trade-off and expand the "efficient frontier."

During some years spreads of developing country over U.S. Treasury bonds went well into double digits, at times over 20%! While such situations are not the norm, they are also not rare, occurring, for example, when one country is experiencing major macro-economic difficulties — such as Mexico in late 1994 and through 1995 — and resulting investor nervousness spills over into almost all other emerging markets. The bonds' high yields, their wide risk premiums and substantial movements have produced very attractive rates of return for this asset class, accompanied, of course, by outsized volatility. Exhibit 1 displays the rates of return for one type of emerging market bonds — Brady bonds — since their inception, along with those for government bonds of the United States and of industrialized countries. Clearly, Brady bonds compare very favorably with the other issues. They well outperformed Treasury bonds over the 1990-1997 period, due to their hefty risk premium on top of Treasuries and the general narrowing of credit spreads over that time. The spread narrowing, in turn, reflected improved credit fundamentals of the Brady bond countries as a group, as well as increasing investor acceptance of the securities. Of course, this narrowing was not smooth, which shows up in the comparative volatilities of the asset classes, as shown in Exhibit 2. Brady bonds also compare favorably with non-dollar government bonds (and with the World Government Bond Index, a market weighted average of U.S. and non-U.S. industrialized country bonds). Currency movements impart a great deal of volatility to non-dollar bonds. While this element of risk is absent in Brady bonds, their volatility is still greater, but, as Exhibit 2 shows, they offered a superior return over the period.

Exhibit 1: Annualized (Non-Compounded) Monthly Rates of Return
May 1990 (Inception of Brady Index) to
April 1997 (Salomon Brothers' Monthly ROR Data)

	Percentage
U.S.	8.533
Non-U.S.	10.917
WGBI	9.678
Brady	19.760

Exhibit 2: Standard Deviation of Monthly Rates of Return
May 1990 (Inception of Brady Index) to April 1997 (Salomon Brothers' Monthly ROR Data)

	Percentage
U.S.	1.261
Non-U.S.	2.566
WGBI	1.752
Brady	4.063

Is this comparison of emerging market bonds to those of industrialized countries valid? From one perspective it is. They are all government issues and, therefore, should carry the lowest yield among issuers in their respective countries. (On this, see the next section.) From a different perspective, though, the comparison may be inappropriate. Brady and most developing country Eurobonds are dollar denominated. Hence, they are not "government bonds" with respect to the currency in which they are denominated. Their substantial risk of default imposes a high risk premium on the bonds, much like high-yield corporate issues which must offer a yield in excess of that of the government bonds of the currency country. For this reason, a number of institutional investors — especially those who accessed the developing country bond market relatively early in its development — consider them a high-yield issue, belonging in the same class, so to speak, as high-yield corporate bonds. In fact, as spreads on high-yield corporates contracted during the 1990s, many investors looked to Brady bonds and other emerging market bonds as high-yield alternatives.

There is much to be said for this latter line of reasoning. Indeed, the sovereign risk analysis described in a later section is in many ways similar to that performed for corporate bonds. Yet there are good reasons to consider developing country bonds in a global government bond portfolio. When all is said and done, we are analyzing countries. The currency risk, the current account deficit, the ability to service debt from tax revenue, the inflation factor are all *macro*-economic concerns. Hence, many of the tools used to analyze bonds issued by foreign industrialized countries, properly amended, are useful for these bonds. Furthermore, a number of emerging market countries have graduated, or are expected to graduate, from developing to developed status. Finally, emerging market bonds "fit" into a global portfolio because they have low to negative correlation with non-dollar developed country bonds, as Exhibit 3 shows. This is an attractive attribute in an increasingly interrelated global financial market. Perhaps more surprising is that, despite their dollar denomination, Brady bonds have had a relatively low correlation with U.S. Treasury issues.

In short, developing country bonds present an excellent diversification tool, allowing an expansion of a global portfolio's "efficient frontier." This combination of high yield, potentially high rates of return, macro-economic/country choice, and diversification benefits points to emerging market bonds as an important ingredient to a well-rounded global portfolio.

Exhibit 3: Correlation Coefficients
May 1990 - April 1997

	U.S. Treasuries	World Gov't Bond Index	Non-Dollar WGBI	Brady Index
U.S. Treasuries	1.000	0.603	0.390	0.400
World Gov't Bond Index	0.603	1.000	0.966	0.025
Non-Dollar WGBI	0.390	0.966	1.000	–0.090
Brady Bond Index	0.400	0.025	–0.090	1.000

EMERGING MARKET FIXED INCOME SECURITIES

There are four segments to the emerging debt market: bank loans, Eurobonds, local issues and Brady bonds.

A Brief History

Institutional investor interest in emerging market debt securities predates the creation of Brady bonds, although the Brady Plan and its resulting bonds certainly were the catalysts for their acceptance into the more traditional institutional portfolios. Low savings rates had forced many developing countries to look abroad for financing development and other projects intended to raise domestic living standards.

Capital was provided by official sources, such as governments and international agencies, and by commercial banks. The latter largely took the form of U.S. dollar-denominated loans, and were tied to a floating interest rate, usually LIBOR. When short-term interest rates surged during the early 1980s, debt service became very difficult. Coupled with the second "oil price shock" (most developing nations are petroleum importers) and recessions in industrialized countries which reduced their imports from the developing world, sizable portions of developing countries' income and output had to be sent abroad. This led to a number of debtor nations defaulting on their borrowings (the preferred term then was "moratorium").

The idea spread to more countries, until a veritable "LDC (less developed countries) debt crisis" was created. During the early stages of the crisis, the responses of bank lenders was similar to those applied to corporate defaults, that is, trying to work out the problem through maturity extensions, new money, and other traditional means. However, over time the situation deteriorated, affecting the creditworthiness of the banks themselves. Many major U.S. and some foreign commercial banks wrote off much of the value of these loans, and attempted to sell the remainder. Inter-bank trading of these loans therefore constituted the original primary market for distressed LDC debt. But since banks as a whole were trying to dispense of their remaining loans, prices remained depressed for a long time. Debt-equity swaps were successful to some extent, but their potential was limited. A number of non-bank investors entered the market at this time. However, these were typically speculators, as most of the loans were non-performing.

Bank Loans

The market for developing country loans still exists today, but primary trading activity has shifted to the Bradys and Eurobonds. Some of the original loans, though, are performing — Morocco, for example, has continually serviced its obligations. Those that are non-performing are sold with or without past due interest. Bank loans are offered to investors as assignments or by way of participations. The advent of the Brady Plan has created a new type of loan trading strategy — purchasing a non-performing loan in anticipation of it becoming "Bradied."

Eurobonds

Developing countries have issued (and defaulted) on their foreign bonds for at least 100 years. In the modern era, these countries' Eurobonds have had an excellent credit record, having been serviced even during the years of the bank LDC loan crisis and subsequent defaults. This may explain why yields on developing country Eurobonds are significantly lower than the same country's Brady issues.

Other possible reasons include the relatively small size of these obligations compared to bank debt and their resulting Brady issues, so that defaulting on them is much less economical, and the perceived need of having at least one unblemished market to access when necessary. But a more fundamental reason may be the nature of bonds relative to loans. The latter involve a small and relatively homogeneous group of creditors. A default leads to negotiations in which the health of the country is a concern to the creditors, since they likely wish to maintain a good relationship with the debtor, who may well provide more business in the future. Bondholders, by contrast, are a large, diverse group who, in the event of default, wish to recoup as much as possible *now* and have less to gain by working to preserve the long-run health of the debtor. In this respect, Brady bonds are more like Eurobonds, and deserve a narrower yield spread than loans.

Eurobonds are sold by the sovereign countries directly, by various government agencies as well as by state-run and large private corporate entities. The Eurobond market is the source of "new money" bond issues (as opposed to the Bradys which primarily repackage "old money.") Included in this category are Yankee bonds (developing country bonds issued in the U.S.) and the more recent global bonds (issued simultaneously in a number of world markets).

Local Issues

A number of developing countries have well-functioning and relatively liquid domestic debt markets. Because of historically high and variable inflation rates, these securities tend to be limited to money market maturities and floating rate notes and, if longer in term, are denominated in dollars. U.S. and other foreign investors have increased their interest in and allocation to these assets in recent years (notwithstanding a net withdrawal of funds during the period surrounding the Mexican devaluation), becoming more comfortable with the credit as well as the currency risk inherent in them. Because of the currency factor, these bonds contain another layer of complexity, as will be explained later.

Brady Bonds

In the midst of the developing country debt crisis of the 1980s, various attempts were made at resolution, each ending in failure. Simply extending new loans did not go over well with the creditor banks, as they had tried that in the early years of the crises with counterproductive results. And the increased supply of loans only depressed prices further. International lending agencies also resisted providing new funds, as borrower countries did not meet mandated targets. The Brady Plan differed from previous approaches in a number of respects. First, it addressed the underlying fundamental economic problems of the debtor countries (such as protected markets and controlled prices), which had generally not been done before.

With respect to the bank loans, the plan's innovation was to focus on enhancing the value of *existing* loans rather than extension of new money. In some cases the original loan amount was discounted. In others, the coupon was set at below market rates. By effectively decreasing the supply of loans, these features raised the value of the loans in the secondary market. By lowering the debt burden of the borrowers, the risk premium was reduced, adding to the loan's value. And by transforming the loans into bonds, their appeal to investors was enhanced.

Finally, for some of the bonds, U.S. Treasury zero-coupon securities were purchased to serve as collateral for the principal payment, and high grade money market securities for a portion of the interest. The result of all this was the creation of a new market, that of Brady bonds. Most of the bonds are U.S. dollar denominated, and a host of different payment features exist: fixed- and floating-rate (and hybrids); partially collateralized and un-collateralized; bullet and amortizing bonds. Brady bonds now command the lion's share of emerging markets debt trading volume.

TOOLS OF ANALYSIS

Begin with a U.S. Treasury bond, of arbitrary maturity. Assume the bond is purchased on its coupon date and the investor has a 1-year horizon, which avoids accrued interest calculations on both the purchase and sale dates, as well as reinvestment rates for the coupon payments.[1] For simplicity, assume the full coupon is paid annually. Let

P = current price of bond
C = coupon
P^* = expected sale price of bond
ROR = expected rate of return

---

[1] In the appendix to the following work, the 1-year horizon assumption is relaxed and the complications of reinvestment in the presence of potential default is dealt with: Steven I. Dym, "Integrating Emerging Market Bonds into a Global Portfolio," Chapter 3 in *The Handbook of Emerging Fixed Income and Currency Markets* (New Hope, PA: Frank J. Fabozzi, 1997).

Then

$$P = \frac{C + P^*}{1 + ROR} \tag{1}$$

Solving for the expected rate of return,

$$ROR = C/P + (P^* - P)/P \tag{2}$$

The bond's rate of return equals its current yield plus any capital gain or loss. We can use the familiar duration approximation to write:

$$ROR = cy - Dur \bullet \Delta y \tag{3}$$

where cy is the bond's current yield, y its yield to maturity, Dur its (modified) duration and Δ denotes change.

Dollar-Denominated Brady or Eurobonds

How do equations (1) through (3) change for dollar-denominated emerging market bonds? Because there is no foreign-exchange risk, the structure of equations (1) and (2) are the same. Obviously, the current yield is higher, as the bond contains a hefty risk premium for possible default. In addition, the final term of equation (3) must explicitly incorporate the possible change in the risk premium and its effect on the bond's price on the horizon date. For this, we will use the following notation:

t = yield of corresponding maturity Treasury bond
r = credit risk spread of emerging market bond
Dur_t = Duration with respect to Treasury yield change
Dur_r = Duration with respect to credit spread change

Then equation (3) is modified to:

$$ROR = cy - Dur_t \cdot \Delta t - Dur_r \cdot \Delta r \tag{4}$$

A change in Treasury yields will affect the bond's price, as will a shift in the risk premium the market applies to the bond. The two duration measures are not necessarily the same. If it is a fixed rate bond, then only if the bond is uncollateralized will the durations be equal. They will obviously differ if it is a floating-rate issue, but here, too, the measures depend on the existence of collateral.[2]

Clearly, understanding the determinants of the risk premium is crucial. The greater the risk of default, the higher the risk premium. What determines the market's assessment of a country's default risk? This is the central idea of sovereign risk, analysis of which is briefly summarized in the next subsection.

---

[2] For the actual durations, see Steven I. Dym, "Price Sensitivity and Risk Measures for Brady Bonds," Chapter 10 in *The Handbook of Emerging Fixed Income and Currency Markets*.

Sovereign Risk

Many measures, too numerous to mention, are relevant to assessing expected default for a developing economy.[3] An efficient approach is to compartmentalize these measures into three categories: structural, solvency and serviceability. In addition to making the analysis more manageable by removing redundancies, this categorization produces a "term structure" of expected default rates, akin to the well-known notion of term structure of interest rates.

Structural Factors

Measures classified as structural factors describe the long-term fundamental health of the country. These measures include economic variables such as reliance on a particular commodity for export earnings and the inflation experience of the country, welfare indicators such as per-capita GNP, and social/economic measures such as income distribution. More subjective factors are the perceived integrity of the country and its integration into the world economy. Structural variables are generally not directly linked to default. But countries with poor such fundamentals are likely to develop economic problems that do bring on default. Further, given two countries with similar other variables, the one with the inferior structural measures will likely have a lower tolerance to adverse economic shocks and default earlier.

Solvency Factors

Compared to the longer-term structural variables, the solvency class contains intermediate-term measures of a country's health. (A loose analogy to an industrialized country's yield curve would be to put business cycle variables affecting interest rates into the intermediate class and savings rate and productivity measures into the long term class.) In particular, solvency variables should reflect the country's ability, over time, to meet its central government debt obligations. Both internal and external debt are included, but debt denominated in foreign currency must be distinguished from own currency borrowing, as will be shown later. In either case, we will see that a crucial element is whether the country's economy is growing at a rate in excess of the real cost of its borrowing.

Serviceability Factors

Serviceability factors are of short-term, if not immediate, concern. They reflect the country's foreign exchange reserve position relative to its obligations Despite good or improving fundamentals and strong solvency measures, a developing country may be forced into a liquidity type crisis if its reserves are deficient or likely to become so when a foreign debt payment is due.

---

[3] For a discussion of the approach by Standard & Poor's sovereign ratings, see David T. Beers and Marie Cavanaugh," Sovereign Credit Rating: A Primer," and Helena Hessel, "Rating the Transition Economies," Chapters 6 and 7, respectively, in *The Handbook of Emerging Fixed Income and Currency Markets*.

The importance of these sovereign risk measures lies in the link between them and the probability of the country defaulting on its obligations. A deterioration in any of the factors raises the likelihood of default. Should a default occur, the investor's rate of return falls precipitously, with the precise ROR depending on the recovery value of the bonds.[4] Our concern here is with the effect of an increase in the likelihood of default on the bond's value, even if a default does not actually occur. In equation (4), this raises the value of the risk premium, *r*, reducing the rate of return according to the bond's credit spread duration. For example, suppose the outlook for inflation in a developing country worsens, although it is not yet reflected in current price trends, and the currency is little affected. Since this is a structural factor, it impacts the risk premium on the country's longer-term bonds more than its shorter maturity issues. On the other hand, a temporary decline in foreign exchange reserves will have a greater effect on shorter-term bonds, reducing their rates of return more than for longer-term securities.[5]

Local Currency Issues

An investment in the local currency obligations of developing countries brings another variable into the analysis: foreign exchange rate movements. Here, equation (1) must be amended as follows:

$$P/e = \frac{(C + P^*)/(e^*)}{1 + ROR} \tag{5}$$

where e is the spot exchange rate of the local currency for one U.S. dollar, and e^* is its expected rate at the end of the 1-year holding period. The investment's rate of return then includes an additional term:

$$ROR = (C/P) + (P^* - P)/P - (e^* - e)/e \tag{6}$$

Exchange rate movements can profoundly affect rates of return. Looked at this way, there is nothing special about currency risk for emerging market bonds compared to that of foreign currency denominated industrialized country bonds. But, in fact, there is.

Market participants need little reminding that developing country currencies can quickly lose much of their value. This type of risk — which we can call "wipe-out" risk — is essentially absent in industrialized countries' currencies. During stable periods, this risk is low, and a developing country's currency can behave and react to the fundamental variables in a manner qualitatively similar to that of an industrialized country. But when debt ratios, as modeled in a later sec-

---

[4] A methodology for estimating expected rate of return over a long-term horizon for various recovery and reinvestment rates, as well as different default probabilities, is found in the appendix to Dym, "Integrating Emerging market Bonds into a Global Portfolio."

[5] This analysis relates default probability movements to changes in the credit risk premium, then the latter to its effect on the bond's price, hence its rate of return. In Steven I. Dym, "Identifying and Measuring the Risks of Developing Country Bonds," *Journal of Portfolio Management* (Winter 1994), a methodology to go directly from implied default rates to bond price changes is presented.

tion, rise to unsustainable levels, or a special event occurs — such as runaway inflation, a loan default, renouncement of a currency peg, or a coup — the wipe-out risk parameter takes over, overpowering any of the other fundamental variables until confidence is restored (or, in the extreme, a new currency regime is imposed).

Let w be the probability of this occurring by the end of the horizon. Then equation (6) needs to be modified to

$$P/e = \frac{(1-w)\cdot(C+P^*)/e^*}{1+ROR} \tag{7}$$

Examine equation (7) from the perspective of a *required ROR*. Notice what this does to the currency's *spot* value, e. Given an expectation for P^*, a higher wipe-out risk, w, must lower P/e, in order to generate the required *ROR*. P will fall, too, but the less developed the economy, the more likely this risk to be translated into currency depreciation.

Responses to Shocks

Using the above analysis, it is easy to examine the effects of various economic shocks on developing country bonds and see how they differ from their effects on industrialized country issues. Exhibit 4 summarizes a few examples. Notice how, for example, economic growth affects Brady and Eurobonds differently from domestic bonds of a developed country. The textbook response of greater economic activity is higher interest rates, as liquidity becomes tighter (unless offset by the central bank). But in the case of developing countries, because the country's economic condition is reflected in the credit spread, the yield on its dollar-denominated bonds actually falls, as the improving economic conditions reduce the probability of default.

In the next section we develop a more rigorous framework for analyzing the relationships between the various economic variables in Exhibit 4 and sovereign risk measures.

Exhibit 4: Responses of Securities to Various Economic Shocks

Economic shock	Industrialized country bond	Dollar-denominated Brady or Eurobond	Local currency emerging market bond
Faster growth	Yield rises; stronger currency unless inflation accelerates	Sovereign risk decreases as solvency improves; hence credit spread on borrowings narrows	Yield rises; currency strengthens
Higher inflation	Yield increases, currency *may* depreciate unless central bank tightens	Sovereign risk increases, hence credit spread widens	Yield increases currency depreciates
Global capital tightening	Yield rises, but degree depends on the country's global sensitivity	Underlying U.S. rate rises, credit spread increases as well, as debt service costs rise	Same as dollar denominated bond
Trade deficit worsening	Yield may fall due to decline in economic activity; currency surely depreciates	Sovereign risk increases, raising credit spread	Yield increases; currency falls for both sovereign risk and trade reasons

THE NEW BUDGET MATH

Budget math is not new. The relationships among a country's macro-economic variables and its debt burden are important for industrialized as well as developing countries. Indeed, recent years have witnessed a renewed interest in these calculations even for developed nations since they are a crucial element in considering a country's entry into the European Monetary Union. Therefore, we start the analysis by developing the budget math relevant to any country. Then we introduce a new variable — foreign debt — of paramount concern to developing countries, and show how this affects the analysis.

Review of "Standard" Budget Math

Some new notation is necessary. Let:

d = ratio of stock of government debt to *nominal* GDP
b = share of operational budget deficit in GDP
r = real interest rate on domestic government debt
g = real growth rate of economy

Recognizing that the level of debt increases with the budget deficit plus the interest on outstanding debt, it is easily shown that:[6]

$$\Delta d = b + d \cdot (r - g) \tag{8}$$

Investors and international agencies worry if the d ratio is rising. As a solvency factor in our breakdown of sovereign risk, its unconstrained rise will result in instability. Thus, if r is greater than g, this suggests that in order to prevent d from rising, b should be negative (a budget surplus), or at least declining. Conversely, if g is greater than r, this means b can be positive, but with an upper limit. Of course, government spending can influence g. During a recession, for example, an increase in b may raise g, but d will be reduced only if the resulting impact on real interest rates is not larger than the increase in growth.

Highlighting Foreign Debt

When a government funds a substantial portion of its deficit abroad, as is the case with most developing countries that have large capital development needs together with low savings rates, its foreign debt must be explicitly recognized. Assume the foreign debt is dollar denominated. Let:

d_f = ratio of dollar denominated government debt, valued in domestic currency, to GDP
r_f = real interest rate on U.S. debt

[6] The development of this relationship, as well as the two that follow in this section, is provided in Steven I. Dym, "Budget Arithmetic for Developed and Developing Countries," unpublished paper.

If we allow the dynamics of the currency to follow purchasing power parity, then we find:

$$\Delta d = b + d \cdot (r - g) + d_f \cdot (r_f - r) \tag{9}$$

Notice that r_f includes the risk premium paid by the country to foreign lenders. Increasing growth is still the best way to reduce the overall debt/GDP ratio. But if $r_f < r$, then accessing foreign markets reduces the ratio as well. However, increasing the foreign debt share to take advantage of this interest rate differential increases the country's exposure to foreign lenders, tending to raise the risk premium included in r_f. The next section relates foreign borrowing to the current account deficit.

Current Account Deficit and Foreign Debt Dynamics

Foreign borrowing is an important element in a government's overall debt/GDP ratio, as shown above, and hence a solvency factor in the country's sovereign risk. In addition, the foreign debt to GDP ratio is a serviceability factor. A high ratio can bring on a liquidity crisis when foreigners are unwilling to roll over the country's foreign currency denominated debt. Whereas the previous section was concerned with *government* debt in both domestic and foreign form, here we examine the *total* stock of *foreign* debt. A deficit on the country's foreign account increases its foreign indebtedness. If c is the ratio of the current account deficit to GDP, then it can be shown that:

$$\Delta d_f = c + d_f \cdot (r_f - g) \tag{10}$$

Higher growth can offset a rising current account deficit, as long as the country's foreign borrowing rate does not exceed the growth rate.

We now have a basic understanding of sovereign risk. A change in this risk affects the bond's risk premium, in turn impacting its price via spread duration as shown above. A change in U.S. Treasury yields affects the bond's price via its Treasury duration. But it will also affect sovereign risk through its influence on the country's foreign debt service. The next section pulls all this together by looking at dynamic decision making for a truly global portfolio.

TRULY GLOBAL PORTFOLIO MANAGEMENT

A truly global fixed income portfolio — from a dollar-based investor's perspective — consists of U.S., foreign industrialized, and developing country debt instruments. With the tools above, the portfolio manager can make analytically sound global portfolio allocation decisions. A few examples are provided below.

Increase in U.S. Interest Rates

Suppose a portfolio manager expects an increase in U.S. interest rates more than implied by the yield curve. Obviously, this calls for a reduced exposure to U.S. bonds. Deciding which foreign industrialized countries to shift the portfolio's exposure to depends on the degree the foreign country's interest rates responds to the U.S. move, and on the effect of the new yield differential on the foreign currency, requiring a country by country analysis. Dollar-denominated emerging market bonds will, as a group, likely underperform (ignoring the foreign exchange effect on developed country bonds), as the higher U.S. rate is directly reflected in the bonds. But their risk spreads will likely widen as well, since debt service costs will rise. The degree of this effect depends on the foreign debt/GDP ratio, as developed above, and the maturity structure of this debt. Further, the rise in U.S. rates removes the incentive of some investors in emerging markets, who, when rates dropped at home, had left U.S. government issues in search of higher yielding dollar bonds. Their departure from the emerging markets raises the spreads. Developing countries' own currency denominated bonds should be hurt as well, for the same reason as the foreign developed country bonds, plus this sovereign risk effect.

Global Capital Tightening

As summarized in Exhibit 4, a tightening of global capital will raise interest rates in industrialized countries, with the individual country effects dependent on the degree of global sensitivity present in the country's domestic capital markets.[7] U.S. rates will rise as well, according to its sensitivity, bringing developing country dollar denominated bonds down along with it. Here, though, it is not clear that Brady and Eurobonds will underperform industrialized country bonds. This is because in this case the latter are directly affected by the global shock, while the former's effect is via U.S. rates. But risk spreads also widen, as the higher dollar interest rates increase borrowing costs, with the size, of course, dependent upon the country's reliance on foreign borrowing.

Flight to Quality

Clearly a movement by investors to higher quality issuers will force a major widening of developing country credit spreads. While these countries will suffer most, there will be some spillover to a handful of weaker developed nations. U.S. bonds will be affected the least; indeed, they may rally as global funds enter the country as a haven. This will help the Bradys and Eurobonds, given their dollar denomination. However, the net effect will be negative, as the risk spread widening will dominate the beneficial effect of the U.S. bond rally.

---

[7] Estimates for these global sensitivities can be found in Steven I. Dym, "Global and Local Risk Components of Foreign Bonds," *Financial Analysts Journal* (March-April 1992).

Chapter 11

Risk and Relative Value in the Brady Bond Market

Luis F. Martins, Ph.D.
Emerging Markets Research Analyst
Fidelity Investments

Jonathan M. Kelly
Portfolio Manager
Fidelity Investments

INTRODUCTION

The last few years have witnessed an explosion in interest and investment in emerging market debt (EMD). In 1996, the Emerging Markets Trading Association (EMTA) estimates that $5.3 trillion of EMD was traded.[1] The most liquid type of EMD is the Brady bond, which experienced nearly $2.7 trillion of dollar volume traded. Brady bonds came into existence in the late 1980s and early 1990s, and are restructured sovereign debt securities that evolved from defaulted commercial bank debt.

At present, there is an estimated $150 billion in outstanding face amount. They have been issued by a number of countries, have long tenors, and are mostly dollar denominated (see Exhibit 1). While all coupon payments are semiannual, there are a number of different coupon structures such as fixed rate, floating rate, and step-up; some Brady bonds contain both step-up and floating coupons. Many have either amortizing or capitalizing structures. Some Brady bonds have collateral in the form of U.S. Treasury zero-coupon bonds and/or AA rated securities which guarantee both principal and/or some coupon payments. They have also been eligible for participation at par in their local countries' privatizations.

Because of their complex structure, Brady bonds pose a number of interesting analytical challenges to the investor with a general familiarity of fixed income techniques. In this chapter we begin with a review of interest rate duration

[1] Emerging Markets Traders Association, "1996 Debt Trading Volume Survey," March 1997.

The authors wish to acknowledge the contribution of Constantin Petrov.

for fixed- and floating-rate bonds. Next, we discuss the price risk in the Brady bond market and introduce two case studies — the Argentine FRB and the Brazilian EXIT and New Money Bond (NMB). We then show how to calculate stripped spread and stripped spread duration (the spread and duration of a Brady bond excluding its collateral) and how to use these measures as relative-value tools in the Brady market. The limitations of collateral stripping in a relative value framework are then explained. Once the concept of stripping is understood, we can compare stripped spread duration with effective spread duration and show how they are used for different purposes. Finally, we combine effective interest rate duration and effective spread duration and revisit both the Argentine FRB and Brazil EXIT - plus - NMB case studies.

INTEREST RATE DURATION

To measure the sensitivity of a U.S. Treasury bond to parallel shifts in the *assumed flat* U.S. Treasury yield (and, consequently) spot curve, investors use the conventional interest rate duration. For a *fixed-rate semiannual coupon bond* this duration measure (in years) is:

$$D = \frac{1}{2}\frac{\sum_{t=1}^{N} tCF(t)(1+y/2)^{-t}}{P} \tag{1}$$

Exhibit 1: Characteristics of Selected Types of Brady Bonds

Brady Bond Type	Coupon Type*	Maturity	Collateral	Amortize
Par Bond	Fixed (can step-up)	30 years	yes	no
Discount Bond	Float; L + 13/16%	30 years	yes	no
Front-Loaded Interest Reduction Bonds (FLIRB)	Fixed (step-up) then Float; L + 13/16%	up to 18 years	partial	yes
New Money Bonds	Float; L + 13/16%	15 years	no	yes
Debt Conversion Bond (DCB)	Float; L + 13/16% or	up to 25 years	no Fixed (step up)	yes
Past Due Interest (PDI)	Float; L + 13/16% or Fixed (step-up)	20 years	no	yes
Capitalization Bond (C)	Fixed; step up	20 years	no	yes
Floating Rate Bond (FRB)	Float; L + 13/16%	12 years	no	yes
Exit Bond	Fixed	24 years	no	yes
Interest Reduction Bond (IRB)	Fixed; step-up	18 years	partial	yes
Interest Arrears Bonds	Float; L + 13/16%	up to 17 years	no	yes

* L = 6-month LIBOR

In equation (1) the yield to maturity, y, of the bond is equal to any of the U.S. Treasury spot rates, since the yield curve is assumed flat, N is the number of coupons in a semiannual bond, P is the bond's clean price, t is the time period (in half-years) between the settlement date and t-th cash flow, $CF(t)$ is the t-th cash flow, and D is the interest rate duration for the fixed-rate bond.

For a (small) parallel shift of the U.S. Treasury (yield) spot curve we have:

$$\Delta P = \frac{-P}{1 + y/2} D \Delta y + \text{second and higher order terms} \tag{2}$$

where Δ is the "small change in..." operator. The quantity $-D/(1+y/2)$ is usually referred to as the *modified interest rate duration.* That is,

$$\text{Modified duration} = \frac{-D}{1 + y/2} \tag{3}$$

Modified interest rate duration is commonly used by participants in the U.S. Treasury market to determine the price sensitivity of a security to changes in interest rates. An alternative to calculating modified interest rate duration by calculating equation (1) and then dividing by $(1 + y/2)$ is by changing rates up and down by a small number of basis points and determining how the price would change. The average percentage price change is then computed and is the duration measure. This procedure is the one that is used by software vendors to calculate modified interest rate duration.

For noncallable Treasury securities, modified interest rate duration is a good estimate of the price sensitivity of a security to a small change in interest rates. In contrast, there are securities with embedded options (e.g., callable securities and floating-rate notes with caps) for which modified interest rate duration may give a misleading estimate of the security's price sensitivity to changes in interest rates. The reason is as rates change, the expected cash flows change because of the embedded options. To determine the duration for such securities, the average percentage price change is calculated when rates are increased and decreased, as explained above. The resulting duration measure is called *effective interest rate duration.* The difference between effective and modified interest rate duration is that the prices used in the effective interest rate duration calculation reflect how changes in interest rates affect the cash flows. We will use the effective interest rate duration concept throughout this chapter.

Next we look at how to extend the concept of interest rate duration to a risk-free floating-rate note. For a floating-rate note, at some future time j, the coupon rate $C(t)$ begins to adjust in response to changes in market interest rates. Normally j=1, that is the coupon rate adjusts for the first time at the end of the initial interest period. (However, as shown in Exhibit 1, for some emerging market bonds, such as FLIRB's, we have an initial period where the bond is a fixed, usually step-up, coupon bond followed by a period where the bond is a floating-rate coupon bond. In this case j is the number of periods for which the bond pays a fixed (or step-up) coupon.) Following is the equation for D_{float}, the interest rate duration for a floating-rate note:[2]

$$D_{\text{float}} = D_{\text{fixed}} - \frac{\sum_{t=j+1}^{N} \partial C(t)/\partial y(1+y/2)^{-(t+1)}}{P} \tag{4}$$

where D_{fixed} is the duration of a fixed-rate bond which is otherwise identical to the floating-rate bond. Note that $\partial C(t)/\partial y$ in equation (4) must be evaluated for each t, $j+1 \le t \le N$.

Equation (4) tells us that the interest rate duration of a floating-rate bond equals the duration of a fixed-rate but otherwise identical bond minus a quantity that reflects the sensitivity of the floating-rate bond's coupon to changes in market interest rates.

Assuming that the floating-rate bond's coupon adjusts perfectly (i.e., one for one) to changes in market interest rates (for a LIBOR floater, since we are already assuming flat yield and spot curves and consequently a flat forward 6-month LIBOR strip) this is equivalent to assuming a constant LIBOR-Treasury spread, $\partial C(t)/\partial y = 1$ for each period t, $j+1 \le t \le N$, so that

$$D_{\text{float}} = D_{\text{fixed}} - \frac{\sum_{t=j+1}^{N} (1+y/2)^{-(t+1)}}{P} \tag{5}$$

Notice that equations (1) and (5) are valid measures of interest rate duration for fixed- and floating-rate bonds to estimate the component of price sensitivity due to U.S. interest rate changes for both collateralized and uncollateralized dollar-denominated Brady bonds. This is because the entire stream of payments (both coupons and principal) is subject to U.S. interest rate risk.

From equation (5) we can see that floating-rate coupon bonds trading at a deep enough discount can have a negative interest rate duration. In fact, deep discount floaters (like most Brady floaters) have a high enough yield to keep the first term in equation (5) small and the second large, thus ensuring their difference is negative. A negative interest rate duration means that, holding sovereign spreads constant, the price of the floating-rate bond should rise along with U.S. Treasury rates. This is the opposite of fixed-rate bonds, whose prices fall whenever interest rates rise.

In column 10 of Exhibit 2 we show effective interest rate duration for several fixed- and floating-rate Brady bonds. The pricing in the exhibit is as of market closing on 2/7/97. The rows corresponding to purely floating-rate bonds have been shadowed. Except for those floaters with short maturities (for example, the Brazilian IDU) and those selling at an insufficiently deep discount (the Philippines DCB and FLIRB bonds), we see that their effective interest rate durations are all negative. For fixed-rate bonds, the durations are all positive.

---

[2] See John D. Finnerty, "Measuring the Duration of a Floating-Rate Bond," *Journal of Portfolio Management* (Summer 1989), pp. 67-72.

Exhibit 2: Relative Value Measures for Selected Brady Debt

(1) Security	(2) Bid	(3) Ask	(4) Current Yield	(5) Stripped Yield	(6) Stripped Spread	(7) Blended Yield	(8) Spread Dur	(9) WAL	(10) Effective Duration	(11) Eff. Conv.	(12) Eff. Spread Dur.
Argentina Disc	82.125	82.375	7.80	11.75	529	9.63	7.63	26.1	1.73	73.9	5.07
Argentina FRB	**90.500**	**90.688**	**7.41**	**9.66**	**348**	**9.66**	**4.17**	**5.2**	**-0.14**	**-1.1**	**3.98**
Argentina Par	66.688	66.938	8.22	11.85	541	9.35	7.28	26.1	11.99	241.8	4.56
Brazil C	79.281	79.469	5.66	10.94	453	10.94	7.81	12.2	7.49	76.8	7.40
Brazil DCB	**80.875**	**81.125**	**8.12**	**10.58**	**419**	**10.58**	**7.05**	**11.2**	**-0.85**	**-7.3**	**6.69**
Brazil Disc	82.094	82.344	7.93	11.63	516	9.64	7.70	27.2	1.56	76.1	5.224
Brazil EI	**90.219**	**90.406**	**7.22**	**9.49**	**326**	**9.49**	**4.77**	**6.2**	**-0.14**	**-1.4**	**4.56**
Brazil IDU	**98.094**	**98.219**	**6.65**	**7.87**	**197**	**7.87**	**2.11**	**2.3**	**0.35**	**0.4**	**2.03**
Brazil Par Bond	66.344	66.594	7.51	11.52	506	9.26	7.51	27.2	12.14	251.7	4.84
Brazil Exit	75.625	75.625	8.04	10.53	418	10.53	5.94	9.3	5.70	50.9	5.64
Brazil FLIRB	76.500	76.500	5.88	10.64	429	10.52	6.92	9.2	2.39	5.6	6.16
Brazil NMB 1994	**85.625**	**86.000**	**7.66**	**10.17**	**387**	**10.17**	**5.79**	**8.2**	**-0.42**	**-3.4**	**5.51**
Bulgaria Disc A	57.500	58.125	11.28	20.02	1368	13.58	5.52	27.5	3.25	127.7	3.06
Bulgaria IAB	**52.625**	**53.000**	**12.37**	**17.16**	**1081**	**17.16**	**6.25**	**11.5**	**-2.73**	**-22.2**	**5.76**
Bulgaria FLIRB A	39.000	40.125	5.61	18.16	1179	17.80	7.21	10.5	2.53	1.3	6.25
Ecuador IEB	**86.000**	**88.000**	**7.42**	**11.07**	**492**	**11.07**	**3.96**	**5.0**	**-0.02**	**-1.4**	**3.76**
Ecuador Par	44.375	44.688	7.83	16.06	965	10.76	6.57	28.1	13.91	323.3	3.445
Ecuador PDI (cap)	**58.313**	**58.563**	**5.19**	**13.79**	**735**	**13.79**	**8.42**	**14.1**	**-0.59**	**17.3**	**7.88**
Ecuador Disc	66.750	67.125	9.82	15.75	933	11.80	6.26	28.1	1.78	73.9	3.95
Jordan PAR	62.000	64.000	6.25	12.18	572	9.70	7.68	26.9	12.59	261.9	5.01
Mexico Disc D	90.875	91.125	7.06	10.67	424	8.67	7.34	22.9	1.79	54.6	4.32
Mexico Par B	76.313	76.563	8.16	10.87	445	8.64	6.80	22.9	11.17	201.0	3.98
Mexico Aztec	**99.937**	**100.125**	**7.56**	**11.62**	**536**	**8.40**	**4.59**	**11.1**	**1.52**	**20.9**	**2.29**
Mexico Global 11.375% 9/15/16	109.250	109.500	10.39	10.27	378	10.27	8.20	19.6	7.94	105.5	7.80
Mexico Global 11.5% 2026	109.550	109.800	10.47	10.45	389	10.45	9.04	29.3	8.80	141.3	8.59

Exhibit 2 (Continued)

(1)	(2)	(3)	(4)	(5)	(6)	(7)	(8)	(9)	(10)	(11)	(12)
Security	Bid	Ask	Current Yield	Stripped Yield	Stripped Spread	Blended Yield	Spread Dur	WAL	Effective Duration	Eff. Conv.	Eff. Spread Dur.
Nigeria PAR	69.000	69.625	8.98	12.67	626	9.58	6.59	23.8	11.35	213.5	3.93
Panama IRB	77.813	78.313	4.47	8.74	233	8.67	8.03	10.9	5.14	30.3	7.36
Panama PDI	88.750	89.125	4.55	8.82	231	8.82	10.38	15.9	1.38	39.8	9.95
Peru FLIRB w/I	59.438	59.938	5.42	10.46	399	10.38	9.15	13.5	7.06	61.7	8.48
Peru PDI w/I	64.750	65.250	6.13	10.12	367	10.12	8.63	13.3	6.60	54.3	8.21
Philippines DCB B	**97.250**	**97.875**	**6.57**	**7.94**	**167**	**7.94**	**5.08**	**6.8**	**0.20**	**-0.2**	**4.89**
Philippines FLIRB B	**95.000**	**95.250**	**5.32**	**8.04**	**177**	**8.00**	**5.65**	**7.1**	**1.58**	**3.1**	**5.12**
Philippines Par B	89.125	89.625	7.07	8.47	204	7.62	7.30	20.8	11.00	181.1	4.56
Poland Disc	98.125	98.375	6.70	8.52	199	7.99	9.28	17.7	1.35	43.0	7.51
Poland PDI	84.500	85.250	4.69	7.90	145	7.90	8.77	13.0	8.56	99.4	8.44
Poland RSTA	63.250	64.250	5.06	8.36	183	7.68	9.58	27.7	13.95	298.8	6.95
Poland Par	57.000	57.500	5.22	8.33	178	7.62	9.96	27.7	14.72	323.8	6.97
Venezuela DCB DL	**89.250**	**89.500**	**7.33**	**9.98**	**377**	**9.98**	**4.40**	**5.9**	**0.00**	**-1.5**	**4.20**
Venezuela Disc	86.000	86.625	7.53	11.61	518	9.21	7.10	23.1	1.72	63.5	4.30
Venezuela FLIRB A	**90.000**	**90.563**	**7.52**	**10.08**	**388**	**10.08**	**3.84**	**5.1**	**-0.19**	**-1.5**	**3.66**
Venezuela Par B	77.000	77.438	8.72	11.71	529	9.16	6.77	23.1	11.05	199.6	4.09

Exhibit 3: FRB Bid Price versus Long Bond Yield

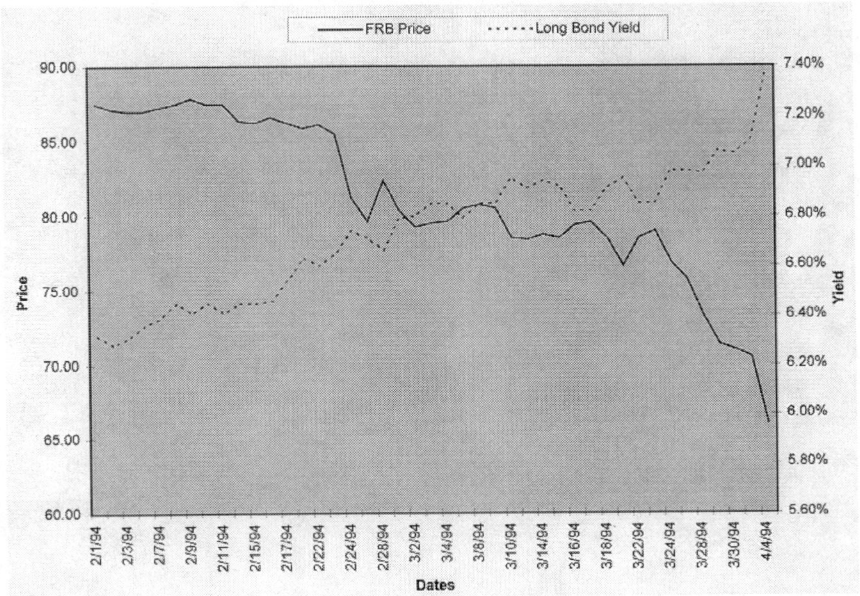

PRICE RISK OF EMERGING MARKET DEBT

Computing the interest rate duration of a Brady bond is an important first step in understanding its risk. However, interest rate duration by itself is a poor overall risk measure for the Brady market. To illustrate this, consider the performance of the J.P. Morgan Floating Rate Brady Bond Index in 1994. The index fell by more than 12% even though the yield on its base rate, 6-month LIBOR, rose from 3.375% to 7%. Clearly, there was more to the risk picture than interest rate duration.

In order to examine this more closely, we reviewed the performance of the Argentine FRB which is priced at a discount and has a floating-rate coupon of LIBOR + 13/16%. The FRB has a final maturity on March 31, 2005 and began amortizing in March 1996. In Exhibit 3 we show time series plots for both the bid-side price of the Argentine FRB and the long bond yield from February 1 through April 4 of 1994. We see that corresponding to a yield *rise* of 106 bps (from 6.32% on 2/1/94 to 7.38% on 4/4/94) we have a FRB price *drop* of $21.50 (from $87.50 to $66), or in percent terms, a whooping –24.5% (in just two months)! During this crisis the FRB (and more generally the Brady bond market) exhibited downside volatility more characteristic of an equity market than of a bond market.[3]

[3] See Raul Elizade, "Latin American Debt and Equity Market Relationships," *ING Barings Emerging Markets Weekly Report* (December 28, 1995), pp. 9-19.

Exhibit 4: Empirical versus Theoretical Interest Rate Duration

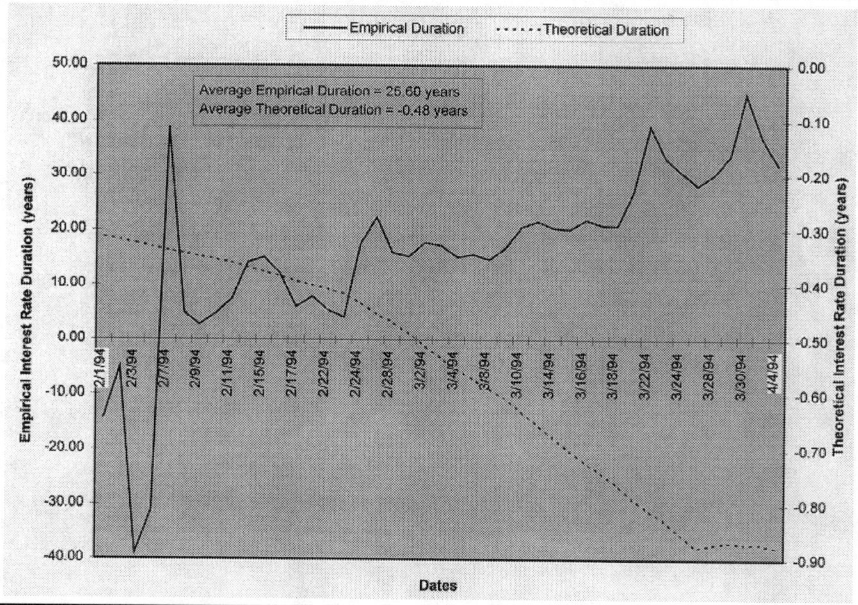

Consistent with equation (3) we define the FRB's *empirical interest rate duration* as follows:

$$D^{t}_{\text{empirical}} = -\frac{\Delta P_{FRB}}{P_{FRB}^{t-(1\text{-month})}}\frac{1}{\Delta Y_{\text{longbond}}} \tag{6}$$

where

$$\Delta P_{FRB} = P^{t}_{FRB} - P_{FRB}^{t-(1\text{-month})}$$

$$\Delta Y_{\text{longbond}} = Y^{t}_{\text{longbond}} - Y_{\text{longbond}}^{t-(1\text{-month})}$$

In Exhibit 4 we plot this empirical interest rate duration for the FRB together with its theoretical interest rate duration defined by equation (3). Note that for most of the sampling period the empirical duration is a positive number that increases, almost monotonically, from 2/9/94 until 4/4/94. The average value of this empirical duration for the sampling period was 25.6 years! Also note that the theoretical interest rate duration is a small negative number that decreases monotonically during the sampling period due to the bond's falling price. The average value of this theoretical duration for the sampling period is -0.46 years. These high empirical durations imply that the FRB behaved less like a deep discount floater, for which the price should have increased moderately with increasing rates, and more like a 25-year U.S. Treasury zero-coupon bond.

Nonetheless, the explanation is straightforward. The duration as given by equation (4) predicts the response to small changes of the Treasury rates *only* if nothing else changes. Hence, key to the derivation (and application) of equation (2) for the computation of the change in price of a floating-rate bond is the phrase "holding the sovereign spread constant." However, when interest rates started to rise early in 1994, sovereign spreads also started widening.

There were several reasons for the spread widening. First, many investors in emerging market debt were forced out of leveraged positions. Moreover, non-leveraged investors also decided to liquidate part of their positions. For cross-over investors this was attractive because yield opportunities could be found closer to home in the new higher rate environment. For both cross-over and dedicated investors concerns about future deterioration of sovereign creditworthiness, due to rising global interest rates and the associated decrease of capital flows into emerging economies,[4] also led to a liquidation of some positions. Thus, the rise in global rates led to the anticipation of a fall in creditworthiness in some emerging countries, which in turn put upward pressure on the spreads of their external debt.

The initial widening then triggered still more liquidations and associated spread widening. The cycle then reinforced itself to the point where spreads would widen or narrow based on what the Treasury market did that morning.[5] The positive correlation between Treasury rates and sovereign spreads exaggerated the effect of the Treasury rate movements, making both fixed- and floating-rate bonds behave as if their respective observed interest rate duration were longer than their theoretical duration value. In particular, for floating-rate bonds, Treasury backups were associated with price falls (i.e., these bonds behaved like debt instruments with positive interest rate duration). Thus, the severe spread widening and associated price depreciation overcame the effect of the negative interest rate duration, which in isolation would have led to price appreciation in a rising rate environment.

In Exhibit 5 we plot time series for both the price and sovereign spread of the FRB, again for the time period from 1/3/94 through 4/4/94. We see that after February 3, prices started dropping in step with the widening of the sovereign spread. As a matter of fact, the correlation between the two (for both the entire sample period and the sub-sample 2/3/94-4/4/94) is equal to −1.0!

In Exhibit 6, which covers the same period, we plot two 5-day-trailing rolling correlations between the FRB prices, and (1) the FRB sovereign spreads and (2) the long bond yield. If the FRB were to behave as a typical deep discount floater we would expect the rolling correlation between FRB prices and the long bond yields to always be a small positive number. Instead the correlation is usually a large negative number (close to −1), as would occur with a long duration zero-coupon bond. The correlation between prices and spreads is also close to −1. These two rolling correlations confirm that, beginning in early February 1994, rising rates

---

[4] For a prescient piece on this topic, see Guillermo Calvo, Leonardo Leiderman, and Carmen Reinhart, "Capital Inflows and Real Exchange Rate Appreciation in Latin America — The Role of External Factors," *IMF Staff Papers* (March 1993), pp. 108-151.

[5] See Vincent Palermo, "Brady Bonds — Tales of the Unexpected," *Emerging Markets Investor* (December 1994), pp. 54-55.

did lead to liquidations, which led to widening spreads, which in turn led to more liquidations. Hence, even though the tightening of U.S. rates sparked the liquidation process, the price of the bonds is not *directly* determined by the path that rates followed, but rather by the behavior of the sovereign spreads. Keep in mind that U.S. interest rates are only one factor affecting spreads. Idiosyncratic events, such as a dramatic change in economic policy, can also trigger a deterioration in a country's creditworthiness, which in turn can widen spreads and cause prices to fall.

Exhibit 5: Bid-Side Prices and Sovereign Spreads

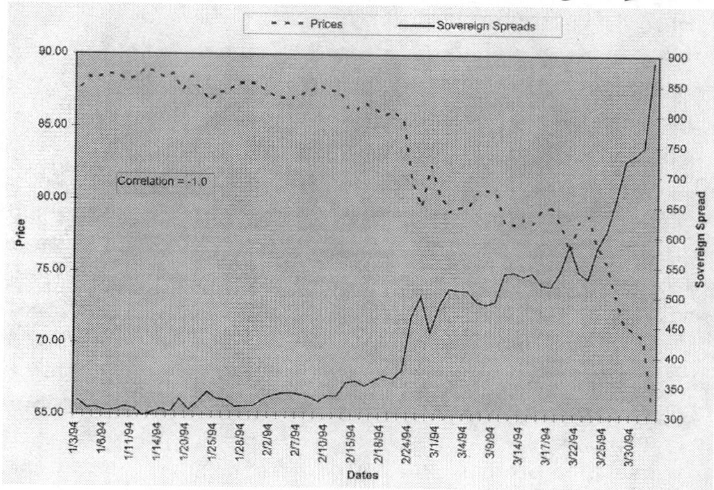

Exhibit 6: Trailing 5-Day Rolling Correlations Between Prices and Sovereign Spreads and Between Prices and the Long Bond Yields

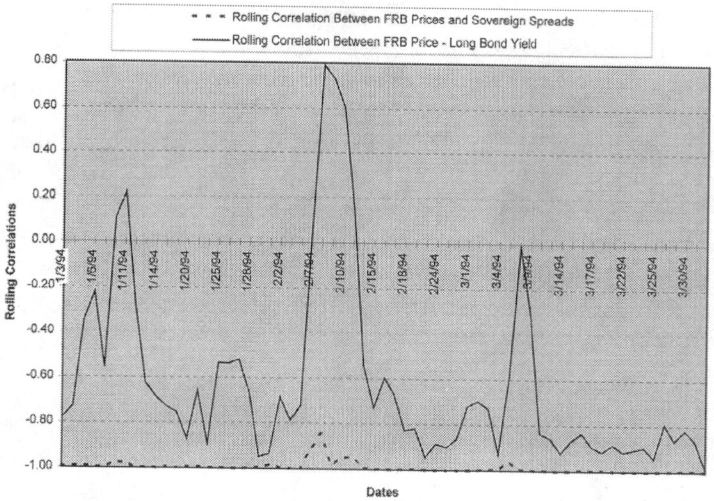

Exhibit 7: EXIT and NMB Bid Prices versus Long Bond Yield

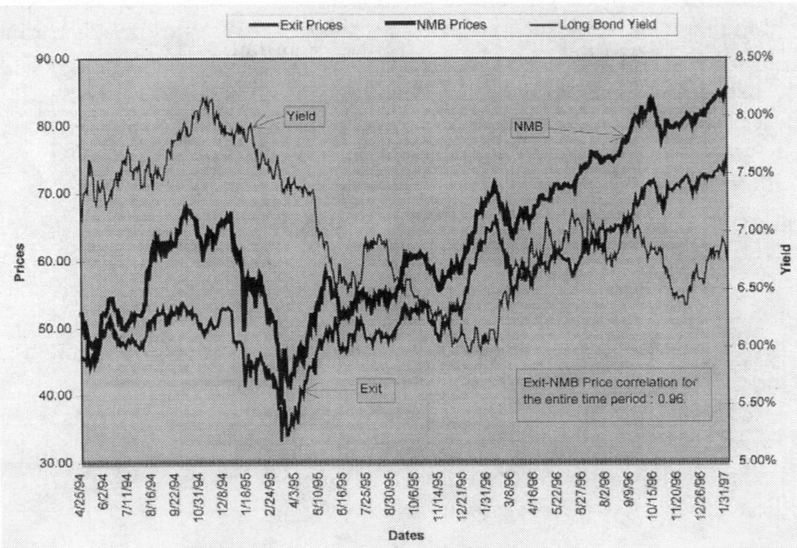

We therefore conclude that simply knowing the interest rate duration of an emerging market debt instrument is insufficient for characterizing the price risk of that bond. As a result we will need an additional measure that will translate sovereign spread volatility into price volatility. This measure is *spread duration.* In the FRB case study we see that the effect of positive spread duration (i.e. a widening of spreads leading to a drop in prices) vastly outweighed the negative theoretical interest rate duration.

A second case study that further justifies the need for a spread duration measure is described by the time series plots in Exhibit 7. These time series are for the prices of the Brazilian NMB, a *floating-rate* bond with a negative interest rate duration, and the Brazilian EXIT, a *fixed-rate* bond with a positive interest rate duration (see Exhibit 2). The analysis is from 4/25/94 through 2/3/97, a period which experienced both rising and falling interest rates. Moreover, despite their differing floating versus fixed structures, their prices have always tracked each other very closely. In fact, for the entire time period the correlation between the two was 0.96.

In Exhibit 8 we plot 5-day-trailing rolling correlations between the EXIT and NMB bid-side prices, together with the long bond yield time series. Once again we notice that irrespective of whether yields are falling or rising the rolling correlation is usually positive. In fact, of the 696 trading days, the rolling correlation is positive for 608 trading days (i.e., 87%).

If sovereign spreads had remained constant throughout the entire time sample, the EXIT would be expected to outperform during interest rate rallies and the NMB during interest rate increases. This did not take place because, once again, sovereign spreads changed substantially and the spread effect far outweighed the interest rate effect. In Exhibit 9 we plot sovereign spreads for the two bonds. Similar to the experience with prices, we notice a very high degree of correlation between the two spreads. The value of this correlation for the entire data sample was 0.95 (i.e., the same as for the two price series). Hence, the price of the bonds is mostly determined by the sovereign spread changes, instead of by interest rate changes.

From the two case studies above we conclude that tools other than interest rate duration are needed to control the price volatility in a portfolio of emerging market debt. Those tools are stripped and effective sovereign spread duration. We introduce the tools in the sections to follow.

In the same way we need duration measures that are specific to the emerging debt markets, we will also need specific yield measures to assess relative value. In the investment grade and high-yield markets, the relative value of a bond is found by calculating the yield-to-maturity from the price and future cash flows, and then comparing this to the yield-to-maturity of other bonds with similar credit and maturity/interest rate duration characteristics.

Exhibit 8: EXIT-NMB 5-Day Rolling Correlation of Prices versus Long Bond Yield

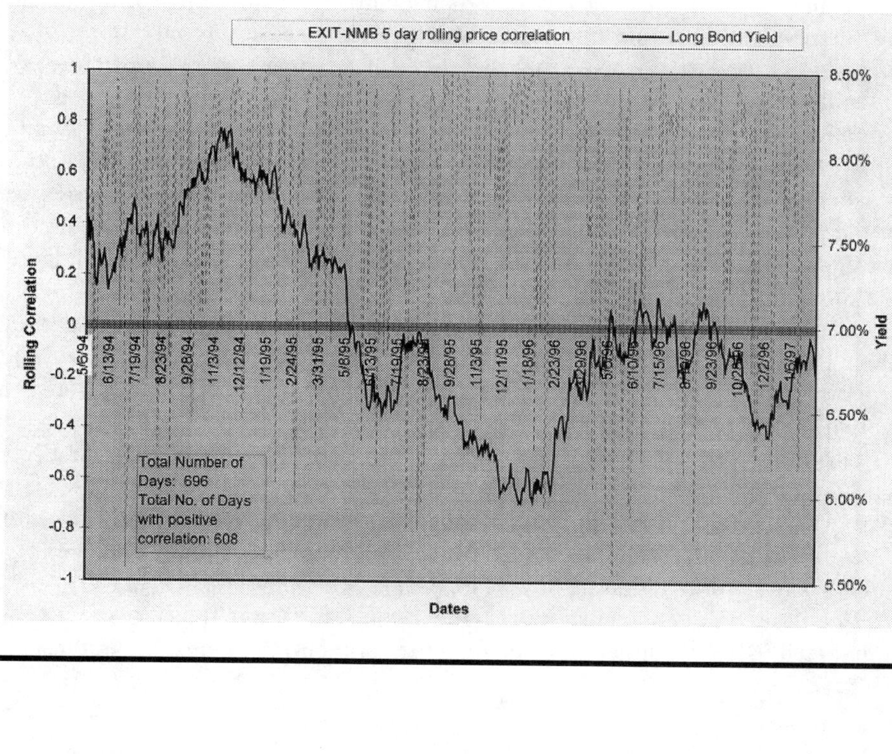

Exhibit 9: EXIT and NMB Sovereign Spreads versus Long Bond Yield

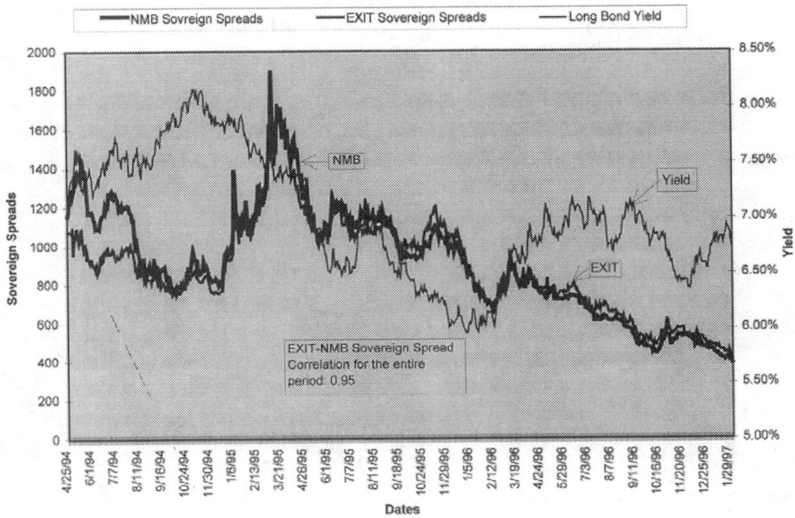

One of the special features of Brady bonds is their credit enhancement by investment grade collateral. Consequently the yield-to-maturity represents a *blended yield* of future cash flows — some of them fully exposed to sovereign credit risk only while others are largely insensitive to credit risk. In order to measure the true credit risk/spread of these securities, we must first *strip* the collateral enhancement from the Brady bond so that future cash flows representing pure sovereign credit risk are obtained. *Hence, stripping removes the effect of any credit enhancements, and focuses only on the credit of the sovereign.* The yield-to-maturity thus obtained is called the *stripped yield.* Similarly we can obtain a stripped spread and a stripped spread duration. These will be two relative value tools we use later in the chapter.

UNDERSTANDING BRADY BOND RELATIVE VALUE TOOLS

The credit enhancements present in Brady bonds can be of two general types: (1) a *principal guarantee* where either the entire principal or a fraction of it (50% in the case of the Vietnam Par bond) is backed by U.S. Treasury strip collateral, and (2) a *rolling interest guarantee* (RIG), backed by AA rated collateral, and which guarantees the payment of the next n coupons following a default by the underlying sovereign credit. The "rolling" feature means that once a coupon payment is made by the sovereign issuer, the guarantee rolls to cover the next n coupons. Some bonds have both a principal guarantee and a RIG (for example, the Mexican

Par and Argentine Discount). Others have only principal guarantee (Poland Par). Still others simply have a RIG which only lasts for part of the life of the bond (for example, the RIG on the Bulgaria FLIRB expires once the bond becomes a floater).

Below we show how to strip the two types of collateral described above. We will start, however, by reviewing the definition of yield-to-maturity (YTM), which in the case of the Brady universe is referred to as a blended yield because no distinction is made between cash flows exposed to sovereign risk and those which are collateralized. Blended yield (BY) is defined as:

$$P = \sum_{i=1}^{N} \frac{CF_i}{(1 + BY/2)^i} \tag{7}$$

where CF_i is the cash flow on coupon date i.

Valuation of the Principal Collateral

If Z_N is the yield of the U.S. zero-coupon bond with the same maturity as the Brady bond with principal collateral, the value of this collateral, PV_P, is given by:

$$PV_P = \frac{100}{(1 + Z_N/2)^{2N}} \tag{8}$$

where N is the remaining maturity of the Brady (in years).

Valuation of the Rolling Interest Guarantee Using the Modified Cash Flow Method

Assume that n, the number of coupon payments covered by the rolling interest rate guarantee, is two. The exact value of the rolling interest guarantee, RIG, would be trivial to calculate if the guarantee did not roll forward. If the collateral provided a guarantee only for the first two coupon payments (and reverted to the issuer if not used) those payments would represent AA rated credit risk, and their present value would then be determined using AA spot rates, similar to what is done with the principal collateral. However the guarantee does roll forward and, consequently, *may* guarantee the third and fourth, the fifth and sixth coupon payments, etc. This approach to valuing the RIG is called the *modified cash flow (MCF) method*. The MCF method is an attempt to model an interest guarantee that if not used for any given coupon payment rolls immediately forward. According to the MCF method, the RIG is valued by decomposing it into two components, as described below.[6]

---

[6] See Edward Bartholomew, "Valuing the Rolling Interest Guarantee: A Comparison of Approaches," J.P. Morgan Securities, Inc. (September 8, 1995).

Component 1 of the RIG

If the underlying sovereign credit defaults today, the next two coupon payments are guaranteed by the AA rated collateral. Then, insofar as the next two coupon payments are concerned, the investor has no exposure to the sovereign. Instead, the investor is exposed to AA rated credit risk. The value of *Component 1* of the RIG will then be equal to the present value of the next two coupon payments of the Brady bond, discounted using a zero-coupon curve for AA rated credit. This curve is nothing more than the zero-coupon U.S. dollar swap curve. Thus, in the general case:

$$\text{RIG Component 1} = G = \sum_{j=1}^{n} \frac{C_j}{(1 + Z_j/2)^j} \tag{9}$$

where C_j is the j-th coupon payment.

Hence Component 1 of the RIG, denoted by G, is the value of the guarantee if it did not roll forward.

Component 2 of the RIG

Component 2 of the RIG applies to all coupons after the next n. Consider the m-th coupon payment, with $m > n$. Even though this coupon is not guaranteed today because it is not one of the next n coupons directly covered by the interest guarantee, it turns out that since this guarantee is *rolling* the investor is *not* subjected to *full sovereign credit exposure* between now and the m-th coupon date. Recalling that *rolling* implies that once a coupon payment is made by the issuer, the guarantee rolls to include the next n coupons, it follows that if the sovereign makes the (m-n)-th coupon payment, the m-th coupon becomes automatically covered by the interest guarantee. Thus, insofar as receiving the m-th coupon payment is concerned, the investor is subject to sovereign credit risk until the (m-n)-th coupon date. Between the (m-n)-th and the m-th coupon dates the investor is only exposed to AA rated credit risk.

For a semiannual paying bond, to find the present value of the m-th coupon payment, C_m, we first present value this payment to the (m-n)-th coupon date using the (n/2)-year forward swap rate (m-n)/2 years forward, and then we find the present value of this *modified cash flow* to the present date using the sovereign spot rate with maturity (m-n)/2 years. (See Exhibit 10.) Hence:

$$\text{PV(Coupon } m) = \frac{1}{(1 + \text{sovereign}_{(m-n)}/2)^{(m-n)}} \frac{C_m}{(1 + {}_{(m-n)}f_n/2)^n}$$

$$= \frac{Q_m}{(1 + \text{sovereign}_{(m-n)}/2)^{(m-n)}}$$

$$Q_m = \frac{C_m}{(1 + {}_{(m-n)}f_n/2)^n} \tag{10}$$

Exhibit 10: Modified Cash Flow Q_m

The Modified Cash Flow, Q_m, on coupon date $(m-n)$, but not coupon date m, is the component of the m-th coupon payment that is exposed to sovereign risk.

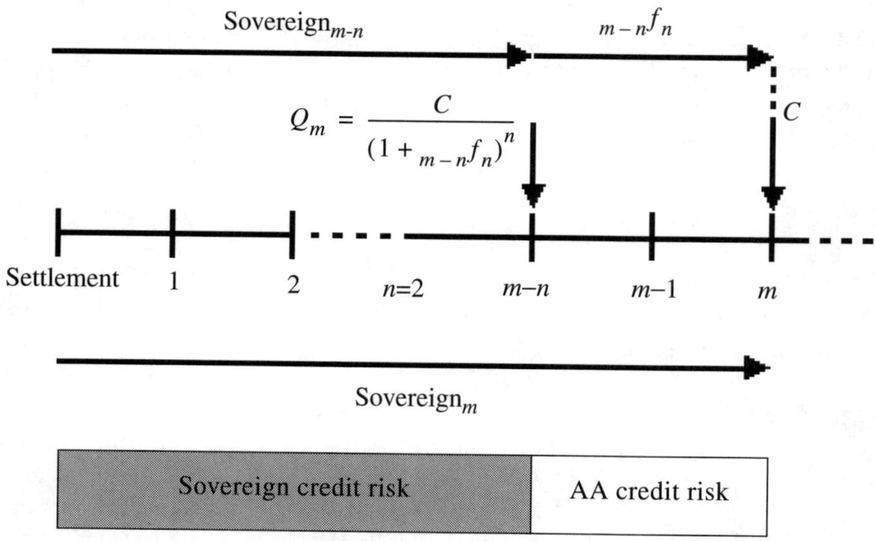

Credit exposure for coupon m $(m>n)$: sovereign risk exposure between settlement and coupon date $(m-n)$; AA risk exposure between coupon date $(m-n)$ and coupon date m.

---

where ${}_{(m-n)}f_n$ is the $(n/2)$-year forward U.S. dollar swap rate $(m-n)/2$ years forward and Q_m is the modified cash flow due on m-th coupon date.

If we assume that the sovereign spot curve is flat, the sovereign rate in equation (10) is the same for all maturities and equal to the internal rate of return of the sovereign (i.e., non-collateralized) cash flows (SIRR). With this assumption, the contribution of the m-th coupon to the second component of the RIG is

$$(\text{RIG Component 2})_m = \frac{Q_m}{(1+\text{SIRR}_{(m-n)}/2)^{(m-n)}} - \frac{C_m}{(1+\text{SIRR}_m/2)^m} \quad (11)$$

Hence,

$$\text{RIG Component 2} = \sum_{m>n}^{N} (\text{RIG Component 2})_m \quad (12)$$

Equations (11) and (12) show that the value of the second component of the RIG is due solely to the "rolling" character of the guarantee: every coupon payment is not exposed to sovereign risk between settlement and that coupon date but to a blended "sovereign plus AA rated" credit risk. Notice that if the guarantee is not rolling, for any coupon after the next n, n becomes zero in equations (10) and (11) since the guarantee expires. In this situation, $Q_m = C_m$ in equation (10), the right hand side of equation (11) becomes exactly zero, and only Component 1 of RIG remains.

Valuation of the Rolling Interest Guarantee Using the Implied Probability of Default Method

The implied probability of default (IPD) method for valuing the RIG[7] assumes that the conditional probability of default on any coupon date, given no prior default, is a constant equal to p_d. For a given static U.S. Treasury yield curve, the cash flows are uniquely determined, save for the possibility of a default on a payment date. It is further assumed that (1) if the issuer defaults there is no recovery, except for the value of the payments provided by the RIG and (2) the investor is risk neutral.

There are three components to a collateralized bond's price: (1) the present value of the principal, (2) the sum of the present values of interest payments received under the no-default scenario weighted by the probability of receiving each one, and (3) the sum of the present values of interest collateral account payments weighted by the total probability of receiving them. Mathematically, this is expressed as:

$$P = PV_P + \sum_{j=1}^{N}\left[\frac{C_j/2}{(1+Z_j/2)^j}(1-p_d)^j + \frac{IC_j}{(1+Z_j/2)^j}p_d(1-p_d)^{j-1}\right] \quad (13)$$

In equation (13) IC_j is the present value on coupon date j of the set of interest payments received in case of default of the j-th coupon payment. To find p_d we solve equation (13) iteratively by inserting values for this probability of first default until P equals the market price for the Brady bond.

The second term in the summation in equation (13) is the expected present value of coupon payments made from the RIG collateral account. This is nothing more than the *value* of the RIG:

$$\text{RIG} = \sum_{j=1}^{N}\left[\frac{IC_j}{(1+Z_j/2)^j}p_d(1-p_d)^{j-1}\right] \quad (14)$$

The value of the RIG is smaller than the amount of collateral necessary to guarantee the interest payments. To illustrate this, we will assume that the U.S. zero-coupon curve is flat with rates equal to Z. Equation (14) for the RIG value becomes:

$$\text{RIG} = IC\sum\frac{p_d(1-p_d)^{j-1}}{(1+Z/2)^j} = \text{IC}\frac{p_d}{(p_d+Z/2)}\left(1-\left(\frac{1-p_d}{1+Z/2}\right)^N\right) \quad (15)$$

---

[7] See Adrian Devenyi and Steven Kugelmass, "Stripped Spreads for Brady Assets," Bear Stearns Fixed Income Research (June 5, 1997).

From equation (15), we see that the RIG is less than *IC* since it is obtained by multiplying the former by two factors, both of which are smaller than one. This result will also hold if the U.S. zero-coupon curve is not flat.

Using equation (14), equation (13) can be rewritten as:

$$P^* = P - PV_P - \text{RIG} = \sum_{j=1}^{N} \frac{C_j/2}{(1 + (Z_j + SS)/2)^j} \tag{16}$$

where

$$\sum_{j=1}^{N} \frac{C_j/2}{(1 + (Z_j + SS)/2)^j} = \sum_{j=1}^{N} \left[\frac{C_j/2}{(1 + Z_j/2)^j} (1 - p_d)^j \right] \tag{17}$$

In equation (16), P^* is the value of non-guaranteed cash flows, or the *stripped price,* and *SS* is the stripped spread. Note that multiplying the value of a cash flow by a survival probability is equivalent to discounting it with an additional spread. This is the stripped spread for a Brady bond. It is the compensation to the investor for the risk of default by the issuer and is associated only with the sovereign payments after the value of the collateral has been removed.

Note also that the IPD and MCF methods to value the RIG can be shown to be perfectly equivalent.[8,9]

In Exhibit 11, we apply equations (8), (13), (15), (16), and (17) to the Mexican Par bond, for settlement on 8/1/97, to examine the value added by the RIG, assuming that the U.S. yield curve is flat at 6.4%. The next coupon date (j=1) is 9/30/97 and the present value of IC_1 is \$8.715 which is the upper bound on the RIG and is associated with Mexico defaulting between settlement and the next coupon date.

Going forward the MCF method to value the RIG will be used.

Stripped Yield

From equations (8), (9), and (10) and assuming that the sovereign risk curve is flat so that $\text{sovereign}_m = SIRR = SY$, for all m, we have:

$$P = G + \sum_{j=1}^{N-n} \frac{Q_{j+n}}{(1 + SY/2)^j} + PV_P \tag{18}$$

where *SY* is the stripped yield of the collateralized bond and *G* is component 1 of the RIG. Equation (18) can be rewritten as:

$$\Pi = \sum_{j=1}^{N-n} \frac{Q_{n+j}}{(1 + SY/2)^j} \qquad \Pi = P - G - PV_P \tag{19}$$

---

[8] See Devenyi and Kugelmass, "Stripped Spreads for Brady Assets."

[9] See Daniel Peirce, "A Valuation Framework for Rolling Interest Guarantees," *Bank of Boston Emerging Markets Bi-Weekly* (February 23, 1996), pp. 4-7.

Exhibit 11: Decomposition of Mexican Par Bond Value

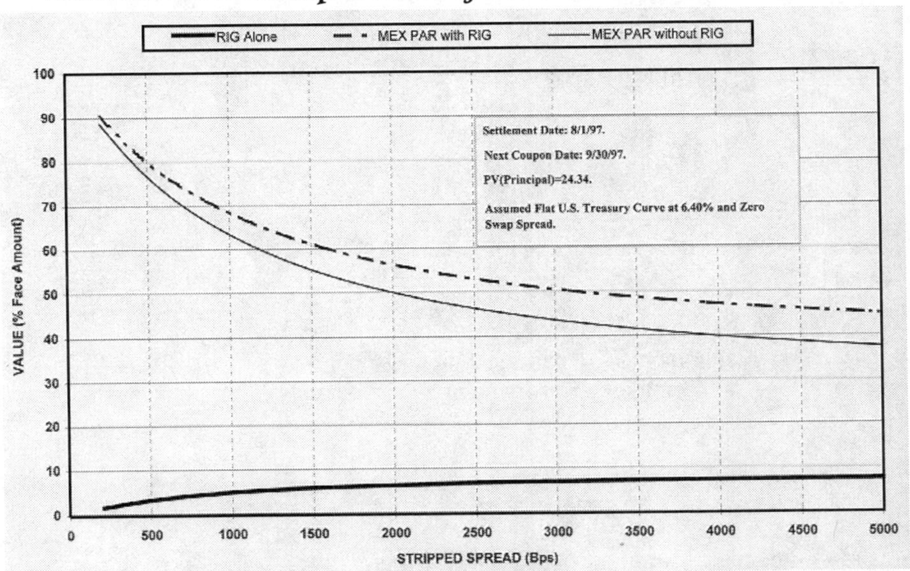

where Π is called the *sovereign risk value*. Hence, the stripped yield is the internal rate of return of an annuity with price Π with the same coupon dates as the corresponding Brady bond but maturing on coupon date N-n, and with annuity payments equal to Q_j, $n+1 \leq j \leq N$. (See Exhibit 12.)

Stripped Spread

The static stripped spread, SS, is defined as follows:

$$\Pi = \sum_{j=1}^{N-n} \frac{Q_{n+j}}{(1+(Z_j+SS)/2)^j} \tag{20}$$

The stripped spread is the *single* spread over the U.S. Treasury zero-coupon curve that when used to discount each modified cash flow recovers the sovereign risk value, Π, for the *particular* Brady. In Exhibit 13 we show stripped spreads for two Brazilian Bradys: the EI bond and the DCB.

A closer look at Exhibit 13 reveals, however, a limitation of the stripped spread measure.[10] Since both the EI and the DCB are *pari passu* liabilities of Brazil, it is inconsistent to value a EI and a DCB cash flow falling on the same date using different discount rates. But that is exactly what we are doing when we use the EI and DCB "zero coupon curves" obtained from the U.S. Treasury zero curve by addition of the two different stripped spreads.

---

[10] See Daniel Nadler, Pantelis Tsoucas, and Casimir Wierzynski, "Brady Bond Valuation and the Universe of Credit Structures," *Goldman Sachs Fixed Income Research* (January 1996).

Exhibit 12: Stripped Yield on Brady Bond

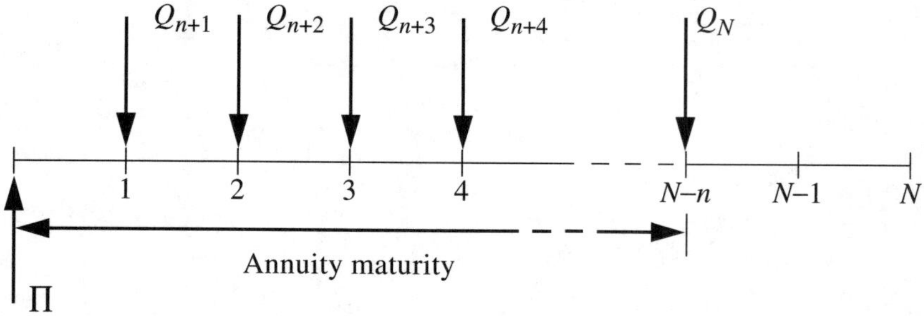

{1, 2, 3, ..., N–3, N–2, N–1, N} = Brady bond coupon paying dates
N = total number of remaining coupons
$\prod = P - G - PV_P \equiv$ price of annuity
Q_j = annuity cash flows

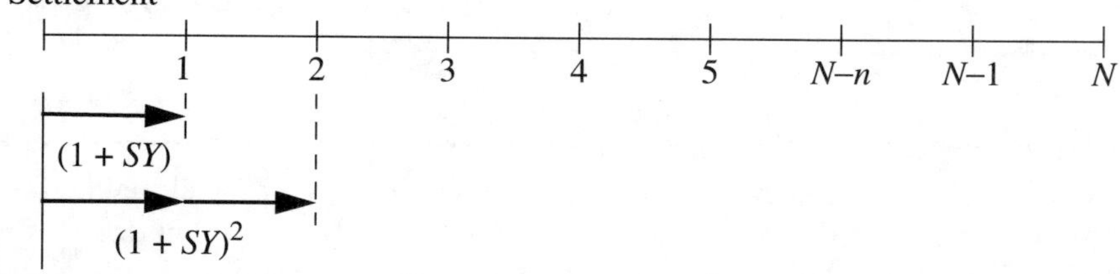

Stripped yield on Brady bond with maturity N, coupon c, and RIG covering n coupon payments is the internal rate of return on an annuity with price $\prod$, maturity N–n, and coupons Q_j, $n < j \leq N$.

Exhibit 13: Static Stripped Spread (As of Close on 2/7/97)

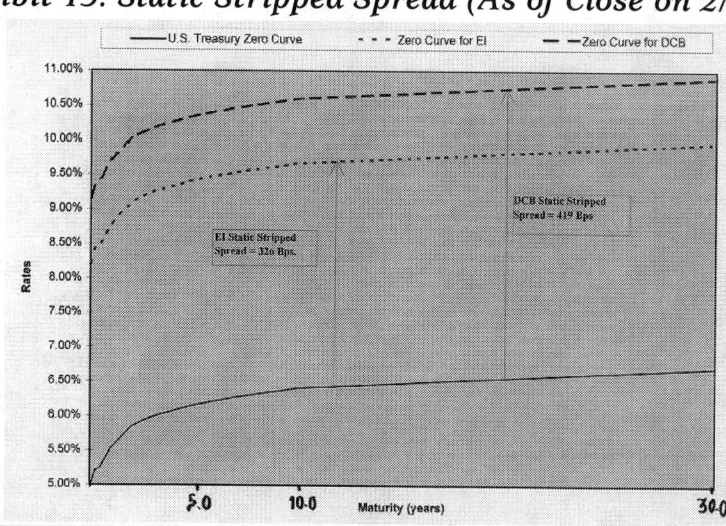

Investors should thus look at the DCB's stripped spread simply as a rough measure of value that enables them *to compare* the value of the DCB against that of any other Brazilian bond, and not as a means of obtaining a term structure of credit risk (a sovereign credit curve) in Brazil.

Stripped Spread Duration

The *stripped spread duration* (on the "sovereign risk value"), D_{spread}, is defined as (in years):

$$D_{spread} = \frac{1}{2}\frac{\sum_{j=1}^{N-n} t_j Q_{j+n}(1+(Z_j+SS)/2)^{-j}}{\Pi} \qquad (21)$$

where t_j is the time period (in years) between the settlement date and the j-th cash flow.

If the sovereign credit curve is assumed to be flat and undergo a parallel shift equal to ΔSS, we see that *the percent change in the sovereign risk value* due to this change in stripped spread, assuming that U.S. rates remain constant, is equal to:

$$(\Delta\Pi)/\Pi = (-D^{mod}_{spread})\Delta SS;\ -D^{mod}_{spread} = -1/(1+SY/2)D_{spread} \qquad (22)$$

where D^{mod}_{spread} is the modified stripped spread duration.

Effective Spread Duration

The *effective spread duration* is defined by the expression:

$$(\Delta P)/P = -D^{eff}_{spread}\Delta SS \qquad (23)$$

The effective spread duration thus allows investors to compute *the percent change in the clean price* of a Brady bond if stripped spreads change by a small amount ΔSS and if interest rates remain constant. Only if the Brady bond is uncollateralized is $\Pi = P$ and the effective spread duration is *equal* to the modified spread duration.

Weighted Average Life

Many Brady bonds are amortizing securities, i.e. the principal is returned throughout the life of the security instead of simply on the maturity date. For amortizing bonds, maturity is not a good measure of the longevity of this form of debt. Instead, a preferred measure of longevity is the weighted *average* elapsed time until the principal is fully returned. The commonly used measure, the *weighted average life* (WAL), is the weighted average time to principal repayment with the amount of the scheduled principal pay-downs as the weights:

$$WAL\text{ (in years)} = \frac{\sum_{i=1}^{N} t_i Amort_i}{FA} \qquad (24)$$

In equation (24) *FA* is the face amount outstanding on the issue date, t_i is time period (in years) between the settlement date and the *i*-th cash flow, and $Amort_i$ is the amortization payment (principal repayment) on the *i*-th cash flow date. For bullet bonds $Amort_j = 0$ for $j<N$ and $Amort_j = FA$ for $j=N$. Hence, the WAL for a bullet bond is t_N, its term to maturity. WAL thus expresses that average number of years that each dollar of principal will be outstanding. The sooner the principal is returned, the shorter the average life.

Notice that if prior to amortizing, the bond capitalizes (part of) the coupon payments (such as the Brazilian C-bond), the denominator in equation (24) becomes FA_{max}, i.e., the face value of the bond at the end of the capitalization schedule. FA_{max} is thus the maximum face value that is reached during the life of the bond.

HOW TO USE STRIPPED SPREAD DURATION AND STRIPPED SPREAD AS RELATIVE-VALUE TOOLS

Similar to other bond markets, stripped yields and spreads on Brady bonds increase with stripped spread duration simply because repayment risk increases over time. Stripped spreads together with stripped spread duration thus constitute one of the relative value tools used in emerging debt markets.[11] Similar to the U.S. bond market (a world of similar bonds that repay principal at maturity and trade close to par value), where investors build yield curves by fitting a curve in the maturity-yield space to the on-the-run bonds, investors in the emerging debt markets build sovereign curves in the stripped spread duration — sovereign spread space. This is shown in Exhibit 14.

When building a sovereign yield curve, we must decide whether the Brady bond repayment risk rises in a linear, polynomial, log, or log-linear fashion. Following the reasons advanced by Raul Elizade,[12] we have decided to fit a *logarithmic interpolation curve* to the set of stripped spread-versus-stripped spread duration points. We selected a logarithmic fit since they produce forward rates that are bound to reasonable levels and are more "sensible" than forward rates obtained using other fits, such as the linear.

In addition, an econometric model developed to explain the behavior of stripped spreads as a function of a set of independent variables found that one of the statistically significant variables was stripped spread duration.[13] Furthermore, Domville and Segal have shown that taking the natural logarithm of the stripped spread duration produced the best results.

---

[11] See Raul Elizade, "Observations on the Brazilian Yield Curve," *ING Barings Emerging Markets Weekly Report*, (February 16, 1996).

[12] See Raul Elizade, "Emerging Market Yield Curves: The March Towards Reason," *ING Barings Emerging Markets Weekly Report* (January 3, 1997), pp. 13-23.

[13] See Lucia Domville and Richard Segal, "A Brady-Global Trading Model: Techniques for Arbitraging 39 Liquid Bonds," *Santander Investment Emerging Markets Fixed-Income Research* (May 6, 1997).

Exhibit 14: Brazil Sovereign Spread Curves on 2/7/96 and 2/7/97

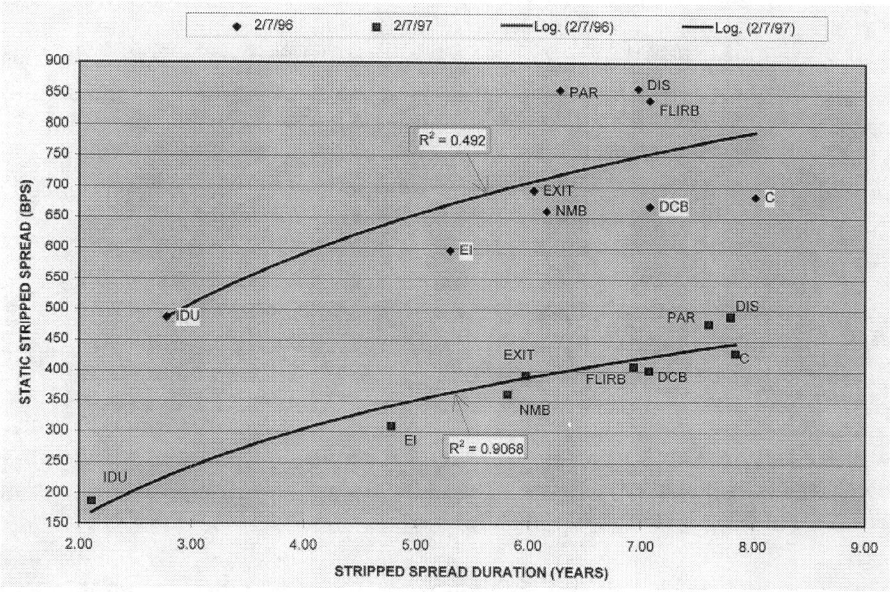

We will use the statistical R^2 as a measure of the explanatory power of the interpolated sovereign curve. When the R^2 of the regression is low, the logarithmic sovereign curve provides poor explanatory power and suggests that the scatter of stripped spread-versus-sovereign spread duration points is determined by the market without regard to forward rate considerations. This dispersed distribution of stripped spreads corresponds to a segmented, thin, and immature market. For example, if we look at the Brazil sovereign curve on 2/7/96 (see Exhibit 14), we notice a relatively low R^2 value, 0.492, and a corresponding substantial dispersion of the data points around the logarithmic curve.

According to Raul Elizade, the following three key factors are crucial in narrowing the dispersion of stripped spreads around the interpolated sovereign curve: (1) a wider and deeper scope of market participants; (2) greater market liquidity; and, (3) the emergence of derivative instruments used to strip collateral out of a bond and give investors access to the sovereign only cash flows.[14] As the Brady market more fully developed and deepened during 1996, the values of R^2 have become much higher. In Exhibit 14, we show that by 2/7/97, the R^2 for the Brazilian sovereign curve had increased to 0.907. As evidence of this increased efficiency, notice how the Brazilian FLIRB, which was particularly cheap relative to a similar spread duration instrument (the DCB) in February 1996, had tightened significantly by February 1997.

[14] See Elizade, "Emerging Market Yield Curves: The March Towards Reason."

Finally, from an analysis of Exhibit 14, we observe an anomaly in the Brazilian yield curve: the pricing of the Brazilian collateralized instruments, the Par and Discount bonds. On 2/7/96 these bonds appeared to be abnormally cheap relative to their non-collateralized counterparts. By 2/7/97 this anomaly still persisted, although not as pronounced as in 2/7/96, and on a stripped spread duration basis the collateralized bonds were still cheap. This anomaly is also observed in other sovereigns with collateralized Brady bonds: the Par and Discount bonds trade at a discount in comparison to similar stripped spread duration non-collateralized instruments. This anomaly will be addressed later in this chapter.

LIMITATIONS OF THE STRIPPED YIELD AS A RELATIVE VALUE MEASURE

Since the IPD and the MCF methods to value the RIG are mathematically equivalent, the following critique applies to both methods and, indeed, to any simple internal rate of return adjustment method to value the RIG. We will develop the critique below around the MCF method.

Even though the MCF method to strip the collateral from a collateralized bond is internally consistent, it contains a serious structural flaw that limits its usefulness as the sole relative value measure. In reality the RIG is a "default option"[15] where the underlying is the "creditworthiness of the issuer."[16] If this creditworthiness drops below a critical, or "exercise," value the sovereign cannot make the coupon payments and the option is exercised by having those payments being made out of the AA rated securities held as collateral.

One unit of RIG has value because it allows an investor to be long an amount delta (the "option delta") of a AA rated bond with maturity n (the number of coupons covered by the RIG). The closer delta gets to one, the closer the sovereign gets to defaulting. At each point in time the default option should be priced like any other option: by arbitrage pricing through the construction of a riskless hedge,[17] and not by the simplistic mechanical MCF process already described in this chapter. Using the option framework, we notice that in the MCF, the delta is always one, even if sovereign spreads are very tight and, by implication, there is a small probability of an early sovereign default.

In addition, the RIG is valued as if it will always be in place for the life of the bond, even for a credit with an extremely wide spread and, by implication, a reasonable likelihood of an early default. Even in this situation, the MCF continues to mechanically move up cash flows for the entire life of the bond. These

---

[15] See Vincent Palermo, "Brady Bond Collateral Stripping: Calculations, Uses, and Limitations," *Merrill Lynch Emerging Debt Monthly* (June 27, 1996), pp. 19-22.

[16] See Stijn Claessens and George Pennacchi, "Estimating the Likelihood of Mexican Default from the Market Prices of Brady Bonds," *Journal of Financial and Quantitative Analysis* (March 1996), pp. 109-126.

[17] See John Cox and Mark Rubinstein, *Options Markets* (Englewood Cliffs, NJ: Prentice Hall, 1985).

shortcomings, as pointed out by Vincent Palermo,[18] are "not a problem specific to the MCF method (alone), but merely an amplification of the weakness of conventional yield measures, which themselves grow less relevant as the likelihood of restructuring increases."

As a result, if we use, albeit inaccurately, the option analogy to describe the MCF method of pricing the RIG, we get the following description: the investor is long an American option on an *n*-period AA rated bond, which is always deep in the money (delta = 1) even for very tight spreads and with a maturity equal to the remaining life of the Brady bond, even for very wide spreads (i.e., even if the country is near default). We thus see that by using the MCF to price the RIG we are *overpricing* the true default option that this guarantee represents.

Now, remember that a collateralized bond contains a sovereign coupon strip with value equal to the "sovereign risk value," a zero-coupon bond for the principal repayment, and the RIG. If the MCF method overprices the RIG, then it underprices the sovereign risk value. Thus, in reality, the collateralized bond is trading at a tighter stripped spread than the one calculated using the MCF to value the RIG. This explains, at least partially, the anomaly of why Pars and Discounts have historically always traded cheap to the sovereign curve, when using the MCF method to price the RIG. Given the confusion surrounding the RIG, some market participants have decided to completely ignore its value and only consider the U.S. Treasury guaranteed principal. This will tend to lower the stripped yield and spread.

In Exhibit 15 we plot the sovereign curves for Brazil for the same trade dates as shown in Exhibit 14, but now ignore the RIG in the stripped calculations for the Par and Discount (and the partial RIG for the FLIRB). When comparing these exhibits we observe the following:

1. The anomaly of the Par and Discount bonds being cheap to the curve got attenuated in 2/7/96 and was completely gone by 2/7/97, if investors do indeed ignore the RIG in the pricing of collateralized bonds.
2. The fit of the logarithmic curves to the trading data, as measured by the R^2, is better if the RIG is ignored.
3. When the RIG is ignored, the Brazilian sovereign curve appears to be largely efficient on 2/7/97 (i.e., all mispricings have been arbitraged out).

In Exhibit 16 we compare the stripped spreads for the Brazilian collateralized bonds calculated considering the RIG and with the RIG ignored.

Finally, there is another type of investor who believes that stripped yield, even with the RIG ignored, is misleading and should instead use the blended yield as a measure of relative value. Because many investors face short-selling constraints that prevent them from selling the U.S. Treasury zero necessary to "earn" the stripped yield, these investors claim that since they can earn blended yield, but not stripped yield, they consequently should look simply at blended yields and

[18] See Palermo, "Brady Bond Collateral Stripping: Calculations, Uses and Limitations," pp. 19-22.

effective spread duration. In the remainder of this section we will show that this statement is inaccurate if there are enough investors who consistently trade using stripped yield as a pricing convention.

In order to demonstrate why this reasoning is wrong, we must first recognize that if the yield curve is perfectly flat and remains unchanged during a 1-year horizon period, the realized return on either a bond or an annuity is its yield to maturity. Now, let SY^* be the stripped yield on a collateralized bond, calculated neglecting the contribution of the RIG. This bond can be modeled as a portfolio of a zero-coupon bond yielding S_N and a sovereign coupon strip yielding SY^*. If we assume a horizon period equal to one year, the Treasury yield curve remains perfectly flat, and the stripped spread remains constant, the realized return on this portfolio is its yield. Thus, in this static world,

Exhibit 15: Brazil Sovereign Spread Curves on 2/7/96 and 2/7/97 (RIG Neglected)

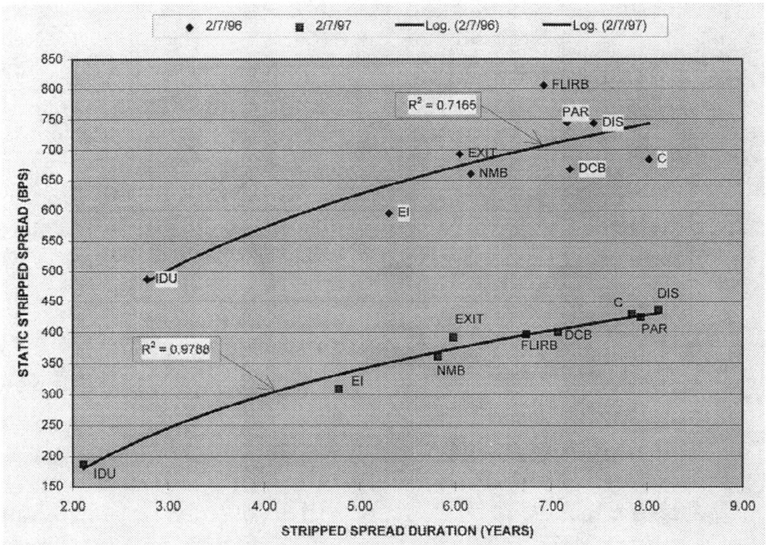

Exhibit 16: Brazilian Stripped Spreads Calculated Either With or Without the RIG

	Trade Date: 2/7/96			Trade Date: 2/7/97		
	Stripped Spread with RIG (bps)	Stripped Spread without RIG (bps)	Difference	Stripped Spread with RIG (bps)	Stripped Spread without RIG (bps)	Difference
FLIRB	840	806	34	408	397	11
Par	856	745	111	478	425	53
Discount	859	744	115	490	436	54

$$
\begin{aligned}
\text{1-year return} &= \text{weight of coupon strip} \times SY^* + \text{weight of zero} \times S_N \\
&= \left(P - \frac{100}{(1+S_N/2)^N}\right) / P \times SY^* + \left(\frac{100}{(1+S_N/2)^N}\right) / P \times S_N \\
&= SY^* - PV_P \times (SY^* - S_N) < SY^*;\ [\text{since} SY^* > S_N] \qquad (25)
\end{aligned}
$$

Let BY be the blended yield at the beginning of the horizon period. Assuming a static world, it can be demonstrated that at the horizon date the blended yield will be some other number BY^* smaller than BY.[19] In this world, at the horizon date the price of our collateralized bond is P^*, larger than P. P^* together with the structure of the bond at horizon date will determine a value for BY^* according to Equation (7). The blended yield is thus endogenous and non-constant in our static world where the *exogenous variable* is the stripped yield which is *assumed* to be the accepted benchmark for finding relative-value in Bradys.

It can be shown that

$$BY < \text{one year return} \qquad (26)$$

Putting together equations (25) and (26) it follows that in a simple static world where SY^* is assumed to be the exogenous variable describing the idiosyncrasies (i.e., the universally accepted yield-measure benchmark) of emerging market debt:

$$BY < \text{1-year holding period return} < SY^* \qquad (27)$$

From equation (27) we see that blended yield is not the correct relative value measure for *any* investor, including those who cannot short the U.S. Treasury collateral, as long as the current widespread use of stripped yield measures continues in the future. The proof that the stripped yield (and not the blended yield) has been used consistently up to now as a pricing convention by a substantial portion of investors, and thus “the market,” is given by the increasing efficiency of the sovereign curves in the stripped spread-stripped spread duration space.

In Exhibit 17 we calculate returns for every Par bond outstanding as of 2/7/97. To calculate these holding period returns we assume that both U.S. rates and sovereign stripped spreads remain constant and that all coupon payments are reinvested at 6-month LIBOR until the horizon date. The trade date is 2/7/97. We also show the stripped and blended yields for all Par bonds.

From an analysis of Exhibit 17, it can be seen that even though the U.S. Treasury and swap curves are not flat, the result given in equation (27) still holds. That is, for every Par bond, the 1-year holding period return is always bounded by the bond’s stripped and blended yields. The pick-up in horizon period total return over the bond’s blended yield varies between a minimum of 58 basis points (for the Philippines) and a maximum 166 basis points (for Ecuador), with the average pick-up being equal to 105 basis points.

---

[19] The proof is available from the authors.

Exhibit 17: Stripped Yield (RIG Neglected), Blended Yield, and One-Year-Horizon Return in an Unchanged Environment for all Par Bonds, 2/7/97

Security	Stripped Yield (no RIG)	Blended Yield	One-Year Return	Stripped Yield minus Return (Bps)	Return minus Blended Yield (Bps)
Argentina Par	11.17%	9.35%	10.46%	71	111
Brazil Par	10.93%	9.26%	10.28%	65	102
Ecuador Par	14.57%	10.76%	12.42%	215	166
Jordan PAR	11.77%	9.70%	10.92%	85	123
Mexico Par B	10.07%	8.64%	9.55%	53	90
Nigeria PAR	11.82%	9.58%	10.77%	105	119
Philippines Par B	8.21%	7.62%	8.20%	1	58
Poland Par	8.29%	7.62%	8.28%	1	69
Venzuela Par B	10.92%	9.16%	10.20%	71	104

These results thus challenge the notion that stripped yield and/or spread (neglecting the contribution of the RIG) cannot be earned unless the investor shorts the U.S. Treasury collateral. Indeed, as pointed out by Palermo, "if market pricing conventions are consistent over time, the stripped spread can be translated into total returns in a surprisingly self-fulfilling manner."[20] Consequently even for those investors who cannot short the U.S. strip, the stripped yield, and not the blended yield, is the pricing convention to use.

STRIPPED SPREAD DURATION VERSUS EFFECTIVE SPREAD DURATION

In Exhibit 18 we compare the relative performance of two Mexican bonds for the time period 8/1/96 to 10/3/96. The two bonds are the Mexican Par, a collateralized (both principal and RIG) fixed-rate bullet bond maturing in 2019, and the UMS 26, a fixed-rate non-collateralized bullet bond maturing in 2026.

In Part A of Exhibit 18 we show the movement of U.S. rates. For all practical purposes, the U.S. yield curve can be considered unchanged for that period. The relative outperformance of one of the two bonds will be largely a function of relative stripped spread changes and relative magnitudes of the spread duration.

In Part B1 of Exhibit 18 we show the effective and modified spread duration for 8/1/96, as well as the stripped spreads for both bonds for both 8/1/96 and 10/3/96. In Part B2 we show the holding period return for both bonds. We notice that even though the stripped spread of the Par bond tightened by more than the stripped spread of the UMS 26, the latter posted the higher horizon period return.

[20] See Vincent Palermo, "Total Return of Collateralized Brady Bonds," *Merrill Lynch Emerging Markets Debt Monthly* (December 20, 1996), pp. 30-32.

Exhibit 18: Total Return Outperformance of Pure-Sovereign-Play Bonds

(A) U.S. Treasury Environment

Maturity	8/1/96 — Yield	10/3/96 — Yield
1 year	5.74	5.58
2 years	6.11	6.01
3 years	6.24	6.16
5 years	6.42	6.35
10 years	6.65	6.60
30 years	6.85	6.84

Source: The Bloomberg

(B) Mexico

(B1) Relevant Stripped Yields, Stripped Spreads, and Spread Durations

	Stripped Yields (%)	Aug. 1 Stripped Spread Duration (Years)	Aug. 1 Modified Stripped Spread Duration (Years)*	Aug. 1 Effective Spread Duration (Years)	Aug. 1 Stripped Spread (Bps)	Oct. 3 Stripped Spread (Bps)
Mex Par	14.42	5.95	5.55	3.20	768	573
Mex UMS 26	12.47	7.98	7.51	7.51	562	461
Spread Difference (Bps)					206	112

*Calculated from equation (22) using the stripped yields and Stripped Spread Duration numbers given in this Exhibit.

Source: Fidelity Investments

(B2) Holding Period Total Return

	Aug. 1 Total Return Index	Oct. 3 Total Return Index
Mex Par	100	111
Mex UMS 26	100	114
Total Return Difference (Bps)		–3

Source: J.P. Morgan

As pointed out by Michael Cembalest, the reason for the outperformance of the UMS 26 has to do with its higher effective spread duration.[21] The relevant spread duration for estimating price sensitivity to stripped spread changes is the spread duration of the entire bond's cash flows, i.e., the effective spread duration. It is not the stripped spread duration which measures only the sensitivity of the sovereign risk cash flows to spread changes. For uncollateralized bonds the modified stripped spread duration and the effective spread duration are one and the same. This can be see in Exhibit 18, Part B1, by comparing the relevant columns for the UMS 26 bond.

[21] See Michael Cembalest, "Trends in Relative Value," *J.P. Morgan Emerging Markets Outlook* (October 11, 1996), pp. 8-9.

Exhibit 19: Comparison of Three Brazilian Floaters

(A) Brazil on 2/7/97

	(1)	(2)	(3)	(4)	(5)	(6)	(7)	(8)
Security	Bid Price	Stripped Yield	Stripped Spread	Blended Yield	Stripped Spread Dur.	WAL	Eff. Interest Rate Duration	Eff. Spread Dur.
Brazil DCB	80.875	10.60%	419	10.60%	7.04	11.2	-0.85	6.69
Brazil Disc	82.094	11.63%	514	9.66%	7.71	27.2	1.52	5.26
Brazil NMB 1994	85.625	10.18%	387	10.18%	5.79	8.2	-0.42	5.51

Source: Fidelity Investments

(B) Expected 3-month holding period returns for unchanged interest rate scenario and a stripped spread tightening equal to 50 bps

Security	Expected Returns
Brazil DCB	5.62
Brazil Disc	4.88
Brazil NMB 1994	4.94

Source: Fidelity Investments

(C) Break-Even Analysis: If for the coming three months interest rates remain unchanged and the stripped spread tightening for the DCB is equal to 50 bps, for each of the other two bonds what is the spread tightening that gives the same return?

Security	Expected Returns	Str. Spread Tight (Bps)
Brazil DCB	5.62	50.0
Brazil Disc	5.62	63.5
Brazil NMB 1994	5.62	62.0

Source: Fidelity Investments

From Exhibit 18, Part B1, we see that the Par bond spread tightened by 206 basis points versus 112 for the UMS 26 (a ratio of 1.84 times). Since the modified stripped spread duration of the UMS 26 is only 7.51 versus 5.55 for the Par bond (a ratio of 1.35 times) the Par should have outperformed if modified stripped spread duration was the appropriate variable to transform spread changes into return. However, the UMS 26 outperformed the Par bond and the reason is the corresponding effective spread duration was 7.51 versus 3.20 (a ratio of 2.35 times greater than the spread tightening ratio of 1.84 times).

As a second example, we look at three Brazilian floaters: the DCB, the Discount, and the NMB. The trade date is 2/7/97 and the relevant value measures are given in Part A of Exhibit 19. From column (5) we see that the Discount bond has the largest stripped spread duration (7.71), followed by the DCB (7.04), and the NMB (5.79).

Next we perform a scenario analysis in which we assume a 3-month holding period return, an unchanged interest rate environment, and a parallel spread tightening of 50 basis points for the portion of the sovereign curve between the NMB and the Discount bond. The unchanged interest rate scenario should (except for roll down) remove the return component due simply to interest rate duration; stripped spread sensitivity will be the key return driver.

From Part B of Exhibit 19 we see that under these assumptions, the best performing bond is the DCB, followed by the NMB. The Discount bond placed third. This ranking based on the expected returns cannot be explained only in terms of *stripped* spread duration. However, looking at the effective spread duration (column (8) in Part A of Exhibit 19), we get our explanation. The relationship between the effective spread duration and expected returns is one-to-one: the DCB has the highest effective spread duration (6.69), followed by the NMB (5.51), and the Discount bond (5.26).

Finally, in Part C of Exhibit 19 we show a break-even analysis in which we calculate the necessary spread tightening for the Discount and NMB bonds to generate the same horizon period return as the DCB, when it tightens by 50 basis points. In this way we can design an iso-return sovereign curve change corresponding to a given U.S. Treasury scenario. This is another way to think about relative-value.

PUTTING IT ALL TOGETHER: COMBINING EFFECTIVE INTEREST RATE DURATION AND EFFECTIVE SPREAD DURATION

In our first look at the FRB and the EXIT-plus-NMB case studies it might have appeared that the effective interest rate duration is a meaningless measure of price sensitivity for emerging market debt for two reasons. First, the FRB, a floating-rate bond, saw its price drop while interest rates rose (see Exhibit 3). Second, the NMB and the EXIT, respectively, a floating- and a fixed-rate bond, exhibited a high degree of correlation since the issuance of the Brazilian Brady bonds, even though throughout this time period there were episodes of both rising and falling interest rates (see Exhibits 7 and 8). We will now consider the predictive power of combining effective interest rate duration with effective spread duration to compute price changes for emerging market debt. We will start by re-analyzing the EXIT-plus-NMB example (see Exhibit 20).

The period under consideration is the two weeks from 9/10/96 to 9/24/96. In Exhibit 20, Part A, we show the effective duration, both interest rate and spread, for both bonds on 9/10/96. We notice that the spread duration is very similar for both bonds. However, the EXIT had a positive Treasury duration, similar in value to its spread duration, whereas the NMB had a small negative interest rate duration.

In Part B of Exhibit 20 we show the two week price and spread changes for both bonds as well as the long bond yield change. We use this yield change as a proxy for the interest rate change, $\Delta\mathbf{y}$, used in equation (3) to compute the corresponding price change.

Exhibit 20: Computation of Price Changes for the Brazilian NMB and EXIT Bond

(A) Effective Interest Rate and Spread Durations on 9/10/96

Security	Effective Interest Rate Duration	Effective Spread Duration
EXIT	5.45	5.40
NMB	–0.86	5.36

Source: Fidelity Investments

(B) Spread, Prices, and Long Bond Yields on 9/10/96 and 9/24/96

	EXIT Stripped Spread (Bps)	NMB Stripped Spread (Bps)	EXIT Price (Bid)	NMB Price (Bid)	Long Bond Yield
9/10/96	580	531	66.00	79.00	7.12%
9/24/96	521	483	69.00	81.44	6.99%
Change	–59	–48	3.00	2.44	–0.13%

Source: Fidelity Investments

(C) Computation of the First Order Approximation to the Price Change Using the Interest Rate and Spread Durations

$$\frac{\Delta P}{P^{9/10/96}} = -D_{spread}^{9/10/96} \times \Delta Spread - D_{int.\ rate}^{9/10/96} \times \Delta Long\ Bond\ Yield + \text{higher order terms}$$

EXIT Bond: $$\frac{\Delta P}{P^{9/10/96}} = -5.40 \times (-0.0059) - 5.45 \times (-0.0013) = 3.91\%$$

therefore, $\Delta P = 2.58$

NMB: $$\frac{\Delta P}{P^{9/10/96}} = -5.36 \times (-0.0048) - (-0.86) \times (-0.0013) = 2.46\%$$

therefore, $\Delta P = 1.95$

The return due to *both* a sovereign spread *and* interest rate change is found by superimposing equations (3) and (23). We thus get the equation shown in Part C of Exhibit 20. Neglecting higher-order terms, i.e., interest rate and spread convexities, as well as the fact that the Treasury yield curve is not flat and it does not undergo a parallel shift, we calculate a price change for the EXIT bond equal to \$2.58. The actual price change was \$3.00. Thus, the linear approximation got 86% of the actual price change. For the NMB we computed a price change equal to \$1.95 (versus \$2.44, 80% of the actual price change). Note that had we only used the interest rate component to compute the price change for the EXIT we would have obtained \$0.46 (only 16% of the actual change), while for the

NMB the result would have been –$0.09 (a negative price change corresponding to the negative interest rate duration and rates rallying).

Hence, even in the case of the EXIT where the magnitudes of the spread and interest rate duration are very similar, the interest rate component of the price change severely underpredicts the return. The reason is that the volatility of sovereign spreads is much higher than the yield volatility of U.S. Treasuries. From Exhibit 20 we see the spread compression for the EXIT bond was 59 basis points, whereas the yield of the long bond rallied by 13 basis points (4.5 times smaller than the sovereign spread change). Furthermore, our simple linear model correctly shows that the EXIT bond is the best performer of the two bonds. This is due to a combination of a larger spread compression (associated with, basically, the same value of effective spread duration for both bonds) and a larger interest rate duration.

We thus conclude that effective interest rate duration combined with the effective spread duration is a valid approximation of price changes given a U.S. Treasury and sovereign spread forecast.

Using the tools described, we can now easily understand the performance of the FRB in early 1994 mentioned at the start of the chapter. Between 2/1/94 and 4/4/94 the long bond backed up by 106 basis points (from 6.32% to 7.38%). However the sovereign spread widened by 563 basis points (from 326 basis points to 889 basis points). From Exhibit 4, we see the average effective interest rate duration during the period was –0.48. The average value of the effective spread duration was 5.48. We thus have a spread widening which was 5.3 times larger than the rate backup, and a positive average spread duration which was 11.4 times larger (in absolute value) then the negative interest rate duration. As a result, the component of price volatility associated with sovereign spread volatility easily overwhelmed the component due to interest rate volatility. No wonder, then, that the price of the FRB plummeted in early 1994.

Chapter 12

Global Performance Attribution

Gifford Fong
President
Gifford Fong Associates

Daihyun Yoo
Research Associate
Gifford Fong Associates

Zandra M. Zelaya
Application Specialist
Gifford Fong Associates

INTRODUCTION

This chapter will focus on the performance attribution of a portfolio composed of fixed income assets and derivatives of multiple countries. The distinctive feature of a performance attribution analysis of a global portfolio is that individual security returns depend on both local market performance and foreign exchange returns. Each local currency return is governed by the country's term structure of interest rates. Thus, this analysis needs to be performed with the term structure of interest rates of multiple countries and foreign exchange rates as well as a global fixed income index.

The purpose of global fixed income attribution analysis is to identify the factors that contribute to the realized performance and to give a quantitative assessment of the contribution of each factor to the total return. To meet this goal the performance attribution analysis is to answer the following six questions:

1. How does each element of the manager's return compare to the same elements of return of the benchmark?
2. What is the return of investing in the pure default-free fixed income market?
3. Has the manager successfully anticipated interest rate changes?
4. Has the manager successfully selected the issuing sector and quality groups that enhance the portfolio's performance?
5. Has the manager improved returns by selecting individual bonds because of company fundamentals?
6. Has the manager successfully anticipated foreign exchange rate fluctuations and/or hedged the exchange risk?

Before we examine the details of the analysis, we have to pay attention to some aspects peculiar to global performance attribution analysis. They are as follows:

1. The availability of an appropriate global index that represents all markets included in the global portfolio.
2. The consistent treatment of the foreign tax withholdings in the portfolio returns and the global benchmark index returns calculations.
3. The use of a unified accounting method for tracking the portfolio and cash transactions of each country's portfolio. Because the settlement date conventions are different from each country, the trade day accounting method is the appropriate standard of bookkeeping in global performance attribution.

Suppose the global portfolio is composed of securities denominated in n currencies. Then the global portfolio can be regarded as a portfolio of n currency sub-portfolios. Thus, we will focus on the analysis of a single currency sub-portfolio in terms of the home currency.

In the evaluation of bond portfolio performance, the first step is the measurement of the total return of the portfolio over the evaluation period. The next step is the identification of the factors that contributed to the realized performance and a quantitative assessment of the contribution of each factor to the total return.

THE MEASUREMENT OF TOTAL RETURN

The measurement of total return is done at two levels: (1) the portfolio level and (2) the individual security level. Currency sub-portfolio total return can be measured by the same approach as the global portfolio.

Calculating the Total Return of a Portfolio

The total return of a portfolio can be calculated by using the general accounting identity that the ending market value of the portfolio is the sum of the beginning market value, net transfers into the account, interest accrual over the evaluation period, and capital gains minus the administrative expenses.

The cash flows can occur due to two reasons. One is from internal transactions of buying or selling the securities. In this case, there is no transfer of fund into or out of the account. However, cash contributions or withdrawals are regarded as external transactions. Coupon payments also belong to the external transactions. These external transactions constitute the transfer into or out of the account. Because the performance of a portfolio must reflect the effect of cash flows occurring during the period, the modified version of the Dietz method is used to calculate the total return over the evaluation period. This method is described below.

Let

V_{PB} = the beginning market value of the portfolio in home currency
V_{PE} = the ending market value of the portfolio in home currency
TIA_k = the kth transfer into account in home currency
TOA_k = the kth transfer out of account in home currency
AEP = the administrative expenses in home currency

Total return of the portfolio in home currency, R_H, is

$$R_H = \frac{V_{PE} - V_{PB} - \sum_I TIA_I + \sum_J TOA_J + AEP}{\bar{V}_{PB}} \tag{1}$$

where

$$\bar{V}_{PB} = V_{PB} + \sum_I TIA_I \cdot t_I - \sum_J TOA_J \cdot t_J - AEP \cdot t_K$$

and

$$t_i = \frac{\text{Ending date} - \text{Payment date for transfer}}{\text{Ending date} - \text{Beginning date}}$$

Calculating the Total Return of a Security

Total return of a bond i in local currency using the modified Dietz method is:

$$r_{L,i} = \frac{(P_{E,i} + I_{E,i}) - (P_{B,i} + I_{B,i}) + CPN_{paid,i}}{P_{B,i} + I_{B,i} - CPN_{paid,i} \cdot t_c} \tag{2}$$

where

$r_{L,i}$ = the total return of a bond in local currency
$P_{B,i}$ = the beginning market price of the bond
$I_{B,i}$ = the accrued interest at the beginning date
$P_{E,i}$ = the ending market price of the bond
$I_{E,i}$ = the accrued interest at the end date
$CPN_{paid,i}$ = the coupon income paid during the evaluation period
t_c = (End date – Coupon date)/(End date – Beginning date)

The total return of the bond i in home currency can be measured by adding the foreign exchange return, X_t, to the return of the bond i in local currency.

$$r_{H,i} = (1 + r_{L,i})(1 + X_i) - 1 \tag{3}$$

IDENTIFICATION OF FACTORS AND ANALYSIS OF THE SOURCES OF RETURNS

The return of the global portfolio can be decomposed into local returns and foreign exchange returns. The local return can be decomposed into two parts. One depends on the changes in the interest rate environments of the countries included in the portfolio which are beyond the manager's control. The other part depends on the management process, such as interest risk management, credit risk management, and individual security selection. The foreign exchange return depends also on two factors. One is the foreign exchange return that is beyond the control of the manager. The other is the foreign exchange hedging return that is under the control of the manager.

The total return of the portfolio in home currency, R_H, can be decomposed into four major sources of returns:

$$R_H = \mathrm{I} + \mathrm{C} + \mathrm{X} + \mathrm{H} \tag{4}$$

Where

I = the effect of the external interest rate environment
C = the contribution of the management process
X = the foreign exchange return
H = the foreign exchange hedging return

The first level of the decomposition differentiates local currency return and foreign exchange return. The second level of the decomposition is performed within the local market returns. The local return is composed of two parts: the effect of the external interest rate environment and the management contribution. If we separate the effect of circumstances that are outside the control of the portfolio manager from the effect of the portfolio management process, we can gain valuable insight into the nature of the portfolio performance.

Security Level Analysis

Uncontrollable Components

If the sub-portfolio at the currency level has no element of management, its return is solely due to the environment. This portfolio can be considered to be randomly selected from an available universe of fixed income securities. As a proxy for this management free randomly selected portfolio, we can use the total of all default-free securities, best approximated by all outstanding Treasury issues of the country.

We can achieve a more refined analysis of the external factor component by partitioning the actual holding period return on the Treasury index into two sources: return that would be realized if interest rates did not change and the return due to the actual interest rate change.

The return on the default-free securities under the market-implicit scenario of no change in the forward rates can be measured by the spot rates as follows:

$$S1_i = \text{1-period spot rate} \tag{5}$$

The return attributable to the actual change in forward rates of the country is then:

$$S2_i = \text{Total return of the Treasury index of the country} - S1_i \tag{6}$$

Controllable Components

We can attribute the difference between the actual portfolio (or security) return in local currency and the actual Treasury index return to the management process.

In evaluating the management contribution, consider the means by which the management process can affect the portfolio (or security) return. Three principal management skills that have an effect on performance include interest rate risk management, sector/quality management, and selection of individual securities. Thus, a partitioning of the management contribution is as follows:

1. return from interest rate risk management,
2. return from sector/quality management, and
3. return attributable to the selection of specific securities.

Interest rate risk management (which might more correctly be called duration management) is an important tool of a bond portfolio manager and one that typically has the largest impact on performance. The successful application of this skill is related to the ability of the manager to anticipate interest rate changes. Holding long duration portfolios during periods of decreasing interest rates and short duration portfolios during periods of rate increases will typically result in superior performance. Being short when rates decline or long when rates go up will have a negative impact on performance.

Within a local currency return, interest rate risk management can be decomposed into three factors: duration, convexity, and yield curve shape changes effects.

Duration measures the effects of a parallel shift in the yield curve. If the yield curve change is not parallel, the magnitude of the yield curve shift will vary depending upon where the measurement is made. Consistent with the concept of using the Treasury index to measure the unmanaged interest rate effect, we use the duration of the Treasury index as the point for measuring the amount of the parallel yield shift.

As part of the maturity management analysis, a regression of the changes of the spot rate curve is computed. The shift in rates for the Treasury index is then:

$$\Delta R = a + b \cdot D_T \tag{7}$$

where

ΔR = change in the spot rate curve
a = intercept of the regression of the changes of the spot rate curve
b = slope of the regression line of the changes of the spot rate curve
D_T = beginning of month Treasury Index duration

The duration return component of interest rate management can then be expressed as:

$$S3_i = -(D_i - D_T) \cdot \Delta R \tag{8}$$

where

$S3_i$ = duration return component of the bond i
D_i = beginning of month security i's duration
D_T = beginning of month average adjusted Treasury index duration
ΔR = shift in Treasury yield at Treasury index duration

Duration can be thought of as measuring the effect of minute (or local) changes in rates on price (a first-order effect), while convexity can be thought of as measuring the change in duration as rates shift (a second-order measure). This second-order yield shift effect is calculated as:

$$S4_i = \tfrac{1}{2}(C_i - C_T) \cdot \Delta R^2 - (C_i - C_T) \cdot b + (D_i - D_T) \cdot D_T \cdot b \tag{9}$$

where

$S4_i$ = convexity return component from the shift in the level of interest rates
C_i = adjusted convexity of the bond i at the beginning of the month
C_T = adjusted convexity of the Treasury index at the beginning of the month

The convexity management return component of interest rate management actually results from two effects. The first effect is from the change in the level of interest rates. The other effect measured by convexity can be thought of as a "twist" effect (i.e., the effect of rotation in the yield curve).

The parameters of duration and convexity do not measure effects resulting from changes in the shape of the yield curve (i.e., a downward sloping curve changing to a "humped" curve). We classify such effects as a "yield curve shape change" as opposed to duration and convexity effects. Yield curve shape change ends up being the residual component of the interest rate risk management component after the duration and convexity effects are eliminated.

$$S5_i = -\sum_m (D_{im} - D_{Tm}) \cdot \Delta R_m - S3_i - S4_i \tag{10}$$

where

$S5_i$ = yield curve shape change return component
D_{im} = m year functional duration of the bond i
D_{Tm} = m year functional duration of the Treasury index
ΔR_m = the changes in m-year spot rate

Sector and quality management allocates the portfolio among the alternative issuing sectors and quality groups of the bond market. There may be spread relationships among the individual sector/quality groups that the manager may be able to exploit. Having a portfolio concentrated in high-quality industrial issues, for instance, during a period when high quality industrials generally perform better than other sectors, would increase the portfolio return.

The ability to select the right issuing sector and quality group at the right time constitutes the sector/quality management skill. The sector/quality return component can be measured by the following formula:

$$S6_i = -D_t \cdot \Delta s_k + H \cdot s_{kB} \tag{11}$$

where

$S6_i$ = sector/quality component return
H = holding period in years
s_{kB} = beginning spread for the sector k to which bond i belong
Δs_k = changes in the spread for sector k during the evaluation period

Selectivity, or individual bond picking, is the skill of selecting specific securities within a given sector/quality group to enhance the portfolio return. Individual securities show specific returns over and above the performance of their sector/quality group. While sector /quality management means selecting the right market segment, selectivity means concentrating on the bonds, within that segment, whose specific returns are the most advantageous. As with the other two management skills, selectivity is involved with initial portfolio construction as well as in subsequent activities such as purchases, sales, or swaps, within a sector quality group.

$$S7_i = R_{L,i} - (S1_i + S2_i) - (S3_i + S4_i + S5_i + S6_i) \tag{12}$$

where $R_{L,i}$ = total return of bond i in local currency.

Foreign Exchange Return

The foreign exchange return component derives from the changes in foreign exchange rates over the period. In this sense, this component is outside the control of the manager after a position in bond i is taken. The foreign exchange return can be measured by the following equation:

$$S8_i = \frac{X_E - X_B}{X_B} \tag{13}$$

where

$S8_i$ = the foreign exchange return component of bond i in home currency
X_B = the beginning exchange rate
X_E = the ending exchange rate

Then the total return of bond i in terms of home currency becomes

$$S9_i = (1 + R_{L,i})(1+ S8_i) - 1 \tag{14}$$

Trading Activity Return

Trading activity (timing) is not a separate skill, but rather an aspect of each of the skills identified above. Trading activity by shifting a portfolio from short to long duration or vice versa is really an element of maturity management, rather than an independently exercised ability. Without trading activity, there would be no maturity management. Similarly, trading activity is an essential part of sector/quality management and a part of choosing the proper bonds within a given sector/quality group. To provide a meaningful analysis of the portfolio return, the trading activity component must be included in the calculation of the return components.

Each component of the total portfolio return is the weighted average of component return of each individual bond in the global portfolio. Thus, the xth component of the portfolio return can be represented as follows:

$$P_X = \sum_i \omega_i \cdot SX_i \qquad \text{for } X = 1, 2, 3, \ldots, 9 \tag{15}$$

where

P_X = the xth component return of the portfolio
ω_i = the weight of bond i calculated using the beginning home currency prices,
SX_i = the xth component return for bond i

Then the trading activity return of the portfolio, $P9$, is:

$$P9 = R_H - \sum_{X=1}^{8} P_X \tag{16}$$

where R_H = Total return of the portfolio in home currency.

At the portfolio level or currency sub-portfolio level, there can be an additional component of currency hedging return if the manager takes a foreign exchange hedging position. Popular currency hedging instruments are currency futures and currency options. The currency hedging component is measured by the following formula.

$$P_{10} = \frac{F_E - F_B}{F_B} \tag{17}$$

where

P_{10} = the currency hedging component return
F_B = the beginning market price of the currency hedging instrument
F_E = the ending market price of the currency hedging instrument

MARKET INDEX

To determine whether the manager added value by outperforming the established benchmark and how the manager achieved the return, we must specify a benchmark against which the manager will be measured. It is done by performing the return analysis for the chosen bogey as well, thus allowing a direct comparison of the resulting components of return between the actual portfolio and the specialized bogey. Two types of benchmarks can be used in evaluating global fixed income portfolio managers. One is the market indexes published by dealer firms such as the Salomon World Government Bond Index. The other is a customized index that includes a set of securities that contains all of the securities from which a manager normally chooses, weighted by the market values of the individual securities.

ILLUSTRATION

Here we illustrate the return attribution model using a hypothetical portfolio for the period May 31, 1994 to June 30, 1994. We show particularly how it answers the six questions about management. Exhibit 1 shows the holdings of the portfolio and the transactions during the period. Also shown for each security are the beginning and ending par amount, prices, and the capital gain or loss.

Exhibit 2 shows the results of the performance attribution analysis for the portfolio. The "Evaluation Period Return" column describes the return and components of return for the portfolio over the evaluation period. The "Bond Equivalent Annualized Return" column is the annualized return and components of return for the portfolio over the evaluation period. The "Market Index" column shows the evaluation period return of a market index (benchmark). The index selected for this example is the Salomon Brothers' World Government Bond index.

Section I of Exhibit 2, the "Interest Rate Effect," is the return over the evaluation period stemming from the external internal rate environment. We can interpret this return as the cost of being in the bond market. Therefore, this component of return is considered out of the manager's control. Here we use the Salomon Brothers' World Government Bond Index for the interest rate effect; other indexes can be used when appropriate. The interest rate effect is further decomposed into two sub-components: the expected interest rate effect and the unexpected interest rate effect. The former is the return on default-free securities under the market-implicit scenario of no change in the forward rates. This simulates the effect of return from rolling down the spot rate curve. The unexpected interest rate effect is the return attributable to the actual change in forward rates.

The "Interest Rate Management Effect," reported in Section II, shows the option-adjusted default-free return for the portfolio. This component of return shows whether the manager has successfully anticipated interest rate changes. The interest rate management effect is broken into three sub-components: (1) duration effect (which is the effect on the return due to the magnitude of the yield curve shift); (2) convexity effect (which is the return component of managing the convexity of the portfolio); and, (3) yield curve shape change effect (which is the return due to the change in the shape of the yield curve, i.e., the residual return component not measured by duration and convexity).

Exhibit 1: Hypothetical Portfolio and Transactions

CUSIP	Bond Description	Initial/Last Date	Beg/End Par Value ($000)	Beg/End Price ($)	Capital Gain/Loss
539830AF	Lockheed Martin	5/31/96	2000	98.00	1.41
		6/30/94	1500	98.75	
887315BB	Time Warner	5/31/94	1000	105.5	0.06
		6/30/94	1000	105.00	
912810CC	U.S. Treasury Bond	5/31/94	1000	106.62	0.63
		6/30/94	1000	106.62	
912810DS	U.S. Treasury Bond	5/31/94	1500	131.77	1.72
		6/30/94	2000	133.21	
912827WW	U.S. Treasury Note	5/31/94	2500	108.34	0.66
		6/30/94	2500	108.34	
912827ZX	U.S. Treasury Note	5/31/94	1000	104.18	0.86
		6/30/94	1500	104.46	
913994CE	United Kingdom	5/31/94	500	102.21	0.71
	Treasury Government	6/30/94	500	102.21	
913994CJ	United Kingdom	5/31/94	1000	102.71	0.70
	Treasury Government	6/30/94	1000	102.71	
9139959D	United Kingdom	5/31/94	1000	104.87	0.70
	Treasury Government	6/30/94	1000	104.87	
984994CT	Japanese Government Bond	5/31/94	5000	105.81	2.68
		6/30/94	5000	102.42	
984994CX	Japanese Government Bond	5/31/94	5000	103.62	0.37
		6/30/94	5000	100.46	
984994SY	Japanese Government Bond	5/31/94	5000	108.17	6.27
		6/30/94	5000	108.17	
JYM50000	Japanese Currency Futures	5/31/94	–25000	98.54	
		6/30/94	–25000	104.72	

Exhibit 2: Results of the Performance Attribution Analysis

	Evaluation Period Return (%)	Market Index Evaluation Period Return (%)
I. Interest rate effect		
1. Expected	0.363	0.373
2. Unexpected	0.359	−1.092
Subtotal	0.722	−0.719
II. Interest rate management effect		
3. Duration	−0.368	0
4. Convexity	−0.006	0
5. Yield curve shape change	0.019	0
Subtotal (options adjusted)	−0.355	0
III. Other management effects		
6. Sector/Quality	1.287	0
7. Bond selectivity	−0.773	0
8. Transaction costs	0	0
Subtotal	0.514	0
IV. Trading activity return	0.359	0
V. Currency return		
9. Foreign exchange	0.864	2.145
10. Currency hedging	−0.105	0
Subtotal	0.759	2.145
VI. Total Return (sum of I, II, III, IV, and, V)	1.999	1.426

"Other Management Effects" are shown in Section III, divided into three effects. The sector/quality effect is the return component, which shows whether the manager successfully selected the sector and quality groups that performed better over the evaluation period. The bond selectivity effect is the return component due to the selection of individual bonds in the portfolio. Transactions costs refers to the hypothetical effect of transactions on the portfolio's return.

Section IV describes the trading activity return. Section V disaggregates the currency return into two components. The foreign exchange component measures the change in portfolio value from exchange rate changes before hedging, while the currency hedging component incorporates the behavior of currency derivatives.

"Total Return" is the time-weighted total return for the evaluation period. This is the sum of the "Interest Rate Effect," "Interest Rate Management Effect," "Others Management Effects," "Trading Activity," and "Currency Returns." Exhibit 3 shows the decomposition of return on the individual security basis.

Exhibit 3: Decomposition of Return of Individual Securities

CUSIP	Bond Description	Initial/ Last Date	Beg/End Par Value ($000)	Market Expected Rate of Change	Int. Rate Effect: Duration/Convexity/ Yield Curve	Sector Effect: Sector/ Selectivity	Currency Exchange Return (%)	Local Currency Return (%)	Base Currency Return (%)
539830AF	Lockheed Martin	5/31/96	2000	0.352	–0.979	1.546	0	1.415	1.415
		6/30/94	1500	–0.535	–0.185	1.213			
					0.003				
887315BB	Time Warner	5/31/94	1000	0.352	–1.201	1.10	0	0.066	0.066
		6/30/94	1000	–0.535	–0.245	0.583			
					0.010				
912810CC	U.S. Treasury Bond	5/31/94	1000	0.352	–0.372	0.00	0	0.636	0.636
		6/30/94	1000	–0.535	0.003	1.19			
					–0.011				
912810DS	U.S. Treasury Bond	5/31/94	1500	0.352	–0.744	0.00	0	1.722	1.722
		6/30/94	2000	–0.535	–0.105	2.761			
					–0.008				
912827WW	U.S. Treasury Note	5/31/94	2500	0.352	0.176	0.00	0	0.666	0.666
		6/30/94	2500	–0.535	0.42	0.674			
					–0.043				
912827ZX	U.S. Treasury Note	5/31/94	1000	0.352	–0.054	0.00	0	0.868	0.868
		6/30/94	1500	–0.535	0.028	1.129			
					–0.053				

Exhibit 3 (Continued)

CUSIP	Bond Description	Initial/ Last Date	Beg/End Par Value ($000)	Market Expected Rate of Change	Int. Rate Effect: Duration/Convexity/ Yield Curve	Sector Effect: Sector/ Selectivity	Currency Exchange Return (%)	Local Currency Return (%)	Base Currency Return (%)
913994CE	United Kingdom	5/31/94	500	0.397	−0.139	0.00	2.814	0.713	3.547
	Treasury Government	6/30/94	500	2.450	0.201	−2.583			
					0.387				
913994CJ	United Kingdom	5/31/94	1000	0.397	−0.181	0.00	2.814	0.7070	3.540
	Treasury Government	6/30/94	1000	2.450	0.371	−2.232			
					−0.098				
9139959D	United Kingdom	5/31/94	1000	0.397	0.002	0.00	2.814	0.752	3.587
	Treasury Government	6/30/94	1000	2.450	−0.090	−2.196			
					0.189				
984994CT	Japanese Government Bond	5/31/94	10000	0.176	−0.935	0.00	6.093	−2.814	3.107
		6/30/94	10000	3.870	0.034	−6.027			
					0.068				
984994CX	Japanese Government Bond	5/31/94	10000	0.176	−0.968	0.00	6.093	−2.814	3.107
		6/30/94	10000	3.870	0.034	−6.027			
					0.068				
984994SY	Japanese Government Bond	5/31/94	20000	0.176	0.375	0.00	6.093	0.373	6.489
		6/30/94	20000	3.870	−0.039	−3.809			
					−0.199				
JYM50000	Japanese Currency Futures	5/31/94	50000	0.00	0.000	0.00	0.00	0.00	6.272
		6/30/94	50000	0.00	0.000	0.00			
					0.000				

SUMMARY

Global fixed income performance measurement involves calculation of the total return in home currency realized by a manager over some evaluation period. Global performance evaluation determines whether a manager added value by outperforming an established benchmark and how the manager achieved the return. It identifies the sources of return. In the global fixed income area, returns are composed of local returns and foreign exchange returns. The local returns at each currency level can be attributed to (1) elements beyond the manager's control, such as the interest rate environment, and (2) elements that the management process contributes to, such as interest rate risk management, sector/quality allocations, and individual bond selection. To refine the return attribution of a global fixed income portfolio, a breakdown of the interest rate risk management component may be accomplished, which further reveals the sources of management skill. The foreign exchange return at the portfolio level or currency level can be decomposed into (1) pure foreign exchange return and (2) currency hedging return. For global fixed income strategies that rely upon the hedging tools, this framework can be a useful monitoring tool.

Chapter 13

Approaches to Global Fixed Income Performance Attribution

Robert C. Kuberek
Vice President and Principal
Wilshire Associates Incorporated

INTRODUCTION

Investment managers add value through timing, security selection, and trading. For multi-currency fixed income portfolios, timing involves choosing the right countries, picking the right duration and position on the yield curve in each country, and selecting the right currencies. In institutional portfolios these decisions are generally made relative to a recognized, broad market benchmark. In addition to timing, investment managers add value through security selection and trading. This is the art and practice of valuing individual issues relative to their markets and identifying issues that are underpriced or overpriced relative to their fair market or intrinsic value.

Much of the focus of analytical work on performance attribution — and the focus of this chapter — is on the attribution of what has just been described as timing. Did the manager correctly anticipate an increase in German interest rates or a weakness in the pound? Did the French bond market outperform the U.K. bond market? Did U.S. corporate spreads narrow while mortgage spreads widened and what was the effect on the portfolio?

Yet in spite of the level of interest and the effort that has been expended, there is little agreement among practitioners on how to account for these effects. This is probably because the best choice of frameworks depends on the investment process and on the purpose of the analysis. In other words, one size does not fit all.

The attribution process begins with a description of the process that generates returns. The description must be consistent with the investment process and with the purpose to which the analysis is to be put. The model may be simple, for example defining portfolio returns in terms of the returns of segments of a broad

The author would like to thank Jack Saunders and Brian Raab for their assistance with this chapter.

market benchmark. Alternatively, the process may be elaborate, for example defining returns in terms of a sophisticated factor risk model.

Where the investment process begins with country selection, for example, the appropriate attribution framework emphasizes the country allocation decision. In contrast, where the investment process is based on yield curve forecasts, country allocation loses relevance—market exposure is the key. In addition, if the purpose of the attribution analysis is to communicate a general picture of how the portfolio performed and why, perhaps in relation to global events that are commonly acknowledged, the appropriate framework may emphasize key strategic issues such as country and currency selection. Alternatively, where the purpose of the analysis is diagnostics, the framework may focus in great detail on differential risk factor exposure and issue selection. Attribution models come in all shapes and sizes and there are probably at least as many useful schemes as there are participants.

The purpose of this chapter is to describe and compare three of the leading approaches to multi-currency fixed income performance attribution. These are

1. The allocation/duration approach
2. The yield/exposure approach
3. The factor model approach

As will be shown, these three approaches are differentiated primarily by the description of the return-generating process that each one uses.

The allocation/duration framework is arguably the most widely recognized and probably developed out of the approach that has been used for equity portfolios for some time. This approach focuses on the country selection decision, the duration decision within each country, and the currency decision.[1] Selection is a residual.

In some ways an improvement on the allocation/duration framework, the more modern yield/exposure framework recognizes that market exposure in a given country can be achieved with a 20% allocation in 5-year duration bonds or with a 10% allocation in 10-year duration bonds. Either way, the exposure of the portfolio to local changes in interest rates is essentially the same; therefore the market exposure is the same.

Finally, the most precise and detailed of the three frameworks uses a factor model.[2] The factor model represents a detailed description of returns in terms of a set common risk factors. The factor model approach derives from the work of

---

[1] The costs and effects of hedging can be analyzed easily within all three of these frameworks. However, in the interest of clarity, the presentation here will not deal with these issues.

[2] Both the allocation/duration and yield/exposure frameworks could be said to be factor models where the factor exposures are simply the portfolio weights (or, in the case of the yield/exposure model, weighted durations). However, because of the simplicity of these models and their reliance on index returns to define the factors, these models are not commonly referred to as factor models.

Benjamin King[3] and of Kalman Cohen and Jerome Pogue[4] in the mid-1960s, which was popularized by Wilshire and other firms in the 1970s and 1980s. The original fixed income risk model described in this chapter was developed at Wilshire in the mid-1980s and has been in continuous use by Wilshire's clients since that time. The model decomposes returns in multi-currency portfolios in terms of yield curve movements and currency changes. A major advantage of the factor model approach is that it can produce the smallest return residuals of the three approaches.

Other approaches are in use,[5] and the ones described here are not necessarily the best for every purpose — but these approaches are widely employed and commonly understood. They represent alternative generic types of attribution that have broad application in a variety of activities, including marketing of investment management services, client communication, internal diagnostics, and compensation.

THE ALLOCATION/DURATION APPROACH

The allocation/duration framework probably developed out of methods that have been used to attribute performance in equity portfolios for many years. The basic multi-currency equity framework decomposes performance into three components: country, currency, and selection. However, to adapt this framework to multi-currency fixed income portfolios, portfolio managers had to recognize that within each country the duration decision is extremely important in explaining performance. Therefore a fourth component, duration-within-country, was added, resulting in the complete allocation/duration decomposition explained below. This attribution framework is still in wide use today and is one of the simplest and most practical.

The following notation will be used in describing the allocation/duration approaches:

w_{pi} = portfolio weight in country i
w_{bi} = benchmark weight in country i
d_{pi} = portfolio duration in country i
d_{bi} = benchmark duration in country i
y_i = risk free rate in country i
s_{bi} = benchmark local currency spot return in country i
x_i = spot currency return in country i, relative to a base currency

[3] Benjamin King, "Market and Industry Factors in Stock Price Behavior," *Journal of Business* (1966), pp. 139-190.
[4] K.J. Cohen and J.A. Pogue, "An Empirical Evaluation of Alternative Portfolio Selection Models," *Journal of Business* (1967), pp. 166-193.
[5] The approaches to attribution described here follow the convention that the return components *add* to the total return difference from the benchmark. Alternative multiplicative schemes are also in use.

Market Model

The allocation/duration attribution scheme is derived from the following description of base currency return:[6]

$$r = \sum_i w_i y_i \Delta t + \sum_i w_i d_i (s_{bi} - y_{bi}\Delta t)/d_{bi} + \sum_i w_i x_i \tag{1}$$

In other words, portfolio returns result from the accumulation of yield, changes in interest rates by country, and changes in exchange rates by country.

For the benchmark this reduces simply to

$$r_b = \sum_i w_{bi} s_{bi} + \sum_i w_{bi} x_i$$

In other words, this model is consistent with the representation of the benchmark return as the weighted sum of the local market returns and the currency returns.

By defining the appropriate additional term, the market model given by equation (1) can be rewritten as

$$r = \sum_i w_i y_i \Delta t + \sum_i w_i d_i \delta_i + \sum_i w_i x_i$$

where the δ_i represent the (negative of) the average yield change in country i. This makes it possible to write the attribution very concisely.

Return Attribution

The allocation/duration model attributes value added by country, as follows:

Source	*Components of Return*[7]
Country	$(w_{pi} - w_{bi})(s_{bi} - \overline{s_{bi}})$
Duration	$w_{pi}(d_{pi} - d_{bi})\delta_i$
Currency	$(w_{pi} - w_{bi})x_i$
Selection/trading	*residual*

In this framework, value-added is separated into four components. The first is country allocation. Essentially, this is the value-added to being overweighted in countries that outperformed, or underweighted in countries that underperformed, the average country in the benchmark.

[6] For simplicity, in this and all subsequent developments, the currency interaction term is ignored. In practice, this term contributes almost nothing to management return in conventional institutional portfolios.

[7] The decomposition here and in what follows is of return *differences* to the benchmark. Explaining these management effects is the objective of performance attribution. If attribution of *total* return is desired, a cash benchmark can be used.

The second component of performance is duration-within-country. This measures the value-added by being longer than the benchmark in a country where interest rates fell or shorter than the benchmark in a country where interest rates rose. In this way it is possible to add value through interest rate changes even though the portfolio's country weights match those of the benchmark. The duration component is portfolio-weighted to assure internal consistency.

The third component of performance is currency. This component measures the value-added to being overweighted in currencies that appreciated, or underweighted in currencies that depreciated, relative to the base currency. In the absence of hedges (currency forwards, swaps, futures and options), the currency weights are the same as the country weights. Because of this many portfolio managers use hedges to manage their currency exposure independently.

The performance that is not explained by country allocation, duration within country, and currency exposure is attributed to selection and trading. An important goal of performance attribution is to explain as much of the performance as possible with the market factors, or in this case, country allocation, duration, and currency. For example, some of the residual trading effect can be explained by shortening the period of the attribution, to weeks or days, and linking together the results to months, quarters, and years. This way, changes in portfolio structure that occur during the month are attributed to the decisions that they represent. Nevertheless, a certain residual generally remains to issue selection and trading. In particular, the allocation/duration framework is unable to explain variations in performance across securities that stem from yield curve effects rather than true issue specific effects. As a consequence, these yield curve effects show up as selection/trading.

THE YIELD/EXPOSURE APPROACH

In practice, management of multi-currency fixed income portfolios tends to focus on four sources of value: market exposure, currency exposure, sector and yield curve exposure within markets, and individual issue selection. Market exposure combines country allocation and duration and represents the exposure of the portfolio to changes in interest rates country-by-country. As noted earlier, market exposure in a given country can be achieved with a 20% allocation in 5-year duration bonds or with a 10% allocation in 10-year duration bonds. Either way the exposure of the portfolio to local changes in interest rates is essentially the same, so the market exposure is the same.

Currency exposure arises naturally as countries are overweighted or underweighted in the portfolio relative to the index. However, through the use of hedges, portfolio managers frequently alter the currency exposures that would otherwise result from their bond holdings. Moreover, in many organizations the currency decision is made by different managers in an entirely different way from the market decision.[8]

Sector and yield curve exposures within markets also contribute to return differences from the benchmark. Since the most common multi-currency benchmarks consist exclusively of government bonds, any use of corporate bonds will tend to add value (and risk) to the portfolio relative to the benchmark. Similarly, differential weighting of different parts of the yield curve can add value by adding yield, further distinguishing the portfolio from the benchmark. Together, the values added through sector and yield curve exposure are accumulation effects: value is added not as the result of market surprises, but simply as the result of the passage of time.

Finally, individual issue selection contributes to return differences from the benchmark. Most portfolios have some degree of issue selection. Often, enhanced index strategies focus exclusively on this source of value-added. Issue selection represents that part of the portfolio's return that is not explained by the portfolio's market exposures, currency exposures, and differential yield through the use of corporate bonds or yield curve weightings. Factors affecting issue selection include unexpected upgrades and downgrades of issue quality and unexpected corporate actions, such as exercise of options. Issue selection is also affected by sector and yield curve exposure. Yield spread changes that affect corporate sectors and changes in the shape of yield curves show up in this category of the attribution.

The following notation will be used in describing the yield/exposure approach:

w_{pi} = portfolio weight in country i
w_{bi} = benchmark weight in country i
d_{pi} = portfolio duration in country i
d_{bi} = benchmark duration in country i
y_{pi} = portfolio yield in country i
y_{bi} = benchmark yield in country i
s_{bi} = benchmark local currency spot return in country i
x_i = spot currency return in country i, relative to a base currency

Market Model

The attribution scheme is derived from the following description of base currency return:

---

[8] Interestingly, currency hedges can affect market exposures. To see this, consider a 3-month forward, yen from marks. The equivalent cash position is a long 3-month yen bill and a short 3-month mark bill. Each of these hypothetical bills has a non-zero duration. Each one's value will depend, in part, on local interest rates. Thus, adding the 3-month forward to the portfolio increases the Japanese *market* exposure (the exposure to interest rate changes) by a little, as well as the yen currency exposure, and reduces the German market exposure by a little, as well as the mark currency exposure. On the other hand, pure interest rate contracts, such as bond futures, create market exposure but no currency exposure (except insofar as settlement balances are allowed to build up unhedged or un-reallocated).

$$r = \sum_i w_i y_i \Delta t + \sum_i w_i d_i (s_{bi} - y_{bi} \Delta t) / d_{bi} + \sum_i w_i x_i \qquad (2)$$

In this description of return, or market model, returns arise from the portfolio's yield, which incorporates any yield spread in a market that results from the use of corporate bonds or from the portfolio's positioning along the yield curve, from market exposure (which is measured using the benchmark's return), and from currency exposure.

As before, this reduces for the benchmark simply to

$$r_b = \sum_i w_{bi} s_{bi} + \sum_i w_{bi} x_i$$

which is just the sum of the country returns (in local currency) and the currency returns.

As in the allocation/duration model, by defining the appropriate additional term, the market model given by equation (2) can be rewritten as

$$r = \sum_i w_i y_i \Delta t + \sum_i w_i d_i o_i + \sum_i w_i x_i$$

where

$$o_i = (s_{bi} - y_{bi} \Delta t) / d_{bi}$$

the excess return of the benchmark per year of benchmark duration, i.e., the (negative of the) average yield change in country i. Thus, returns arise primarily from yield, from yield changes, and from currency returns.

Careful examination of equation (2) shows that it is identical in form to equation (1). The difference — and it is a subtle one — is in the definition of the yield *y*. To accommodate convention, in the allocation/duration model *y* is defined as the risk-free rate. Here, in contrast, it is a measure of portfolio yield. This allows the yield/exposure model to account for the effects of yield premiums, as explained below.

Return Attribution

The yield/exposure framework attributes returns as follows:

Source	Components of Return
Yield	$w_{pi} y_{pi} \Delta t - w_{bi} y_{bi} \Delta t$
Market exposure	$(w_{pi} d_{pi} - w_{bi} d_{bi}) o_i$
Currency	$(w_{pi} - w_{bi}) x_i$
Selection/trading	*residual*

The yield component measures the yield pick-up in the portfolio relative to the benchmark by being invested in higher yielding securities (for example, in corporate bonds or mortgages). Also, the effect of extending maturity along a positively sloped yield curve will show up in this term.

Market exposure captures the effect of differential interest rate exposures after taking out the effect of term spreads, which is captured in the yield term. The market exposure component can be thought of as resulting from the combination of country-weighting and duration-within-country decisions. Thus a large country weighting offset by a short duration within the country might result in a neutral or even negative net market exposure, where using the allocation/duration framework the portfolio would have a large positive country bet and a large negative duration bet. It is this rationalization of the market bets in the portfolio that makes the yield/exposure framework attractive.

The currency effect is defined precisely the same way in the yield/exposure model as in the allocation/duration model. This component measures the value-added to being overweighted in currencies that appreciated, or underweighted in currencies that depreciated, relative to the base currency.

As before, the performance that is unexplained by the market factors, in this case yield, market exposure and currency, is left to selection and trading. However, in the yield/exposure model slightly more of the return typically is explained by the market factors. This is because the yield component picks up the accumulation effects related to yield premiums. For example, high yield bonds, such as corporate bonds or mortgages, will have a yield premium to the sovereign debt issues in the most widely used global benchmarks. Where this yield premium shows up in the residual in the allocation/duration model, it shows up in the yield component in the yield/exposure model.

THE FACTOR MODEL APPROACH

The factor model approach uses the idea that if we know the exposures of the bond or bond portfolio to a set of risk factors, we can then infer the factor returns for a given period from a cross-section. Wilshire's fixed income risk model, which was developed originally for the U.S. market in the mid 1980s, uses three yield shifts to represent term structure risk in each country. The yield shifts are prespecified from a Taylor Series in such a way as to maximize the ability of the model to explain a wide variety of yield curve movements in a very specific mathematical sense[9] using as few factors as possible. Because the model was developed from first principles instead of from data, the model has been easily generalized to global developed markets without the need for re-parameterization.

---

[9] Robert C. Kuberek, "An Approximate Factor Model for U.S. Treasuries," *Proceedings of the Seminar on the Analysis of Security Prices* (Chicago, IL: The University of Chicago Center for Research in Securities Prices, November 1991)

Exhibit 1: Yield Curve Shift Components

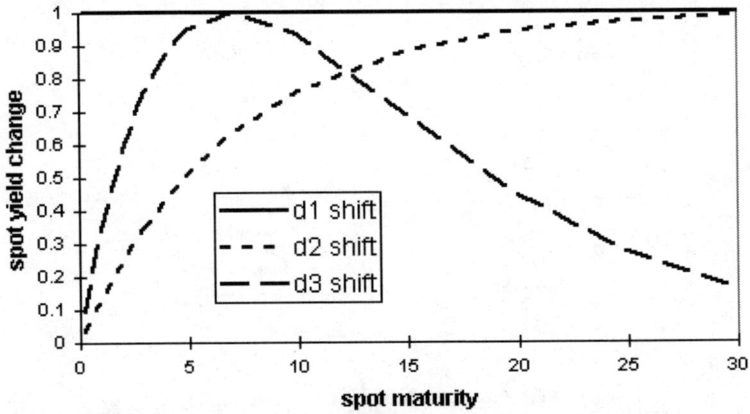

Exhibit 1 shows the yield curve shifts generated by the Taylor Series. The idea of the model is that actual yield curve shifts can always be approximated as some composite of these three basic types of yield curve shifts. Moreover, tests of the model using yield curve data and actual bond returns have proven this model to provide a very accurate description of yield curve risk.

Because the risk factors are yield curve shifts, there is a measure of duration associated with each one. Therefore, simply by regressing bond excess returns on their durations with respect to the three yield curve shifts using large market cross-sections, it is possible to infer the returns associated with each of the risk factors. These returns can then be used for attribution.

There are three major advantages to this way of specifying the factor model:

1. Effective duration, as conventionally defined, *is* the first factor.
2. The risk factors (yield shifts) correspond to events that portfolio managers can imagine actually happening, such as steepening of the yield curve.
3. The yield shifts are pre-specified from first principles, so the model does not depend in any way on a specific historical data sample. This guarantees that the model is robust over time and across countries.

The following notation will be used in describing the factor model:

d_{1bi} = benchmark effective duration in country i
d_{2bi} = benchmark effective d_2 country i (steepening risk)
d_{3bi} = benchmark effective d_3 in country i (curvature risk)
y_{bi} = benchmark yield in country i
s_{bi} = benchmark local currency spot return in country i

Here the ds are measures of duration with respect to each of the three types of yield curve shift in the model.

Exhibit 2: Actual versus Fitted Yield Curve Shifts: U.S. Market 6/28/96 to 7/31/96

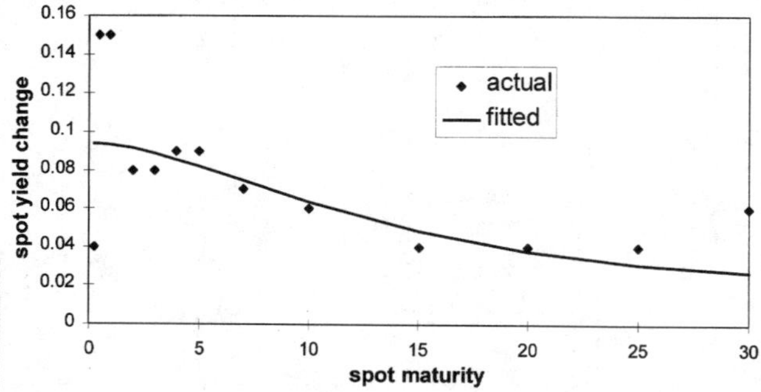

Yield Curve Shift Components

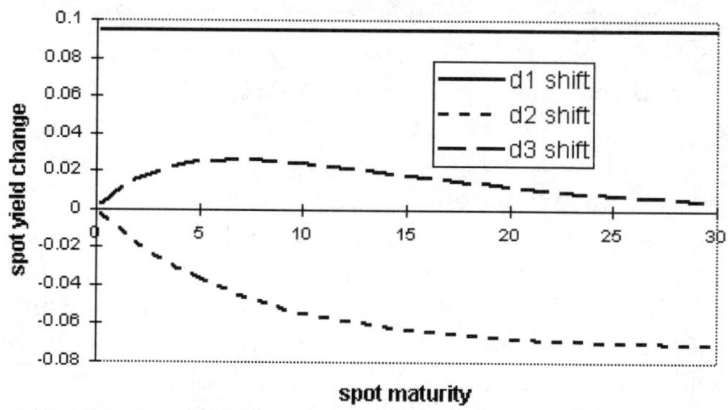

Factor Model

The factor model decomposes local currency benchmark returns as follows:

$$s_{bi} = y_{bi}\Delta t + d_{1bi}\Delta q_{1i} + d_{2bi}\Delta q_{2i} + d_{3bi}\Delta q_{3i} \tag{3}$$

In other words the benchmark return in country i is the sum of the yield and the components of total return due to each of the three types of yield curve shift that combined to produce the actual total yield curve shift in country i over that period. In this factorization, the ds are scaled so that the Δq are, loosely speaking, the negative of the amounts of each type of yield curve shift. For example, if the curve had steepened by 100 basis points in country i during the performance period, then Δq_{2i} would have a value of approximately −1.0.

Exhibit 2 shows how the yield curve shifts combine to explain actual yield curve movements. The top graph in Exhibit 2 shows the actual versus the fitted yield curve shifts for the U.S. market over the period from 6/28/96 to 7/31/96. The smooth curve represents the sum of the component shifts that are plotted in the bottom graph of Exhibit 2.

Wilshire has estimated this model across all the countries in the developed market universe. In every case the maximum cross-sectional R-squared is near one, while the median R-squared statistics are comparable across all countries in the universe, indicating that the model performs comparably well in every country. Interestingly, in spite of the excellent performance of the model for the U.S. market, the three shift model does not always perform better in the U.S. than in other countries.

Attribution Framework

We will use the following notation for the attribution framework:

w_{pi} = portfolio weight in country i
w_{bi} = benchmark weight in country i
d_{1pi} = portfolio effective duration in country i
d_{1bi} = benchmark effective duration in country i
d_{2pi} = portfolio effective d_2 in country i (steepening risk)
d_{2bi} = benchmark effective d_2 country i (steepening risk)
d_{3pi} = portfolio effective d_3 in country i (curvature risk)
d_{3bi} = benchmark effective d_3 in country i (curvature risk)
y_{pi} = portfolio yield in country i
y_{bi} = benchmark yield in country i
s_{bi} = benchmark local currency spot return in country i
x_i = spot currency return in country i, relative to a base currency

Market Model

The attribution model is derived from the following description of returns. First, the benchmark local currency return is factored by cross-sectional regression, country by country, as follows:

$$s_{bi} = y_{bi}\Delta t + d_{1bi}\Delta q_{1i} + d_{2bi}\Delta q_{2i} + d_{3bi}\Delta q_{3i}$$

In this factorization, the Δq are, loosely speaking, the negative of the amounts of each type of yield curve shift that occurred in country i during the performance period. For example, if the curve steepened by 100 basis points in country i during the performance period, then Δq_{2i} would have had a value of approximately -1.0.

The description of base currency portfolio return that results from this factorization of the benchmark return is

$$r = \sum_i w_i y_i + \sum_i w_i(d_{1i}\Delta q_{1i} + d_{2i}\Delta q_{2i} + d_{3i}\Delta q_{3i}) + \sum_i w_i x_i \tag{4}$$

Return Attribution

The attribution by country is then given as follows:

Source	*Components of Return*
Yield	$w_{pi}y_{pi}\Delta t - w_{bi}y_{bi}\Delta t$
Duration	$(w_{pi}d_{1pi} - w_{bi}d_{1bi})\Delta q_{1i}$
Steepening/Flattening	$(w_{pi}d_{2pi} - w_{bi}d_{2bi})\Delta q_{2i}$
Curvature Change	$(w_{pi}d_{3pi} - w_{bi}d_{3bi})\Delta q_{3i}$
Currency	$(w_{pi} - w_{bi})x_i$
Selection/trading	*residual*

As with the yield/exposure model, the yield component measures the yield pick-up in the portfolio relative to the benchmark by being invested in higher yielding securities (for example, in corporate bonds or mortgages). Also, the effect of extending maturity along a positively sloped yield curve will show up in this term.

The duration component captures the effect of differential exposures to parallel yield curve movements by country.[10] For example, if short rates generally moved upward in country *i* and the portfolio's weighted effective duration contribution in country *i* was less than the benchmark, the portfolio would underperform the benchmark from this source. Likewise, steepening/flattening captures the effect of differential exposures to yield curve steepening or flattening relative to the benchmark, while curvature captures the effect of differential exposures to this aspect of yield curve movements, by country.

The currency effect is defined precisely the same way in this model as in the yield/exposure and allocation/duration frameworks. This component measures the value-added to being overweighted in currencies that appreciated, or underweighted in currencies that depreciated, relative to the base currency.

Finally, again as before, the performance that is unexplained by the market factors, in this case yield, effective duration, steepening, curvature, and currency, is left to selection and trading. Again, more of the return is typically explained using the factor model than in either of the other, simpler schemes. This is because the factor model captures term structure effects explicitly, such as twists and changes in curvature, that would be averaged out and that would show up in the residual under the allocation/duration and yield/exposure frameworks.

[10] When measuring parallel yield curve movements in combination with non-parallel movements, it is necessary to decide whether parallel movements are to be defined off the short end of the curve, the long end of the curve, or some other part of the curve. The model illustrated here defines parallel shift components off the short end.

Exhibit 3: Summary of the Features of the Three Leading Attribution Models

	Framework	Components	Comments
(1)	Allocation/duration	Country	
		Duration-within-country	relative to benchmark
		Currency	
		Selection/Trading	residual
(2)	Yield/exposure	Yield	including effects of yield premiums
		Market	focuses on market exposure
		Currency	same as allocation/duration
		Selection/Trading	residual
(3)	Factor model	Yield	same as yield/exposure
		Duration	parallel shift effects
		Steepening/Flattening	
		Curvature	
		Currency	same as above
		Selection/Trading	residual

SUMMARY

Exhibit 3 summarizes the features of the three leading attribution models described in this chapter. Of the three approaches the allocation/duration (or variants) is probably the most widely used. It is intuitive, easy to explain, and consistent with the way attribution is frequently done for equity portfolios. However, one drawback of this approach is that it fails to recognize that the same market exposure can be obtained with differing combinations of weights and durations within countries.

The second approach, the yield/exposure model, recognizes that the same market exposure can be obtained with differing combinations of weights and durations within countries. Additionally, this model potentially accounts for more return because it picks up in the yield component the effects of yield premiums earned by owning higher yielding securities, such as corporates and mortgages. Like the allocation/duration model, however, the yield/exposure model also fails to account for return differences that result from changes in the shape of the yield curve, as distinct from changes in the level of interest rates.

The factor model approach is the most elaborate and precise of the three approaches. Like the yield/exposure model, the factor model approach accounts for yield premiums associated with owning higher yielding securities. However, the factor model approach also explicitly accounts for yield curve effects, such as steepening and changes in curvature, that would otherwise show up in unexplained residual, to be attributed to selection and trading.

Index

F

J

K

L

Q

R